Blackburn College - Lumpkin Library

0 00 51 0001080 9

Macmillan/McGraw-Hill READING

Mc Graw Hill **Macmillan**
McGraw-Hill

D1511795

learning through listening

Students with print disabilities may be eligible to obtain an accessible, audio version of the
pupil edition of this textbook. Please call Recording for the Blind & Dyslexic at 1-800-221-4792
for complete information.

The *McGraw·Hill* Companies

 **Macmillan
McGraw-Hill**

Published by Macmillan/McGraw-Hill, of McGraw-Hill Education, a division of The McGraw-Hill Companies, Inc.,
Two Penn Plaza, New York, New York 10121.

Copyright © 2005 by Macmillan/McGraw-Hill. All rights reserved. The contents, or parts thereof, may be reproduced in print
form for non-profit educational use with Macmillan/McGraw-Hill Reading, provided such reproductions bear copyright
notice, but may not be reproduced in any form for any other purpose without the prior written consent of The McGraw-Hill
Companies, Inc., including, but not limited to, network storage or transmission, or broadcast for distance learning.

Printed in the United States of America

2 3 4 5 6 7 8 9   073/043   09 08 07 06 05 04

Macmillan/McGraw-Hill READING

Authors

James Flood

Jan E. Hasbrouck

James V. Hoffman

Diane Lapp

Donna Lubcker

Angela Shelf Medearis

Scott Paris

Steven Stahl

Josefina Villamil Tinajero

Karen D. Wood

Macmillan
McGraw-Hill

Computer Center

Managing the

Art Center

Working with Words Center

Phonics Center

Reading and Listening Center

Writing Center

cat
dog

Classroom

Math Center

$1^2 3 4 5$

Teacher Directed
Small Group
Instruction

TEACHING TIP

MANAGEMENT
Provide children in each group with their own list of centers they will go to. Children can check off each center after finishing their work. Early finishers can read a book from the Reading Center.

Sample Management Plan

Group 1	Group 2	Group 3	Group 4
With Teacher	Phonics Center or Word Center	Writing Center or Reading Center	Cross-Curricular Center
Phonics Center or Word Center	**With Teacher**	Cross-Curricular Center	Writing Center or Reading Center
Writing Center or Reading Center	Cross-Curricular Center	**With Teacher**	Phonics Center or Word Center
Cross-Curricular Center	Writing Center or Reading Center	Phonics Center or Word Center	**With Teacher**

Creating CENTERS

Establishing independent Centers and other independent activities is the key to helping you manage the classroom as you meet with small groups.

Reading and Listening

Set up a classroom library that includes the following books organized in baskets: ABC Books, Leveled Books, and other independent reading titles on each group's independent reading level. Also, see the Theme Bibliography on pages T54 and T55 for suggestions. Children can use the Reading Center for:

- Self-selected reading
- Paired reading
- Listening to selections in the Listening Library

TEACHING TIP

ASSESSMENT In each center provide a basket for finished work. You may also wish to provide a date stamp and ink pad for children to date their work.

Writing

Children can practice their fine motor and handwriting skills, as well as their writing skills, at the Center. Children can use the Writing Center for:

- Drawing or writing about their own experiences
- Practice in forming the letters of the alphabet
- Responding to literature
- Journal writing

Phonics

Children can practice the phonemic awareness and phonics skills they are learning. Phonics Center activities may include:

- Matching capital and lowercase letters
- Matching letters and pictures
- Sorting pictures
- Identifying beginning, medial, and ending sounds

Working with Words

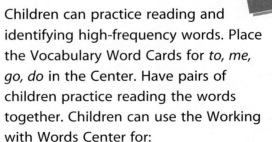

Children can practice reading and identifying high-frequency words. Place the Vocabulary Word Cards for *to, me, go, do* in the Center. Have pairs of children practice reading the words together. Children can use the Working with Words Center for:

- Matching word cards
- Reading words
- Using words in sentences
- Playing word games

Cross-Curricular

CENTERS

Set up Cross-Curricular Centers to help extend selection concepts and ideas.
Suggestions for Cross-Curricular Centers can be found throughout the unit.

Science

- Apple ID, 186T
- Moon Shapes, 203B
- Mammals, 205/206B
- Favorite Foods, 209B
- Favorite Pets, 217/218B
- Nature Alphabet, 222F
- Make a Mural, 223B
- Planting in Mud, 229/230B

Math

$3 + 2$

- Guessing Game, 198F
- Count and Check, 210F
- May I Measure?, 222F
- Cats of a Different Color, 233B
- Dog Pictures, 241/242B

Social Studies

- Safety First, 186T
- Backyard Maps, 193/194B
- Watch It Grow, 197B
- Pottery, 198F
- Different Kinds of Homes, 210F

Art

- Make a Cat, 199B
- Paperbag Pumpkin, 235B

Additional Independent Activities

The following independent activities are offered as a means to practice and reinforce concepts and skills taught within the unit.

LEVELED BOOKS: The Easy, Independent, and Challenge books review the skills children have been learning each week.

EASY

Ron Is In

INDEPENDENT

You Are IT!

CHALLENGE

Ron's Radishes
by Roy Tanner
illustrated by Andrea Wallace

INDEPENDENT WRITING: At the end of each week, there are Easy, Independent, and Challenge writing activities that allow children to apply the skills they have learned up to this point.

McGraw-Hill Reading

Theme Chart

MULTI-AGE Classroom

Using the same global themes at each grade level facilitates the use of materials in multi-age classrooms.

GRADE LEVEL	Experience	Connections
	Experiences can tell us about ourselves and our world.	Making connections develops new understandings.
Kindergarten	**My World** We learn a lot from all the things we see and do at home and in school.	**All Kinds of Friends** When we work and play together, we learn more about ourselves.
Subtheme 1	At Home	Working Together
Subtheme 2	School Days	Playing Together
1	**Day by Day** Each day brings new experiences.	**Together Is Better** We like to share ideas and experiences with others.
2	**What's New?** With each day, we learn something new.	**Just Between Us** Family and friends help us see the world in new ways.
3	**Great Adventures** Life is made up of big and small experiences.	**Nature Links** Nature can give us new ideas.
4	**Reflections** Stories let us share the experiences of others.	**Something in Common** Sharing ideas can lead to meaningful cooperation.
5	**Time of My Life** We sometimes find memorable experiences in unexpected places.	**Building Bridges** Knowing what we have in common helps us appreciate our differences.
6	**Pathways** Reflecting on life's experiences can lead to new understandings.	**A Common Thread** A look beneath the surface may uncover hidden connections.

Themes: Kindergarten – Grade 6

Expression	Inquiry	Problem Solving	Making Decisions
There are many styles and forms for expressing ourselves.	By exploring and asking questions, we make discoveries.	Analyzing information can help us solve problems.	Using what we know helps us evaluate situations.
Time to Shine We can use our ideas and our imagination to do many wonderful things.	**I Wonder** We can make discoveries about the wonders of nature in our own backyard.	**Let's Work It Out** Working as part of a team can help me find a way to solve problems.	**Choices** We can make many good choices and decisions every day.
Great Ideas	In My Backyard	Try and Try Again	Good Choices
Let's Pretend	Wonders of Nature	Teamwork	Let's Decide
Stories to Tell Each one of us has a different story to tell.	**Let's Find Out!** Looking for answers is an adventure.	**Think About It!** It takes time to solve problems.	**Many Paths** Each decision opens the door to a new path.
Express Yourself We share our ideas in many ways.	**Look Around** There are surprises all around us.	**Figure It Out** We can solve problems by working together.	**Starting Now** Unexpected events can lead to new decisions.
Be Creative! We can all express ourselves in creative, wonderful ways.	**Tell Me More** Looking and listening closely will help us find out the facts.	**Think It Through** Solutions come in many shapes and sizes.	**Turning Points** We make new judgments based on our experiences.
Our Voices We can each use our talents to communicate ideas.	**Just Curious** We can find answers in surprising places.	**Make a Plan** Often we have to think carefully about a problem in order to solve it.	**Sorting It Out** We make decisions that can lead to new ideas and discoveries.
Imagine That The way we express our thoughts and feelings can take different forms.	**Investigate!** We never know where the search for answers might lead us.	**Bright Ideas** Some problems require unusual approaches.	**Crossroads** Decisions cause changes that can enrich our lives.
With Flying Colors Creative people help us see the world from different perspectives.	**Seek and Discover** To make new discoveries, we must observe and explore.	**Brainstorms** We can meet any challenge with determination and ingenuity.	**All Things Considered** Encountering new places and people can help us make decisions.

Contents

I Wonder

*We can make discoveries about
the wonders of nature in our own backyard.*

"The Little Turtle" a poem by *Vachel Lindsay*

Subtheme: In My Backyard
YOU ARE IT! **186Q**

SKILLS			
Phonics	**Comprehension**	**Vocabulary**	**Beginning Reading Concepts**
• **Introduce** Initial /r/r • **Review** /r/r, /f/f; Blending with Short *a, i, o*	• **Introduce** Main Idea • **Review** Main Idea	• **Introduce** High-Frequency Words: *to* • **Review** *to, the, that*	• **Introduce** On, Off

You Are IT!

Is It You? **198C**

SKILLS			
Phonics	**Comprehension**	**Vocabulary**	**Beginning Reading Concepts**
• **Introduce** Initial /p/p • **Introduce** Final /p/p • **Review** /p/p; Blending with Short *a, i, o*	• **Introduce** Compare and Contrast • **Review** Compare and Contrast	• **Introduce** High-Frequency Words: *me* • **Review** *me, to, you*	• **Introduce** Inside, Outside

Is It You?

Unit Planner

You Are IT!

Is It You?

	WEEK 1 You Are IT!	**WEEK 2** Is It You?
📖 **Leveled Books**	**Easy Book:** *Ron Is In* **On-Level Book:** *You Are IT!* **Challenge Book:** *Ron's Radishes*	**Easy Book:** *The Mop Man* **On-Level Book:** *Is It You?* **Challenge Book:** *The Picnic*
☑️ **Tested Skills**	☑ **Phonics and Decoding** Initial /r/r, 186Y–186, 188C–188, 190C–190 Initial /f/f, 190C–190 Blending with Short *a*, *i*, *o*, 192C–192, 196C–196 ☑ **Comprehension** Main Idea, 189E–189, 195A–195 ☑ **Vocabulary** High-Frequency Word: *to*, 191C–191 *to*, *the*, *that*, 197C–197 ☑ **Beginning Reading Concepts** On, Off, 187E–187	☑ **Phonics and Decoding** Initial /p/p, 198K–198, 202C–202 Final /p/p, 200C–200, 202C–202 Blending with Short *a*, *i*, *o*, 204C–204, 208C–208 ☑ **Comprehension** Compare and Contrast, 201C–201, 207A–207 ☑ **Vocabulary** High-Frequency Word: *me*, 203C–203 *me*, *to*, *you*, 209C–209 ☑ **Beginning Reading Concepts** Inside, Outside, 199C–199
Language Arts	**Writing:** Letter Formation, 186Y–186 Interactive Writing, 198A–198B	**Writing:** Letter Formation, 198K–198, 200C–200 Interactive Writing, 210A–210B

Curriculum Connections	**Writing:** Name That Cat, 186S **Science:** Apple ID, 186T **Social Studies:** Safety First, 186T **Social Studies:** Backyard Maps, 193/194B **Social Studies:** Watch It Grow, 197B	**Writing:** Giving Art, 198E **Math:** Guessing Game, 198F **Social Studies:** Pottery, 198F **Art:** Make a Cat, 199B **Science:** Moon Shapes, 203B **Science:** Mammals, 205/206B **Science:** Favorite Foods, 209B
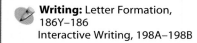 CULTURAL PERSPECTIVES	Jumping Rope, 191B	

Go, Lad, Go

Mud Fun

Ron and Me

WEEK 3 — Go, Lad, Go!

Easy Book: *Lin Did It!*
On-Level Book: *Go, Lad, Go!*
Challenge Book: *Let's Go!*

☑ **Phonics and Decoding**
Initial /l/*l*, 210K–210, 212C–212, 214C–214
Initial and Final /p/*p*, 214C–214
Review Blending with Short *a*, *i*, *o*, 216C–216, 220C–220

☑ **Comprehension**
Main Idea, 213G–213, 219A–219

☑ **Vocabulary**
High-Frequency Word: *go*, 215C–215
go, *to*, *me*, *you*, 221C–221

☑ **Beginning Reading Concepts**
Over, Under, 211C–211

✎ **Writing:** Letter Formation, 210K–210
Interactive Writing, 222A–222B

Writing: Animal Favorites, 210E

Math: Count and Check, 210F

Social Studies: Different Kinds of Homes, 210F

Social Studies: Safety Signs, 221B

Science: Favorite Pets, 217/218B

Camouflage, 215B

WEEK 4 — Mud Fun

Easy Book: *Pam and the Pup*
On-Level Book: *Mud Fun*
Challenge Book: *Fun on the Farm*

☑ **Phonics and Decoding**
Initial /u/*u*, 222K–222, 226C–226
Medial /u/*u*, 224C–224, 226C–226
Blending with Short *u*, *o*, 228C–228, 232C–232

☑ **Comprehension**
Compare and Contrast, 225C–225, 231A–231

☑ **Vocabulary**
High-Frequency Word: *do*, 227C–227
do, *go*, *I*, *and*, *me*, 233C–233

☑ **Beginning Reading Concepts**
Up, Down, 223C–223

✎ **Writing:** Letter Formation, 222K–222, 224C–224
Interactive Writing, 234A–234B

Writing: Words and Pictures, 222E

Math: May I Measure? 222F

Science: Nature Alphabet, 222F

Science: Make a Mural, 223B

Science: Planting in Mud, 229/230B

Math: Cats of a Different Color, 233B

Counting, 227B

WEEK 5 — Ron and Me

Easy Book: *We Have Fun!*
On-Level Book: *Ron and Me*
Self-Selected Reading of Challenge Books

☑ **Phonics and Decoding**
Initial /r/*r*, /p/*p*, /l/*l*, 234K–234, 238C–238
Final /p/*p*, 236C–236
Blending with Short *u*, *o*, *i*, 240C–240, 244C–244

☑ **Comprehension**
Main Idea, 237C–237
Compare and Contrast, 243A–243

☑ **Vocabulary**
High-Frequency Words: *to*, *me*, *go*, *do*, 239C–239, 245C–245

☑ **Beginning Reading Concepts**
On, Off; Inside, Outside; Over, Under; Up, Down, 235C–235

✎ **Writing:** Interactive Writing, 246A–246B

Writing: Make an *Rr* Book, 234E

Science: Sun Spots, 234F

Science: Kinder-Garden, 245B

Social Studies: Map Time, 234F

Social Studies: Our Town, 239B

Art: Paperbag Pumpkin, 235B

Math: Dog Pictures, 241/242B

WEEK 6 — Review, Assessment

Self-Selected Reading

☑ **Assess Skills**

Phonics and Decoding
Initial /r/*r*, /p/*p*, /l/*l*, /u/*u*
Final /p/*p*
Medial /u/*u*
Blending with Short *a*, *i*, *o*, *u*

Comprehension
Main Idea
Compare and Contrast

Vocabulary
High-Frequency Words: *to*, *me*, *go*, *do*

Beginning Reading Concepts
On, Off
Inside, Outside
Over, Under
Up, Down

☑ **Unit 4 Assessment**

☑ **Standardized Test Preparation**

LITERATURE

DECODABLE STORIES These four-color stories in the Pupil Edition consist of words containing the phonetic elements that have been taught, as well as the high-frequency words. The stories reinforce the comprehension and concepts of print skills. These are also available as Independent Leveled Books.

LEVELED BOOKS These engaging stories include the high-frequency words and words with the phonetic elements that are focused on. They reinforce the comprehension skills and correlate to the unit themes.

Easy	Independent	Challenge
• *Ron Is In*	• *You Are IT!*	• *Ron's Radishes*
• *The Mop Man*	• *Is It You?*	• *The Picnic*
• *Lin Did It!*	• *Go, Lad, Go!*	• *Let's Go!*
• *Pam and the Pup*	• *Mud Fun*	• *Fun on the Farm*
• *We Have Fun!*	• *Ron and Me*	

ABC BIG BOOK Children build alphabetic knowledge and letter identification as they enjoy a shared reading of this story that correlates to the theme. Little book versions of the stories are also available.
• *Allie's Adventure from A to Z*

LITERATURE BIG BOOKS Shared readings of the highest-quality literature reinforce comprehension skills and introduce children to a variety of genres.
• *The Apple Pie Tree*
• *Nature Spy*

READ ALOUDS Traditional folk tales, fables, fairy tales, and stories from around the world can be shared with children as they develop their oral comprehension skills and learn about other cultures.
• *Every Time I Climb a Tree*
• *The Playground of the Sun and Moon*
• *The Clever Turtle*
• *How Many Spots Does a Leopard Have?*

LISTENING LIBRARY
Recordings of the Big Books, Independent Books, and Unit Opener and Closer Poetry.

SKILLS

PUPIL EDITION Colorful practice pages help you to assess children's progress as they learn and review each skill, including phonics, high-frequency words, readiness, comprehension, and letter formation.

PRACTICE BOOK Practice pages in alternative formats provide additional reinforcement of each skill as well as extra handwriting practice.

BIG BOOK OF PHONICS RHYMES AND POEMS Traditional and contemporary poems emphasize phonics and rhyme and allow children to develop oral comprehension skills.

READING FOR INFORMATION This lively big book introduces important study skills.

WORD BUILDING MANIPULATIVE CARDS
 Letter and word cards to utilize phonics and build children's vocabulary. Includes high-frequency word cards.

LANGUAGE SUPPORT BOOK
ESL Parallel teaching and practice activities for children needing language support.

SONGS FROM A–Z
Recordings of short lively songs to reinforce letter sounds.

McGraw-Hill School
TECHNOLOGY

Phonics CD-ROM Provides interactive lessons for additional phonics support.

interNET CONNECTION Extend lessons through Research and Inquiry Ideas.

Handwriting CD-ROM provides practice activities.

Visit www.mhschool.com/reading

Resources for Meeting Individual Needs

	EASY	INDEPENDENT	CHALLENGE	LANGUAGE SUPPORT

UNIT 4

You Are IT!

EASY

📘 **Easy Book**
Ron Is In
Teaching Strategies 186, 187, 188, 189, 190, 191, 192, 195, 196, 197
Alternate Teaching Strategy T22–T26
💿 **Writing** 198B

💿 **Phonics CD-ROM**

INDEPENDENT

You Are IT!
Teaching Strategies 186–192, 195–197
Alternate Teaching Strategy T22–T26
💿 **Writing** 198B

📘 **Challenge Book**
Ron's Radishes

💿 **Phonics CD-ROM**

CHALLENGE

📘 **Challenge Book**
Ron's Radishes
Teaching Strategies 186, 187, 188, 189, 190, 191, 192, 195, 196, 197
💿 **Writing** 198B

💿 **Phonics CD-ROM**

LANGUAGE SUPPORT

Teaching Strategies 186, 187, 188, 189, 190, 191, 192, 195, 196, 197
Alternate Teaching Strategy T22–T26
💿 **Writing** 198B

💿 **Phonics CD-ROM**

Is It You?

EASY

📘 **Easy Book**
The Mop Man
Teaching Strategies 198, 199, 200, 201, 202, 203, 204, 207, 208, 209
Alternate Teaching Strategy T26–T30
💿 **Writing** 210B

💿 **Phonics CD-ROM**

INDEPENDENT

Is It You?
Teaching Strategies 198–204, 207–209
Alternate Teaching Strategy T26–T30
💿 **Writing** 210B

📘 **Challenge Book**
The Picnic

💿 **Phonics CD-ROM**

CHALLENGE

📘 **Challenge Book**
The Picnic
Teaching Strategies 198, 199, 200, 201, 202, 203, 204, 207, 208, 209
💿 **Writing** 210B

💿 **Phonics CD-ROM**

LANGUAGE SUPPORT

Teaching Strategies 198, 199, 200, 201, 202, 203, 204, 207, 208, 209
Alternate Teaching Strategy T26–T30
💿 **Writing** 210B

💿 **Phonics CD-ROM**

Go, Lad, Go!

EASY

📘 **Easy Book**
Lin Did It!
Teaching Strategies 210, 211, 212, 213, 214, 215, 216, 219, 220, 221
Alternate Teaching Strategy T25, T26, T31, T32, T35
💿 **Writing** 222B

💿 **Phonics CD-ROM**

INDEPENDENT

Go, Lad, Go!
Teaching Strategies 210–216, 219–221
Alternate Teaching Strategy T25, T26, T31, T32, T35
💿 **Writing** 222B

📘 **Challenge Book**
Let's Go!

💿 **Phonics CD-ROM**

CHALLENGE

📘 **Challenge Book**
Let's Go!
Teaching Strategies 210, 211, 212, 213, 214, 215, 216, 219, 220, 221
💿 **Writing** 222B

💿 **Phonics CD-ROM**

LANGUAGE SUPPORT

Teaching Strategies 210, 211, 212, 213, 214, 215, 216, 219, 220, 221
Alternate Teaching Strategy T25, T26, T31, T32, T35
💿 **Writing** 222B

💿 **Phonics CD-ROM**

Mud Fun

EASY

📘 **Easy Book**
Pam and the Pup
Teaching Strategies 222, 223, 224, 225, 226, 227, 228, 231, 232, 233
Alternate Teaching Strategy T26, T30, T33–T35
💿 **Writing** 234B

💿 **Phonics CD-ROM**

INDEPENDENT

Mud Fun
Teaching Strategies 222–228, 231–233
Alternate Teaching Strategy T26, T30, T33–T35
💿 **Writing** 234B

📘 **Challenge Book**
Fun on the Farm

💿 **Phonics CD-ROM**

CHALLENGE

📘 **Challenge Book**
Fun on the Farm
Teaching Strategies 222, 223, 224, 225, 226, 227, 228, 231, 232, 233
💿 **Writing** 234B

💿 **Phonics CD-ROM**

LANGUAGE SUPPORT

Teaching Strategies 222, 223, 224, 225, 226, 227, 228, 231, 232, 233
Alternate Teaching Strategy T26, T30, T33–T35
💿 **Writing** 234B

💿 **Phonics CD-ROM**

Ron and Me

EASY

📘 **Easy Book**
We Have Fun!
Teaching Strategies 234, 235, 236, 237, 238, 239, 240, 243, 244, 245
Alternate Teaching Strategy T24–T35
💿 **Writing** 246B

💿 **Phonics CD-ROM**

INDEPENDENT

Ron and Me
Teaching Strategies 234–240, 243–245
Alternate Teaching Strategy T24–T35
💿 **Writing** 246B

📘 **Challenge Book**
Challenge Book Choice

💿 **Phonics CD-ROM**

CHALLENGE

📘 **Challenge Book**
Challenge Book Choice
Teaching Strategies 234, 235, 236, 237, 238, 239, 240, 243, 244, 245
💿 **Writing** 246B

💿 **Phonics CD-ROM**

LANGUAGE SUPPORT

Teaching Strategies 234, 235, 236, 237, 238, 239, 240, 243, 244, 245
Alternate Teaching Strategy T24–T35
💿 **Writing** 246B

💿 **Phonics CD-ROM**

INFORMAL

Informal Assessment

- Phonological Awareness, 186V, 188B, 190B, 192B, 196B, 198H, 200B, 202B, 204B, 208B, 210H, 212B, 214B, 216B, 220B, 222H, 224B, 226B, 228B, 232B, 234H, 236B, 238B, 240B, 244B
- Phonics and Decoding, 186Y, 188C, 190C, 192C, 196C, 198K, 200C, 202C, 204C, 208C, 210K, 212C, 214C, 216C, 220C, 222K, 224C, 226C, 228C, 232C, 234K, 236C, 238C, 240C, 244C
- Comprehension, 187B, 189B, 189E, 195A, 197B, 199B, 201B, 201C, 207A, 209B, 211B, 213B, 213G, 219A, 221B, 223B, 225B, 225C, 231A, 233B, 235B, 237B, 237C, 243A, 245B
- High-Frequency Words, 191C, 197C, 203C, 209C, 215C, 221C, 227C, 233C, 239C, 245C
- Beginning Reading Concepts, 187E, 199C, 211C, 223C, 235C

Performance Assessment

- Research and Inquiry Project, 186O, 246C
- Interactive Writing, 198A–198B, 210A–210B, 222A–222B, 234A–234B, 246A–246B
- Listening, Speaking, Viewing Activities, 198B, 210B, 222B, 234B, 246B
- Portfolio
  Writing, 198A–198B, 210A–210B, 222A–222B, 234A–234B, 246A–246B
  Cross-Curricular Activities, 186S, 186T, 193/194B, 197B, 198E, 198F, 199B, 203B, 205/206B, 209B, 210E, 210F, 217/218B, 221B, 222E, 222F, 223B, 229/230B, 233B, 234E, 234F, 235B, 239B, 241/242B

Practice

- **Phonics and Decoding**
  /r/r, 186, 188, 190, 234, 238; /f/f, 190; /p/p, 198, 200, 202, 214, 234, 236, 238; /l/l, 210, 212, 214, 234, 238; /u/u, 222, 224, 226
  Blending with Short *a, i, o, u*, 192, 196, 204, 208, 216, 220, 228, 232, 240, 244
- **Comprehension**
  Main Idea, 189, 195, 213, 219, 237
  Compare and Contrast, 201, 207, 225, 231, 243
- **High-Frequency Words**
  to, me, go, do, 191, 197, 203, 209, 215, 221, 227, 233, 239, 245
- **Beginning Reading Concepts**
  On, Off, 187; Inside, Outside, 199; Over, Under, 211; Up, Down, 223; Positional Terms, 235

FORMAL

Unit 4 Assessment

- **Phonics and Decoding**
  Initial /r/r
  Initial /f/f
  Initial and Final /p/p
  Initial /l/l
  Initial and Medial /u/u
  Blending with Short *a, i, o, u*
- **Comprehension**
  Main Idea
  Compare and Contrast
- **High-Frequency Words**
  to, me, go, do
- **Beginning Reading Concepts**
  On, Off
  Inside, Outside
  Over, Under
  Up, Down

Diagnostic/Placement Evaluation

- Phonemic Awareness Assessment
- Placement Tests
- Informal Reading Inventories
- Running Records

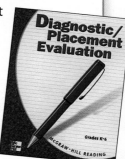

Test Preparation

- Standardized Test Preparation Practice Book

Assessment Checklist

Student .... Grade ....

Teacher ....

	You Are IT!	Is It You?	Go, Lad, Go!	Mud Fun	Ron and Me	Assessment Summary
LISTENING/SPEAKING						
Participates in oral language experiences						
Listens and speaks to gain knowledge of culture						
Speaks appropriately to audiences for different purposes						
Communicates clearly (gains increasing control of grammar)						
READING						
Demonstrates knowledge of concepts of print						
Uses phonological awareness strategies, including						
• Identifying rhyming words						
• Identifying sounds: initial, final, and medial						
• Segmenting (syllables, sounds)						
• Blending (onset/rime, sounds)						
• Deleting syllables						
Uses letter/sound knowledge, including						
• Applying letter-sound correspondences to begin to read						
• Phonics and Decoding: initial /r/ R,r						
• Phonics and Decoding: initial, final /p/ P,p						
• Phonics and Decoding: initial /l/ L,l						
• Phonics and Decoding: initial, medial /u/ U,u						
• Blending with a, i, o, u						
Develops an extensive vocabulary, including						
• High-frequency words: to, me, go, do						
Identifies the main idea of a selection						
Compare and contrast information in a selection						
Recognizes and responds to various types of texts						
Conducts research using various sources						
Reads to increase knowledge						
WRITING						
Writes his/her own name						
Writes each letter of the alphabet						
Uses phonological knowledge to write messages						
Gains increasing control of penmanship						
Composes original texts						
Uses writing as a tool for learning and research						

+ Observed   — Not Observed

Introduce the Theme

I Wonder

We can make discoveries about the wonders of nature in our own backyard.

Big Books

The **Apple Pie Tree**
BY Zoe Hall
ILLUSTRATED BY
Shari Halpern

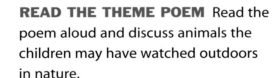

The Little Turtle

There was a little turtle.
He lived in a box.
He swam in a puddle.
He climbed on the rocks.
He snapped at a mosquito.
He snapped at a flea.
He snapped at a minnow.
And he snapped at me.

He caught the mosquito.
He caught the flea.
He caught the minnow.
But he didn't catch me.

Vachel Lindsay

 Listening Library

Allie's Adventure
From A to Z

Written by Ellen Dreyer Illustrated by...

NATURE SPY
written by SHELLEY ROTNER and KEN KREISLER
photographs by SHELLEY ROTNER

READ THE THEME POEM Read the poem aloud and discuss animals the children may have watched outdoors in nature.

DISCUSS THE POEM Ask children to tell things the poem taught them about turtles. Ask how they think the poet learned these things.

THEME CONNECTIONS

Theme Summary The weeks in Unit 4 relate to the unit theme, *I Wonder*. This thematic link will help children to make connections from their own experiences with nature to the literature of the unit.

My Backyard Literature selections presented within the first two weeks are also related to the subtheme *In My Backyard*. These stories include experiences with nature that are familiar to many children.

Wonders of Nature Selections for the third and fourth weeks are tied to the subtheme *Wonders of Nature*. These stories enable children to expand their knowledge as they make discoveries about nature beyond their local world.

The fifth week of the unit gives children the opportunity to reread their favorite literature selections and discuss the main theme of *I Wonder*.

Research and Inquiry

Theme Project: Nature Collages

PARTNERS

Tell children that they will create collages of the wonderful things they find in nature.

List What They Know Help children create lists of natural things they think they might find and collect for their collages.

Ask Questions and Identify Resources Help children generate questions about things on their list.

QUESTIONS	RESOURCES
• Why do acorns fall from trees? • What are rocks and pebbles made from?	• books about nature • Web sites • teacher

Create a Presentation Have pairs of children gather nature items from their backyards at home and the playground, such as flower petals, seeds, acorns, feathers, leaves, and small pebbles. Show pairs how to arrange the items in an interesting way and glue them to construction paper. Have pairs dictate a sentence about their collages as you record them.

Other Resources

SCHOOL/HOME CONNECTION

Take-Home Books
Theme-related daily activities and decodable stories will encourage children's learning at home.

THEME BIBLIOGRAPHY For a listing of theme-related books and multimedia resources see pages T54–T55.

TECHNOLOGY

 Signs of Nature
(National Geographic)

 Where Does It Come From?
(National Geographic)

 Help children log on to
www.mhschool.com/reading,
where they can find more information about apple trees.

You Are IT!

Phonics	Comprehension	Vocabulary
• Initial /r/r • Blending	• Main Idea	• to

Literature Resources

Big Books

Big Book of Phonics Rhymes and Poems
pages 19, 44, 45

ABC Big Book
pages 187A–187B

Literature Big Book
pages 189A–189B

Reading for Information Big Book
page 24

Read Aloud

Every Time I Climb a Tree

page 191A

Student Books

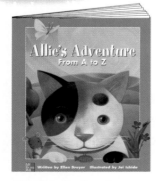

ABC Little Book
pages 187A–187B

Easy
page 197A
Decodable

Independent
pages 193/194A–193/194B, 197A
Decodable
Story also available in Pupil Edition

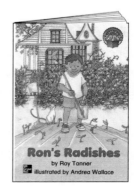

Challenge
page 197B
Patterned

Center Activities for the Week

Center Activities

Activities take 15–20 minutes each.

Phonics

Sort *Rr*

Objective: Identify words that begin with /r/.

- ◆ Display items and pictures at the Center.
- ◆ Ask children to sort items by placing items that begin with /r/ in the *Rr* box.

MATERIALS
- Shoe box labeled *Rr*
- Items and pictures of items that begin with *Rr* and some that do not begin with *Rr*

Writing

Name That Cat

Objective: Recognize ABC order.

- ◆ Have children trace and cut out cats.
- ◆ Ask them to name their cats. Have them print the name on the back of the cat.
- ◆ Put the class cats in ABC order.

MATERIALS
- Templates of cats
- Construction paper

Reading and Listening

Self-Selected Reading

Objective: Compare personal experiences with those described in a book.

Place the literature for the week and the corresponding audiocassettes or CDs in the Reading Center. You may also include the following books from the Theme Bibliography on pages T54–T55.

- ◆ *My Backyard Garden* by Carol Lerner
- ◆ *My Spring Robin* by Anne F. Rockwell
- ◆ *Planting a Rainbow* by Lois Ehlert

MATERIALS
- Listening Library cassettes and CDs
- Books

Science

Apple ID

Objective: Identify and describe parts of an object.

◆ Show children an apple half.

◆ Invite them to describe the texture, colors, and smell of the apple.

◆ Point out the stem, skin, seeds, core, and pulp.

Social Studies

Safety First

Objective: Communicate information and ideas using appropriate media.

◆ Talk about safe and fair play.

◆ Have children brainstorm rules that will ensure safe, fair play.

◆ Have children draw pictures of fair play. Help them write the appropriate safety rule under their picture.

MATERIALS
• Index cards
• Poster board
• Markers
• Crayons

Working with Words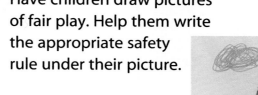

MATERIALS
• Word cards for *to* and *in*
• Aluminum tin filled with sand
• Index cards, two per child

Trace and Write

Objective: Recognize high-frequency words.

◆ Show the cards for *to* and *in*.

◆ Have children trace each word in the sand.

◆ Ask them to copy the words on index cards.

You Are IT!

Suggested Lesson Planner

READING AND LANGUAGE ARTS

- ● **Phonological Awareness**

- ● **Phonics** initial /r/r; blending with short *a, i, o*

- ● **Comprehension**

- ● **Vocabulary**

- ● **Beginning Reading Concepts**

- ● **Listening, Speaking, Viewing, Representing**

DAY 1

Focus on Reading Skills

Develop Phonological Awareness, 186W–186X
"R is for Ribbon" *Big Book of Phonics Rhymes and Poems,* 45

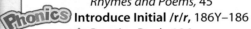 **Introduce Initial /r/r,** 186Y–186
- ◆ Practice Book, 186
- ◆ Phonics/Phonemic Awareness Practice Book, 99–100

- ◆  **CD-ROM**

 Read the Literature

Read *Allie's Adventure from A to Z* **Big Book,** 187A–187B
Shared Reading

Build Skills
- ☑ On, Off, 187E–187
- ◆ Practice Book, 187

DAY 2

The Apple Pie Tree
BY Zoe Hall
ILLUSTRATED BY Shari Halpern

Focus on Reading Skills

Develop Phonological Awareness, 188A–188B
"Rainbow Riddle" *Big Book of Phonics Rhymes and Poems,* 44

 **Review Initial /r/r,** 188C–188
- ◆ Practice Book, 188
- ◆ Phonics/Phonemic Awareness Practice Book, 101–102

- ◆  **CD-ROM**

Read the Literature

Read *The Apple Pie Tree* **Big Book,** 189A–189B
Shared Reading

Build Skills
- ☑ Main Idea, 189E–189
- ◆ Practice Book, 189

- ● **Cross Curriculum**

◆ Science, Social Studies, 186T

◆ Science, Social Studies, 186T

- ● **Writing**

◆ **Writing Prompt:** Write about what happens next to Allie and Zack.

 Journal Writing, 187B
Letter Formation, 186Y

◆ **Writing Prompt:** Write about what you learned about apple trees from *The Apple Pie Tree.*

 Journal Writing, 189B
Letter Formation, 188C

Read EVERY DAY

DAY 3

Every Time I Climb a Tree

Focus on Reading Skills

Develop Phonological Awareness, 190A–190B
"Rainbow Riddle" and "Ferris Wheel Fun" *Big Book of Phonics Rhymes and Poems,* 44, 19

**Review /r/r, /f/f,** 190C–190
◆ Practice Book, 190
◆ Phonics/Phonemic Awareness Practice Book, 99–102

◆ **CD-ROM**

Read the Literature

Read "Every Time I Climb a Tree" Teacher Read Aloud, 191A–191B
Shared Reading
Read the Reading for Information Big Book, 24–25
Maps

Build Skills

☑ **High-Frequency Word:** *to* 191C–191
◆ Practice Book, 191

◆ Cultural Perspectives, 191B

◆ **Writing Prompt:** What is your favorite kind of tree? Draw it and explain what you like about it.

DAY 4

You Are IT!

Focus on Reading Skills

Develop Phonological Awareness, 192A–192B
"Ron the Cat"

**Review Blending with Short *a, i, o,*** 192C–192
◆ Practice Book, 192
◆ Phonics/Phonemic Awareness Practice Book, 103

◆  **CD-ROM**

Read the Literature

Read "You Are IT!" On-Level Decodable Story, 193/194A–193/194B

☑ Initial /r/r; Blending
☑ Main Idea
☑ High-Frequency Word: *to* Concepts of Print

Build Skills

☑ Main Idea, 195A–195
◆ Practice Book, 195

◆ Social Studies, 193/194B

◆ **Writing Prompt:** What game do you like to play with your friends? Write about it.
Journal Writing, 193/194B
Letter Formation Practice Book, 193–194

DAY 5

Ron Is In
You Are IT!
Ron's Radishes
by Ray Tanner
illustrated by Andrea Wallace

Focus on Reading Skills

Develop Phonological Awareness, 196A–196B
"Ron the Cat"

Review Blending with Short *a, i, o,* 196C–196
◆ Practice Book, 196
◆ Phonics/Phonemic Awareness Practice Book, 104

◆ **CD-ROM**

Read the Literature

Read "Ron Is In" Easy Decodable Story, 197A
Reread "You Are IT!" On-Level Decodable Story, 197A
Read "Ron's Radishes" Challenge Patterned Book, 197B
Guided Reading
☑ Initial /r/r; Blending
☑ Main Idea
☑ High-Frequency Word: *to* Concepts of Print

Build Skills

☑ High-Frequency Words: *to, the, that,* 197C–197
◆ Practice Book, 197

◆ Social Studies, 197B

◆ **Writing Prompt:** Write about your favorite thing in your neighborhood.

Interactive Writing, 198A–198B

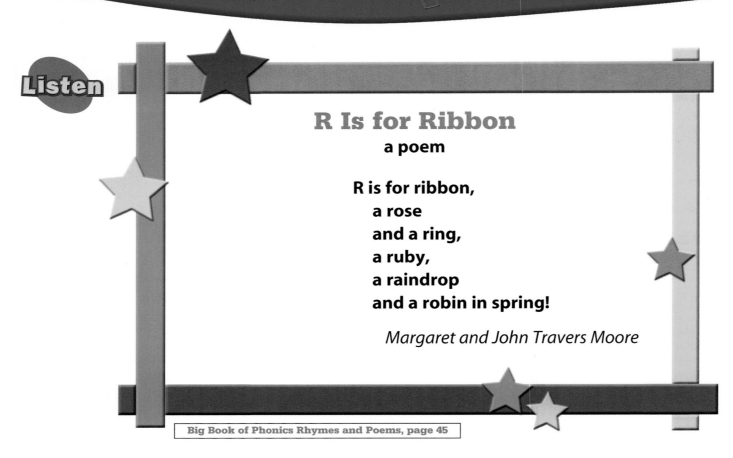

Listen

R Is for Ribbon
a poem

R is for ribbon,
    a rose
    and a ring,
    a ruby,
    a raindrop
    and a robin in spring!

Margaret and John Travers Moore

Big Book of Phonics Rhymes and Poems, page 45

Identify Rhyming Words · · · · · · · Phonological Awareness · · · · · · ·

Teach   Ask children to listen as you recite "R Is for Ribbon." Then read the poem again, pausing before the end of lines three and six to encourage children to supply the rhyming word.

MODEL: Listen to these rhyming words: *ring, spring*. Can you think of another word that rhymes with *ring* and *spring*?

Practice   Say each word below. Ask children to suggest words that rhyme with each word. If some children have trouble producing rhymes, ask others to help. Remind them to think of words that have the same ending sounds: *ring* and *spring, rose* and *nose*.

> ring: wing, sting, thing, sing
> rose: nose, goes, toes, hose
> rain: pain, gain, train, mane
> run: bun, won, done, ton

Listen for Beginning Sounds · · · · · · · · Phonemic Awareness · · · · · · · · · · ·

Teach Display the Phonics Picture Poster (picture side only) for *rabbit*. Have the puppet say *rabbit*. Have children listen for the beginning sound as you repeat the word. Then say the following words from the poem: *ribbon, rose, ring, ruby, raindrop,* and *robin*. Explain that each of these six words begin with the same sound, /r/. Have children say the /r/ sound with you.

Practice Say the pairs of words in the box below. Ask children to say *rabbit* when they hear the /r/ sound at the beginning of both words.

ribbon/dog	*race/ran*	*root/fan*
rip/rake	*run/fall*	*raccoon/rainbow*

MATERIALS
- Phonics Picture Poster: *rabbit*
- **puppet**

· ·

INFORMAL ASSESSMENT Observe children as they identify rhyming words and beginning sounds. If children have difficulty, see Alternate Teaching Strategies: Unit 3, T29; and Unit 4, T22.

Read Together

From Phonemic Awareness to Phonics

Objective: Identify /r/R, r

IDENTIFY THE LETTER FOR THE SOUND Explain to children that the letters *R, r* stand for the sound /r/. Ask children to say the sound with you.

Display the Big Book of Phonics Rhymes and Poems, page 45. Point to the letters in the corner and identify them. Have children make the /r/ sound as you point to the letters.

REREAD THE POEM Reread the poem, pointing to each word. Ask children to raise a finger when you point to and say a word that begins with /r/.

FIND WORDS WITH R, r Have children find words that begin with R, r and put self-stick notes under them.

SOLVE THE RIDDLE Tell children you are going to play a game with words that begin with *R, r* from the poem. Then say the sentence: *I'd like to smell a _____ (rose).* Ask a volunteer to say the word to finish the sentence. Continue with the following sentences.

> **The present had a (ribbon).**
> **I have a (ring) on my finger.**

Rr

R is for ribbon,
a rose
and a ring,
a ruby,
a raindrop
and a robin in spring!
Margaret and John Travers Moore

Big Book of Phonics Rhymes and Poems, page 45

186X

Initial /r/ r

Rr
rabbit

Phonics Picture Posters and Cards

Children will:

☑ identify and form *R, r*

☑ identify /r/ *R, r*

MATERIALS

- Phonics Picture Posters

ADDITIONAL RESOURCES

- Practice Book, page 186
- Phonics/Phonemic Awareness Practice Book, pages 99–100
- **Phonics** CD-ROM

Phonics Song

Ricky the Rabbit

Ricky the Rabbit rides his bike,
Rides his bike, rides his bike,
Ricky the Rabbit rides his bike,
Then he stops to rest.

Sung to the tune of "The Wheels on the Bus"

From Songs from A to Z

Introduce

TEACH

Phonemic Awareness Warm-Up Have children sing the song "Ricky the Rabbit" with you. Then say the words from the song without the /r/ sound. Have children add the /r/ sound to say the words: est/rest; abbit/rabbit; icky/Ricky; ides/rides. Continue with other words.

Identify /r/ R, r Say the word *rabbit* slowly, emphasizing the /r/ sound. Display the Phonics Picture Poster for *rabbit*. Point to the letters *R, r* and explain that *R, r* stands for the sound /r/. Have children repeat the /r/ sound after you.

Form R, r Review the capital and lowercase forms with children. With your back to them, trace the letters one at a time in the air with your finger. Ask children to do the same. Then, give children small squares of paper and have them write *R* on one side and *r* on the other side.

PRACTICE

Can You Find the *Rr*?

Materials: Phonics Picture Cards
rabbit, turtle, monkey, pig, rope

◆ Place the Phonics Picture Cards around the room.

◆ Invite volunteers to find the *Rr* card and identify the picture on the card.

ON LEVEL

✓ ASSESS/CLOSE

Have children complete page 186 of the Pupil Edition or the Practice Book. For a different approach to this skill, see page T23 for the **Alternate Teaching Strategy.**

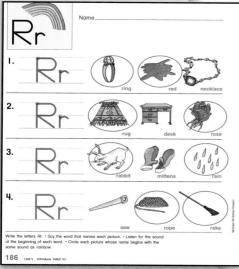

Rr Name_____

1. Rr ring red necklace

2. Rr rug desk rose

3. Rr rabbit mittens rain

4. Rr saw rope rake

Write the letters *Rr*. • Say the word that names each picture. • Listen for the sound at the beginning of each word. • Circle each picture whose name begins with the same sound as rainbow.

186 Unit 4 Introduce Initial /r/

Pupil Edition page 186

Meeting Individual Needs
Activities

Form the Letter

Materials: modeling clay

◆ Show children how to roll modeling clay into a long roll.

◆ Invite children to use clay to form a capital *R*. Then have them trace the clay *R* as they say the letter name. Have children repeat the process for lowercase *r*.

EASY

Making Alphabet Cards

Materials: crayons, drawing paper

◆ Have children brainstorm words that begin with /r/, such as *run, rabbit, red, race, rip,* and *rag.*

◆ On one side of the drawing paper, ask children to draw a picture of one of the words. On the back of the card, children can print *Rr.*

◆ Ask children to say the names of their pictures and use the words in sentences.

CHALLENGE

Show the Word!

◆ Ask children to pantomime the following action words that begin with the letter *r*: *run, roll, race, rip, rake.*

◆ Then repeat the words and have children trace the letters *R* and *r* in the air with their fingers.

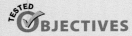

Allie's Adventure
From A to Z
Written by Ellen Dreyer   Illustrated by Jui Ishida

Big Book

TESTED OBJECTIVES

Children will:

☐ track print from left to right.

☐ recognize ABC order in the story.

☐ make predictions.

☑ identify the main idea of the story.

ELLEN DREYER lives in New York City. She has written many books for young readers. She says, "My cat Dixie loves having adventures and then curling up on her special pillow."

JUI ISHIDA grew up in Japan and now lives in California. She had a cat just like Allie in Japan, and misses her very much.

Build Background

Develop Vocabulary   Show children a picture of a cat. Invite children to demonstrate cat actions and sounds.

Make a word web of the cat actions on the board.

Read the Big Book

Preview and Predict   Show the cover of the Big Book, and read aloud the title, author, and illustrator. Discuss the cover, asking children if they can tell what the book is about.

Set Purposes   Show children the cover again and point out the second half of the title, *From A to Z*. As you read the story, ask children to listen for what the cat might do that involves the letters of the alphabet.

Read the Story   Point to the highlighted words in the first few sentences you read. Help children identify the initial letters in the words. Continue to point out the ABC words as you read the story. *Concepts of Print*

Point to the letter *r* in the sentence "Allie needs a rest!" Ask children to make the /r/ sound. *Letter Identification*

Invite a volunteer to point to the highlighted word in a sentence. Ask children what letter the word begins and ends with. *Concepts of Print*

LANGUAGE SUPPORT

ESL   Take a picture walk with children through the first few pages of the story to help them develop vocabulary. Use gestures and facial expressions to help children understand the meaning of the words *quick, rested, tired,* and *excited*.

This is **Allie**.

Allie sees a **butterfly**.

Allie's Adventure, pages 2–3

Literature Response

LISTENING/SPEAKING

Return to Predictions Ask children if they predicted any of Allie's adventures before reading the story.

Discuss the Story Ask volunteers to answer the questions using complete sentences.

Why do you think the story is called *Allie's Adventure from A to Z*? (Answers will vary) *Main Idea*

What word at the beginning of the story starts with the letter *a*? (Allie) What letter comes next in the alphabet? (b) What word in the story starts with the letter *b*? (butterfly) *Literal: Letter Identification*

Does Allie act like a real cat? (Answers will vary.) *Inferential: Fantasy and Reality*

Who can find the word that starts with the capital *Z*? What is it? (Zack) *Concepts of Print*

WRITING

Journal Writing Ask children to write and draw about a favorite activity that Allie did in the story. Invite them to explain their drawings to a friend.

Allie is **excited**.

Allie's Adventure, page 29

INFORMAL ASSESSMENT

RECOGNIZE ABC ORDER

How to Assess
Write three children's names on three strips of paper. Have children circle the beginning letter in each name and then arrange the names in ABC order.

Follow-Up
Provide children with letter cards to arrange in ABC order.

 **Activity**

ABC Activity

ABC CATS Provide templates of cat faces. Have children trace and cut out cat faces that show a collar beneath. Make sure the collar is large enough for a child to write on. Then ask children to name their cats, printing the name on the collar, and first initial on the back. Children can put their cats in ABC order.

 Ann

 Bob

 Cal

This is **Allie**.

Allie sees a **butterfly**.

Allie sees a **cow**.

Allie sees a **door**.

Allie sees some **eggs**.

Allie sees lots of **feathers**.

Allie pushes the **gate**.

Allie sees a **hole**.

Allie sees an **insect**.

Allie **jumps**!

A hole is no place for a **kitten**.

Allie sees some **lettuce**.

Allie does not see the **mouse**.

Allie sees a tiny **nose**.

She puts her paw **on** the nose.

Allie's Adventure Big Book

The mouse runs past the **pumpkins**!

The mouse is very **quick**.

Allie needs a **rest**!

Allie curls up in a **sunny** spot.

She is very **tired**.

Allie wakes **up**.

She hears a **voice**.

Allie **walks** toward the voice.

Allie is **excited**.

A boy is **yelling** her name.

Zack missed Allie.

Allie's Adventure Big Book

187D

On, Off

TESTED

OBJECTIVES

Children will:

☑ identify *on* and *off*

MATERIALS

- *Allie's Adventure from A to Z*

TEACHING TIP

VOCABULARY You may wish to add the words in the Beginning Reading Concepts lessons in this unit to the Word Wall.

Introduce

Allie's Adventure from A to Z

TEACH

Recognize On and Off Display the cover of the Big Book *Allie's Adventure from A to Z* and have children recall the story. Turn to page 12 and ask: *Where is the beetle?* (on Allie's nose) On pages 30–31, ask: *Where is the boy?* (on the porch) *Is the cat on the porch?* (No. The cat is not on the porch.) Look for other examples of *on* or *off* in the story.

PRACTICE

Off and On

◆ Place a book *on* a chair and then take it *off* the chair. Tell what you did in a complete sentence. (I put a book *on* the chair, then I took the book *off* the chair.)

◆ Model one other *on/off* sentence and then have several children suggest their own *on/off* sentence and act it out.

ON LEVEL

✓ ASSESS/CLOSE

Have children complete page 187 of the Pupil Edition or Practice Book. For a different approach to teaching this skill, see page T24 for the **Alternate Teaching Strategy.**

Name

1.

2.

3.

4.

Draw a circle around the picture that shows something that is on. • Draw a line under the picture that shows something that is off.

Unit 4 Introduce On, Off 187

Pupil Edition page 187

Meeting Individual Needs
Activities

Musical Chairs

Materials: one fewer chair than there are children, tape player and music tapes

◆ Discuss the rules of "Musical Chairs," emphasizing the words *on* and *off*.

◆ One child controls the music. While music plays, the children walk around the chairs. When it stops, they find a chair and sit *on* it. Music plays again, they get *off* the chairs and walk around.

◆ One chair is removed in each round of the game.

EASY

On or Off?

Materials: drawing paper, crayons or markers

◆ Have children fold a sheet of paper in half. In the first half, they draw a snowman with a hat on its head. In the second half, they draw a snowman with the hat off its head.

◆ Have them turn the paper over. Repeat the process by drawing a snowman with a scarf on and off.

CHALLENGE

Follow Directions

Materials: hat, block, book, coat

◆ Give children opportunities to follow your directions, such as: *Put the hat on. Take the block off the table.*

◆ If necessary, model doing the action yourself, then have children do the same.

LANGUAGE SUPPORT

187

Phonological Awareness

DAY 2

Listen

Rainbow Riddle

Have you seen colors like red, green, and blue
After a summer rain is through?

A ribbon of violet, yellow, and green—
The loveliest ribbon you ever have seen.

Can you guess before this riddle is through
That a rainbow is what I'm describing to you?

Big Book of Phonics Rhymes and Poems, page 44

Segment Syllables

Phonological Awareness

Teach   Read "Rainbow Riddle." Then clap the erasers to show the syllables in the word: *sum-mer*. Tell children the word *summer* has two word parts. Encourage the class to clap along with you.

> MODEL: Listen to the word *colors*. Listen again. *Co-lors*. It has two word parts. Say and clap the parts with me: *co-lors*.

Practice   Say each word in the box below. Ask a child to clap the erasers together for each syllable. Have children in the class decide whether or not the child clapped the correct number of times.

co-lors	sum-mer	rib-bon
vi-o-let	love-li-est	rid-dle

MATERIALS
- chalkboard erasers

Listen for Beginning Sounds

Teach   Tell children that you are a lion cub. Roar /rrrrrrrrr/ and let children do the same. Hold up the picture of the rabbit and say *rabbit*. Use a roaring /r/ to emphasize the beginning sound. Repeat for *robin, risky, ribbon, riddle, rainbow*. Explain to the children that each of these words start with the same sound /r/.

Practice   Have children pretend to be lion cubs. Ask some volunteers to say a word that begins with /r/. Have children roar when they hear a word that begins with /r/. Then have them say the word aloud.

INFORMAL ASSESSMENT   Observe children as they segment syllables and identify beginning sounds. If children have difficulty, see Alternate Teaching Strategies: Unit 3, T35; and Unit 4, T22.

MATERIALS
- **Phonics Picture Cards:** *rabbit*

Read Together

From Phonemic Awareness to Phonics

Objective: Identify /r/ R, r

IDENTIFY THE LETTER FOR THE SOUND
- Explain to children that the letters *R, r* stand for the sound /r/. Ask children to say the sound with you.
- Display the Big Book of Phonics Rhymes and Poems, page 44. Point to the letters in the corner and identify them. Have children make the /r/ sound as you point to the letters.

REREAD THE POEM
- Reread the poem, pointing to each word. Ask children to raise a finger when you point to and say a word that begins with /r/.

LOOK FOR WORDS
- Tell children that there are six words in the poem that begin with *r*. Ask volunteers to find each word. Then help children read aloud the *r* words.

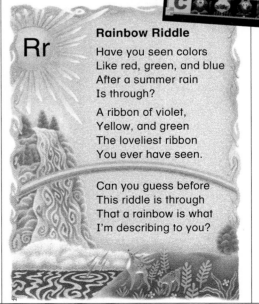

Rr

Rainbow Riddle

Have you seen colors
Like red, green, and blue
After a summer rain
Is through?

A ribbon of violet,
Yellow, and green
The loveliest ribbon
You ever have seen.

Can you guess before
This riddle is through
That a rainbow is what
I'm describing to you?

Big Book of Phonics Rhymes and Poems, page 44

188B

Initial /r/ *r*

Rr
rabbit

Phonics Picture Posters and Cards

OBJECTIVES

Children will:
- ☑ identify /r/ *R, r*
- ☑ write and use letters *R, r*

MATERIALS
- Phonics Picture Posters
- letter cards
- index cards

ADDITIONAL RESOURCES
- Practice Book, page 188
- Phonics/Phonemic Awareness Practice Book, pages 101–102
- **Phonics** CD-ROM

♪ Phonics Song ♪

Ricky the Rabbit

Ricky the Rabbit rides his bike,
Rides his bike, rides his bike,
Ricky the Rabbit rides his bike,
Then he stops to rest.

*Sung to the tune of
"The Wheels on the Bus"*

From **Songs from A to Z**

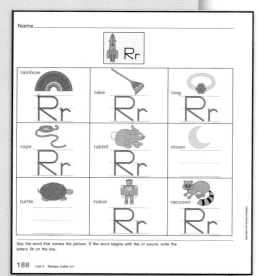

Pupil Edition page 188

Review

TEACH

Phonemic Awareness Warm-Up Have children sing the song "Ricky the Rabbit" with you. Then tell children riddles for objects that begin with the /r/ sound. Say, *I'm thinking of a color that begins with the /r/ sound.* (red) Repeat with the words *rabbit, rain,* and *rainbow.*

Identify /r/ *R, r* Display Phonics Picture Poster *Rr.* Remind children the letters *Rr* stand for the sound /r/. Distribute *Rr* letter cards. Say the following words: *run, rip, bag, rice, ray, can, duck.* Ask children to hold up their letter cards when they hear a word that begins with /r/.

Form *R, r* Review how to form the letters *Rr* with children. Have them practice writing with their finger on the desk. Then distribute index cards and have children write *Rr* at the top of the card. Then have children draw a picture of something that begins with the /r/ sound.

PRACTICE

Find the *R*'s

Materials: Tactile ABC Cards

◆ Give children Tactile ABC Cards or sandpaper letter cards, including the cards for *R* and *r*.

◆ Invite children to identify the *R* and *r* cards.

◆ Ask children to make the /r/ sound and write *R, r*. Then invite children to say a name that begins with *R* and an animal whose name begins with *r*.

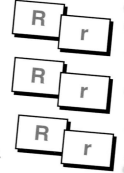

ON LEVEL

✓ ASSESS/CLOSE

Have children complete page 188 of the Pupil Edition or the Practice Book. For a different approach to this skill, see page T23 for the **Alternate Teaching Strategy.**

Meeting Individual Needs
Activities

Yarn Letters

Materials: yarn, drawing paper, paste

◆ Have children form a capital and a lowercase *R* on paper with paste.

◆ Have children use yarn to cover the glue and form the *R* and *r*.

◆ When the string is dry, children trace the letters with their fingers and say the letter name and its sound.

EASY

Draw a Picture

Materials: crayons, drawing paper

◆ Have children brainstorm words that begin with *r*, such as *rug, river, rain, rake,* and *ring*.

◆ Have children draw a picture that includes two /r/ words.

◆ Ask them to label the objects they draw with *R* and *r*, and to say a sentence with one of the words that begins with *r*.

CHALLENGE

Make Labels!

Materials: self-stick labels

◆ Encourage children to write the letters *R* and *r* on self-stick labels.

◆ Invite children to label objects in their classroom that begin with the letter *r*, such as *raincoat, ring, rag, ruler, raisins,* and *rug*.

◆ Have children trace the letters on the labels and say /r/.

LANGUAGE SUPPORT

The Apple Pie Tree
BY Zoe Hall
ILLUSTRATED BY Shari Halpern

Big Book

OBJECTIVES

Children will:
- [ ] develop vocabulary
- [x] understand the main idea of the story
- [ ] listen responsively to a story

 ZOE HALL loves to bake pies and used her own recipe in this book. Her first book "It's Pumpkin Time" won several major awards.

 SHARI HALPERN grew up in Massachusetts and used one of her mother's apple pies as a model for the art in this book. She lives in New Jersey with her husband Paul, who is a puppet maker, and her two cats.

LANGUAGE SUPPORT

ESL Cut an apple in half. Help children describe the texture, colors, and smell of the apple. Then identify the parts of the apple: stem, skin, seeds, core, and pulp. Provide a labeled picture of an apple for children to color.

Build Background

Develop Vocabulary Hold up an apple or a picture of an apple, and talk about where children might get one. (apple trees, farm stands, grocery stores) Then, draw the trunk of a tree on chart paper. Invite volunteers to add bark, branches, leaves and apples.

Story Pop-Out Cards from *The Apple Pie Tree*

Read the Big Book

Track the print as you read the story. *Concepts of Print*

Preview and Predict Display the cover and read the title together. Name the author and illustrator and share some information about them. Then invite children to take a picture walk through the first few pages of the book. Ask them to predict what will happen in the story.

Set Purposes Tell children you will read to find out what happens to the apples on the tree.

Read the Story Read the entire story aloud, tracking the print. *Concepts of Print*

Have children look at the pictures of the tree on pages 5–7.

MODEL: The apple tree changes from winter to spring. In the winter picture I see no leaves on the tree. In the spring picture I see leaves and a bird's nest. *Main Idea*

But in spring, leaves grow on every branch.

Look! Two robins are building a nest in our tree.

The Apple Pie Tree, pages 6–7

Literature Response

LISTENING/SPEAKING

Return to Predictions Discuss the predictions children made before reading the story. How does the apple tree change in the summer? (The tree is covered with big round apples.) *Literal: Story Details*

Discuss the main idea of the book.

MODEL: Let me think about what this story was mainly about. It tells all the ways the apple tree changes during the year. *Main Idea*

WRITING

Journal Writing Have children draw an apple tree in one of the seasons: winter, spring, summer, or fall. Display the book and review what the tree looks like in each season. Ask them to write something about the tree. Then have them compare their pictures.

The Apple Pie Tree, page 27

INFORMAL ASSESSMENT

How to Assess
If a child is having difficulty identifying main idea, use the skills lesson on page 189E.

 Activity

Retell the Story

Let children make a mural to show the events in *The Apple Pie Tree*. Draw lines to divide the paper into four sections. Label the sections: Winter, Spring, Summer, Fall. When the class finishes drawing or painting pictures to show what happened in each season, ask volunteers to use the pictures to retell the story.

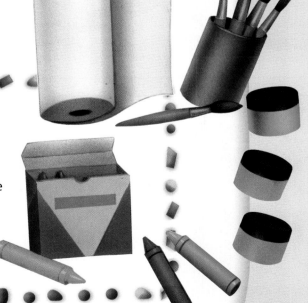

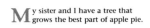

The Apple Pie Tree

BY Zoe Hall

ILLUSTRATED BY
Shari Halpern

My sister and I have a tree that grows the best part of apple pie.

Can you guess what that is?

3

Apples!
And every year,
we watch our apple tree grow.

In winter, our apple tree
is brown and bare.

4   5

But in spring,
leaves grow
on every branch.

Look! Two robins
are building a nest
in our tree.

6   7

Tiny pink flower buds
appear on the branches.
The robins chirp loudly,
guarding their eggs.

8   9

Just when the flower buds open,   baby robins break through the eggshells.

10   11

Now our tree is covered with blossoms.
And the baby robins begin to grow feathers.

12   13

When breezes blow,
the petals fall to the ground.
Mama and Papa Robin
teach their little birds to fly.

Some days it rains,
and the wind blows hard.
But our apple tree is strong.
And the robins are safe
in the branches.

Small green apples grow
where the blossoms used to be.

Soon it is summer.
The apples get bigger and bigger.

The little robins have grown up.
But they visit every day.

The branches bend down low.
They are covered with
big, round apples.

Now it is autumn.
The apples are red and ready to be picked!
We fill our basket to the brim.

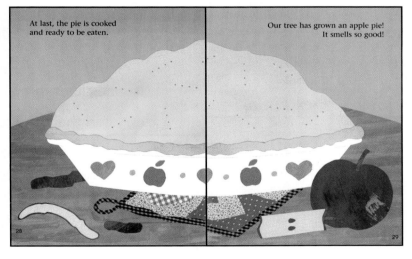

Mom and Dad help us
peel the apples, cut them up,
and pile them into a pie shell.
Then we sprinkle cinnamon
and sugar over the top.

Mom puts the pan in the oven.

At last, the pie is cooked
and ready to be eaten.

Our tree has grown an apple pie!
It smells so good!

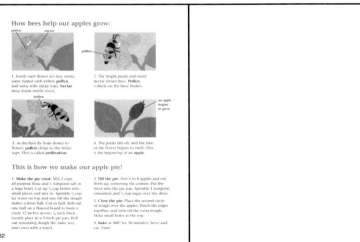

And it tastes delicious!
There's nothing as good
as an apple pie
you grew yourself.

How bees help our apples grow:

1. Inside each flower are tiny stems, some tipped with yellow **pollen**, and some with sticky tops. **Nectar** deep inside smells sweet.

2. The bright petals and sweet nectar attract bees. **Pollen** collects on the bees' bodies.

3. As the bees fly from flower to flower, **pollen** clings to the sticky tops. This is called **pollination**.

4. The petals fall off, and the base of the flower begins to swell. This is the beginning of an **apple**.

This is how we make our apple pie!

1. **Make the pie crust:** Mix 2 cups all-purpose flour and 1 teaspoon salt in a large bowl. Cut up ⅓ cup butter into small pieces and mix in. Sprinkle ⅓ cup ice water on top and mix till the dough makes a loose ball. Cut in half. Roll out one half on a floured board to form a circle 12 inches across, ⅛ inch thick. Gently place in a 9-inch pie pan. Roll out remaining dough the same way, and cover with a towel.

2. **Fill the pie:** Peel 6 to 8 apples and cut them up, removing the centers. Put the slices into the pie pan. Sprinkle 1 teaspoon cinnamon and ½ cup sugar over the slices.

3. **Close the pie:** Place the second circle of dough over the apples. Pinch the edges together, and trim off the extra dough. Make small holes in the top.

4. Bake at 400° for 50 minutes. Serve and eat. Yum!

Main Idea

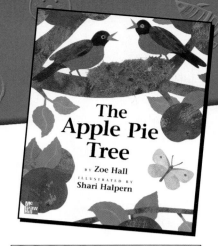

The Apple Pie Tree
by Zoe Hall
ILLUSTRATED BY Shari Halpern

The Apple Pie Tree

OBJECTIVES

Children will:

☑ use story details to determine the main idea

MATERIALS

• *The Apple Pie Tree*

TEACHING TIP

INSTRUCTIONAL Give children practice finding the main idea by talking about something they did. Ask: *What was the most important thing you did during _____ (name of activity)?*

Introduce

TEACH

Decide Upon a Main Theme Display the cover of *The Apple Pie Tree* and ask children to recall the story. Point to pictures of the apple tree and encourage children to discuss what is happening in each one. Ask children what the author was trying to tell the reader about the apple tree. Encourage children to discuss what the book is mainly about. Point out that all books have one very important idea.

PRACTICE

What Is the Main Idea?

◆ Invite children to choose a book from the classroom library.

◆ Read the book together.

◆ Have children complete the following sentence: *This story is mainly about _____.*

ON LEVEL

✓ ASSESS/CLOSE

Have children complete page 189 of the Pupil Edition or the Practice Book. For a different approach to this skill, see page T25 for the **Alternate Teaching Strategy.**

Name_____

1.

The cat sat on a mat.

The cat ran to Mom.

2.

Nan is mad.

Sam is sad.

Look at each picture. • Then read the sentences. • Draw a line under the sentence that tells what the picture is all about.

Unit 4 Introduce Main Idea 189

Pupil Edition page 189

189E *You Are IT!*

Meeting Individual Needs
Activities

Changing Seasons

Materials: drawing paper, crayons

◆ Remind children that the story they read was about an apple tree. Help them name the four seasons of the year.

◆ Have pairs of children divide a sheet of paper into four squares and draw pictures of the apple tree in each season.

◆ Encourage partners to describe the apple tree in each picture.

EASY

Find the Main Idea

Materials: On-Level Decodable Stories, writing paper

◆ Distribute an On-Level Decodable Story to each child.

◆ Have children pick a picture and write or dictate a sentence that tells the main idea of the picture.

◆ Encourage children to share their main idea sentence and picture.

CHALLENGE

All About Pictures

Materials: picture book, oaktag strips

◆ Point to illustrations in a picture book.

◆ Ask children what is happening in each picture.

◆ Write captions, based on their descriptions, on oaktag strips.

◆ Read each caption. Explain that it tells the most important idea about the picture.

LANGUAGE SUPPORT

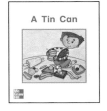
A Tin Can

On a Dot

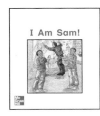
I Am Sam!

Listen

Rainbow Riddle
a poem

Have you seen colors
Like red, green, and blue
After a summer rain
Is through?
A ribbon of violet,
Yellow, and green
The loveliest ribbon
You ever have seen.
Can you guess before
This riddle is through
That a rainbow is what
I'm describing to you?

Ferris Wheel Fun
a poem

Fasten my seat belt.
This feels fun!
I'm on the Ferris wheel
For ride number one!

It's going fast!
And faster still.
Ferris wheel fun
Is such a thrill!

Big Book of Phonics Rhymes and Poems, pages 44, 19

Delete Syllables · · · · · Phonological Awareness · · · · · ·

Teach Read the poems. Clap the word *riddle* and explain that the word has two syllables, *rid-dle*. If we take away the last syllable in *riddle*, the word *rid* is left.

MODEL: Pretend that it is raining. Tap the syllables of the words as you chant: *pit-ter, pat-ter, pit-ter, pat-ter.* Ask children if they can hear the syllables in these words. Begin the chant again: *pit-ter, pat-ter, pit-ter, pat-.* Pause and let children say the missing syllable. (ter)

Practice Have children say and tap the syllables in these words. Say the words again, and have children delete the last syllable.

pit-ter (pit)	be-fore (be)	rain-drop (rain)
ri-ver (ri)	feath-er (feath)	fall-ing (fall)

Listen for Beginning Sounds

Teach   Have children draw a rainbow on their pieces of construction paper. Tell them that you will be reading a poem and want them to hold up their rainbows high in the air every time they hear a word that starts with the /r/ sound.

Practice   Read "Rainbow Riddle" to the children slowly. Elongate the initial /r/ sound in such words as *rain, ribbon, rainbow,* and *riddle.*

MATERIALS
- construction paper
- crayons or markers

INFORMAL ASSESSMENT   Observe children as they delete syllables in words and identify beginning sounds. If children have difficulty, see Alternate Teaching Strategies on T22.

Read Together

From Phonemic Awareness to Phonics

Objective: Identify /r/ R, r and /f/ F, f

IDENTIFY THE LETTERS
Display the Big Book of Phonics Rhymes and Poems, pages 19 and 44. On each page, point to the letters, identify them, and say the sounds they stand for: /r/ and /f/.

REREAD THE POEMS Reread the poems, tracking the print and emphasizing the words with initial /r/ or /f/. Have children repeat the words after you.

FIND WORDS WITH R, r, F, f
Have children use their fingers to frame words in the poems that begin with R, r, F, or f.

Rr

Rainbow Riddle

Have you seen colors
Like red, green, and blue
After a summer rain
Is through?

A ribbon of violet,
Yellow, and green
The loveliest ribbon
You ever have seen.

Can you guess before
This riddle is through
That a rainbow is what
I'm describing to you?

Ff

Ferris Wheel Fun

Fasten my seat belt.
This feels fun!
I'm on the Ferris wheel
For ride number one!

It's going fast!
And faster still.
Ferris wheel fun
Is such a thrill!

Big Book of Phonics Rhymes and Poems, pages 44, 19

190B

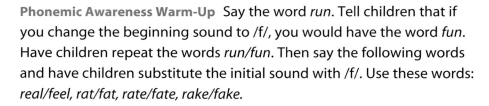

Phonics Picture Posters and Cards

TESTED

OBJECTIVES

Children will:

☑ identify and discriminate between /r/ *R, r* and /f/ *F, f*

☑ write and use letters *R, r* and *F, f*

MATERIALS

- letter cards
- Phonics Picture Posters
- index cards

ADDITIONAL RESOURCES

- Practice Book, page 190
- Phonics/Phonemic Awareness Practice Book, page 99
- **Phonics** CD-ROM

TEACHING TIP

INSTRUCTIONAL Have children act out words that begin with /r/ and /f/. Have them say the name of the initial letter, its sound, and the word as they perform each action.

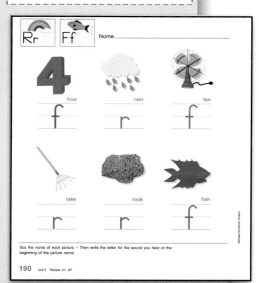

Pupil Edition page 190

190C *You Are IT!*

Review

TEACH

Phonemic Awareness Warm-Up Say the word *run*. Tell children that if you change the beginning sound to /f/, you would have the word *fun*. Have children repeat the words *run/fun*. Then say the following words and have children substitute the initial sound with /f/. Use these words: *real/feel, rat/fat, rate/fate, rake/fake.*

Identify and Discriminate Between /r/ *R, r* and /f/ *F, f* Display the Phonics Picture Posters for *Rr* and *Ff*. Identify the sounds the letters stand for. Give children letter cards for *Rr* and *Ff*. Say a sentence, such as: *Ron had fun.* Have children raise the *Rr* or the *Ff* letter card if they hear a word that begins with that letter.

Form *R, r* and *F, f* Display letter cards for *Rr* and *Ff* and review the capital and lowercase forms with children. Give each child four index cards. Write *R, r, F* and *f* on the chalkboard. Have children write each of these letters on a card. Then have children exchange cards with a partner. Partners write the missing form of each letter on the cards.

PRACTICE

Self-Stick Note Match

Materials: picture cards for initial /r/ and /f/, self-stick notes

◆ Write *r* and *f* on three self-stick notes each.

◆ Display three pictures whose names begin with /r/ and three that begin with /f/. Have children name them with you.

◆ Ask volunteers to name each picture, its initial sound, and its initial letter, and label the picture with the appropriate self-stick note.

ON LEVEL

✓ ASSESS/CLOSE

Have children complete page 190 of the Pupil Edition or the Practice Book. For a different approach to this skill, see page T23 for the **Alternate Teaching Strategy.**

Meeting Individual Needs
Activities

Picture Sort

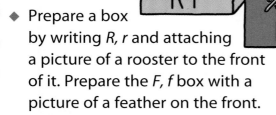

Materials: picture cards for initial /r/ and /f/, two boxes

◆ Prepare a box by writing *R, r* and attaching a picture of a rooster to the front of it. Prepare the *F, f* box with a picture of a feather on the front.

◆ Have children select a picture card, name the word, and put the card in the box for the correct initial sound.

EASY

Rainbow Concentration

Materials: index cards, crayons, or paint

◆ Give each partner three index cards. One partner draws pictures of things that begin with /r/ on the index cards. The other partner draws /f/ words on the index cards.

◆ On the back of each card, children draw a rainbow.

◆ Children put their cards together, mix them up, and spread the cards on the table, rainbow side up.

◆ Children match cards with the same initial sound.

CHALLENGE

Play Simon Says

◆ Preview /r/ and /f/ words that you will use in the game. Point to pictures or act out each word as you say it. Have children repeat each word.

◆ Tell children to listen for /r/ and /f/ words as you play a game of "Simon Says."

◆ Play the game, emphasizing words that begin with /r/ and /f/. For example, say: *Simon says put your hands on your face. Rub your hands together.*

LANGUAGE SUPPORT

Every Time I Climb a Tree

a poem by David McCord

Every time I climb a tree
Every time I climb a tree
Every time I climb a tree
I scrape a leg
Or skin a knee
And every time I climb a tree
I find some ants
Or dodge a bee
And get the ants
All over me
And every time I climb a tree
Where have you been?
They say to me
But don't they know that I am free
Every time I climb a tree?
I like it best

To spot a nest
That has an egg
Or maybe three
And then I skin
The other leg
But every time I climb a tree
I see a lot of things to see
Swallows rooftops and TV
And all the fields and farms there be
Every time I climb a tree
Though climbing may be good for
   ants
It isn't awfully good for pants
But still it's pretty good for me
Every time I climb a tree.

Oral Comprehension

LISTENING AND SPEAKING Use these questions to encourage children to respond to the poem. Remind children to speak clearly and with a volume that is appropriate for the classroom.

- Whom do you think is telling this poem? (The speaker is a child who enjoys climbing trees.)

- What kinds of things happen when the speaker climbs a tree? (Possible answer: Accidents happen.)

- What does the speaker like about climbing trees? (The speaker likes to be able to see nature up close and far away.)

Activity Ask children to pretend they are a bird in a tree. Have them describe what they might see. Check that children demonstrate skills of providing information and reporting. You may wish to make a class list of their ideas.

▶**Linguistic**

Reading for Information

Can you follow the footsteps?
Start at **X**.

24
25

Reading for Information Big Book, pages 24–25

Objective: Read a Map

DISCUSS THE BIG BOOK Talk with children about maps they have seen or used. Explain to children that the map in the Big Book shows what the boy from the poem "Every Time I Climb a Tree" did one day.

- Turn to pages 24 and 25 in the Big Book and show children the map. Explain that a map shows how to get to different places.

- Read aloud the question at the bottom of page 25. Then discuss the map.

- Ask: *Where is the boy's starting point?* (his house) *Where does the boy go first?* (the hammock) *Where else does he go?* Then discuss children's own experience with maps. Ask: *Where else have you seen maps?* (Answers will vary.)

CULTURAL PERSPECTIVES

JUMPING ROPE Share that jump rope is a game children around the world like to play. In the United States, children play a game with two jump ropes called *Double Dutch*. In Colombia, a popular jump-rope game is called *Resortte-Chicle.* Indonesian children play a game called *Lompat Tali.* Point out these countries on a map.

Activity Help children interview each other to find out what games they most enjoy playing. Have children draw a portrait of the person they've interviewed and write the person's name at the bottom of the paper. Invite volunteers to share their work.

▶ Spatial/Interpersonal

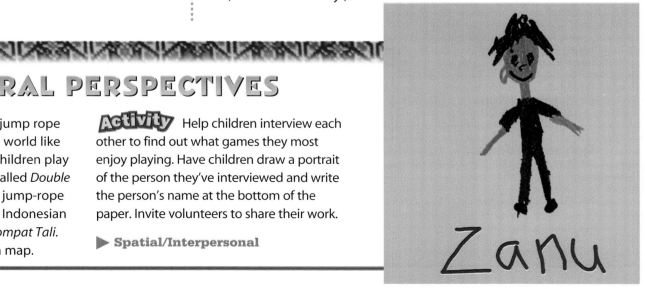

Zanu

Vocabulary: *to*

OBJECTIVES

Children will:
☑ identify and read the high-frequency word *to*

MATERIALS

- pocket chart
- word cards

TEACHING TIP

WORD WALL Add the word *to* to the Word Wall. Point to the word and have children spell it as you point to each letter. Then have children count the number of letters and write the word in the air.

Name_____ | to

1. Nan ran <u>to</u> Dad.

2. Dad ran <u>to</u> Ron.

3. Ron ran <u>to</u> Mom.

4. Mom ran <u>to</u> Min.

Read the sentence. • Draw a line under the word *to* in the sentence.

Unit 4 Introduce High-Frequency Words: *to* **191**

Pupil Edition page 191

Introduce

| to |

Vocabulary Cards

TEACH

Introduce *to* Say aloud the following sentences: *I ran to the tree. I ran to the house.* Have children act out the sentences by running in place.

Place the following word cards in a pocket chart: *I, ran, to, the.* Place a picture of a tree in the last position in the pocket chart. Point to each word or picture as you read the sentence aloud: *I ran to the (tree).* Tell children to pay special attention to the word *to*.

Then repeat the procedure with the sentence: *I ran to the* (picture of house). Ask volunteers to point to the word *to*.

PRACTICE

I Like *To* Read

Materials: word cards *to*

◆ Give each child a word card for *to*.

◆ Say several sentences. Have children hold up their card each time you say the word *to*.

ON LEVEL

✓ ASSESS/CLOSE

Have children complete page 191 of the Pupil Edition or Practice Book. For a different approach to teaching this skill, see page T26 for the **Alternate Teaching Strategy.**

Meeting Individual Needs
Activities

Sandy *To*

Materials: word cards *to*, sand or salt tray, index cards, crayons or markers

◆ Give children the word card *to*.

◆ Have children write the word in a sand or salt tray.

◆ Then, using index cards, have them make their own word cards to take home.

EASY

To Poem

◆ Write these lines of poetry on the chalkboard and read them aloud: *I like it best/To spot a nest.*

◆ Have children rewrite the last line by replacing the last three words.

◆ Explain that the lines do not have to rhyme.

◆ Have children share their poems.

CHALLENGE

Play a Game

Materials: drawing paper for game board, number cube, markers

◆ Make a simple board game with squares. Write *to* in some squares, and other words in other squares.

◆ Have children roll the number cube and move a marker around the board.

◆ When they land on the word *to*, they read it aloud and score a point.

LANGUAGE SUPPORT

191

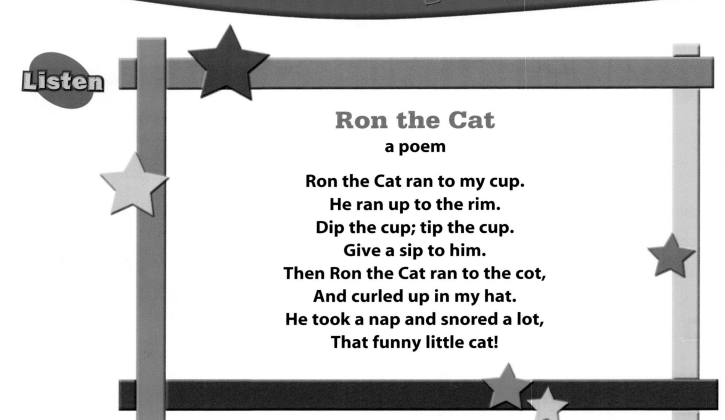

Listen

Ron the Cat
a poem

Ron the Cat ran to my cup.
He ran up to the rim.
Dip the cup; tip the cup.
Give a sip to him.
Then Ron the Cat ran to the cot,
And curled up in my hat.
He took a nap and snored a lot,
That funny little cat!

Blend Onsets and Rimes

Phonological Awareness

Teach   Read "Ron the Cat" to the children. Reread the line "He took a nap and snored a lot." Tell children the sounds *n-ap* make the word *nap*. Have children repeat the sounds and the word with you: *n-ap: nap*.

MODEL: Listen to me say the following words. I will blend the beginning sound with the rest of the word to make the whole word *t-ook: took*. Listen again, *r-an; ran*. Now I'll make the sounds, and you say the word with me, *r-im*. What's the word? *(rim)*

s-ip sip!
s-ip sip!
s-ip sip!
s-ip sip!
s-ip sip!

Practice   Have children chant the following segmented sounds. As a group, say the onsets and rimes together to form words.

R-on (Ron)	s-ip (sip)	n-ice (nice)
f-ur (fur)	l-ap (lap)	r-im (rim)

Blend Sounds

Teach Display the Phonics Picture Card (picture side only) for *fish*. Tell children the word *fish* has three sounds: /f/-/i/-/sh/. Have children repeat the sounds and the word with you: /f/-/i/-/sh/: *fish*.

Then display the Phonics Picture Cards for *dog, cat*, and *pig*. Repeat the same process for these words.

Practice Tell children you will say the sounds of other words. Have children blend the sounds to say the words. Use these words: *rat, cab, fan, ran, wish, duck, rock, rain.*

MATERIALS
• Phonics Picture Cards: *fish, dog, cat, pig*

INFORMAL ASSESSMENT Observe children as they blend onsets and rimes and blend sounds to make words. If children have difficulty, see Alternate Teaching Strategies: Unit 1, T33; and Unit 4, T22.

Read Together

From Phonemic Awareness to Phonics

Objective: Focus on Print

LISTEN FOR SOUNDS Read the poem "Ron the Cat." To help children recall that the word *ran* has three sounds, say the word aloud, segmenting the sounds.

/r/ - /a/ - /n/

IDENTIFY THE LETTERS Write the word *ran* on the chalkboard. Point to the letters, one at a time, and have children identify each one. Then say the sound each letter stands for. Repeat for the word *rat.*

COMPARE WORDS Ask children to look closely at the words on the chalkboard and tell how they are the same and how they are different.

COUNT THE LETTERS Write the word *ran* on the chalkboard in large print. Set out several sheets of colored paper and some tape. As you say the name of each letter in the word, have a volunteer cover the letter with a piece of colored paper. Have children count the number of colored papers to determine the number of letters in

the word. Repeat with the word *rat.*

LOOK AT MORE WORDS Write the words *rim* and *rid* on the chalkboard. Repeat the letter identification, comparison, and letter counting with this pair of words.

DAY 4
Short *a, i, o*
Blending

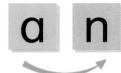

OBJECTIVES
TESTED

Children will:
- ☑ identify /a/ *a*, /i/ *i*, and /o/ *o*
- ☑ blend and read short *a, i,* and *o* words
- ☑ write short *a, i,* and *o* words

MATERIALS
- letter cards

ADDITIONAL RESOURCES
- Practice Book, page 192
- Phonics/Phonemic Awareness Practice Book, pages 110, 116, 122
- **Phonics** CD-ROM

TEACHING TIP

WORD FAMILIES Make word cards for *rat, cat, sat, Nat, fat, mat, ran, can, man, Nan, Dan* and *fan*. Have children play a matching game by turning over two cards and matching words with the same endings.

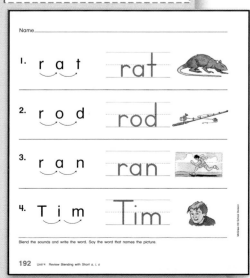

Name_____

1. r a t   rat 🐀

2. r o d   rod

3. r a n   ran 🏃

4. T i m   Tim 👦

Blend the sounds and write the word. Say the word that names the picture.

192   Unit 4   Review Blending with Short a, i, o

Pupil Edition page 192

192C   *You Are IT!*

Review

TEACH

Model Blending with Short *a, i, o* Display the *a* letter card and say /a/. Have children repeat the /a/ sound as you point to the *a* card. Place the *n* card to the right of the *a* card. Point to each letter as you blend the sounds together and have children repeat after you: *an.*

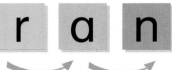

Place the *r* card to the left of *an* to show *ran*. Point to the cards as you blend to read *ran,* and have children repeat after you.

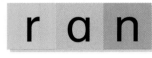

Continue modeling and guided practice using *rot, Ron, rat, rod, rid,* and *ram.*

PRACTICE

Rhyme a Word

Materials: letter cards *a, c, d, i, m, n, o, r, s, t*

- ◆ Arrange the cards on a chalkboard ledge or in a pocket chart.
- ◆ Form the word *cot.* Track the print as you blend the sounds and read the word. Have children read with you.
- ◆ Take away the *c* card and ask volunteers to add a new letter to make a word that rhymes with *cot.*
- ◆ Repeat for other phonograms, such as *-id* and *-an.*

ON LEVEL

✓ ASSESS/CLOSE

Have children complete page 192 of the Pupil Edition or the Practice Book. For a different approach to this skill, see page T23 for the **Alternate Teaching Strategy.**

Meeting Individual Needs
Activities

Picture and Word Match

Materials: picture and word cards for *rat, Ron, rod, ran, ram* and *rip*, drawing paper, crayons

◆ Mix up the cards.

◆ Have children sort the cards by matching the word and picture cards.

◆ Have children fold a paper into thirds, write *a, i,* and *o* at the top of the sections and draw a picture for each vowel.

EASY

Make a Word

Materials: letter cards *a, d, i, m, n, o, r,* and *t;* drawing paper; crayons or markers

◆ Have children fold the drawing paper in half and in half again. Then have them open the paper.

◆ Tell children to use the letter cards to make four different words.

◆ Tell children to write each word in one section of their drawing paper, and then draw a picture that shows their word.

CHALLENGE

Make Living Words

Materials: letter cards *a, d, i, m, n, o, r,* and *t*

◆ Review the sound of each letter with children.

◆ Give each child a letter card. Say: *If you like to go swimming,* nod *your head. What does* nod *mean?*

◆ Invite children with the letter cards *n, o,* and *d* to arrange themselves to make the word *nod.*

◆ Repeat for other /a/, /i/, and /o/ words.

LANGUAGE SUPPORT

Read the Story

Ron ran to Tom.

2

"You are IT!" said Ron.

3

☑ **Initial /r/ r**

☑ **High-Frequency Word:** *to*

☑ **Main Idea**

☐ **Concepts of Print**

PREVIEW AND PREDICT

Read the story title, and discuss the cover illustration with children. Ask *What do you think the title* You Are IT! *means?* Take a picture walk through the first few pages of the book, and ask *What game do the children seem to be playing?*

You Are IT!

SET PURPOSES

Ask children what they might want to find out as they read. Then ask *Who do you think will be the last person to be IT?*

AS YOU READ

Have children track print as they read. Use the following prompts:

- **Page 2** Have children point to the word *to* on this page, read it, and spell it. *High-Frequency Words*

- **Page 6** If children have difficulty reading the word *ran*, have them cover up the *r* in *ran* and blend *a-n* to make *an*. Then have them blend all the letters together, *r-a-n, ran*. *Graphophonic Cues*

- **Page 8** Ask children to find two words on this page that begin with /r/. Have them read the words aloud. (Ron, ran) *Initial* r

- **Page 8** After reading this page, ask children what the story is about. (The story is about children who play a game of tag and bring Dad into the game.) *Main Idea*

Pupil Edition pp. 193–194

Tom ran to Nan.

4

"You are IT!" said Tom.

5

TEACHING TIP

To put books together:

1. Tear out the story page.

2. Cut along the dotted line.

3. Fold each section on the fold line.

4. Assemble the book.

193/194A *You Are IT!*

Nan ran to Dad.

6

"You are IT!" said Nan.

7

Ron, Tom, and Nan ran.

8

Read the Story

RETURN TO PREDICTIONS

After reading the story, ask children to think back to their predictions and ideas. Did they guess the children were playing tag? Did they guess that Dad would be the last person to be IT?

RETELL THE STORY

Ask four volunteers to pretend to be Ron, Tom, Nan, and Dad in the story. Have the children retell the story in order as they role-play the story events.

WRITING

Journal Writing Invite each child to write one rule for a favorite tag game, such as *When you play "Freeze Tag," you have to freeze when you are touched.*

CENTER Activity

Cross Curricular: Social Studies

BACKYARD MAPS In the learning center, place a variety of aerial-view maps of backyards, such as the ones found in gardening books. Invite children to study the maps and use art supplies to create a map of a backyard they think would be ideal for a game of "Tag" or "Hide and Seek."

▶ **Visual/Spatial**

INFORMAL ASSESSMENT

INITIAL /r/ r

HOW TO ASSESS Ask children to look at pages 2–4, and read all the words that begin with *r*. (Ron, ran)

FOLLOW UP Make a list of words that begin with *r*. Have children read each word and underline the letter *r*.

You Are IT!

McGraw Hill

| You Are IT! |

Review

OBJECTIVES
TESTED ✓

Children will:
☑ identify the main idea of a story

••••••••••••••••••••••••••••••••

MATERIALS
• *You Are IT!*

TEACHING TIP
INSTRUCTIONAL Ask children to explain how to play tag. Point out that some children may play by different rules. Discuss what the label *IT* means in tag.

TEACH

Identify the Main Idea Display the cover of the book *You Are IT!* and reread the story together. Then ask children how the story begins, what happens, and how the story ends. Explain that the main idea is the most important idea in the story. It tells what the story is about. Encourage volunteers to tell in one sentence what the story is about. Then ask children to think of a favorite television show or movie. Have volunteers take turns telling, in one sentence, what the show or movie was about.

PRACTICE

What's It About?

◆ Show children how to fold paper into fourths.

◆ Encourage them to tell a story about an activity they like to do with their parents.

◆ Have them draw four pictures about the activity.

◆ Call on volunteers to show their pictures and tell the main idea of the story.

ON LEVEL

✓ ASSESS/CLOSE

Have children complete page 195 of the Pupil Edition or the Practice Book. For a different approach to this skill, see page T25 for the **Alternate Teaching Strategy.**

Name_____

1. A cat is on the cot.

Ron and Nan sat on the cot.

2. Ron ran to Dad and Nan.

Mom and Dad sat.

Look at each picture. • Then read the sentences. • Draw a line under the sentence that tells what the picture is all about.

Unit 4 Review Main Idea 195

Pupil Edition page 195

195A *You Are IT!*

Meeting Individual Needs
Activities

Draw a Book Cover

Materials: book, drawing paper, crayons

◆ Display the cover of a book from the classroom library.

◆ Invite children to draw a book cover for *You Are IT!* that shows the main idea of the story.

◆ Have children talk about the book cover in class.

EASY

Write a Story

Materials: drawing paper, crayons

◆ Invite pairs of children to think of another game like *You Are IT!*

◆ Have them draw pictures to illustrate their game.

◆ Encourage children to tell the main idea of their game.

CHALLENGE

Act Out a Story

◆ Reread *You Are IT!* or another familiar story with children.

◆ Encourage children to decide what the story is mainly about. Two children might act out what the story is about while another child states the main idea.

LANGUAGE SUPPORT

Phonological Awareness

Listen

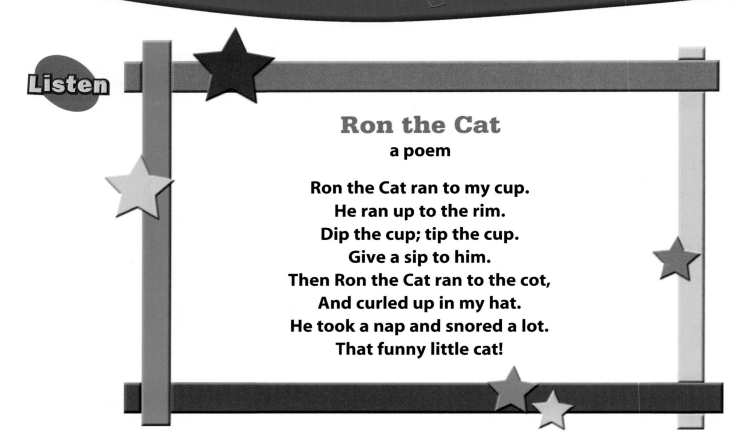

Ron the Cat
a poem

Ron the Cat ran to my cup.
He ran up to the rim.
Dip the cup; tip the cup.
Give a sip to him.
Then Ron the Cat ran to the cot,
And curled up in my hat.
He took a nap and snored a lot.
That funny little cat!

Segment Onsets and Rimes

Phonological Awareness

Teach Say the poem with the children. Reread the line "Ron the Cat ran to my cup." Then say the word *cup*. Segment the onset and rime of *cup, c-up*. Do the same for the word *ran, r-an*.

MODEL: Listen to me say the following words. I will say the entire word first. Then I will say the beginning sound followed by the rest of the word: *wait, w-ait; sip, s-ip*. What about the word *jump*? How do I break it apart? *j-ump*.

c–

up!

Practice Ask children to work with a partner. Say each word below and have one child in each pair say the beginning sound and the other say the rest of the word.

hug; h-ug	food; f-ood
fork; f-ork	knife; kn-ife

Segment Sounds

Phonemic Awareness

Teach Tell the children that Ron the Cat is a very silly cat. He likes to tip the cup and make words spill out. When they spill out, the words break apart. Say the word *leaf*. Roll the cubes in the cup and dump them out. Point to each cube as you segment sounds: l-ea-f. Ask children to put the word back together again. *(leaf)*

Practice Continue to say words, having children roll the cubes and dump them out of the cup. Ask children to pick up the cubes one at a time, as they say individual sounds. Use these words: *man, had, tin, rid, tan, rod, ham, and hen.*

MATERIALS
- cup or mug
- 3 cubes

INFORMAL ASSESSMENT Observe children as they blend onsets and rimes and segment sounds. If children have difficulty, see Alternate Teaching Strategies: Unit 1, T33; Unit 2, T29; and Unit 4, T22.

Read Together

From Phonemic Awareness to Phonics

Objective: Identify Words with the Same Endings

LISTEN FOR FINAL SOUNDS
Read the fifth and sixth lines of the poem "Ron the Cat." Ask children where Ron curled up.

> in   my   hat

Write the word *in* on the board. Tell children that you think that Ron the Cat eats from a tin. Write the word *tin* next to *in*. Encourage children to tell how the two words are alike. Say the words again, emphasizing the final two sounds.

> /i/-/n/

NAME RHYMING WORDS
Invite children to name other words that rhyme with *in* and *tin*. Write their responses on the board, framing the letters *i* and *n*.

PLAY A GAME Write the words listed on the board on index cards, using one card for each word. Add a few other word cards with words that do not rhyme with *in* and *tin*. Place all the cards in a box or bag. Invite volunteers to pull out a card and place it in a hat if it ends with the same letters as *in* and *tin*.

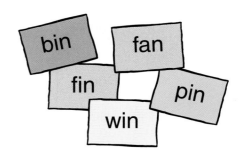

196B

Short *a, i, o*
Blending

TESTED OBJECTIVES

Children will:

- ☑ identify /a/ *a*, /i/ *i*, and /o/ *o*
- ☑ blend and read short *a, i,* and *o* words
- ☑ write short *a, i, o* words

MATERIALS

- letter cards

ADDITIONAL RESOURCES

- Practice Book, page 196
- Phonics/Phonemic Awareness Practice Book, pages 110, 116, 122
- **Phonics** CD-ROM

TEACHING TIP

WRITE WORDS Use adding machine tape to write the *–an* word ending five times. Say the following words and have volunteers write the beginning sound next to the word ending: ran, man, tan, Nan, Dan.

Name _____

1. (cat) mat
   cat

2. [fishing pole] ran (rod)
   rod

3. [boy with baby] Mom (Dad)
   Dad

4. [fish] (fin) fan
   fin

Draw a circle around the word that names the picture. • Say the word. • Then write the word.

196 Unit 4 Review Blending with Short a, i, o

Pupil Edition page 196

196C *You Are IT!*

Review

TEACH

Model Blending with Short *a, i, o* Display the *i* letter card and say /i/. Have children repeat the sound /i/ as you point to the *i* card.

Place the *d* card to the right of the *i* card. Point to each letter as you blend the sounds together and have children repeat after you: *id*.

Place the *r* card to the left of *id* to show *rid*. Point to the cards as you blend to read *rid*, and have children repeat after you.

Continue modeling and guided practice using *rod, Ron, fan, tin, rat, dim,* and *nod*.

PRACTICE

Word Riddles

Materials: letter cards *a, c, d, i, m, n, o, r, s, t*

- ◆ Display the letter cards.
- ◆ Tell children to listen to the clues so they can name the secret word. For example, say: *I take a nap on this. It rhymes with* hot. *What is it? (cot)*
- ◆ Once children guess the word, have them use the letter cards to make the word.

ON LEVEL

✓ ASSESS/CLOSE

Have children complete page 196 of the Pupil Edition or the Practice Book. For a different approach to this skill, see page T23 for the **Alternate Teaching Strategy.**

Meeting Individual Needs
Activities

One Doesn't Belong

Materials: Word Building Cards *bib, cap, cat, fan, ham, top*; index cards; paper clips

◆ On the index cards, write the word for a picture card on one side, and a word different by one letter on the other side. For example, *cat/cot* and *ham/had*. Clip each to a picture card.

◆ Children put the word card by the picture card so the correct word is face up.

EASY

cat

Flip Books

Materials: stapler, scissors, drawing paper, crayons or markers, consonant letter cards

◆ Prepare flip books by stapling several sheets of folded drawing paper. Cut each book into three parts by cutting about three-fourths of the way up each sheet.

◆ On each center page write a phonogram, such as *-an, -in,* and *-ot.*

◆ Have children write a letter on a left page. Then have them flip to make a word and draw its picture on a right page.

CHALLENGE

Listen for Words

Materials: word cards for short *a, i, o* words

◆ Review the words on the cards with children by saying the sounds and blending them together with children.

◆ Discuss what each word means.

◆ Give out the word cards so that each child has one.

◆ Tell children to listen as you say a sentence. If you say a sentence with their word, they should stand up.

LANGUAGE SUPPORT

196

Leveled Books

Meeting Individual Needs

EASY

TESTED OBJECTIVES

☑ Initial /r/ R, r
☑ Main Idea
☐ Concepts of Print
☑ Vocabulary: *to*

Guided Reading

PREVIEW AND PREDICT Ask children to look at the cover illustration and predict what the story might be about. Point to each word as you read aloud the title. Then conduct a picture walk through the first few pages. Have children predict who Ron is. Before reading, remind children to point to each word as they read it.

READ THE BOOK Use the following prompts to guide children's reading:

Pages 2–3 Ask children to find the words that are the same on both pages. *Concepts of Print*

Page 5 Have children point to the *r* in *Ron* and *ran. Phonics*

Pages 6–7 Ask children to point to the word *to* on each page. *Vocabulary*

Page 8 After you read page 8, ask, *What is this story about?* (Ron runs out of his cage, but Nat finds him.) *Main Idea*

LITERARY RESPONSE Ask children to draw and write about what Ron and Nat might do next.

Ron Is In

McGraw Hill

INDEPENDENT

You Are IT!

McGraw Hill

TESTED OBJECTIVES

☑ Initial /r/ R, r
☑ Main Idea
☐ Concepts of Print
☑ Vocabulary: *to*

Guided Reading

Page 3 Have children point to the quotation marks and read the words the character is saying. *Concepts of Print*

Page 6 Have children point to the word *to* on the page. *Vocabulary*

Page 8 Have children tell what the story is about. *Main Idea*

LITERARY RESPONSE Ask children to write and draw a different ending for the story.

REREAD THE BOOK FOR FLUENCY Encourage children to reread the book alone or with a partner.

Page 2 Have children identify two words that begin with /r/. (Ron, ran) *Phonics*

CHALLENGE

Guided Reading

Ron's Radishes
by Ray Tanner
illustrated by Andrea Wallace

PREVIEW AND PREDICT Ask children to look at the cover illustration and predict what the story might be about. Then conduct a picture walk through the first few pages. Have children speculate what Ron is growing in his garden and introduce the word *radish*.

READ THE BOOK Use the following prompts to guide children's reading:

Pages 2–3 Ask children to point to the same word on both pages that begins with *t* and read it together. *Vocabulary*

Pages 4–5 *Point to the word* Ron. *Let's read this word together. Phonics*

Pages 6–7 *Who can find two words that are the same on these two pages?* (Ron, likes, to) *Concepts of Print*

Page 8 *What is this story about?* (a boy who grows radishes in his garden) *Main Idea*

LITERARY RESPONSE Have children draw a picture of what they would like to grow in a garden and write about it in their journal.

TESTED OBJECTIVES

- ☑ Initial /r/ *R, r*
- ☑ Main Idea
- ☐ Concepts of Print
- ☑ Vocabulary: *to*

INFORMAL ASSESSMENT

MAIN IDEA
HOW TO ASSESS Read a short book from the classroom library. Ask children what the story is about and record the main idea on chart paper.

FOLLOW UP Continue reading books with children and recording each main idea on chart paper.

CENTER Activity

Cross Curricular: Social Studies

WATCH IT GROW Make direction cards that show children how to plant seeds in empty milk containers. Then have children place the containers in different areas of the room. Establish a watering schedule, and have children compare the seeds over a period of several weeks.

▶ **Logical/Spatial**

Vocabulary:
to, the, that

Vocabulary Cards

TESTED OBJECTIVES

Children will:
- ☑ identify and read the high-frequency words *to, the, that*

MATERIALS

- word cards
- picture cards
- pocket chart

TEACHING TIP

WORD WALL Point to the words *to, the,* and *that* on the Word Wall. Then ask children questions, such as: "Where are you going?" Children respond by using the words *to, the,* and *that.*

Review

TEACH

Review *to, the, that* Teach the following rhyme to children: *Do this and that/To the cat. Do that and this/To the fish.* Say the rhyme several times together. Give them word cards for *to, the, that.* Ask them to hold up the correct word card each time you say the word in the rhyme.

Place the following word cards in a pocket chart: *do, this, and, that, to the.* Read the sentence. Give each child a picture card of a cat and a fish, and ask them to put the right picture at the end of the sentence in the pocket chart. Repeat with *Do, that, and, this, to, the.*

PRACTICE

Words in Context

Materials: word cards *to, the, that*

- ◆ Write the rhyme from the Teach section on the chalkboard.

- ◆ Ask children to match the *to, the, that* cards to words on the chalkboard.

- ◆ Ask volunteers to use each of the words in a sentence.

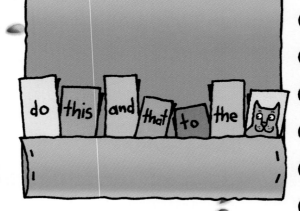

ON LEVEL

✓ ASSESS/CLOSE

Have children complete page 197 of the Pupil Edition or Practice Book. For a different approach to teaching this skill, see page T26 for the **Alternate Teaching Strategy.**

Name_____

1.

The tot ran (to) Dad.

2.

Is (that) the cat?

3.

(The) cat ran to Mom.

4.

(That) cat is Tom.

Read the sentences. 1. Draw a circle around the word *to.* 2. Draw a circle around the word *that.* 3. Draw a circle around the word *the.* 4. Draw a circle around the word *that.*

Unit 9 Review *to, the, that* 197

Pupil Edition page 197

Meeting Individual Needs
Activities

Where Are They?

Materials: cut-out or magnetic letters, including *t*(2), *o*, *h*, *e*, *a*; paper bags

◆ Put ten cut-out or magnetic letters in the bag.

◆ Have children use their sense of touch to find the letters that make up the words *to, the, that.*

EASY

Matching Words

Materials: word cards (2 sets): *the, a, my, that, and, to, we, are*

◆ Place both sets of words face-down and mix them.

◆ Have children turn over two cards trying to make a matching pair.

◆ As they make a match, have them read the word and use it in a sentence.

CHALLENGE

T Words

Materials: word cards (two sets): *to, the, that*

◆ Place all six cards face down.

◆ Have children turn over the cards, trying to make a match.

◆ Ask children to read each word aloud.

LANGUAGE SUPPORT

Interactive Writing

Write a Sentence

GRAMMAR/SPELLING CONNECTIONS

As children brainstorm, model how to use complete sentences by saying something such as *I like apples because they are sweet.*

TEACHING TIP

You may want to carry out the parts of the lesson over a week's time. The **Prewrite** activities may be done on Monday, the **Draft** on Tuesday, **Revise** and **Publish** on Wednesday, **Presentation Ideas** on Thursday, and **Meeting Individual Needs for Writing** on Friday.

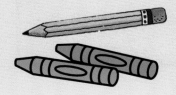

Prewrite

REVIEW THE STORY Remind children that in the story *The Apple Pie Tree,* the two girls had a fruit tree that they loved. Ask: *What kind of fruit grew on the tree? Why did the girls love apples?*

BRAINSTORM Invite children to name their favorite fruits. If they need a prompt, let them find magazine pictures of fruits and name them. Write children's responses on the chalkboard.

apples
oranges
grapes
bananas

Draft

WRITE A SENTENCE Tell children that they are going to write a sentence about their favorite fruit. Explain that they will also make a collage of the fruits they write about.

- At the top of a long horizontal sheet of butcher paper, write the title *Our Favorite Fruits.* Read the words to children, tracking print and have them repeat after you.

- Have children cut out magazine pictures of their favorite fruits or draw small pictures of them and cut them out. Help them to arrange and paste the pictures in collage form on the butcher paper below the title.

- Invite children to name each fruit in their collage. Then write, on a sentence strip, a sentence the children dictate that tells about their favorite fruit. Have children help you write a word or a letter or two, as appropriate. Remind children that sentences begin with capital letters and end with periods.

Revise

Before publishing the collage and sentences, read each sentence aloud as you track the print. Then ask:

- Do we have a picture of the fruits named in each sentence?

- Is there enough space between the words in each sentence?

- Does each sentence begin with a capital letter and end with a period?

- Do we want to add a sentence and a picture for any other fruit?

Publish

Display the collage and sentences on a wall in the classroom or in the school hallway.

Our Favorite Fruits

I like bananas because I like to peel them.

My favorite fruit is an orange because it is *juicy*.

Presentation Ideas

PAINTING A STILL LIFE Place several pieces of fruit into a large fruit bowl. Invite each child to select a few pieces of fruit, arrange them in a pleasant way, and paint a picture of the arrangement. Explain that artists call this kind of painting a "still life." Help children write a sentence about their painting, and read the sentence aloud.

ONE

HAVE A FRUIT SALAD PARTY Invite parents to bring in fruit and join their children for a Fruit Salad Party. Cut the fruit into bite-sized pieces, and place each separate fruit into individual bowls. Then let children and guests choose the fruits they wish to try, and mix them into a salad.

GROUP

Listening and Speaking

- Remind children to speak clearly and slowly as they read aloud the sentences about their paintings.

- When children are making their fruit salads, point out how to politely say *please; thank you;* and *no, thank you,* as the fruit is being served.

TECHNOLOGY TIP

Have children help you type their sentences for the collage on the computer. Then print them out, and let children take their individual sentences home to read with family members.

LANGUAGE SUPPORT

ESL Encourage children to describe the taste, texture, and color of the fruit they eat. Make a list of descriptive words for children to use in sentences.

Meeting Individual Needs for Writing

EASY	ON-LEVEL	CHALLENGE
Fruit Picture Invite each child to draw a picture of a fruit they do *not* enjoy eating. Have them dictate a sentence to you that tells why.	**Fruit Rebus** Have children copy and complete the following sentence frame by drawing a picture of their favorite fruit or cutting it out of a magazine: *I like _____ the best.*	**Make a Pictograph** Invite children to survey their classmates to find out their favorite fruits. Have them create a pictograph by drawing a picture of each fruit named. Then have children explain their findings.

Week 2

Phonics	Comprehension	Vocabulary
• Initial /p/*p*; Final /p/*p* • Blending	• Compare and Contrast	• me

Literature Resources

Big Books

Big Book of Phonics Rhymes and Poems
pages 41, 42

ABC Big Book
pages 199A–199B

Literature Big Book
pages 201A–201B

Reading for Information Big Book
page 26

Read Aloud

The Playground of the Sun and Moon

page 203A

Student Books

ABC Little Book
pages 199A–199B

Is It You?

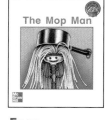

Easy
page 209A
Decodable

Independent
pages 205/206A–205/206B, 209A
Decodable
Story also available in Pupil Edition

Challenge
page 209B
Patterned

Center Activities

Center Activities for the Week

Center Activities

Activities take 15–20 minutes each.

Phonics

Sort Words for /p/

Objective: Sort words that begin or end with /p/.

◆ Have children work in pairs. Partners take turns reading word cards and telling whether the word begins or ends with /p/.

◆ Have children group initial and final *p* words into two piles.

MATERIALS
- Word cards: *pan, pad, pit, pat, pot, top, cap, sip, nap, rip*
- Pencils

Writing

Giving Art

Objective: Respond to audiovisual media in a variety of ways.

◆ Before class, tape yourself reading Silverstein's story.

◆ Have children listen to the tape and follow along with the book.

◆ Invite them to create a "favorite tree" poster.

MATERIALS
- Audio-cassette of *The Giving Tree* by Shel Silverstein
- Copy of the book
- Poster board and art supplies

Reading and Listening

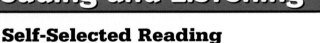

Self-Selected Reading

Objective: Identify the starting and ending point on a printed page.

Place the literature for the week and the corresponding audiocassettes or CDs in the Reading Center. You may also include the following books from the Theme Bibliography on T54–T55.

◆ *My Backyard Garden* by Carol Lerner

◆ *My Spring Robin* by Anne F. Rockwell

◆ *Planting a Rainbow* by Lois Ehlert

MATERIALS
- Listening Library cassettes and CDs
- Books

Working with Words

That Is Me!

Objective: Write and illustrate a sentence.

MATERIALS
- **Drawing paper**
- **Crayons**

◆ Write this sentence on the chalkboard: "That is me!"

◆ Have children copy the sentence and draw a picture of themselves doing something they enjoy.

Social Studies

Pottery

Objective: Gain awareness of the customs of another country.

MATERIALS
- **Self-drying clay**
- **Paint and brushes**

◆ Explain that in Mexico, parents teach children the art of making pottery.

◆ Demonstrate how to make small clay bowls.

◆ Have children paint their dry bowls.

Math 3+2

Guessing Game

Objective: Recognize which containers hold more or less.

◆ Display different fruits and vegetables.

◆ Have children guess how many fruits or vegetables will fit in the different baskets.

◆ Children can check their guesses by filling the baskets.

MATERIALS
- **Various fruits and vegetables**
- **Baskets of various sizes**

Is It You?

Suggested

 **Available on CD-ROM**

Lesson Planner

READING AND LANGUAGE ARTS

- Phonological Awareness
- **Phonics** initial and final /p/p; blending with short a, i, o
- Comprehension
- Vocabulary
- Beginning Reading Concepts
- Listening, Speaking, Viewing, Representing

DAY 1

Allie's Adventure From A to Z
Written by Ellen Dreyer · Illustrated by Jui Ishida

Focus on Reading Skills
Develop Phonological Awareness, 198I–198J
"Pease Porridge Hot" *Big Book of Phonics Rhymes and Poems*, 41

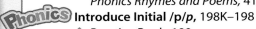 **Introduce Initial /p/p,** 198K–198
- Practice Book, 198
- Phonics/Phonemic Awareness Practice Book, 105–106

-  **CD-ROM**

Read the Literature
 **Read** *Allie's Adventure from A to Z* **Big Book,** 199A–199B
Shared Reading

Build Skills
- ☑ Inside, Outside, 199C–199
- ◆ Practice Book, 199

DAY 2

The Apple Pie Tree
BY Zoe Hall
ILLUSTRATED BY Shari Halpern

Focus on Reading Skills
Develop Phonological Awareness, 200A–200B
"Chicken Soup" *Big Book of Phonics Rhymes and Poems*, 42

 **Introduce Final /p/p,** 200C–200
- Practice Book, 200
- Phonics/Phonemic Awareness Practice Book, 107–108

-  **CD-ROM**

Read the Literature
 **Read** *The Apple Pie Tree* **Big Book,** 201A–201B
Shared Reading

Build Skills
- ☑ Compare and Contrast, 201C–201
- ◆ Practice Book, 201

- **Cross Curriculum**

   Arts, 199B

   Math, Social Studies, 198F

- **Writing**

   Writing Prompt: Write about Allie having a new adventure.

   Journal Writing, 199B
  Letter Formation, 198K

   Writing Prompt: Write about your favorite food. Describe how it tastes.

   Journal Writing, 201B
  Letter Formation, 200C

= **Whole-Day classrooms may extend the day with these optional activities!**

✓ = **Skill Assessed in Unit Test**

DAY 3

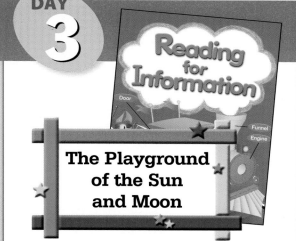

The Playground of the Sun and Moon

Focus on Reading Skills

Develop Phonological Awareness, 202A–202B
"Pease Porridge Hot" and "Chicken Soup" *Big Book of Phonics Rhymes and Poems,* 41–42

 **Review /p/p,** 202C–202
◆ Practice Book, 202
◆ Phonics/Phonemic Awareness Practice Book, 105–108

◆ **Phonics CD-ROM**

Read the Literature

Read "The Playground of the Sun and Moon" Teacher Read Aloud, 203A–203B
Shared Reading
Read the Reading for Information Big Book, 26–27
Maps

Build Skills

☑ High-Frequency Word: *me* 203C–203
◆ Practice Book, 203

 Science, 203B

✎ **Writing Prompt:** Write a poem about the moon and stars.

DAY 4

Is It You?

Focus on Reading Skills

Develop Phonological Awareness, 204A–204B
"Yes, I Did!"
Review Blending with Short *a, i, o,* 204C–204
◆ Practice Book, 204
◆ Phonics/Phonemic Awareness Practice Book, 109

◆ **Phonics CD-ROM**

Read the Literature

Read "Is It You?" On-Level Decodable Story, 205/206A–205/206B

☑ Initial and Final /p/p; Blending
☑ Compare and Contrast
☑ High-Frequency Words: *me*
Concepts of Print

Build Skills

☑ Compare and Contrast, 207A–207
◆ Practice Book, 207

 Science, 205/206B

✎ **Writing Prompt:** Write about a school play you were in.

Letter Formation Practice Book, 205–206

DAY 5

The Mop Man
Picnic
Is It You?
by Anne Miranda
illustrated by Carol Nicklaus

Focus on Reading Skills

Develop Phonological Awareness, 208A–208B
"Yes, I Did!"
Review Blending with Short *a, i, o,* 208C–208
◆ Practice Book, 208
◆ Phonics/Phonemic Awareness Practice Book, 110

◆ **Phonics CD-ROM**

Read the Literature

Read "The Mop Man" Easy Decodable Story, 209B
Reread "Is It You?" On-Level Decodable Story, 209A
Read "The Picnic" Challenge Patterned Book, 209B
Guided Reading
☑ Initial and Final /p/p; Blending
☑ Compare and Contrast
☑ High-Frequency Words: *me*
Concepts of Print

Build Skills

☑ High-Frequency Words: *me, to, you,* 209C–209
◆ Practice Book, 209

 Science, 209B

✎ **Writing Prompt:** Write about your favorite thing to do in your neighborhood.

Interactive Writing, 210A–210B

198H

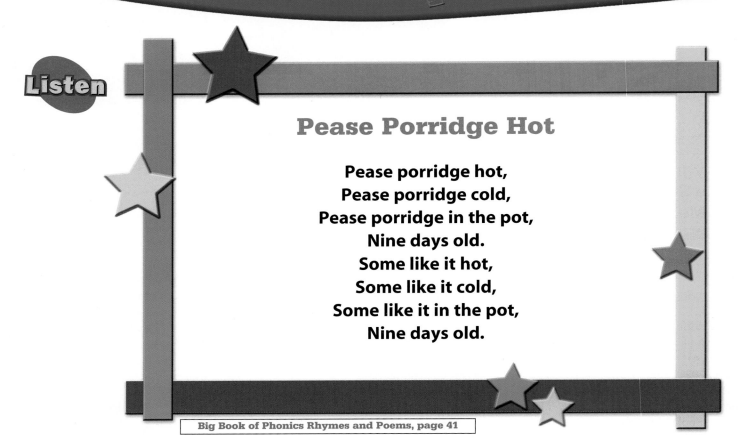

Listen

Pease Porridge Hot

Pease porridge hot,
Pease porridge cold,
Pease porridge in the pot,
Nine days old.
Some like it hot,
Some like it cold,
Some like it in the pot,
Nine days old.

Big Book of Phonics Rhymes and Poems, page 41

Identify Rhyming Words · · · · · · · · Phonological Awareness · · · · · · · · · ·

Teach   Reread the first four lines of the poem several times, having children join in when they are ready. Then read the first four lines again, pausing to have volunteers supply the rhyming words for *hot* and *cold*. Then say the words *hot/pot*. Ask volunteers to say another word that rhymes with *hot* and *pot*. Repeat with *cold* and *old*.

Practice   Separate the children into two groups. Name one group "hot" and the other group "cold." Tell children you will say some words. If the word rhymes with hot, the "hot" group should stand and say the word *hot* and the rhyming word. If the word rhymes with *cold*, the "cold" group should stand up, say the word *cold* and the rhyming word. Use the words in the box.

bold	not	car	spot
told	got	fold	ball

Listen for Beginning Sounds

Teach Say the word *pease* and emphasize the initial /p/ sound. Have the children repeat the sound after you. Then read each line of the poem slowly. Children can hold up a finger every time they hear a word that begins with /p/.

Practice Give students the old magazines and have them find pictures of foods that begin with the /p/ sound. Have the children name the foods in their pictures. Have another child say if the food begins with the /p/ sound. Examples might include *pudding, peas, pear, pizza, pancakes,* and *potato.*

> **MATERIALS**
> • old maga-zines (with pictures or ads of food)

INFORMAL ASSESSMENT Observe children as they identify rhyming words and beginning sounds in words. If children have difficulty, see Alternate Teaching Strategies: Unit 3, T29; and Unit 4, T27.

Read Together

From Phonemic Awareness to Phonics

Objective: Identify Initial /p/P, p

IDENTIFY THE LETTER FOR THE SOUND

• Explain to children that the letter *p* stands for /p/. Say the sound and have children repeat it.

• Then display page 41 in the Big Book of Phonics Rhymes and Poems. Point to the letters in the corner of the page and identify them. Have children repeat the sound /p/ after you.

REREAD THE POEM

• Read the poem again. Explain that you will point to the words that begin with *P, p* as you read.

LOOK FOR P, p

• Write the letters *P, p* on small pieces of paper.

• Volunteers take a letter and find a word in the poem that begins with *P* or *p.*

• After the child finds a word, say the word together. Then the child puts the piece of paper in a pot. Call on other children until all *p* words are identified.

• Afterward, count the pieces of paper to determine how many *p* words are in the poem.

Pease Porridge Hot

Pease porridge hot,
   Pease porridge cold,
Pease porridge in the pot,
   Nine days old.
Some like it hot,
   Some like it cold,
Some like it in the pot,
   Nine days old.

Pp

Big Book of Phonics Rhymes and Poems, page 41

198J

Initial /p/ *P, p*

Pp
pig

Phonics Picture Posters and Cards

☑ OBJECTIVES

Children will:
- ☑ identify the letters *P, p*
- ☑ identify /p/ *P, p*
- ☑ form the letters *P, p*

MATERIALS

- letter cards
- Phonics Picture Posters

ADDITIONAL RESOURCES

- Practice Book, page 198
- Phonics/Phonemic Awareness Practice Book, pages 105–106
- **Phonics** CD-ROM

🎵 Phonics Song 🎵

Penny the Pig

Penny the Pig likes pickles and
    peas,
Pickles and peas, pickles and peas.
Penny the Pig likes pickles and
    peas,
Penny is a pig.

*Sung to the tune of
"Here We Go 'Round
the Mulberry Bush"*
From Songs from A to Z

Introduce

TEACH

Phonemic Awareness Warm-Up Have children sing the song "Penny the Pig" with you. Then say the words without the /p/ sound. Have children add the /p/ sound to say the words: *ig/pig, enny/Penny, ickles/pickles, eas/peas.* Continue with other words.

Identify /p/ *P, p* Write a large *P, p* on the board. Explain to children that *P, p* stands for the sound /p/. Point to the letters and have children repeat the /p/ sound after you.

Form *P, p* Display Phonics Picture Poster *Pp* and review the capital and lowercase forms with children. With your back to them, trace the letters one at a time in the air with your finger. Ask children to do the same. Then, give each child a sheet of paper and help them fold the paper into four boxes. Ask children to write a capital *P* in each box on one side of the paper and a lowercase *p* in each box on the other side.

PRACTICE

Find the *Ps*

Materials: oaktag strips

◆ Say the following words and ask children to write *P, p* on letter strips when they hear a word that begins with /p/: *pen, can, pin, ball, pan, pot, picture.*

ON LEVEL

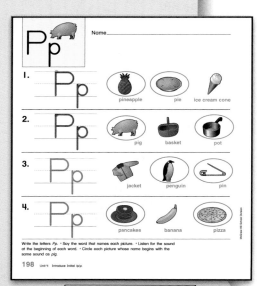

Pupil Edition page 198

☑ ASSESS/CLOSE

Have children complete page 198 of the Pupil Edition or the Practice Book. For a different approach to this skill, see page T28 for the **Alternate Teaching Strategy.**

Meeting Individual Needs
Activities

Pipe Cleaner Letters

Materials: pipe cleaners, fingerpaints

◆ Children bend pipe cleaners to form a capital and lowercase *P*.

◆ Children place the pipe cleaners on paper and paint around the shapes.

◆ Children remove the pipe cleaners and display their pictures.

EASY

Plan a Picnic

Material: drawing paper, crayons

◆ Invite children to think of words that begin with *p* that they might pack for a picnic. Examples include: *pizza, popcorn,* and *pie.*

◆ Have children draw a picnic scene that includes some of the items. Have them write the letter *P, p* on every item that begins with /p/.

CHALLENGE

Powerful Action Words!

◆ Model gestures for words that begin with *p,* such as *push, pull, pat, point,* and *pour.*

◆ Ask children to repeat each word and act it out with you.

◆ Have children trace the letters *P, p* in the air as they say each word.

LANGUAGE SUPPORT

Shared Reading

Allie's Adventure
From A to Z

Written by Ellen Dreyer   Illustrated by Jui Ishida

Big Book

OBJECTIVES

TESTED

Children will:

☐ identify starting and ending points on a page.

☑ identify letters of the alphabet.

☐ use illustrations.

☑ compare and contrast.

☐ listen and respond to the story.

Build Background

Sing a Song   Sing the alphabet song together, shown on page 2 of the *Big Book of Phonics Rhymes and Poems*.

Develop Oral Language   Help children remember Allie's adventures, and make a list of what they remember on the board.

Read the Big Book

Set Purposes   As children reread the story, tell them to look for the words on each page that follow the order of the alphabet.

Read the Story   Show children the starting and ending points on the first few pages of the story. *Concepts of Print*

MODEL: I see that the story starts here. (Point to first word.) This is where I will start reading. It ends here, (Point to last word.) and this is where I will stop. *Concepts of Print*

Invite a volunteer to point out the letter on each page and the word that begins with the letter. *Letter Identification/Word Knowledge*

Ask a volunteer to identify the starting and ending points on a page. Ask another volunteer to trace the path of the words as you read them aloud. *Concepts of Print*

Allie sees some **eggs**.

Allie sees lots of **feathers**.

Allie's Adventure, pages 6–7

Literature Response

LISTENING/SPEAKING

Discuss the Story Ask volunteers to respond to the questions using complete sentences.

What are some of the animals Allie sees? (She sees a butterfly, cow, chicken, insect, and mouse.) *Literal: Story Details*

How are these animals alike? How are they different? (Answers may vary.) *Inferential: Compare and Contrast*

Where do you start reading on page 10? (I start reading on the left.) Where do you stop? (I stop reading at the end of the sentence.) *Concepts of Print*

WRITING

Journal Writing Have children draw pictures of the animals Allie meets and label them with the correct initial letter. Invite them to share their pictures with a friend.

Allie sees a **hole**.

Allie's Adventure, page 10

 SSESSMENT

LETTER IDENTIFICATION

How to Assess
Ask a child to name a favorite animal. Write the animal's name, and have the child identify each letter in the name.

Follow-Up
Write a simple animal name, such as dog or bird. Ask a child to identify the first letter in the name.

Cross Curricular: Art

MAKE A CAT Provide children with paper triangle, circle, rectangle, and oval shapes in various sizes. Invite them to paste the shapes together to make a cat. If necessary, ask them to look carefully for the different shapes in the illustrations.

Inside, Outside

The Apple Pie Tree
BY Zoe Hall
ILLUSTRATED BY
Shari Halpern

The Apple Pie Tree

TESTED OBJECTIVES

Children will:

☑ identify *inside* and *outside*

MATERIALS

- *The Apple Pie Tree*
- box or bag
- small objects

TEACHING TIP

INSTRUCTIONAL Children can work with partners to practice the concepts of *inside* and *outside*. You may wish to pair native English speakers with less-fluent children.

Introduce

TEACH

Discuss Inside and Outside Display the Big Book *The Apple Pie Tree* and recall the story with children. Ask them what the children in the book like to do when they are outside *(watch the robins, watch the tree change, play, pick apples).* Ask what the children in the story like to do when they are inside the house *(bake a pie).* Then use a box or a bag and a small object, such as a pen. Put the pen inside the box and ask: *Where is the pen?* Then take it out and ask: *Is the pen inside the box or outside the box?* Repeat with other small objects.

PRACTICE

Show Inside and Outside

◆ Invite children to take turns asking questions about the box and small objects.

◆ Help children frame questions by suggesting that they say, *Is the _____ inside or outside the box?*

◆ Tell children who are answering the questions to do so by saying, *The _____ is inside (or outside) the box.*

ON LEVEL

✓ ASSESS/CLOSE

Have children complete page 199 of the Pupil Edition or Practice Book. For a different approach to teaching this skill, see page T29 for the **Alternate Teaching Strategy.**

Name_____

1. 2.
3. 4.

1. Draw a circle around the worm that is inside the apple. 2. Draw a circle around the bird that is outside the nest. 3. Draw a circle around the cat that is outside the box. 4. Draw a circle around the dog that is inside the doghouse.

Unit 4 Introduce Inside, Outside 199

Pupil Edition page 199

Meeting Individual Needs
Activities

Inside/Outside the Ring

Materials: construction paper, magazines, scissors, glue

◆ Have children draw a simple outline of a house.

◆ Ask them to cut out magazine pictures of things found inside a house and things found outside a house.

◆ Have children glue the pictures inside or outside the outline. Ask them to use *inside* and *outside* to tell about their work.

EASY

Play a Game

Materials: drawing paper, pencil

◆ Have children draw a large circle.

◆ Have partners take turns giving each other directions, such as: *Draw a flower inside the circle. Draw a bird outside the circle. Draw an apple inside the ring. Draw a nest outside the ring.*

CHALLENGE

Inside/Outside the Box

Materials: small paper bags; small objects such as pencils, stones, paper clips

◆ Give each child a bag and a few small objects.

◆ Give directions, such as: *Put the pencil inside the bag. Put the crayon outside the bag.*

◆ Then have children take turns giving similar directions to follow.

LANGUAGE SUPPORT

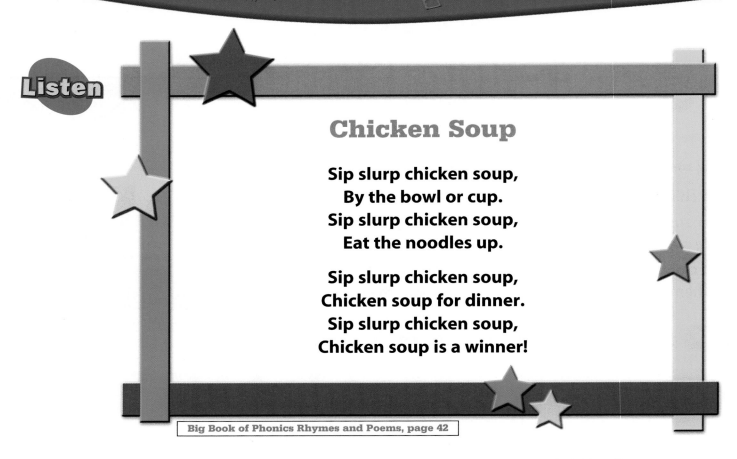
Listen

Chicken Soup

Sip slurp chicken soup,
By the bowl or cup.
Sip slurp chicken soup,
Eat the noodles up.

Sip slurp chicken soup,
Chicken soup for dinner.
Sip slurp chicken soup,
Chicken soup is a winner!

Big Book of Phonics Rhymes and Poems, page 42

Segment Syllables · · · · · Phonological Awareness · · · · ·

Teach   Chant the poem to the class. Then repeat the first line, clapping out the syllables of the words. Do the same for the following three lines. Invite children to clap along with you.

MODEL: Listen to the poem while I clap out the sounds. Feel free to join in with me. "Sip, slurp, chick-en, soup, / By, the, bowl, or, cup. / Sip, slurp, chick-en, soup, / Eat, the, noo-dles, up."

Practice   Read the last four lines. Ask children to stand before the group and clap out the syllables for the words. Review by having the children clap out the syllables for the words in the box.

chick-en	soup	noo-dles
din-ner	win-ner	sip

Listen for Ending Sounds

Teach   Say the word *soup* and emphasize the final /p/ sound. Have the children repeat the sound after you. Tell children the word *soup* has the /p/ sound at the end of the word. Then read each line of the poem slowly. Children should say /p/ after they hear the word *soup*.

Practice   Bring out the drum. Tell the children to "*tap*" the drum. Say the poem aloud. Have them tap the drum each time they hear a word with the final /p/ sound.

> **MATERIALS**
> • drum or can

INFORMAL ASSESSMENT   Observe children as they segment syllables and identify ending sounds. If children have difficulty, see Alternate Teaching Strategies: Unit 2, T29; and Unit 4, T27.

Read Together

From Phonemic Awareness to Phonics

Objective: Identify Final /p/P, p

IDENTIFY THE LETTER FOR THE SOUND
- Explain to children that the letter *p* stands for the sound /p/. Have children repeat the sound after you.
- Display page 42 in the Big Book of Phonics Rhymes and Poems. Point to the letters in the corner and identify them. Have children repeat the sound /p/ after you.

REREAD THE POEM
- Read the poem again as you point to each word. Emphasize words with the final sound of /p/.

- Invite volunteers to find words that end with *p*. Children frame the word using their index fingers.

ACT OUT THE WORDS
- Write the letter *p* on the chalkboard, and have children make the /p/ sound.
- Then say several action words. If the word ends with *p*, volunteers point to the letter and act out the word.

> clap   snap   slip   tap
> sit   hop   run

Pp   **Chicken Soup**

Sip slurp chicken soup,
By the bowl or cup.
Sip slurp chicken soup,
Eat the noodles up.

Sip slurp chicken soup,
Chicken soup for dinner.
Sip slurp chicken soup,
Chicken soup is a winner!

Big Book of Phonics Rhymes and Poems, page 42

Final /p/ *p*

OBJECTIVES

Children will:
- ☑ identify the letters *P, p*
- ☑ identify /p/ *P, p*
- ☑ form the letters *P, p*

MATERIALS
- letter cards
- word cards
- index cards

ADDITIONAL RESOURCES
- Practice Book, page 200
- Phonics/Phonemic Awareness Practice Book, pages 107–108
- **Phonics** CD–ROM

TEACHING TIP

INSTRUCTIONAL To help children distinguish between /p/ and /b/, have them hold two fingers in front of their mouths and say *tap-p-p*. Repeat with *tub-b-b*.

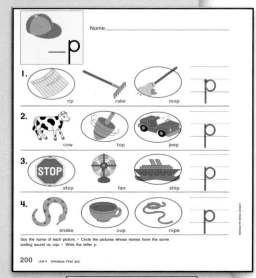

I. rip   rake   mop   p
2. cow   top   jeep   p
3. stop   fan   ship   p
4. snake   cup   rope   p

Say the name of each picture. • Circle the pictures whose names have the same ending sound as *cap.* • Write the letter *p.*

200   Unit 9 Introduce Final /p/

Pupil Edition page 200

Introduce

TEACH

Phonemic Awareness Warm-Up Say: *ap*. Have children add /r/ to make: *rap*. Then say: *ip*. Have children add /r/ to make *rip*. Continue making other words such as: *up/pup*.

Identify /p/ *p* Say the words *cup* and *tap* slowly, emphasizing the final /p/ sound. Write *p* on the board and explain to children that *p* stands for the final sound /p/. Point to the letter and have children repeat the /p/ sound after you.

Form *P, p* Review how to form the letters *Pp* with children. Have them practice writing with their finger on the desk. Then distribute index cards and have children write *Pp* at the top of the card. Then have children draw a picture of something that ends with the /p/ sound.

PRACTICE

Play Simon Says

- ◆ Ask children to do what "Simon" says only if the command includes a word with /p/ at the end.
- ◆ Give directions such as, *Hop on one foot, Clap your hands, Tap your foot, Snap your fingers,* and *Take a step.*
- ◆ Then write the words that end with *p* on the board, read them, and have children use their fingers to write *p* when they hear the final /p/.

ON LEVEL

✓ ASSESS/CLOSE

Have children complete page 200 of the Pupil Edition or the Practice Book. For a different approach to this skill, see page T28 for the **Alternate Teaching Strategy.**

Meeting Individual Needs
Activities

Popcorn *Pp*'s

Materials: glue, construction paper, popcorn

◆ Have children form *P, p* on paper with glue.

◆ Then have them stick pieces of popcorn to the glue.

◆ When the glue dries, invite children to gently trace *Pp* with their finger.

EASY

Our House

Materials: drawing paper, crayons

◆ Have children list household objects that end in *p*, such as *cup, top, pup, cap, mop,* and *map.*

◆ Ask children to draw a picture of a house with at least one of the objects in the drawing.

◆ Have children say each picture word and label it with a *P, p.*

CHALLENGE

On a Search for *P*

◆ Some children will confuse the letters *p* and *d*. To provide practice in differentiating between the letters, write and say words that end in *p* or *d*.

◆ After each word is presented, ask children to repeat the word and say the ending sound.

◆ Have children underline the final letter in each word, name it, and make its sound.

LANGUAGE SUPPORT

Shared Reading

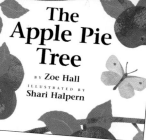

The Apple Pie Tree

BY Zoe Hall

ILLUSTRATED BY Shari Halpern

Big Book

TESTED
OBJECTIVES

Children will:
☐ understand how print is read

☑ compare and contrast

☐ listen responsively to a story

Build Background

Finger Play   Teach the following fingerplay to children.

Two Little Apples

Way up high in the apple tree
Two little apples smiled at me.
I shook that tree as hard as I could.
Down came the apples.
Mmm! They were good!

Develop Oral Language   Have children do simple actions to the fingerplay. Display a copy of "The Apple Pie Tree." Ask children the main idea.

Read the Big Book

Set Purposes   MODEL: We know the story is mainly about how the apple tree changes. When we read today, let's find out about the robins.

Read the Story   As you read the story, track the print. *Concepts of Print*

Have children compare and contrast the clothing worn by the girls throughout the seasons. *Compare and Contrast*

MODEL: In winter the girls wear long-sleeved sweaters. In spring, they wear short sleeves. These are not as warm as their sweaters.

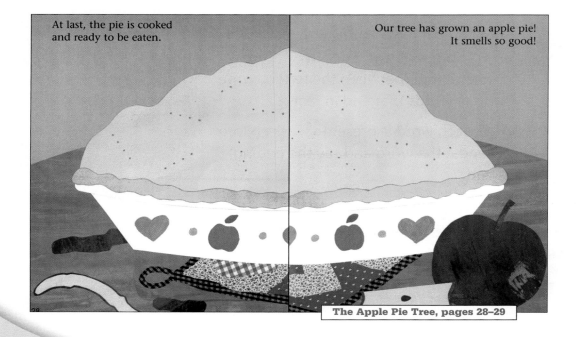

At last, the pie is cooked and ready to be eaten.

Our tree has grown an apple pie! It smells so good!

The Apple Pie Tree, pages 28–29

Literature Response

LISTENING/SPEAKING

Remind children to use eye contact and appropriate gestures when speaking.

Discuss the Story What grows on the tree after the blossoms fall off? (Small green apples grow on the tree.) *Literal: Story details*

Ask children to recall how the baby robins changed during the story. Focus on how they grew, learned to fly, and finally moved away. *Literal: Compare and Contrast*

What do the baby robins grow on their bodies? (They grow feathers.) *Inferential: Use Illustrations*

In what ways have you changed since you were a baby? *Critical: Personal Response*

The Apple Pie Tree, page 27

TEACHING TIP

REALITY OR FANTASY?
Ask if this story could really happen or if it is make-believe. Have children point out the pictures in the story that support their opinions.

Activity

Writing

JOURNAL WRITING Invite children to draw a picture showing the baby robins. On another page in their journal, have them draw a picture showing how the robins looked when they got older. Have them write or dictate a sentence about each picture. Remind them that sentences begin with capital letters.

Baby robins are in a nest.

INFORMAL ASSESSMENT

How to Assess
If children are having difficulty with compare and contrast, they should use the skills lesson that follows on pages 201G–201.

Compare and Contrast

MATERIALS

• *The Apple Pie Tree*

TEACHING TIP

INSTRUCTIONAL Hold up two picture cards of similar objects. Ask children to tell what is the same and different about the pictures.

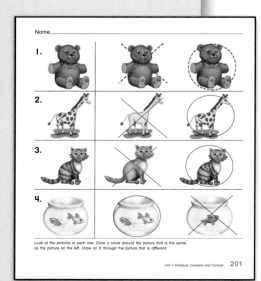

The Apple Pie Tree

Introduce

TEACH

Compare Robins and Trees Reread *The Apple Pie Tree*. After you read page 16, return to page 8. Discuss the ways the robins have changed in the story. Then, direct children to the apple trees on these pages. Ask children to tell how the trees are the same and different.

PRACTICE

Same

Different

All About Apples

Materials: three apples

◆ Bring in three different kinds of apples and show them to children.

◆ Invite children to tell how the apples are the same and how they are different.

◆ Record their answers on the board under the headings *Same* and *Different*.

ON LEVEL

✓ ASSESS/CLOSE

Have children complete page 201 of the Pupil Edition or the Practice Book. For a different approach to this skill, see page T30 for the **Alternate Teaching Strategy.**

Meeting Individual Needs
Activities

Pick a Pair of Apples

Materials: colorful construction paper

◆ Cut out pairs of paper apples, matched by color, shape, and size.

◆ Put the cutouts in a paper bag.

◆ Invite children to pick two apples from the bag and explain how the apples are the same or different.

EASY

Compare and Contrast

Materials: a variety of classroom objects

◆ Set out a tray of common objects.

◆ Challenge children to select two objects from the tray and compare them.

◆ Have children observe the objects carefully to discover the similarities and differences.

CHALLENGE

Talk About Same and Different

Materials: similar objects

◆ Hold up a pair of classroom objects, such as two crayons or two books.

◆ Ask children to hold the objects in their hands.

◆ Invite children to tell how the objects are the same and different.

LANGUAGE SUPPORT

Listen

Pease Porridge Hot
a poem

Pease porridge hot,
Pease porridge cold,
Pease porridge in the pot,
Nine days old.
Some like it hot,
Some like it cold,
Some like it in the pot,
Nine days old.

Chicken Soup
a poem

Sip slurp chicken soup,
By the bowl or cup.
Sip slurp chicken soup,
Eat the noodles up.
Sip slurp chicken soup,
Chicken soup for dinner.
Sip slurp chicken soup,
Chicken soup is a winner!

Big Book of Phonics Rhymes and Poems, pages 41, 42

Delete Syllables
Phonological Awareness

Teach Read the poems to the class. Repeat the line "Chicken soup for dinner." As you say the word *dinner*, place two sticky notes on the chalkboard to represent each syllable. Point to the first sticky note and say *din*. Point to the second and say *ner*. Repeat *din* and then remove the second sticky note. Say, *I took away the sound* ner.

MODEL: "A delicious dinner on my plate. *Chick-en, chick-en.*" (Touch the sticky note that corresponds with each syllable.) *En* is the part someone ate. (Remove the sticky note from the second frame.) What is left on my plate? (Yes, *chick*.)

Practice Repeat the chant using the foods below. Have children delete a syllable, remove the sticky note, and say the remaining word part.

Food	Part someone ate	What is left on my plate?
hot dogs	dogs	hot
meatloaf	loaf	meat
noodles	dles	noo

Listen for Beginning and Ending Sounds

Teach   Tell children the word *porridge* has the /p/ sound at the beginning of the word. Then tell children the word *cup* has the /p/ sound at the end of the word. Have the children repeat the words with you.

Practice   Give half of the class blue sheets of paper. Tell them their paper represents the beginning /p/ sound. Give the other half of the class red sheets of paper. Their paper represents the ending /p/ sound. Then say words that have the /p/ sound. Have students hold up their papers to show whether the word has the beginning or ending /p/ sound.

MATERIALS
- red and blue sheets of construction paper

INFORMAL ASSESSMENT   Observe children as they count the syllables in a word and discriminate beginning and ending sounds. If children have difficulty, see Alternate Teaching Strategies: Unit 1, T24; and Unit 4, T27.

Read Together

From Phonemic Awareness to Phonics

Objective: Identify /p/ *P, p*

IDENTIFY THE LETTERS Display the Big Book of Phonics Rhymes and Poems, pages 41 and 42. Point to the letters *P, p,* identify them, and say the /p/ sound.

REREAD THE POEMS Reread the poems. Point to each word, stressing those that begin or end with /p/.

FIND WORDS WITH *P, p* Have children use the classroom pointer to point out the letters *P* or *p* in the poems. Read the words and have children repeat them after you.

Pease Porridge Hot **Pp**
Pease porridge hot,
  Pease porridge cold,
Pease porridge in the pot,
  Nine days old.
Some like it hot,
  Some like it cold,
Some like it in the pot,
  Nine days old.

Pp **Chicken Soup**
Sip slurp chicken soup,
By the bowl or cup.
Sip slurp chicken soup,
Eat the noodles up.

Sip slurp chicken soup,
Chicken soup for dinner.
Sip slurp chicken soup,
Chicken soup is a winner!

Big Book of Phonics Rhymes and Poems, pages 41, 42

202B

OBJECTIVES

Children will:

☑ identify /p/ *P, p*

☑ write and use letters *P, p*

MATERIALS

- letter cards
- Word Building Cards

ADDITIONAL RESOURCES

- Practice Book, page 202
- Phonics/Phonemic Awareness Practice Book, pages 105–108
- **Phonics** CD-ROM

TEACHING TIP

INSTRUCTIONAL Children can make sound books with pictures that begin or end with a target sound.

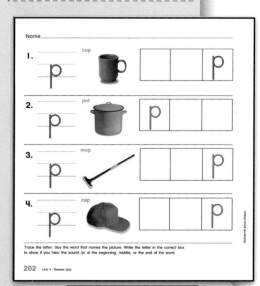

Review

TEACH

Word Building Manipulative Cards

Phonemic Awareness Warm-Up Remind children that the word *cap* has the /p/ sound at the end of the word and *pig* has the /p/ sound at the beginning of the word. Tell children to raise their hands only if they hear you say a word with the /p/ sound at the beginning of it. Say: *pan, pod, top, Pam, map, pad,* and *mop.* Repeat the same process but have children listen for /p/ at the end of the words this time.

Identify /p/ *P, p* Remind children that /p/ can be at the beginning of a word, as in *pig,* or at the end of a word, as in *cap.* Have children point to the picture that shows where they hear the /p/ sound in these words: *pal, lip, hop, pink, petal, top, hip, pen* and *pad.*

Form *P, p* Display letter cards for *P* and *p* and review the capital and lowercase forms with children. Review the words on the chalkboard. Have children write on paper the capital or lowercase forms *P* or *p* in each word.

PRACTICE

Word Card Match

Materials: picture and matching word cards for words with initial and final /p/ *p*

◆ Display the picture cards. Put the matching word cards in a pile facedown on the table.

◆ Have volunteers take a word card from the pile, blend the sounds and read the word aloud, and then match it to its picture.

ON LEVEL

✓ ASSESS/CLOSE

Have children complete page 202 of the Pupil Edition or the Practice Book. For a different approach to this skill, see page T28 for the **Alternate Teaching Strategy.**

Meeting Individual Needs
Activities

Pretty, Pretty Pumpkin Pie

◆ Give a copy of the following rhyme to each child: *Pick a pumpkin from the pile./Pop likes pie, and we like Pop!/We'll bake a pie to make him smile,/A pumpkin pie with plums on top.*

◆ Tell children to follow the rhyme along as you read it. Have them circle words that begin or end with /p/ *p*.

EASY

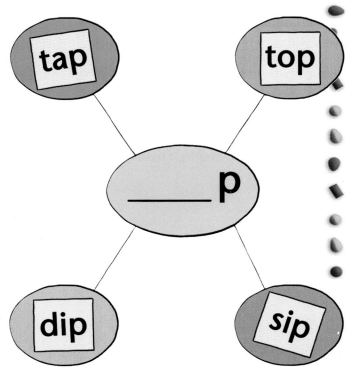

/p/ *p* Pantomime

Materials: word cards for initial and final /p/ *p*

◆ Prepare cards with words that begin or end with /p/ *p*. The words should be easy to act out, such as *tap, pat, nap, dip, sip*.

◆ Have children take turns acting out the cards and having the other children guess the word.

CHALLENGE

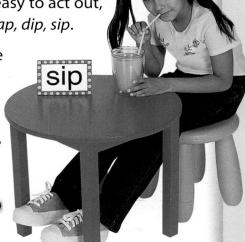

Sound Webs

Materials: self-stick notes with initial and final *p* words on them, chart paper

◆ Blend each word as you say it aloud with children.

◆ Draw two word webs on chart paper. Write *p___* in the center oval of one web and *___p* in the center oval of the other web.

◆ Ask volunteers to pick a self-stick note and read the word on the paper. Have children put the word on the correct web.

tap · top · ___p · dip · sip

LANGUAGE SUPPORT

202

Listen

The Playground of the Sun and Moon
a myth by Margaret Read MacDonald

Some people say that high in the sky, the sun lives in a palace of gold.

Sun looks out his window each morning to see if Moon is in sight.

"Where are you, little Moon? Are you hiding in the nighttime fields? Or are you playing in my blue day skies?"

Sometimes Moon is nearby, drifting pale in the bright daytime. She answers sweetly: "Did you call me, Sun?"

"Sure I called you!" Sun shoots his rays toward her.

"What do you want to play today?" asks Moon shyly.

"Ring of Fortune!" That is what Sun calls his game of chase.

"Oh? And how is it played?"

Then Sun begins to chant the directions:

"I have two rings

Continued on page T2

Oral Comprehension

LISTENING AND SPEAKING Use these questions to encourage children to respond to the myth. Guide children to ask questions if they want more information.

- In what ways are the Sun and Moon different? (The Moon likes darkness and the Sun likes light.)

- What game does Sun like to play? (Sun likes to play "Ring of Fortune" with Moon. Sun chases Moon away in the morning.)

- What does Moon like to do? (She likes to dance and sing all night long.)

- Whom would you rather play with, Sun or Moon? Why? (Answers will vary.)

Activity Have children fold a sheet of paper in half. On one half of the paper, they should draw Sun as they imagine him. On the other half, they should draw Moon. Ask them to label their pictures. Invite volunteers to describe their pictures. Remind children to listen quietly when others are speaking.

▶**Spatial**

Reading for Information

Can you find the playground on the map?

Reading for Information Big Book, pages 26–27

Objective: Read a Map

DISCUSS THE BIG BOOK Remind children that they just listened to a story about the playground of the Sun and Moon. Then display the table of contents for the Big Book and ask them to find the "Playground of the Sun and Moon" map on pages 26–27. Explain that a table of contents can be like a "map" of a book.

- Turn to pages 26 and 27 in the Big Book and show children the map of the park. Reinforce children's understanding that a map is used to show how to get to different destinations.

- Read aloud the questions. Then help children locate the playground. Discuss the purpose of this map.

- Ask: *Where are the ducks?* (They are in the pond.) *If you start at the fountain, what do you pass on the way to the swing set?* (Answers will vary.) *How would you get from the picnic area to the playground?* (Answers will vary.)

CENTER Activity

Cross Curricular: Science

MOON SHAPES The Moon looks like it changes shape over the course of a month. Discuss that these changes in shape are a result of shadows on the face of the Moon.

Activity Provide black construction paper and chalk. Ask children to draw nighttime pictures by using the chalk on black paper. Have children draw at least three items that can be seen at night such as the Moon, stars, street-lights, lightning bugs, and so on. Invite children to write captions for their pictures and share their work with the class.

▶ **Spatial**

203B

Vocabulary: me

me

Vocabulary Cards

OBJECTIVES

Children will:
☑ identify and read the high-frequency word *me*

MATERIALS
- word cards
- pocket chart

TEACHING TIP

WORD WALL Add the word *me* to the Word Wall. Point to the word and have children spell it with you. Then have them think of as many words as they can that rhyme. (Examples: *he, she, be, see, we*)

Introduce

TEACH

Introduce *me* Teach children the following poem: *I am me/Me, me, me./You are you/You, you, you.* Say the poem together several times, and have children point to themselves as they say the first two lines, and to a partner as they say the second two lines.

Place the following words in a pocket chart: *I am me.* Point to each word as you read the sentence aloud. Then give each child a word card *me*. As you read the sentence aloud, have them hold up the card when they hear the word *me*. Repeat the poem you practiced together, and have them hold up the *me* card when they say that word.

PRACTICE

It's ME!

Materials: word cards for *me*

- ◆ Say sentences with the word *me*.
- ◆ Have children hold up their *me* cards and say the word aloud when you say the word *me*.

ON LEVEL

ASSESS/CLOSE

Have children complete page 203 of the Pupil Edition or Practice Book. For a different approach to teaching this skill, see page T26 for the **Alternate Teaching Strategy.**

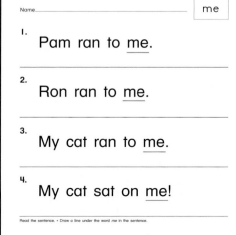

Name_____ me

1. Pam ran to <u>me</u>.

2. Ron ran to <u>me</u>.

3. My cat ran to <u>me</u>.

4. My cat sat on <u>me</u>!

Read the sentence. • Draw a line under the word me in the sentence.

Unit 4 Introduce High-Frequency Words: me **203**

Pupil Edition page 203

Meeting Individual Needs
Activities

Clay Me

Materials: word card *me*, modeling clay

◆ Give each child the word card and modeling clay.

◆ Have children mold clay to make the word *me*.

◆ Invite children to run their fingers over the clay letters, then over the letters on the card, as they say *me*.

 EASY

I or Me?

Materials: word cards *I* and *me*

◆ Make up several sentences with either *I* or *me*. Read them aloud leaving out *I* or *me*.

◆ Have children hold up the word card that completes the sentence as you read.

 CHALLENGE

Me Game

Materials: ball, word cards *I* and *me*

◆ Sit across from a child and say *Roll the ball to me*. Hold up the word card *me*. The child rolls the ball.

◆ Then say: *I roll the ball*. Hold up the word card *I* and roll the ball to another child.

 LANGUAGE SUPPORT

Listen

Yes, I Did!
a poem

Did you nap with the cat on the cot?
No, I did not. No, I did not.
Did you draw a map with Sid?
Yes, I did! Yes, I did!
Did you cook dinner in a pot?
No, I did not. No, I did not.
Did you play all day with Min and Sid?
Yes, I did! Yes, I did!

Blend Onsets and Rimes

Phonological Awareness

Teach Say "Yes, I Did!" with children. Repeat the line "No, I did not. No, I did not." Then tell children the sounds *d-id* make the word *did*. Have children repeat the sounds and the word with you: *d-id*; did.

MODEL: Listen as I blend some sounds to make a word, *n-ot*; not. Listen again, *n-ot*; not. Now I'll make the sounds and you blend them with me: *s-un*. What's the word? *(sun)*

Practice Have children repeat the following segmented sounds and blend them into words with you.

m-ap (map)	s-ink (sink)	d-ot (dot)
v-ery (very)	p-et (pet)	d-ust (dust)
l-et (let)	M-in (Min)	S-id (Sid)

v-ery
very!

Blend Sounds

Teach Read the first line of the poem. As you read, say the word *nap* slowly, so that children can hear each sound clearly. As you say each sound, place a counter in your cup. Then blend the sounds more quickly to say the word *nap*.

Practice Give each child a cup and some counters. Slowly read the second line of the poem, emphasizing the word *not*. Have children drop one counter into their cups for each of the three sounds they hear in /n/ - /o/ - /t/ and then say the word. Repeat this activity using such words as *map, did, pot,* and *Sid.*

MATERIALS
- cups
- counters

INFORMAL ASSESSMENT Observe children as they blend onsets and rimes and blend sounds to make words. If children have difficulty, see Alternate Teaching Strategies: Unit 1, T33; and Unit 4, T27.

Read Together

From Phonemic Awareness to Phonics

Objective: Identify Word Endings

LISTEN FOR RHYMING WORDS Read lines three and four of the poem, and ask children to identify the rhyming words. Write the words on the chalkboard.

> Sid   did

IDENTIFY THE LETTERS Bend a pipe cleaner to make a "magic reading wand" with a loop on one end. Invite a volunteer to place the loop over the two letters the words have in common *(id)*. Ask children to say each word.

NAME OTHER RHYMING WORDS Challenge children to name other words that end with the same letters as *Sid* and *did.* Write their ideas on the board. Invite others to use the reading wand to encircle the two letters the words have in common.

> bid   hid   kid   lid

CLIP THE WORDS Write the following words from the poem on separate index cards: *cot, not, did, Sid.* Place the cards on a table in random order. Read the words aloud, and ask children to find pairs of words with the same ending letters. Have volunteers use clothespins to clip rhyming sets of words together. Invite children to join you in chanting the word pairs.

Short *a, i, o*
Blending

OBJECTIVES

Children will:
- ☑ identify /a/ *a*, /i/ *i*, and /o/ *o*
- ☑ blend and read short *a, i,* and *o* words
- ☑ write short *a, i, o* words

MATERIALS
- letter cards

ADDITIONAL RESOURCES
- Practice Book, page 204
- Phonics/Phonemic Awareness Practice Book, page 109
- **Phonics** CD-ROM

TEACHING TIP

WORD FAMILIES Make one set of cards for the words *nap, map, cap, tap, sip, dip, rip, tip, mop, top.* Have children play a matching game by turning over two cards and matching the word endings.

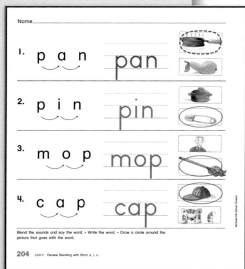

Name_____

1. p a n   pan   [image]
2. p i n   pin   [image]
3. m o p   mop   [image]
4. c a p   cap   [image]

Blend the sounds and say the word. • Write the word. • Draw a circle around the picture that goes with the word.

204 Unit 4 Review Blending with Short *a, i, o*

Pupil Edition page 204

Review

TEACH

Model Blending with Short *a, i, o* Display the *a* letter card and say /a/. Have children repeat the sound /a/ as you point to the *a* card. Place the *p* card to the right of the *a* card. Point to each letter as you blend the sounds together and have children repeat after you: *ap.*

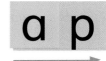

Place the *m* card to the left of *ap* to show *map.* Point to the cards as you blend to read *map,* and have children repeat after you.

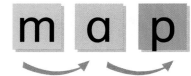
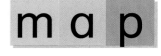

Continue modeling and guided practice using *pad, pot, cap, mop, pin, Pam,* and *man.*

PRACTICE

Complete a Sentence

- ◆ Write the following words on the chalkboard: *pan, cap, dip, nap, sip, mop.*
- ◆ Have children blend and read the words aloud together.
- ◆ Ask children to write one of the words from the chalkboard to complete each sentence you say.

   **ON LEVEL**

✓ ASSESS/CLOSE

Have children complete page 204 of the Pupil Edition or the Practice Book. For a different approach to this skill, see page T28 for the **Alternate Teaching Strategy.**

Meeting Individual Needs
Activities

Sorting Initial and Final /p/ *p*

Materials: word cards for *pan, cap, pin, pot, pit,* and *mop*

◆ Label paper with two columns *p____* and *____p*.

◆ Children take turns selecting a word card and reading it aloud.

◆ Children then place it in the correct column.

EASY

Make a Word

Materials: letter cards *c, d, f, m, n, p, r, s,* and *t*, phonogram cards *pa_, pi_, po_, _ap, _ip, _op*, index cards, crayons or markers

◆ Tell children to use the letter and phonogram cards to make six words. You may want to challenge them to find one letter that makes words with all six phonograms. (*t*)

◆ Have children write each word and then share their words with a partner.

CHALLENGE

Draw a Word

Materials: word cards for *pan, cap, pin, pot, pit, map, mop*; drawing paper cut in the shape of a simple house

◆ Read each card while tracking print.

◆ Give each child a word card and a "house".

◆ Have children draw a girl named Tam or a boy named Tom in the house with the object named on the word card. Have them label their drawings.

pat

LANGUAGE SUPPORT

Read the Story

☑ Initial /p/ *p*

☑ High-Frequency Word: *me*

☑ Compare and Contrast

☐ Concepts of Print

PREVIEW AND PREDICT

Invite children to look at the cover illustration as you read the title. Ask *By looking at the cover, what do you think this story will be about?* Then take a picture walk through the first few pages.

Is It You?

SET PURPOSES

Ask children what they might want to find out as they read. Then ask *Who do you think will play each of the three pigs? Who do you think will play the wolf? Let's read to find out.*

AS YOU READ

Remind children to track print. From time to time, point to the quotation marks and explain why they are used. Then use these prompts:

- **Page 2** Ask children to point to the word that begins with /p/. *(Pam)* Say the word and model how to blend it, *P-a-m, Pam.* Have children repeat after you. *Initial* p

- **Page 3** Ask children to find the word *me* on the page. Then read the sentence with children. *High-Frequency Words*

- **Pages 2 and 6** Have children describe the pigs' houses and tell how they are alike and how they are different. *Compare and Contrast*

- **Page 5** If children have difficulty reading the word *Pat,* remind them to look at the first letter *P,* which makes the sound /p/. *Graphophonic Cues*

Is it Pam?

2

"It is me," said Pam.

3

Pupil Edition pp. 205–206

Is it Pat?

4

"It is me," said Pat.

5

LANGUAGE SUPPORT

ESL To develop story vocabulary, play this game. Have children form a circle. Give one child a mask to wear. Ask each child, one at a time, if he or she is behind the mask. For example, *Is it Manuel?* Then have that child reply *It is not me!* Repeat with each child until you reach the child wearing the mask. Then have that child reply *It is me!*

Is it Ron?

6

"It is not me!" said Ron.

7

It is Min!

8

Cross Curricular: Science

MAMMALS Pigs and wolves are mammals because they give birth to live babies, have hair, and are warm-blooded. Provide animal/nature magazines, scissors, glue, blank two-column charts with the headings, *Mammals* and *Not Mammals,* and a sample chart with pictures of animals. Invite children to find animal pictures of these and glue them in the correct column. ▶ **Logical/Visual**

 *inter***NET** You may wish to explore "Mammals" at
CONNECTION **www.mhschool.com/reading.**

Read the Story

RETURN TO PREDICTIONS

Ask children to think back to their predictions and ideas before reading the story. Did they guess what the story would be about?

RETELL THE STORY

On index cards, write the names of the children who played the parts in the story: *Pam, Pat, Ron, Min.* Challenge children to place the name cards in the order in which they appeared in the story and retell the story using the names as clues.

WRITING

As a class, write a new story ending for *The Three Little Pigs.* Record the new ending on chart paper and invite children to illustrate the new ending.

INITIAL /p/ p

HOW TO ASSESS Give each child a piece of paper with the following words written on it: *Pam, me, you, Pat, Ron, Min, pig.* Ask each child to draw a circle around each word that begins with *p.*

FOLLOW UP Add the initial *p* words to your Word Wall along with several others, such as *pan, pad,* and *pot.*

DAY 4

Compare and Contrast

Is It You?

Mc Graw Hill

Is It You?

TESTED OBJECTIVES

Children will:
☑ compare and contrast to understand a story

MATERIALS

• *Is It You?*

TEACHING TIP

INSTRUCTIONAL Ask children how the classroom looks in the morning. Then ask how it looks during center time. Encourage children to talk about how the room is alike and different at those times.

Review

TEACH

Compare and Contrast Characters Display the cover of *Is It You?* Ask children to recall the story. Then ask how the children in the story are the same. (They are all characters in a play.) Ask them to tell how the children are different. (Three are dressed as pigs and one as a wolf.)

Compare and Contrast Story Details Reread the story. After each page, pause and ask children, *What is different about this house?* (The house is made of straw/sticks/bricks.)

PRACTICE

House Building

Materials: colorful wooden blocks

◆ Distribute wooden blocks and let children build block houses. Talk about the houses, comparing the colors, sizes, and shapes.

◆ Make a chart to show the similarities and differences.

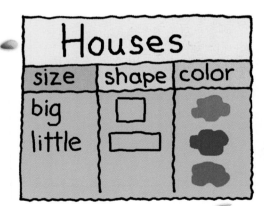

ON LEVEL

✓ ASSESS/CLOSE

Have children complete page 207 of the Pupil Edition or the Practice Book. For a different approach to this skill, see page T30 for the **Alternate Teaching Strategy.**

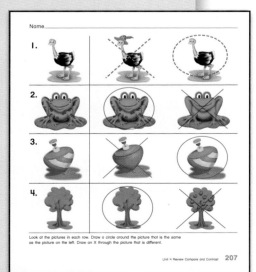

Pupil Edition page 207

207A *Is It You?*

Meeting Individual Needs
Activities

Make Your Own Bouquet!

Materials: pictures of flowers; drawing paper, crayons

◆ Display pictures of flowers.

◆ Ask children to draw a vase and different flowers to create a bouquet.

◆ Invite children to discuss their drawings with a partner and to compare and contrast the different kinds of flowers.

EASY

Fun Time

Materials: drawing paper, crayons

◆ Have children draw a picture of their favorite activity.

◆ Encourage pairs of children to use their drawings to describe their favorite activity.

◆ Then have children compare and contrast their activities by answering the question, *How are they the same and different?*

CHALLENGE

Same and Different

Materials: oaktag cards, apples, oranges

◆ Give each child two cards, one with two smiling faces (for *same*) and one with both a smiling face and a sad face (for *different*).

◆ Have a child show two pieces of fruit. Have the other children hold up the appropriate card for *same* or *different*.

◆ Help children verbalize how the fruits are alike and different.

LANGUAGE SUPPORT

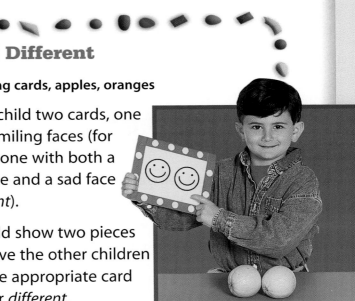

Phonological
Awareness

Listen

Yes, I Did!
a poem

Did you nap with the cat on the cot?
No, I did not. No, I did not.
Did you draw a map with Sid?
Yes, I did! Yes, I did!
Did you cook dinner in a pot?
No, I did not. No, I did not.
Did you play all day with Min and Sid?
Yes, I did! Yes, I did!

Blend Onsets and Rimes

Phonological Awareness

Teach Tell children to listen to the following sounds. Hold out your right hand and say the /k/ sound. Then hold out your left hand and say *ap*. Then clap your hands together and say *cap*. Have children repeat the sounds and motions with you: *c-ap: cap*.

Practice Pick a word from every line of the poem. Have volunteers do the hand motions with you. Remember to have children blend the sounds together to say each word.

n - ap (nap)
m - ap (map)
M - in (Min)
p - ot (pot)
d - ay (day)
d - id (did)

Meeting Individual Needs
Activities

Go Fish for Words

Materials: picture and word cards for *map, rip, mop, pan, pin,* and *pop*

◆ Have pairs of children mix up the cards and place them facedown in a pile. Have each child draw two cards and play "Go Fish."

◆ Encourage children to blend and read the words when they get a pair.

EASY

Rhyming Concentration

Materials: index cards, letter cards *c, d, f, m, n, p, r, s, t;* phonogram cards *_ap, _op, _ip.*

◆ Give children letter and phonogram cards. Have them make a pair of rhyming words for each phonogram.

◆ Have children write their words on separate index cards.

◆ Have children place the index cards facedown to play concentration by matching the rhyming words.

CHALLENGE

Old MacDonald Had a Store

Materials: word cards and picture cards for *mop, pan, cap, map, pad, pin,* and *pot*

◆ Read each card and track print. Have children blend the sounds.

◆ Have children match word and picture cards. Then give a pair to each child.

◆ Sing "Old MacDonald Had a Store." Have children sing their words in the verses of the song.

LANGUAGE SUPPORT

Leveled Books

Meeting Individual Needs

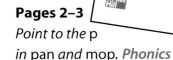

The Mop Man

Guided Reading

OBJECTIVES

- ☑ Initial and final *p*
- ☑ Compare and Contrast
- ☑ Vocabulary: *me*
- ☐ Concepts of Print

PREVIEW AND PREDICT   Ask children to look at the cover illustration and predict what the story might be about. Point to each word as you read aloud the title. Then conduct a picture walk through the first few pages. Have children predict what the mop man is. Before reading, remind children to point to each word as they read it.

READ THE BOOK   Use the following prompts to guide children's reading:

Pages 2–3 *Point to the* p *in* pan *and* mop. *Phonics*

Pages 4–5   *Can you find the question mark and the period? Concepts of Print*

Page 5   *Point to two words that end in* p. *Phonics*

Pages 6–7   *What do the pan and mop look like now? Compare and Contrast*

LITERARY RESPONSE   Ask children to draw and write about what the children might do now with the mop man.

Is It You?

OBJECTIVES

- ☑ Initial and final *p*
- ☑ Compare and Contrast
- ☑ Vocabulary: *me*
- ☐ Concepts of Print

Guided Reading

REREAD THE BOOK FOR FLUENCY   Encourage children to reread the book alone or with a partner.

Page 3   Ask children to point to the word *me* on the page. *Vocabulary*

Pages 2–5   Have children identify the names that begin with /p/. (Pam, Pat) *Phonics*

Pages 2–6   Ask children to tell how the three houses are alike and different. *Compare and Contrast*

Page 7   Ask children to point to the quotation marks and tell who is speaking. (Ron) *Concepts of Print*

LITERARY RESPONSE   Have children draw a picture showing a play they have been in or would like to be in.

CHALLENGE

Guided Reading

PREVIEW AND PREDICT Ask children to look at the cover illustration and the author's and illustrator's name. Then conduct a picture walk through the first few pages. Ask children to predict what the story might be about.

READ THE BOOK Use the following prompts to guide children's reading:

Pages 2–3 Ask the children to point to the word *me*. Read the word together. *Vocabulary*

Page 4 Ask volunteers to point to the first and last words in the sentence. *Concepts of Print*

Page 6 *Point to the word* Pat. *Let's blend these sounds together: P-a-t. Point to the* P. *Phonics*

Page 8 Ask children to find and name all the foods in the story. *How are they the same?* (They begin with *p*.) *How are they different?* (We eat some with our hands and some with forks.) *Compare and Contrast*

LITERARY RESPONSE Ask children to draw a picture showing what they would like to eat and do at a picnic. Have them write about the picnic in their journal.

The Picnic
by Anne Miranda
illustrated by Carol Nicklaus

OBJECTIVES

- ☑ **Initial and final /p/** *p*
- ☑ **Compare and Contrast**
- ☑ **Vocabulary:** *me*
- ☐ **Concepts of Print**

ASSESSMENT

INITIAL AND FINAL *p*
HOW TO ASSESS Write the following words: *Pam, pot, tap, cap*. Have children find the words in the stories, and identify the letter *p*.

FOLLOW UP If children have difficulty, let them hold the letter *p* as they look for each word.

Cross Curricular: Science

FAVORITE FOODS Prepare picture cards showing different foods. Have pairs of children sort the cards into the following food groups: fruits, vegetables, and meats. You may wish to color code the cards on the back so that children can check their work independently.

▶ **Logical**

Vocabulary:
me, to, you

MATERIALS
- word cards

TEACHING **TIP**

WORD WALL Point to the words *me, to,* and *you* on the Word Wall. Then ask volunteers to make up sentences using "to me" or "to you." Call on others to point to the words that are used.

Review

Vocabulary Cards

TEACH

Review *me, to, you* Teach children the following rhyme: *"Hi," said Sue,/ "From me to you."* Say it several times with children. Pass out word cards *me, to, you.* Ask children to hold up the appropriate card as you say each word.

Write each of the words on the chalkboard at the top of a column. Read each one aloud. Ask children to think of words that rhyme with each word and write them in the column under the word. (Examples: *me: he, bee, be, see, we; to: do, Sue, flew, grew, moo, coo; you:* same as for *to.*)

PRACTICE

Words in Context

◆ Say each sentence: *Give _____ the pencil.* (me) *I'll give _____ my crayons.* (you) *Pass the ruler _____ me.* (to)

Give_____ the pencil.

◆ Have children hold up the word card that completes each sentence.

◆ Write the word on the chalkboard, and have children repeat the sentence, adding the word.

ON LEVEL

✓ ASSESS/CLOSE

Have children complete page 209 of the Pupil Edition or Practice Book. For a different approach to teaching this skill, see page T26 for the **Alternate Teaching Strategy.**

Name_____

1.

The cat ran to (you.)

2.

The cat ran (to) me.

3.

The cat sat on (me.)

Read the sentences. Then do the following: 1. Draw a circle around the word you. 2. Draw a circle around the word to. 3. Draw a circle around the word me.

Unit 4 Review me, to, you 209

Pupil Edition page 209

Meeting Individual Needs
Activities

Puzzles

Materials: index cards

◆ Write the letters *m* and *e* on index cards. Cut the cards apart to make puzzle pieces.

◆ Do the same with *t* and *o,* and with *y, o,* and *u.*

◆ Give children several cards, and have them find the matches and read the words.

 EASY

It's ME!

Materials: drawing paper, markers, pencils, mirror

◆ Have children label a sheet of drawing paper *me.*

◆ Have them draw a self-portrait, using a mirror if necessary.

◆ Display the portraits, having other children guess the artists.

 CHALLENGE

Follow Directions

◆ Write the word *me* on chart paper.

◆ Have children follow directions that include the word *me* such as:
Come with me.
Bring a book to me.
Please sit next to me.

 **LANGUAGE SUPPORT**

Interactive Writing

Create a Chart

GRAMMAR/SPELLING CONNECTIONS

Model how to use a picture dictionary to locate the correct spellings of the names of the fruits children write about.

TEACHING TIP

Show children a chart from a social studies book. Explain that charts tell us information, using pictures. Encourage children to find other examples of charts in their books or around the classroom.

Prewrite

REVIEW THE STORY Reread *The Apple Pie Tree,* and discuss the different colors the tree turned as the seasons changed. Ask: *What color is the tree in winter? What color is the tree in the spring?* Tell children that they will work together to make a chart that shows different fruits and their colors.

BRAINSTORM Invite children to name the colors of fruits. If children need prompting, call their attention to the collage of fruit they made last week. Write the name of the fruit and its color name beside it on the chalkboard as children respond.

apple	red
banana	yellow
plum	purple

Draft

CREATE A CHART Tell children that they are going to help make a chart to show the colors of different fruits. Explain that they will be able to see which fruits have the same color and which have different colors.

- On a piece of chart paper, write the title *Fruits Have Different Colors.* Read the title to children as you track the print, word by word. Have children read the title to you.

- Draw a two-column chart under the title and call children's attention back to the chalkboard list.

- Write a color name at the top of the left column, such as *red.* Have children suggest the names of red fruits, such as apples, cherries, and strawberries. Write the fruit names under the color name. Have children write letters or words when they can.

- Repeat with a new color in the right column.

- Divide the class into pairs. Have each pair copy the chart on construction paper, substituting pictures of fruits for the names that appear on the large class chart. Children should write the name of each color heading if they can.

Revise

Before publishing the charts, help each pair read them aloud. Then ask:

- Do you have the correct fruits under each color?

- Do you want to add any other fruits or colors?

- Did you spell each color name correctly?

Publish

Display the class chart on a bulletin board.
Display children's charts around it.

Presentation Ideas

FRUIT CONCENTRATION In advance, draw pictures of fruits on separate index cards and the color names of the fruits on another set of index cards. Mix up the cards and turn them face down. Invite a child to pick two cards, turn them over, read the color word, and see if the fruit picture matches the color word. If the child makes a match, he or she keeps the cards. If a match is not made, he or she turns over the cards. Have children play until all cards are gone.

PICK A FRUIT Invite each child to write his or her name on a sticky note. Have each child go to the class fruit chart, say the name of his or her favorite fruit shown on the chart, and place the sticky note next to the picture of the fruit.

Listening and Speaking

- Remind children to speak clearly as they name the fruits and colors in the concentration game.

- Remind children to watch and listen carefully as classmates place their sticky notes on the class chart and say the name of their favorite fruits.

TECHNOLOGY TIP

Help children type the name of their favorite fruit and its color name on the computer to print out and take home.

LANGUAGE SUPPORT

ESL Bring in some applesauce for the children. After they have tasted it, have them describe the taste of the applesauce.

Meeting Individual Needs for Writing

EASY

Color Book Ask children to think of other things that are the same color as one set of fruits on the class chart. Have children draw a picture of each item on a separate piece of paper and bind the pages together to make their own color books.

ON-LEVEL

Categorize Fruits Brainstorm other ways children could categorize the fruits on their charts. Help children create a new chart that compares fruits by size, shape, or taste (sweet, sour, etc.).

CHALLENGE

Write a Descriptive Sentence Encourage children to make observations about their color charts. Invite them to write a sentence or two about the chart, such as: *The chart shows three red fruits. They are apples, strawberries, and cherries.*

210B

 **Week ③**

Phonics	Comprehension	Vocabulary
• Initial /l/l • Blending	• Main Idea	• go

Go, Lad, Go!

Literature Resources

Big Books

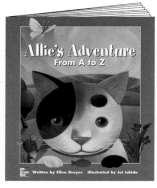

Big Book of Phonics Rhymes and Poems
pages 31, 32, 41

ABC Big Book
pages 211A–211B

Literature Big Book
pages 213A–213B

Reading for Information Big Book
page 28

Read Aloud

The Clever Turtle

page 215A

Student Books

ABC Little Book
pages 211A–211B

Go, Lad, Go!

Easy
page 221A
Decodable

Independent
pages 217/218A–217/218B, 221A
Decodable
Story also available in Pupil Edition

Challenge
page 221B
Patterned

Center Activities

Center Activities for the Week

PHONICS
Sticky *Ll*
page 210E

WRITING
Animal Favorites
page 210E

READING & LISTENING
Self-Selected Reading
page 210E

WORKING WITH WORDS
Build a Word
page 210F

MATH
Count and Check, page 210F

SOCIAL STUDIES
Different Kinds of Homes
page 210F

Safety Signs, page 221B

SCIENCE
Favorite Pets
page 217/218B

Center Activities

Activities take 15–20 minutes each.

Phonics

Sticky *Ll*

Objective: Identify words that contain initial *Ll*.

MATERIALS
- Self-stick notes
- Markers

◆ Have children write *L* or *l* on three self-stick notes.

◆ Ask them to find items or words in the room whose names begin with *L* or *l*.

◆ Have children place a self-stick note on the object or word.

Writing

Animal Favorites

Objective: Understand that sentences are made up of separate words.

MATERIALS
- Handwriting paper
- Pencils
- Pictures of pets

◆ Post these sentences:
I like _____ and _____.
I like _____ best.

◆ Children complete the sentences with names of pets.

◆ Have them tell what they like about the pets.

Reading and Listening

Self-Selected Reading

Objective: Turn the pages of a book in order.

MATERIALS
- Listening Library cassettes and CDs
- Books

Place the literature for the week and the corresponding audiocassettes or CDs in the Reading Center. You may also include books from the Theme Bibliography of pages T54–T55.

◆ *Fireflies, Fireflies Light My Way* by Jonathan London

◆ *I Took a Walk* by Henry Cole

◆ *What's This?* by Caroline Mockford

Math

Count and Check

Objective: Count and record quantities.

- ◆ Fill cups with varying number of buttons.

- ◆ Ask each partner to choose a cup, count the buttons, and record the quantity.

- ◆ Have partners switch cups and check each other's work.

MATERIALS
- Four small cups
- Buttons
- Writing paper

Social Studies

Different Kinds of Homes

Objective: Explore the differences among communities.

- ◆ Display pictures of different homes at the Center.

- ◆ Invite children to draw a picture of one of the homes.

MATERIALS
- Pictures of homes in different regions
- Markers and crayons
- Paper

Working with Words

Build a Word

Objective: Use letters to build simple two, and three-letter words.

- ◆ Have children use letter cards to build words such as *sad, nap, pot, tap, dot, to* and *go.*

- ◆ Ask children to write the words they form in their journals.

MATERIALS
- Letter cards for *a, n, c, d, i, g, o, f, p, r, s, t*
- Journals
- Pencils

Go, Lad, Go

READING AND LANGUAGE ARTS

- **Phonological Awareness**

- **Phonics** initial /l/l; blending with short *a*, *i*, *o*

- **Comprehension**

- **Vocabulary**

- **Beginning Reading Concepts**

- **Listening, Speaking, Viewing, Representing**

DAY 1

Focus on Reading Skills

Develop Phonological Awareness, 210I–210J
"Lightning Bug" *Big Book of Phonics Rhymes and Poems*, 31

 **Introduce Initial /l/l,** 210K–210
- ◆ Practice Book, 210
- ◆ Phonics/Phonemic Awareness Practice Book, 111–112

- ◆  **CD-ROM**

Read the Literature

Read *Allie's Adventure from A to Z* Big Book, 211A–211B
Shared Reading

Build Skills

- ☑ Over, Under, 211C–211
  - ◆ Practice Book, 211

DAY 2

Focus on Reading Skills

Develop Phonological Awareness, 212A–212B
"The Lazy Little Lion" *Big Book of Phonics Rhymes and Poems*, 32

Review Initial /l/l, 212C–212
- ◆ Practice Book, 212
- ◆ Phonics/Phonemic Awareness Practice Book, 113–114

- ◆ **CD-ROM**

Read the Literature

Read *Nature Spy* Big Book, 213A–213B
Shared Reading

Build Skills

- ☑ Main Idea, 213G–213
  - ◆ Practice Book, 213

- **Cross Curriculum**

 Math, Social Studies, 210F

 Math, Science, 213B

- **Writing**

 Writing Prompt: Write about your favorite vegetable.

Letter Formation, 210K

 Writing Prompt: If you were a nature spy, where would you explore?

 Journal Writing, 213B
Letter Formation, 212C

DAY 3

Focus on Reading Skills

Develop Phonological Awareness, 214A–214B
"The Lazy Little Lion" and "Pease Porridge Hot" *Big Book of Phonics Rhymes and Poems,* 32, 41

 **Review /l/l,** 214C–214
◆ Practice Book, 214
◆ Phonics/Phonemic Awareness Practice Book, 111–114

◆ **Phonics CD-ROM**

Read the Literature

Read "The Clever Turtle" Teacher Read Aloud, 215A–215B
Shared Reading
Read the Reading for Information Big Book, 28–29
Chart

Build Skills

☑ High-Frequency Word: *go* 215C–215
◆ Practice Book, 215

 Cultural Perspectives, 215B

 Writing Prompt: What do you think the turtle did after it ran away? Draw a picture and write about it.

DAY 4

Go, Lad, Go

Focus on Reading Skills

Develop Phonological Awareness, 216A–216B
"The Fire Is Lit"
Introduce Blending with Short *a, i, o,* 216C–216
◆ Practice Book, 216
◆ Phonics/Phonemic Awareness Practice Book, 115

◆ **Phonics CD-ROM**

Read the Literature

Read "Go, Lad, Go!" On-Level Decodable Story, 217/218A–217/218B

☑ Initial /l/l; Blending
☑ Main Idea
☑ High-Frequency Words: *go*
Concepts of Print

Build Skills

☑ Main Idea, 219A–219
◆ Practice Book, 219

 Science, 217/218B

 Writing Prompt: Write about a trick you would teach a puppy.

 Journal Writing, 217/218B
Letter Formation Practice Book, 217–218

DAY 5

Lin Did It!

Go!

Go, Lad, Go

by Suzanne Martinucci
illustrated by Thea Kliros

Focus on Reading Skills

Develop Phonological Awareness, 220A–220B
"The Fire Is Lit"
Review Blending with Short *a, i, o,* 220C–220
◆ Practice Book, 220
◆ Phonics/Phonemic Awareness Practice Book, 116

◆ **Phonics CD-ROM**

Read the Literature

Read "Lin Did It!" Easy Decodable Story, 221A
Reread "Go, Lad, Go!" On-Level Decodable Story, 221A
Read "Let's Go!" Challenge Patterned Book, 221B
Guided Reading
☑ Initial /l/l; Blending
☑ Main Idea
☑ High-Frequency Words: *go*
Concepts of Print

Build Skills

☑ High-Frequency Words: *go, to, me, you,* 221C–221
◆ Practice Book, 221

 Social Studies, 221B

 Writing Prompt: Do you have a favorite type of weather? Write about it.

Interactive Writing, 222A–222B

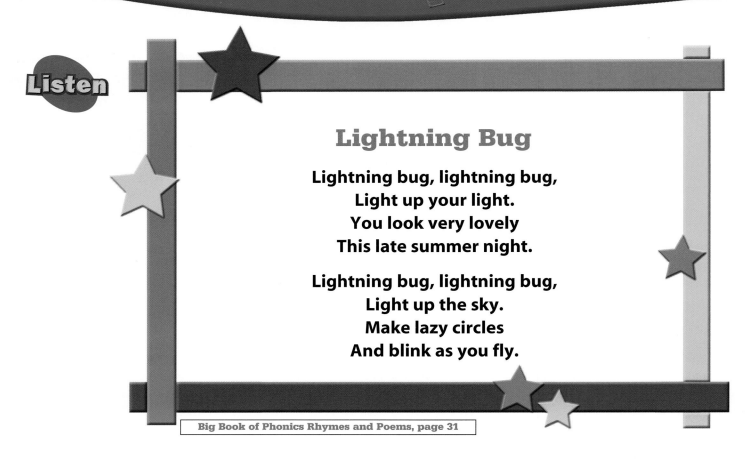

Listen

Lightning Bug

Lightning bug, lightning bug,
Light up your light.
You look very lovely
This late summer night.

Lightning bug, lightning bug,
Light up the sky.
Make lazy circles
And blink as you fly.

Big Book of Phonics Rhymes and Poems, page 31

Identify Rhyming Words · · · · · · · · **Phonological Awareness** · · · · · · ·

Teach   Have the children listen as you read the first stanza of "Lightning Bug." Tell children the words *light* and *night* rhyme because they have the same ending sound. Ask the children which two words rhyme. Then say the following words and have children say the word that does not rhyme with the others: *night, light, pile, right.*

Practice   Say the words below. Ask children to suggest rhymes for each. If they have trouble producing rhymes, offer suggestions. Remind them to think of words that have the same ending sounds.

> sky: fly, my, by
>
> lot: pot, hot, tot
>
> mop: shop, pop, hop

Listen for Beginning Sounds

Phonemic Awareness

Teach *Repeat after me, /l/. Can you hear /l/? Listen for the beginning sound in these words: like, lion, lost, lake.* Explain that the /l/ sound is at the beginning of each of these words.

Practice Read "Lightning Bug" aloud again. Have the students tap their blocks when they hear the /l/ sound at the beginning of a word. Then have children say the beginning sound of the following words: *lion, paint, robot, fish, lake, peel, ladder, loose.*

MATERIALS
- wood or plastic blocks for tapping

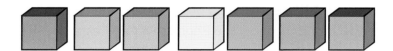

ASSESSMENT Observe children as they produce rhyming words and identify beginning sounds. If children have difficulty, see Alternate Teaching Strategies: Unit 3, T29; and Unit 4, T31.

Read Together

From Phonemic Awareness to Phonics

Objective: Identify Initial /l/ L, l

IDENTIFY THE LETTER FOR THE SOUND Explain to children that the letter *l* stands for the sound /l/. Ask children to say the sound.

Display the Big Book of Phonics Poems and Rhymes, page 31. Point to the letters in the corner. Identify the letters as *l* and say the sound.

REREAD THE POEM Show children how to raise an index finger to show a lowercase *l*. Then read the poem again, pointing to each word. When you say a word that begins with /l/, children raise an index finger.

FIND L, l Slowly read each line of the poem. Ask volunteers to say each word that begins with *L* or *l* as you read. Count the words that begin with the letter *l* with the class.

FIND MATCHING WORDS Have children find two words in the poem that have the same letters. *(Lightning, light)* Then say the words *lightning* and *light*. Point to the words and show that *light* can be found in *lightning*.

Lightning Bug

Lightning bug, lightning bug,
Light up your light.
You look very lovely
This late summer night.

Lightning bug, lightning bug,
Light up the sky.
Make lazy circles,
And blink as you fly.

Ll

Big Book of Phonics Rhymes and Poems, page 31

Initial /l/ l

Phonics Picture Posters and Cards

✓ OBJECTIVES

Children will:
- ☑ identify the letters *L, l*
- ☑ identify /l/ *L, l*
- ☑ form the letters *L, l*

MATERIALS

- letter cards
- **Big Book of Phonics Rhymes and Poems**
- **Phonics Picture Posters**

ADDITIONAL RESOURCES

- Practice Book, page 210
- **Phonics/Phonemic Awareness Practice Book,** pages 111–112
- **Phonics** CD-ROM

Phonics Song

Lucy Lion

Lucy Lion likes to laugh,
Likes to laugh, likes to laugh,
Lucy Lion likes to laugh,
She laughs loudly!

Sung to the tune of "London Bridge"

From **Songs from A to Z**

Introduce

TEACH

Phonemic Awareness Warm-Up Have children sing the song "Lucy Lion" with you. Then sing it again and have children clap once every time they hear a word that begins with the /l/ sound.

Identify L, l Write a large *L, l* on the board and explain that *L, l* stands for the sound /l/. Show the Phonics Picture Poster and have children repeat the /l/ sound after you. Tell children the word *lion* begins with the /l/ sound.

Form L, l Review the capital and lowercase forms of *L, l* with children. With your back to them, trace each letter in the air with your finger. Have them fold a sheet of paper in fourths, and write *L, l* in each of the four boxes. Turn to page 31 in the Big Book of Phonics Rhymes and Poems and reread the poem. Ask children to circle one of the *L, l*'s each time they hear a word that begins with /l/.

PRACTICE

Initial *L* Riddle

◆ Ask children to answer riddles with words that begin with /l/.

◆ Give clues such as: *This object gives you light and rhymes with ramp.* (lamp) *This action word rhymes with book.* (look)

◆ After you write each word, have children write *L* and *l*.

ON LEVEL

✓ ASSESS/CLOSE

Have children complete page 210 of the Pupil Edition or the Practice Book. For a different approach to this skill, see page T32 for the **Alternate Teaching Strategy.**

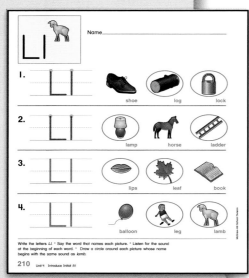

Pupil Edition page 210

Meeting Individual Needs
Activities

Paint a Picture

Materials: drawing paper, finger paints

◆ Have each child pick an object whose name begins with /l/ and paint it with finger paints.

◆ Ask children to paint the letters *L, l* under the picture.

◆ Invite children to share their pictures with the class.

EASY

Silly Sentences

◆ Have children make up silly sentences by using as many words that begin with /l/ as they can. For example: *Liz likes lambs and lakes.*

◆ Ask children to tell their sentences to a partner.

◆ Have the partner write *L, l* for each /l/ word they hear.

CHALLENGE

What's for Lunch?

Materials: lunch box, Tactile ABC Cards for *L, l*

◆ Explain that only things whose names begin with the /l/ sound are inside the lunch box.

◆ Ask: *Which of these things will be in the lunch box? Lemon? Toast?* (*lollipop, lobster, sandwiches, licorice, cake, lettuce*)

◆ Have children repeat each item and answer *yes* or *no.* Then have them trace the tactile cards for *L, l* each time they answer *yes.*

LANGUAGE SUPPORT

Shared Reading

Allie's Adventure
From A to Z

Written by Ellen Dreyer   Illustrated by Jui Ishida

Big Book

Children will:
- ☐ differentiate between words and sentences.
- ☐ review ABC order.
- ☐ classify and categorize.
- ☐ listen and respond to the story.

Build Background

Review the Alphabet   Play "Follow the Leader." The leader starts the game by saying a letter. Children follow the leader by saying the next letter in the alphabet.

Then draw three blank lines on the board. Think of three consecutive letters. Write the first letter in line #1 and the third in line #3. Let children fill in the missing letter. Repeat.

Read the Big Book

Set Purposes   Tell children that as they reread the story, they will be making a list of the different animals Allie meets.

Read the Story   Point to each word as you reread the story. Show children that words are separated by spaces. *Concepts of Print*

MODEL: I see groups of letters. I know that the groups of letters are words. I can see that the words are separated by spaces.

Make the /p/ sound. Have children say it with you. After you read page 17, ask which words begin with that sound. Have them point to the *p* in each word. *Letter Identification*

Invite volunteers to point to each word in the Big Book as you read a few pages. Have them circle the sentence on each page with their finger. *Concepts of Print*

Allie sees a tiny **nose**.

She puts her paw **on** the nose.

Allie's Adventure, pages 16–17

Literature Response

LISTENING/SPEAKING

Discuss the Story Who did Allie meet on the farm? (Allie met a butterfly, hen, insect, and a mouse.) *Literal: Story Details*

Which animals in the story have fur? (cow, mouse) Which animals do not have fur? (butterfly, chicken, insect) *Inferential: Classify and Categorize*

Where do we begin reading on page 20? Where do we stop reading? *Concepts of Print*

WRITING

Draw and Label Invite children to draw a picture of a furry animal and help them label their picture.

The mouse is very **quick**.

20

Allie's Adventure, page 20

ABC Activity

GUESS THE LETTER Have children work in pairs. One child writes a lowercase letter on another child's back with his or her finger. The other child guesses the letter. Children take turns writing and guessing the letters.

INFORMAL ASSESSMENT

DIFFERENTIATE BETWEEN WORDS AND SENTENCES

How to Assess
Turn to Big Book page 32 and read it with children. Ask children to touch each word on the page. Then have them track the sentence.

Follow-Up
Set out word cards to make a sentence. Have children touch each card to track the sentence.

Over, Under

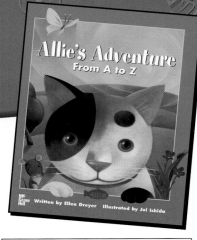

Allie's Adventure from A to Z

Written by Ellen Dreyer   Illustrated by Jui Ishida

TESTED OBJECTIVES

Children will:

☑ understand *over* and *under*

MATERIALS

- *Allie's Adventure from A to Z*
- towel
- small stuffed animal

TEACHING TIP

INSTRUCTIONAL Draw a bridge on the bulletin board. Provide pictures of people and objects which can be attached to the board. Have children practice placing them over and under the bridge.

Introduce

TEACH

Recognize Over and Under Display *Allie's Adventure from A to Z,* and ask children to recall the story. Turn to pages 14–15 and ask: *Where is the mouse? (under the lettuce leaf)* Take a picture walk through the book, and help children find other examples of over and under. Then using a towel and small stuffed animal, demonstrate over and under. Ask such questions as: *Is the bear under the towel? Is the towel over the bear?*

PRACTICE

Show *Over* and *Under*

- ◆ Children, working in pairs, use a chair and objects to demonstrate over and under.

- ◆ Give directions such as: *Pass the book over the chair. Put the book under the chair.*

- ◆ Children then give directions to their partner.

ON LEVEL

✓ ASSESS/CLOSE

Have children complete page 211 of the Pupil Edition or Practice Book. For a different approach to teaching this skill, see page T35 for the **Alternate Teaching Strategy.**

Name _____

1.

2.

3.

4.

1.Draw a ball under the table. 2.Draw a bird under the cloud.
3.Draw a bridge over the water. 4.Draw a kite over the tree.

Unit 4 Introduce Over, Under   211

Pupil Edition page 211

Meeting Individual Needs
Activities

Sing a Song

Materials: outline of a bear, craft sticks, glue, large drawing of a mountain

◆ Have each child cut out the bear outline and glue it to a craft stick.

◆ Have children use their puppets and the drawing to act out the song "The Bear Went Over the Mountain."

◆ Invite children to make up additional verses to focus on over and under.

EASY

Over/Under Picture

Materials: drawing paper, crayons or markers

◆ Have children draw a picture of an outdoor scene. Tell them to include two things that are over other things (*the sun is over the beach*) and two that are under other things (*the boy is under the umbrella*).

◆ Ask children to tell you about the things that are over and under.

LANGUAGE SUPPORT

Weaving Over and Under

Materials: different colored construction paper strips

◆ Prepare sheets of construction paper in which several horizontal "slits" have been cut, leaving an inch uncut at each side.

◆ Demonstrate how to "weave" the strips *over* and *under* the slits.

CHALLENGE

Listen

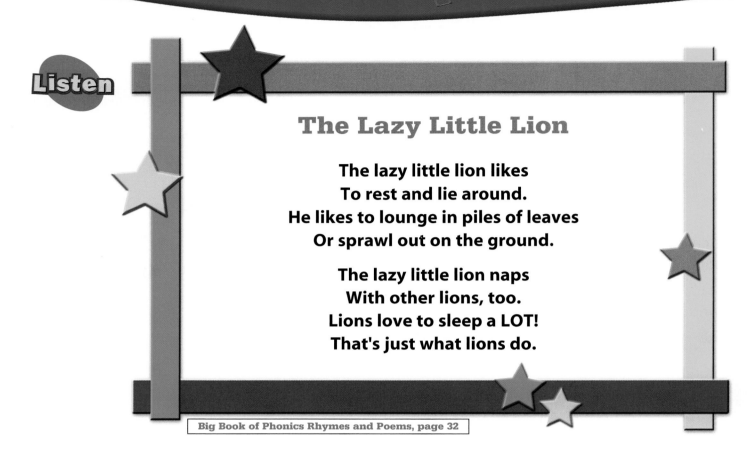

The Lazy Little Lion

The lazy little lion likes
To rest and lie around.
He likes to lounge in piles of leaves
Or sprawl out on the ground.

The lazy little lion naps
With other lions, too.
Lions love to sleep a LOT!
That's just what lions do.

Big Book of Phonics Rhymes and Poems, page 32

Segment Syllables · · · · · · · · · · · · · · Phonological Awareness · · · · · · · · · · · ·

Teach Read the first line of the poem. Have children close their eyes and clap out the syllables in the words *la-zy, lit-tle,* and *likes.*

MODEL: Listen for the two parts of the word *lazy, la-zy.* Now clap as I say each part, *la-zy.* Now clap the syllables as I say the word *little, lit-tle.* How many syllables does *little* have? *(two)* How many syllables are in *likes?* (one)

Practice Say the words below. Ask children to say each word slowly, emphasizing the syllables. If they have trouble, clap the syllables first and have children repeat after you.

oth-er	fan-tas-tic	rest-ing
stop	rocks	sleep-y

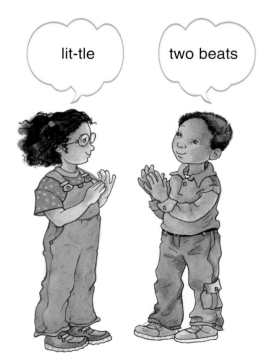

lit-tle

two beats

Listen for Beginning Sounds • • • • • • • • • Phonemic Awareness • • • • • • • • • •

Teach Tell children that both words in the name *Little Lion* begin with the /l/ sound. Have children repeat the /l/ sound and the word with you: /l/; *lion*. Tell children they will play a game in which they will say the beginning sound of names.

MATERIALS
• beanbag

Practice Have children sit in a circle. Hold the beanbag and say: *My name is ___. It begins with the sound ___.* Then pass the beanbag to the child next to you and then repeat the sentences, substituting his/her name and its beginning sound. Continue until all children have had a chance.

 **ASSESSMENT** Observe children as they count syllables in words and identify beginning sounds. If children have difficulty, see Alternate Teaching Strategies: Unit 1, T24; and Unit 4, T31.

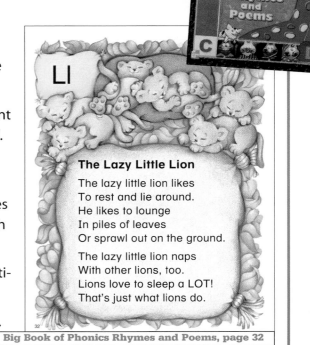

Read Together

From Phonemic Awareness to Phonics

Objective: Identify /l/ L, l

IDENTIFY THE LETTER FOR THE SOUND

• Explain to children that the letters *L, l* stand for the sound /l/. Have children repeat the sound.

• Display the Big Book of Phonics Rhymes and Poems, page 32. Identify the letters *L, l* in the corner of the page and say the letter names. Have children repeat the /l/ sound.

REREAD THE POEM

• Read the poem again, emphasizing the words that begin with /l/ as you point to each word.

FIND L, l

• Use a sheet of paper to isolate each line in the poem. Read the poem line by line.

• Ask volunteers to help you count the words that begin with *L* or *l*.

SUBSTITUTE OTHER ANIMALS

• Have children brainstorm names of other animals that begin with *l.* (lamb, lizard, llama)

• Then pick one animal and substitute its name for the word *lion.*

• Repeat the poem with children.

Ll

The Lazy Little Lion

The lazy little lion likes
To rest and lie around.
He likes to lounge
In piles of leaves
Or sprawl out on the ground.

The lazy little lion naps
With other lions, too.
Lions love to sleep a LOT!
That's just what lions do.

Big Book of Phonics Rhymes and Poems, page 32

212B

Initial /l/ l

Phonics Picture Posters and Cards

Ll
lion

TESTED OBJECTIVES

Children will:
- ☑ identify and use /l/ L, l
- ☑ write the letters L, l

MATERIALS
- Phonics Picture Posters

ADDITIONAL RESOURCES
- Practice Book, page 212
- Phonics/Phonemic Awareness Practice Book, pages 113–114
- **Phonics** CD-ROM

Phonics Song

Lucy Lion

Lucy Lion likes to laugh,
Likes to laugh, likes to laugh,
Lucy Lion likes to laugh,
She laughs loudly!

Sung to the tune of "London Bridge"

From **Songs from A to Z**

Review

TEACH

Phonemic Awareness Warm-Up Have children sing the song "Lucy Lion" with you. Then ask children to name other animals that begin with /l/. If they are having difficulty prompt them with animals such as lamb, llama, or leopard. Sing the song again using these animals.

Identify /l/ L, l Display the Phonics Picture Poster for the letter L, l. Have children make the /l/ sound after you. Then have children say a word that begins with L, l.

Form L, l Display Phonics Picture Poster L, l and review the capital and lowercase forms with children. With your back to them, trace each letter in the air with your finger. Ask children to do the same. Draw a ladder on the board. Ask volunteers to write the letters L, l on different rungs of the ladder as they say the word *ladder*.

PRACTICE

Write the *L*'s

Materials: picture cards

- Show children picture cards. Ask them to write L, l for every picture that shows something whose name begins with /l/, such as, *lamb, ladder, leaf.*
- Have children say the /l/ sound, trace each L, l they wrote, and say a word that begins with /l/.

ON LEVEL

✓ ASSESS/CLOSE

Have children complete page 212 of the Pupil Edition or the Practice Book. For a different approach to this skill, see page T32 for the **Alternate Teaching Strategy.**

Pupil Edition page 212

212C *Go, Lad, Go!*

Meeting Individual Needs
Activities

Make the Letters *L, l*

Materials: modeling clay, drawing paper, crayons

- Have children use modeling clay to form the letters *L* and *l*.

- Children should put the clay letters on a piece of paper and trace around the letters with a crayon while they say the letter's name.

EASY

The Magic Chest

Materials: drawing paper, crayons

- Have pairs of children brainstorm objects that begin with *L* that could be put in a magic chest, such as *ladder, lock, lamp.*

- Ask children to draw a picture of the magic chest and the objects.

- Ask them to label each object with the letters *L, l.*

CHALLENGE

Sort the Words

lap

Materials: word cards

- Place word cards on the chalkboard ledge. Half of the words should begin with /l/.

- Read each word aloud with children.

- If the word begins with /l/, invite a volunteer to place it on the left side of the board and trace the *L, l*. Other words are placed on the right side.

LANGUAGE SUPPORT

NATURE SPY
written by SHELLEY ROTNER and KEN KREISLER
photographs by SHELLEY ROTNER

Big Book

TESTED OBJECTIVES

Children will:
- ☐ ask questions about a topic
- ☐ develop vocabulary to reflect a growing range of knowledge
- ☑ recognize the main idea of a story
- ☐ listen responsively to a story

SHELLEY ROTNER is a photographer and writer whose photographs have appeared in many magazines, including *National Geographic*. She also travels with UNICEF, documenting programs that deal with families and children.

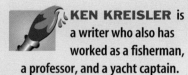

KEN KREISLER is a writer who also has worked as a fisherman, a professor, and a yacht captain. He lives in Manhattan.

LANGUAGE SUPPORT

ESL Take children for a walk outside to collect objects from nature. If this is not practical, you may wish to collect some items yourself. Glue the nature items on paper and label them. Then take children on a picture walk through "Nature Spy" to look for similar objects.

Build Background

Develop Vocabulary Ask children to bring in something they have found from nature. They can take turns naming and describing their item (color, shape, weight). Record observations on a chart.

Read the Big Book

Preview and Predict Display the Big Book cover. Read the title and the author's name. Discuss what it means to *spy*. Point out that Shelley Rotner took the photographs in the book. Ask children to predict what the photographs will show.

Set Purposes Take a picture walk through several pages of the book. Tell children you will read to find out what the Nature Spy sees.

Read the Story Before you read, point to the first word in the first sentence. Explain that this is where you will begin. Track the print as you read the story. *Concepts of Print*

Invite children to describe the leaves on page 11. *Use Illustrations*

Ask children what they think the author and photographer wanted to share. *Main Idea*

MODEL: The photographer took a close-up picture of a flower. I think she wants me to look closely at nature to see new things.

My mother says I'm a curious kid. She calls me a nature spy.

10

Sometimes I look so closely, I can see the lines on a shiny green leaf.

11

Nature Spy, pages 10–11

Literature Response

LISTENING/SPEAKING

Return to Predictions Discuss the predictions children made about the photographs. Ask children to listen politely while others share their ideas.

Discuss the Story Where is the girl looking at the things? (She is outside, in the yard.) *Literal: Story Details*

What does the girl in the story notice up close on the bird? (She sees its feathers.) *Literal: Story Details*

How can you see something up close? (You can bring it closer to your eyes or go closer to it.) *Critical Thinking: Personal Response*

WRITING

Journal Writing Invite children to draw a picture of something from the book. You may also wish to have children collect objects from nature and then choose one to draw. Have them write a sentence that describes their picture.

Nature Spy, page 17 17

INFORMAL ASSESSMENT

How to Assess
If a child is having difficulties identifying the main idea, use the skills lesson on pages 213G–213.

 **Activity**

Retell the Story

Have children pick one item from the book. Have them pretend to be a "nature spy" by looking very closely at the photograph of the item and telling what they see. Children could also use the Story Pop-Out Cards to tell about the items in the story.

NATURE SPY
written by SHELLEY ROTNER and KEN KREISLER
photographs by SHELLEY ROTNER

I like to go outside—to look around and discover things.

7

To take a really close look, even closer

8

and closer.

9

My mother says I'm a curious kid. She calls me a nature spy.

10

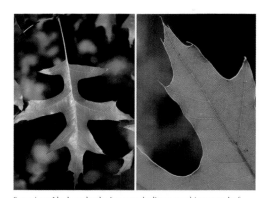

Sometimes I look so closely, I can see the lines on a shiny green leaf,

11

or one small acorn on a branch,

12

or seeds in a pod.

13

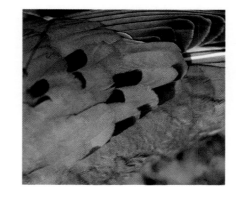

I notice the feathers of a bird.

14

15

or the golden eye of a frog.

16

17

When you look closely, things look so different—
like the bark of a tree or an empty hornet's nest.

18

the seeds of a sunflower, or even a rock.

19

Sometimes there's a pattern, like ice on a frozen pond.

20

or a spider's web, or a butterfly's wing.

21

Everything has its own shape, color,

22

and size.

23

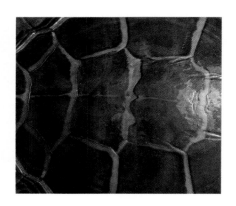

Look closely at a turtle's shell,

24

25

or a dog's fur.

26

27

or even raspberries.

28

or kernels of corn.

29

No matter where you look, up, down

30

or all around.

31

there's always something to see
when you're a nature spy!

32

DAY 2

Main Idea

TESTED OBJECTIVES

Children will:

☑ use the main idea to understand a story

MATERIALS

• *Nature Spy*

TEACHING TIP

AT HOME Invite children to become "nature spies" at home. Ask them to explore their backyards or other nature settings. Have them draw a picture of what they see and talk about their drawings in class.

Nature Spy

Review

TEACH

Understand the Main Idea Display the cover of *Nature Spy* and ask children to recall the story. Explain that the main idea tells the important idea that the writer wants to share. Take a picture walk through the story, asking children to describe some of their favorite parts of the book. Encourage children to share the important idea they learned about studying nature in the book. *(You can see a lot if you look closely at things in nature).* Point out that this important idea is the main idea of the story.

PRACTICE

All About the Main Idea

Materials: drawing paper and crayons

◆ Have children read a new story from the classroom library.

◆ Invite them to draw a picture that shows the main idea of the story they read.

◆ Post the pictures and have children discuss them.

ON LEVEL

✓ ASSESS/CLOSE

Have children complete page 213C of the Pupil Edition or the Practice Book. For a different approach to this skill, see page T25 for the **Alternate Teaching Strategy.**

Name_____

1. Dan can pat the cat.

   Pam can pat the cat.

2. The cap is on the cot.

   Ron is on the cot.

3. The pan and the pot are tan.

   The can is on the pan.

Look at each picture. • Then read the sentences. • Draw a line under the sentence that tells what the picture is all about.

Unit 4 Review Main Idea   213

Pupil Edition page 213

213G   *Go, Lad, Go!*

Meeting Individual Needs
Activities

Picture It

Materials: drawing paper, crayons

◆ Invite children to draw a picture of a school or community activity.

◆ Invite children to complete the following sentence about their pictures: *This picture is mainly about _____.*

◆ Encourage children to share their pictures.

EASY

Draw the Story

Materials: drawing paper, crayons, audiocassette of story

◆ Have children listen to an audiocassette of a story.

◆ Invite children to draw a picture illustrating their favorite part of the story.

◆ Ask children to explain the main idea of their pictures.

CHALLENGE

Comic Strip Fun

Materials: comic strips or cartoons; oaktag strips

◆ Show a simple comic strip or cartoon to children.

◆ Invite children to talk about what is happening in each frame of the comic strip.

◆ Use children's descriptions to complete the following caption on an oaktag strip: *The main idea of this picture is _____.*

LANGUAGE SUPPORT

Listen

The Lazy Little Lion
a poem

The lazy little lion likes
To rest and lie around.
He likes to lounge in piles of leaves
Or sprawl out on the ground.
The lazy little lion naps
With other lions, too.
Lions love to sleep a LOT!
That's just what lions do.

Pease Porridge Hot
a poem

Pease porridge hot,
Pease porridge cold,
Pease porridge in the pot
Nine days old.
Some like it hot,
Some like it cold,
Some like it in the pot
Nine days old.

Big Book of Phonics Rhymes and Poems, page 32, 41

Delete Syllables

Phonological Awareness

Teach   Read the poems. Have children chant each line of "Pease Porridge Hot" after you. Tell children each of the following words has two word parts: *potting, porridge, order.* Have children clap the syllables with you. Say: *If I remove –ing from* potting, *the word pot is left.* Have children repeat the words with you: *potting, pot.*

Practice   Call out a two-syllable word. Ask students to count the syllables in each. Then remove a syllable from each word, and ask students to say the remaining syllable.

> Say *willow* without the *low.* (wil)
> Say *playground* without the *play.* (ground)
> Say *coming* without the *ing.* (come)
> Say *backpack* without the *back.* (pack)

Listen for Beginning Sounds

Teach Say the words *lion, lollipop, likes, lot, leaves* elongating the /l/ sound. Tell children that the words begin with the /l/ sound. Then say the words *pot, pease, porridge, popcorn* elongating the /p/ sound. Tell children that these words begin with the /p/ sound.

Practice Distribute pictures that begin with /l/ or /p/. Line up chairs. Tell children that they can ride with you to the moon. Call on volunteers. Ask them to name their picture and to say the first sound in the name. If the child answers correctly, invite them to sit in the rocket. Continue until all children have boarded. Repeat the procedure for disembarking.

MATERIALS
- pictures of objects that begin with /l/ and /p/

INFORMAL ASSESSMENT Observe children as they delete syllables in a word and identify beginning sounds. If children have difficulty, see Alternate Teaching Strategies on T22 and T31.

Read Together

From Phonemic Awareness to Phonics

Objective: Identify /l/ *L, l* and /p/ *P, p*

IDENTIFY THE LETTERS
Display the Big Book of Phonics Rhymes and Poems, pages 32 and 41. Then point to the letters, identify them, and say the sound each stands for: /l/ and /p/.

REREAD THE POEMS Reread the poems, tracking the print and emphasizing the words with initial /p/ or /l/.

FIND WORDS WITH *L, l, P, p*
Have children place self-stick notes under the words in the poems that begin with *L, l, P,* or *p.*

Ll

The Lazy Little Lion

The lazy little lion likes
To rest and lie around.
He likes to lounge
In piles of leaves
Or sprawl out on the ground.

The lazy little lion naps
With other lions, too.
Lions love to sleep a LOT!
That's just what lions do.

Pp

Pease Porridge Hot

Pease porridge hot,
　Pease porridge cold,
Pease porridge in the pot,
　Nine days old.
Some like it hot,
　Some like it cold,
Some like it in the pot,
　Nine days old.

Big Book of Phonics Rhymes and Poems, pages 32, 41

/l/ *l*, /p/ *p*

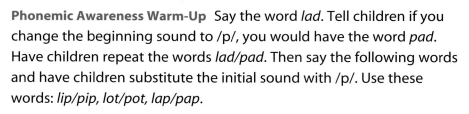

Ll — lion

Pp — pig

Phonics Picture Posters and Cards

OBJECTIVES

Children will:

- ☑ identify and discriminate between /l/ *L, l* and /p/ *P, p*
- ☑ write and use letters *L, l* and *P, p*

MATERIALS

- letter cards
- Phonics Picture Posters

ADDITIONAL RESOURCES

- Practice Book, page 214
- Phonics/Phonemic Awareness Practice Book, pages 105, 111
- **Phonics** CD-ROM

TEACHING TIP

VISUAL DISCRIMINATION

Have children examine tactile models of *L* and *P*. Ask children to see how the lowercase and capital forms of the same letter are the same and different.

Review

TEACH

Phonemic Awareness Warm-Up Say the word *lad*. Tell children if you change the beginning sound to /p/, you would have the word *pad*. Have children repeat the words *lad/pad*. Then say the following words and have children substitute the initial sound with /p/. Use these words: *lip/pip, lot/pot, lap/pap.*

Identify and Discriminate Between /l/ *L, l* and /p/ *P, p* Display the Phonics Picture Posters for *Ll* and *Pp*. Have children say each word and its initial sound and letter with you. Say: *Listen to the sentence I say. Clap each time you hear a word that begins with /p/: Pack pink lemonade in the picnic lunch.* Repeat for /l/ *l.*

Form *L, l* and *P, p* Display letter cards for *L, l, P,* and *p*. Review the capital and lowercase forms with children. Write the sentence you just read on the chalkboard. Read it aloud as you track the print with your hand. Ask volunteers to circle each capital and lowercase *p*. Have children write *P* or *p* on the board to match the ones circled. Repeat the process but have volunteers draw a line under each *l* and then write a capital or lowercase *l* for each underlined one.

PRACTICE

Listening Riddles

- ◆ Tell children a riddle. Explain that you will give clues and they have to figure out the *l* or *p* word that answers the riddle. For example, say:
- ◆ *I am thinking of a word that begins with /l/. I am a baby sheep and I am soft and woolly. (lamb)*
- ◆ *I am thinking of a word that begins with /p/. Heat me and I go pop! What am I? (popcorn)*

ON LEVEL

ASSESS/CLOSE

Have children complete page 214 of the Pupil Edition or the Practice Book. For a different approach to this skill, see page T32 for the **Alternate Teaching Strategy.**

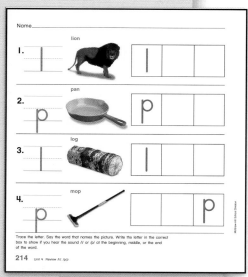

Name _____

1. lion — l

2. pan — p

3. log — l

4. mop — p

Trace the letter. Say the word that names the picture. Write the letter in the correct box to show if you hear the sound /l/ or /p/ at the beginning, middle, or the end of the word.

214   Unit 4 Review /l/ /p/

Pupil Edition page 214

Meeting Individual Needs
Activities

Macaroni Letters

Materials: drawing paper, crayons or markers, glue, macaroni

◆ Have children fold the drawing paper in half. On one half have them write a large *Ll* and on the other half, a large *Pp*.

◆ Then have children glue the macaroni to the letters they made. When dry, have children trace the letters as they say the sound each letter makes.

EASY

What's in Your Lunchbox?

Materials: drawing paper, crayons or markers

◆ Have children fold the drawing paper in half.

◆ On the front have them draw a lunchbox. Have them open the paper and draw things that start with /l/ inside the "lunchbox."

◆ Have partners take turns trying to guess the things that are in the other partner's lunchbox.

CHALLENGE

Charades

Materials: slips of paper, bag

◆ Write *l* and *p* action verbs that can be easily pantomimed on slips of paper.

◆ Preview the words and make sure children understand the meaning of each word.

◆ Have children draw a word from the bag and tell whether it begins with *l* or *p*.

◆ Whisper the word to the child and have the child act it out. The other children guess the word.

LANGUAGE SUPPORT

Listen

The Clever Turtle
a Hispanic folk tale retold by Margaret H. Lippert

Wheet-weedle-whoo, wheet-weedle-whoo, wheet-wheet-wheet-whoo. Every day, Turtle sat by the Amazon River and played her flute. All the birds and animals loved to listen to her play.

One day, a man walking through the forest heard her beautiful music. Wheet-weedle-whoo, wheet-weedle-whoo, wheet-wheet-wheet-whoo.

He stopped to listen. When he saw that a turtle was playing the flute, he thought about dinner.

"Turtle soup would be a treat tonight," he thought. So he picked Turtle up and carried her home.

He put Turtle into a cage made of branches and closed the lid. "Don't let the turtle out of the cage," he said to his children. "Tonight we will have turtle soup." Then the father picked up his hoe and went to work in the garden. The children played in the yard.

Turtle did not want to be made into soup. She started to play her flute. Wheet-weedle-whoo, wheet-

Continued on page T3

Oral Comprehension

LISTENING AND SPEAKING Use these questions to encourage children to respond to the story. Remind children to take turns speaking and listening.

- What does the man hear when he is in the forest? (He hears the turtle playing the flute.)

- What does the turtle make the man think about? (The turtle reminds him of dinner. He decides he wants turtle soup for dinner.)

- How does the turtle trick the children? (He says he is tired from dancing and needs to get out of the cage and go for a short walk. When the children let him out, he walks back into the forest and hides.)

- Is the story of the clever turtle real or make-believe? How do you know? (This story is make-believe. Turtles can't play the flute, dance, or talk.)

Activity Ask children to draw pictures of the man, the children, and the clever turtle. Have them cut the pictures out and attach them to craft sticks to make puppets. Invite groups to retell the story using their puppets. Remind children to speak clearly so everyone can understand them.

▶**Kinesthetic**

Reading for Information

Help the man find the clever turtle.

28   29

Reading for Information Big Book, pages 28–29

Objective: Read a Map

DISCUSS THE BIG BOOK Remind children of the folk tale "The Clever Turtle." Have children recall that at the end of the story, the man hunts for the turtle in the forest.

- Turn to pages 28 and 29 in the Big Book and show children the map of the forest. Remind children that a map tells the best way to get somewhere.

- Read aloud the statement on page 28. Then ask: *What does this map show?* (a forest scene with a twisty path

that leads from the man to the turtle) Then discuss with children the route the man should take.

- Ask: *Which direction should the man go to find the turtle?* (The man should cross the bridge and follow the path.) *What animals will the man see along the way?* (a bird, a warthog, a snake, and a monkey) *Is there another way the man can go to get to the turtle?* (Answers will vary.)

CULTURAL PERSPECTIVES

CAMOUFLAGE Explain that turtles may be found in many countries including Thailand, the Philippines, and the United States. A turtle can pull its head, legs, and tail into its shell and hide in the forest because its shell blends into the surroundings.

Activity Have children draw another animal that could blend easily into a forest. Ask children to label their picture.

▶ Spatial

interNET CONNECTION Help children log on to **www.mhschool.com/reading,** where they can access links to wild animals.

215B

Vocabulary: *go*

OBJECTIVES

Children will:
☑ **identify and read the high-frequency word *go*.**

MATERIALS

• word cards
• pocket chart

TEACHING TIP

WORD WALL Add the word *go* to the Word Wall. Point to the word and have children say it and count the letters. Then ask children to spell the word that means the opposite of *stop*.

Introduce

TEACH

Introduce *go* Teach children the following rhyme: *I go here./I go there./ I go with you/Everywhere!* Say it aloud with them several times. Encourage children to pantomime going somewhere. Give children word cards with the word *go*. Place the words from the rhyme in the pocket chart. Point to each word as you read the sentences aloud. Ask children to hold up the *go* card as you say the word.

PRACTICE

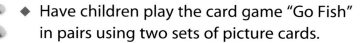
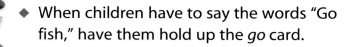

Go Fish!

Materials: picture cards

◆ Have children play the card game "Go Fish" in pairs using two sets of picture cards.

◆ When children have to say the words "Go fish," have them hold up the *go* card.

◆ If a child does not hold up the *go* card while saying the words "Go fish," he or she loses a turn.

ON LEVEL

✓ ASSESS/CLOSE

Have children complete page 215 of the Pupil Edition or Practice Book. For a different approach to teaching this skill, see page T26 for the **Alternate Teaching Strategy.**

Name_____ go

1.
"Go to the cot," I said.

2.
The cat can go to the cot.

3.
I can go to the cot.

4.
We can go and nap.

Read the sentence. • Draw a line under the word go in the sentence.

Unit 4 Introduce High-Frequency Words: go 215

Pupil Edition page 215

Meeting Individual Needs
Activities

Go and Do

Materials: *go* word cards

◆ Give children the *go* word cards. Then give them directions that use the word; for example: *Go to the front of the room. Go to the art center.*

◆ Children hold up their word cards and follow the directions.

EASY

Stop and Go

Materials: octagonal pieces of cardboard

◆ Write *Stop* on one side of the cardboard and *Go* on the other side.

◆ Line up children across the room from you.

◆ Tell them that when you hold up the *Go* side, they may walk toward you. When you hold up the *Stop* side, they must stop.

LANGUAGE SUPPORT

How Many *Go*'s?

◆ Write the following words on chart paper or on the chalkboard: *go, got, so, go, to, goes, do, go, gob.*

◆ Ask children to circle the word *go* every time it appears and to count how many times it appears.

CHALLENGE

215

Listen

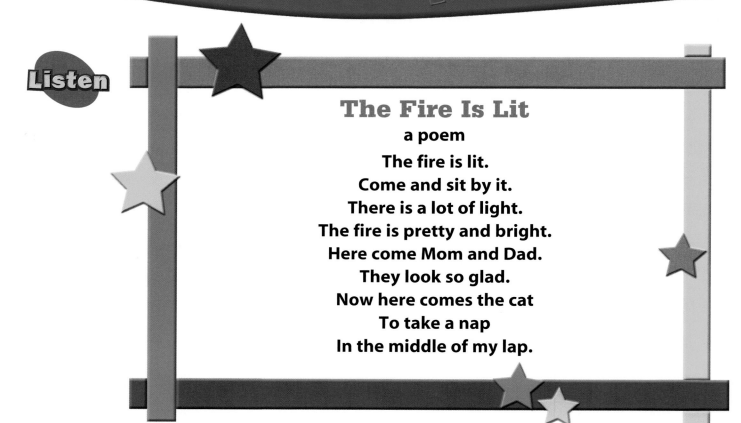

The Fire Is Lit
a poem
The fire is lit.
Come and sit by it.
There is a lot of light.
The fire is pretty and bright.
Here come Mom and Dad.
They look so glad.
Now here comes the cat
To take a nap
In the middle of my lap.

Blend Sounds · · · · · · · · · · · · · · · · **Phonemic** Awareness · · · · · · · · · · · · · ·

Teach   Have children listen as you read the poem aloud. Read the first
line again, isolating the sounds in the word *lit*: The fire is
/l/ - /i/ -/t/. Can you guess the last word in the title? (lit) Yes,
/l/ - /i/ - /t/ is *lit*.

MODEL: Listen to this line. "Come and /s/-/i/-/t/ by it." If I blend
the sounds /s/-/i/-/t/ together, I can make a word: /s/-/i/-/t/, *sit.*
Come and *sit* by it.

Practice   Continue reading lines from the poem. Isolate the sounds in some
words and let children blend the sounds to make a word.

Now here comes the /k/-/a/-/t/ (cat)
To take a /n/-/a/-/p/ (nap)
In the middle of my /l/-/a/-/p/. (lap)

Segment Sounds

Teach Distribute Word Building Boxes with three sections. Say the word *cat*. Point to the first box as you say /k/; point to the second box as you say /a/; and to the third box as you say /t/. Repeat and have children do this with you. Then do the same thing with the word *lot*.

Practice Have a volunteer point to the correct boxes as you say /n/ - /o/ - /t/. Have another child repeat with the same word: /n/ - /o/ - /t/. Move on to the next child. Have him or her use the Word Building Boxes to segment *hot, job,* and *rat*.

MATERIALS
- Word Building Boxes from *Word Building Cards*

INFORMAL ASSESSMENT Observe children as they blend sounds to make a word and segment sounds. If children have difficulty, see Alternate Teaching Strategies on T22, T27, and T31.

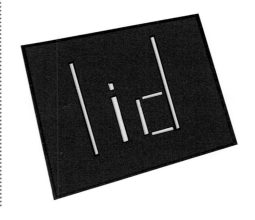

Read Together

From Phonemic Awareness to Phonics

Objective: Associate Sounds with Letters

BRAINSTORM SHORT *o* AND *i* WORDS THAT BEGIN WITH /l/ Write *lot* and *lip* on the chalkboard. Help children brainstorm a variety of three-letter short *o* and *i* words that begin with /l/. Write the words in two columns on the chalkboard.

lot	lip
lob	lid
log	lit

REPEAT DISTINCT SOUNDS Read each listed word. Explain that each word has three letters. Invite children to repeat after you as you reread the list and stretch out each word to say its three sounds. Then name all the letters in each word.

PASTA WORDS Give each child pieces of dry spaghetti, a piece of construction paper, and glue. Invite children to use the pasta pieces to form the letters of a word on the list. Have children glue the pasta pieces to construction paper,

then trace over the letters and say the sound each letter stands for. Children can trade papers to "sound out" classmates' words.

216B

Short *a, i, o*
Blending

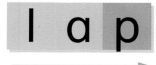

TESTED **OBJECTIVES**

Children will:
- ☑ identify /a/ *a*, /i/ *i*, and /o/ *o*
- ☑ blend and read short *a, i,* and *o* words
- ☑ write short *a, i,* and *o* words

MATERIALS
- letter cards

ADDITIONAL RESOURCES
- Practice Book, page 216
- Phonics/Phonemic Awareness Practice Book, pages 104, 110, 116
- **Phonics** CD-ROM

TEACHING TIP
WORD FAMILIES Make sets of cards for the words *lap, tap, lip, tip, pot, dot, rod, pod, rat, pat, lit* and *sit.* Have small groups play a matching game by turning over two cards and matching word endings.

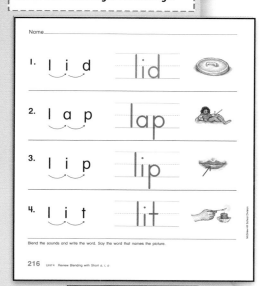

Name_____

1. l i d   lid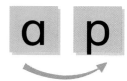
2. l a p   lap
3. l i p   lip
4. l i t   lit

Blend the sounds and write the word. Say the word that names the picture.

216   Unit 4   Review Blending with Short *a, i, o*

Pupil Edition page 216

216C   *Go, Lad, Go!*

Review

TEACH

Model Blending with Short *a, i, o* Display the *a* letter card and say /a/. Have children repeat the /a/ sound as you point to the *a* card. Place the *p* card to the right of the *a* card. Point to each letter as you blend the sounds together and have children repeat after you: *ap.*

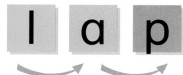

Place the *l* card to the left of *ap* to show *lap.* Point to the cards as you blend to read *lap,* and have children repeat after you.

Continue modeling and guided practice using *lit, lid, lad, lip, lot,* and *Lin.*

PRACTICE

Choose a Word

Materials: word cards for *lap, nap, pan, can, dot, pot*

- ◆ Preview each card and have children blend the sounds as you track the print.
- ◆ Take two word cards at random, and place them on the chalkboard ledge.
- ◆ Ask a volunteer to take one of the cards, show it to the class, and blend the sounds.
- ◆ Repeat for other word pairs.

ON LEVEL

✓ ASSESS/CLOSE

Have children complete page 216 of the Pupil Edition or the Practice Book. For a different approach to this skill, see page T32 for the **Alternate Teaching Strategy.**

Meeting Individual Needs
Activities

Leftovers

Materials: drawing paper, crayons, envelopes, picture cards for *lip, pot, lid, lad, pad, pin, lion,* and *pig*

◆ Label an envelope with each word: *lip, pot, lid, lion, pad,* and *pin.*

◆ Have children read the word on the envelope, find its picture, and put it in its envelope.

◆ Have children draw pictures of the extra words (*lad* and *pig*).

EASY

Missing Vowels

Materials: index cards, paper

◆ Write the following on separate index cards: *l_t, l_p, l_d, L_n,* and *p_l.* Write the vowels *a, i,* and *o* on small squares of paper.

◆ Ask children to use the index cards and vowel squares to make a new word.

◆ Have children write the word.

◆ Have children continue making other words.

CHALLENGE

Poster Sounds

Materials: drawing paper, crayons or markers

◆ Have children work together to make a poster for *Ll* and for *Pp.*

◆ Have children write the capital and lowercase forms of the letter at the top of each poster.

◆ Then have children draw pictures that begin with each letter. Have children share the poster by displaying it in the class.

LANGUAGE SUPPORT

216

Read the Story

☑ **Initial /l/ l**

☑ **High-Frequency Word:** *go*

☑ **Main Idea**

☐ **Concepts of Print**

PREVIEW AND PREDICT

Display the book and name these parts: front and back covers, title. Have children look at the cover illustration as you read the title. Then ask children why they think the story might be titled *Go, Lad, Go!* Then take a picture walk through the first few pages.

Go, Lad, Go!

SET PURPOSES

Have children tell what they want to find out as they read the story. Ask *What do you think Lad will do in this story?*

AS YOU READ

As children read the story, remind them to track the print. Then use the following prompts:

- **Page 2** If children have trouble reading the word *Can,* remind them that the first letter, *c,* often has the /k/ sound. *Graphophonic Cues*

- **Page 3** Ask children to find the word *go* on the page. *High-Frequency Words*

- **Page 7** Have children read the sentence. Then ask them to point to and read the two words that begin with /l/. *(Lad, lap) Initial l*

- **Page 8** After reading this page, have children complete the following sentence orally: Go, Lad, Go! *is about* _____. (Possible Answer: *Go, Lad, Go!* is about a girl who is training her dog, Lad.) *Main Idea*

Can you go to the ?

2

Lad can go to the ● .

3

Pupil Edition pp. 217–218

Can you sit?

4

Lad can sit.

5

LANGUAGE SUPPORT

ESL Develop story vocabulary by having children orally complete the following sentence frame: *I can go to the* _____. Encourage each child to give a different answer, such as *movies, store,* or *library.*

Can you go to the mat?

6

Lad can go to my lap.

7

Lad can nap!

8

Read the Story

RETURN TO PREDICTIONS

Ask children if anyone predicted that the dog would learn to go to the cup and sit. Discuss children's responses.

RETELL THE STORY

Provide an empty cup, a mat, and a stuffed toy dog. Invite pairs of children to act out the story as they retell it.

WRITING

Journal Writing Ask children to write a sentence in their journal about an intelligent dog they have seen before. Have children illustrate their sentences.

CENTER Activity

Cross Curricular: Science

FAVORITE PETS Invite children to use empty boxes, bottles, and art supplies to create a 3-D model of a favorite pet. Have children write a short description of their pets and a description of a trick they would like to teach it.

▶ **Kinesthetic/Interpersonal**

 interNET CONNECTION Help children log on to *www.mhschool.com/reading*, where they can learn more about pets.

INFORMAL ASSESSMENT

CONCEPTS OF PRINT

HOW TO ASSESS Ask each child to complete the following tasks:

- Point to the front cover of the book.
- Point to the back cover of the book.
- Point to the title of the book.
- Turn to page 2. Point to the first word on the page. Point to the last word on the page.

FOLLOW UP Have children complete similar tasks using other books from your class library.

Main Idea

Go, Lad, Go!

Mc Graw Hill

Go, Lad, Go!

OBJECTIVES

Children will:
☑ recognize the main idea to understand a story.

MATERIALS

• *Go, Lad, Go!*

TEACHING TIP

INSTRUCTIONAL Help children understand the relationship between details and main idea of content-area materials. Draw an idea web on the board and invite children to help you complete it.

Review

TEACH

Review Main Idea Remind children that the things the characters do together are story details and the *main idea* is what the story is about. Page through the story *Go, Lad, Go!* and ask children to name things Lad and the girl did together.

Identify Main Idea Ask, *Is the story only about a girl who hugs her dog? Is the story only about a dog taking a nap?* Ask children to tell what the main idea of the story is in their own words. Reinforce that this story is about a girl who is trying to train her new puppy, Lad. Point out that the title, *Go, Lad, Go!,* gives a clue about the main idea of the whole book.

PRACTICE

An Idea Web

◆ Guide children in sorting out main idea and details in *Go, Lad, Go!* by making an idea web.

◆ In the center of the web draw a picture of the girl and her dog.

◆ Have children dictate the important story details for you to write around the center picture.

ON LEVEL

✓ ASSESS/CLOSE

Have children complete page 219 of the Pupil Edition or the Practice Book. For a different approach to this skill, see page T25 for the **Alternate Teaching Strategy.**

Name_____

1. Nan can sit on the cot.

Tim and the cat have a nap.

2. Pam can fit the lid on the pot.

"I have a mop," said Pam.

3. "Sit on my lap," said Mom.

"Pat the cat," said Dad.

Look at each picture. • Then read the sentences. • Draw a line under the sentence that tells what the picture is all about.

Unit 4 Review Main Idea **219**

Pupil Edition page 219

Meeting Individual Needs
Activities

Draw a Main Idea Picture

Materials: drawing paper, crayons

◆ Ask children to think about a favorite story or movie.

◆ Invite children to draw a picture about the story or movie they choose.

◆ Have each child display his or her drawing to a partner and tell what it is about.

EASY

Story Time

Materials: drawing paper, crayons

◆ Ask pairs of children to make up a new story about Lad and his owner.

◆ Have children divide drawing paper into three parts and draw three pictures about their story.

◆ Invite children to share their pictures and tell the main idea of their story.

CHALLENGE

Act It Out

◆ Review the nursery rhyme "Little Boy Blue."

◆ Have children tell the main idea in their own words.

◆ Then have pairs of children act out and tell the main idea of other nursery rhymes.

LANGUAGE SUPPORT

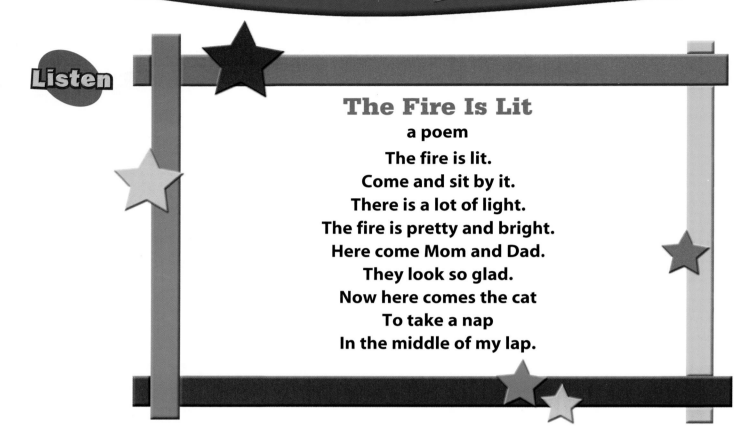

Listen

The Fire Is Lit
a poem

The fire is lit.
Come and sit by it.
There is a lot of light.
The fire is pretty and bright.
Here come Mom and Dad.
They look so glad.
Now here comes the cat
To take a nap
In the middle of my lap.

Blend Sounds · · · · · · · · · · · · · Phonemic Awareness · · · · · · · · · · · · ·

Teach Have children chant the poem with you. When you get to the word *lit* in the first line, say /l/-/i/-/t/. Have the children hold up a finger to count each sound you are making. (three)

MODEL: I am going to blend the sounds /l/-/i/-/t/ to make a word. Blend the sounds faster and faster so that the children hear the word *lit*. Repeat this procedure for the words *lot* and *lap*.

Practice Have the children say each of the words below with you. Again, ask them to hold up a finger for every sound they hear. Be sure to stretch the phonemes so that every child can hear the segmented sounds. Then have the children blend the phonemes and say the word.

/m/-/o/-/m/ (mom)
/t/-/o/-/p/ (top)
/j/-/o/-/b/ (job)
/r/-/i/-/b/ (rib)
/g/-/o/-/t/ (got)

Segment Sounds

Teach Display a *Word Building Box* with three sections. Say the word *Sam*. Point to the first box as you say /s/; point to the second box as you say /a/; and to the third box as you say /m/. Repeat and have children point to the boxes along with you.

Practice Give the Word Building Boxes to a volunteer and have him or her segment sounds so that the whole class can hear. Do this with ten or more children. Use such words as *cot, pit, top,* and *tap.*

MATERIALS
- Word Building Boxes from *Word Building Cards*

INFORMAL ASSESSMENT Observe children as they blend sounds to make words and segment sounds. If children have difficulty, see Alternate Teaching Strategies on T22, T27, and T31.

Read Together

From Phonemic Awareness to Phonics

Objective: Associate Sounds with Letters

LISTEN FOR SOUNDS Read the first line of the poem, and ask children to identify the word that begins with /l/. *(lit)* Write the word on the chalkboard. Read the third line of the poem, and ask children to identify the word with /o/ in the middle. *(lot)* Read the last line of the poem, and ask children to identify the word with /p/ at the end. *(lap)*

lit   lot   lap

SEGMENT SOUNDS Explain that each of these words has three separate sounds. Help children say each word slowly, so each sound is distinct.

ASSOCIATE SOUNDS WITH LETTERS Explain that each sound in the words has a letter that stands for it. For the word *lit*, write ___ *it* on the chalkboard. For the word *lot,* write ___ *ot* on the chalkboard. And for the word *lap,* write ___ *ap* on the board. Tape cardboard cutouts of three *l*'s on the board. Ask a child to place a

letter *l* on the board to complete the first word *lit*. Have the child tape it on the blank and say: /l/-/i/-/t/, *lit*. Continue with *lot* and *lap*.

Short a, i, o
Blending

✓TESTED

⊘OBJECTIVES

Children will:

- ☑ identify /a/ *a*, /i/ *i*, and /o/ *o*
- ☑ blend and read short *a, i,* and *o* words
- ☑ write short *a, i,* and *o* words

MATERIALS

- letter cards

ADDITIONAL RESOURCES

- Practice Book, page 220
- Phonics/Phonemic Awareness Practice Book, pages 104, 110, 116
- *Phonics* CD-ROM

TEACHING TIP

WRITE WORDS Draw a flower with four large petals on the chalkboard. In the center write –*ad*. Say: *lad, dad, pad,* and *mad.* Have children add an initial letter in each petal to form each new word.

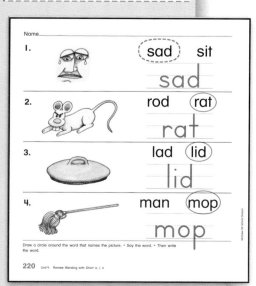

Name _____

1.  (sad) sit

   ___sad___

2. rod (rat)

   ___rat___

3. lad (lid)

   ___lid___

4. man (mop)

   ___mop___

Draw a circle around the word that names the picture. • Say the word. • Then write the word.

220   Unit 4   Review Blending with Short a, i, o

Pupil Edition page 220

220C   *Go, Lad, Go!*

Review

TEACH

Model Blending with Short *a, i, o* Display the *i* letter card and say /i/. Have children repeat the /i/ sound as you point to the *i* card.

Place the *d* card to the right of the *i* card. Point to each letter as you blend the sounds together and have children repeat after you: *id.*

Place the *l* card to the left of *id* to show *lid.* Point to the cards as you blend to read *lid,* and have children repeat after you.

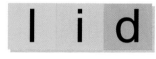

Continue modeling and guided practice using *lad, lap, man, fit, dip, rod,* and *pat.*

PRACTICE

Complete a Sentence

◆ Write on the chalkboard the following words: *dip, fit, lap, sad, lid, lot.*

◆ Have children blend the words as you track the print.

◆ Tell children to listen to the sentence you say and to find the word from the board that completes it. Say sentences such as: *Babies like to sit on a person's ___. (lap) Unscrew the ___ of the jar. (lid)*

ON LEVEL

✓ ASSESS/CLOSE

Have children complete page 220 of the Pupil Edition or the Practice Book. For a different approach to this skill, see page T32 for the **Alternate Teaching Strategy.**

Meeting Individual Needs
Activities

What's the Vowel?

Materials: three boxes; drawing paper; word cards for *lip, lit, pot, pat, lap, fit, sit, mat, tap, rip, Pop,* and *mop*

◆ Label each box: *a, i,* or *o.*

◆ Have children blend the sounds on each card, and put each card in the box that shows its middle sound.

EASY

Word Bingo

Materials: counters, paper bag, word bingo cards, word cards for *pat, lap, lid, tip, tot, pod, map, mop, rip,* and *sad*

◆ Prepare bingo cards by drawing a 3 x 3 inch grid on papers. Write nine words in random order on each grid.

◆ Have partners take turns drawing word cards at random.

◆ Have children put a counter on their card if a word is called. Repeat until one player has bingo.

CHALLENGE

Act It Out

◆ Write the following words on the chalkboard: *lip, pin, pan, pot, lap,* and *lot.*

◆ Have volunteers blend the words and tell what each word means.

◆ Have children work together in a skit. Tell them to circle two of the words from the board and include those words in their skit.

◆ Have children perform their skit for class.

LANGUAGE SUPPORT

Meeting Individual Needs

Lin Did It!

EASY

Guided Reading

OBJECTIVES

- ☑ Initial /l/ *L, l*; Blending
- ☑ Main Idea
- ☑ Vocabulary: *go*
- ☐ Concepts of Print

PREVIEW AND PREDICT Ask children to look at the cover illustration and predict what the story might be about. Point to each word as you read aloud the title. Then conduct a picture walk through the first few pages. Have children predict what Lin will do. Before reading, remind children to point to each word as they read it.

READ THE BOOK Use these prompts.
Pages 2–3 Have children identify a word that begins with /l/ *L*. *Phonics*

Page 4 Point to the first word on the page and have children read it with you. *Can you find this word again on this page? Vocabulary*

Page 6 Point out the exclamation mark and explain its use. Ask: *Why is Mom excited?* (Lin is almost in first place.) *Concepts of Print*

Page 8 *What is the story about?* (It tells about how Lin won the race.) *Main Idea*

LITERARY RESPONSE Ask children to draw and write about Lin's race. Encourage them to share their writing and drawings.

Go, Lad, Go!

INDEPENDENT

Guided Reading

OBJECTIVES

- ☑ Initial /l/ *L, l*; Blending
- ☑ Main Idea
- ☑ Vocabulary: *go*
- ☐ Concepts of Print

REREAD THE BOOK FOR FLUENCY Encourage children to reread the book alone or with a partner.

Cover Have children identify the commas on the cover. *Concepts of Print*

Page 3 Ask children to point to the word *go* on this page. *Vocabulary*

Page 7 Ask children to find the word on the page that begins with *l*. *Let's blend the sounds to read the word: l-a-p, lap. Phonics*

Page 8 *What is this story about?* (A girl is training her new puppy, Lad.) *Main Idea*

LITERARY RESPONSE Ask children to draw where they would like to take a nap.

CHALLENGE

Guided Reading

Let's Go!
by Suzanne Martinucci
illustrated by Thea Kliros

PREVIEW AND PREDICT Ask children to look at the cover illustration and predict what the story might be about. Then conduct a picture walk through the first few pages.

READ THE BOOK Use the following prompts to guide children's reading:

Pages 2–3 Point to *go* on page 2. *Let's read this word together.* Then have children point to and read the same word on page 3. *Vocabulary*

Pages 4–5 Have children find the word that begins with /l/ *L* on these pages. *Phonics*

Page 7 Ask children to find a capital *L* and a lowercase *l* on page 7. *Concepts of Print*

Page 8 *What is this story about?* (children who are visiting a park) *Main Idea*

LITERARY RESPONSE Ask children to write in their journal about a park they would like to visit.

OBJECTIVES

☑ Initial /l/ *L, l*; Blending
☑ Main Idea
☑ Vocabulary: *go*
☐ Concepts of Print

ASSESSMENT

VOCABULARY: *go*
HOW TO ASSESS Have children identify the word *go* throughout the story. Then ask them to make up sentences using *go*.
FOLLOW UP For children who are having difficulty, help them place green dots under the word *go* so that the word can be easily identified.

Cross Curricular: Social Studies

SAFETY SIGNS Encourage children to talk about safety signs they have seen. Guide the discussion with examples of safety, such as wearing a bike helmet and swimming with an adult. Then have children draw posters to illustrate safety. Invite volunteers to talk about their posters in class.

▶ **Spatial/Linguistic**

Vocabulary:
go, to, me, you

Vocabulary Card

TESTED

OBJECTIVES

Children will:
☑ identify and read the high-frequency words *go, to, me, you*

MATERIALS
- word cards
- picture cards

TEACHING TIP

WORD WALL Point to the words *go, to, you,* and *me* on the Word Wall. Have children read the words. Then challenge them to make up statements or questions using any two of the words.

Review

TEACH

Review *go, to, me, you* Say the following sentences aloud: *Where did you go? Tell it to me.* Repeat them several times with children. Pass out word cards *go, to, me, you.* Ask children to hold up each card as you say the word in the sentences.

Have children practice saying the sentences to each other and answering the question with other sentences that use *go, to, me, you.*

PRACTICE

Fill in the Rebus

Materials: picture cards, word cards

- ◆ Make several picture cards to use in rebus sentences, such as a beach and a store. Also provide cards for the words *a, and, the, I, we, you, go,* and *to.*

- ◆ Have children make sentences using their word cards combined with their picture cards.

- ◆ Have children read their rebus sentences aloud.

ON LEVEL

✓ ASSESS/CLOSE

Have children complete page 221 of the Pupil Edition or Practice Book. For a different approach to teaching this skill, see page T26 for the **Alternate Teaching Strategy.**

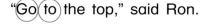

Name

1.

"Go to the top," said Ron.

2.

"You can go," said Dad.

3.

"Go," Mom said to me.

Read the sentences. Then do the following: 1. Draw a circle around the words go and to. 2. Draw a circle around the word you. 3. Draw a circle around the word me.

Unit 4   Review go, to, me, you   **221**

Pupil Edition page 221

Meeting Individual Needs
Activities

Go!

◆ Write these sentences and read them aloud to children: *Let's go to the park. Let's go into the playhouse. Ann and Tom go outside.*

◆ Have volunteers circle the word *go* in each sentence.

◆ Have children dictate other sentences to you that include the word *go*.

 EASY

Word Cubes

Materials: blank six-part spinners or word cubes made out of empty milk cartons

◆ In each blank space on the spinner, or on each side of the word cube, write one of the following words: *go, the, me, that, to, you.*

◆ Have children spin the spinner or roll the cube and read the word, then use it in a sentence.

◆ Children score one point for each correctly used word.

CHALLENGE

Where Can We Go?

Materials: drawing paper, pencils, markers, crayons

◆ Invite children to help you make a picture list of places children can *go*.

◆ Then read the list aloud, beginning each sentence with *"You can go to …"*

◆ Combine the illustrations in a book and add it to the class library.

LANGUAGE SUPPORT

Interactive Writing

Write a Nature Riddle

GRAMMAR/SPELLING CONNECTIONS

During the Draft stage, remind children that complete sentences begin with a capital letter and end with a period.

TEACHING TIP

During the Prewrite stage, hold *Nature Spy* upside down as if you are about to read. Wait to see if children notice, and if not, ask them what is wrong with the way you are holding the book. Then model holding the book in the correct position, and point out the front and back covers.

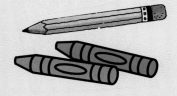

Prewrite

REVIEW THE STORY Reread *Nature Spy* with children. Talk about the story pattern. For example, the pictures show an animal or something from nature, and then the photographs show a closer look. Ask: *What things in this book have you seen before? What other things have you seen in nature?*

BRAINSTORM Encourage children to describe some of the interesting things they have noticed outside. If necessary, prompt them by showing them a few items, such as a leaf, a seashell, or a pine cone. Write children's responses on the chalkboard.

leaf

shell

pine cone

Draft

WRITE A NATURE RIDDLE Tell children that they are going to work together to write a book of riddles about nature.

- Explain that you are going to write some clues that describe one of the items on the class list. Fold a piece of construction paper

in half. Choose one of the items and write two simple clues on the outside of the folded paper, such as: *It is on a tree. It has lines on it.*

- Read the clues with children as you track the print. Ask children to guess, using a complete sentence. (It is a leaf.)

- Open the folded paper and write the answer inside. Then draw a picture of a leaf.

- Ask a volunteer to choose another nature item. On a new folded piece of paper, have children help you write a new riddle. Continue until you have at least five riddles.

- Divide children into five groups. On the inside of the card, have each group draw a picture of the answer to the riddle. Encourage children in each group to read the riddle to each other.

Revise

Before publishing the nature riddles, read each one with children as you track the print. Then ask:

- Does each clue sentence begin with a capital letter and end with a period?

- Do the clues match the picture?

Publish

Display the nature riddles along the chalk-board ledge or on top of a bookcase.

It is yellow in the middle.
It has white petals.

It is a daisy.

Presentation Ideas

WHAT AM I? Have children take turns reading the riddle cards and ask the class to guess the answers. The person who guesses correctly may read another riddle, then choose someone else to guess.

RIDDLE POINTS Form two teams of children. Read a riddle card to Team A and let them collectively guess the answer. If they are correct, award them one "riddle point." Then ask Team B to guess the next riddle. Alternate until all riddles are read.

Listening and Speaking

- Remind children to speak slowly and loudly enough so that everyone in the class can understand them.

- Tell children that when they listen to clues, they should try to picture the nature item in their mind as a way to figure out what it is.

TECHNOLOGY TIP

Help children use a computer encyclopedia or the Internet to find information about their nature items. This information can be used when writing clues.

LANGUAGE SUPPORT

ESL Bring in nature items for ESL children to use when writing nature riddles. Help children focus their clues on how the item feels when they touch it, and how it looks.

Meeting Individual Needs for Writing

EASY

Use Picture Cards Give pairs of children picture cards with items from nature. Have pairs divide the cards and hide them from their partners. Have partners give each other clues about the picture on each card and guess what the item is. When finished, help each pair write a sentence about one picture.

ON-LEVEL

Describe It! Hold up an item from nature and have children write as many words to describe it as possible. Have them count the words in the list. Then repeat with another item.

CHALLENGE

Classmate Riddles Invite children to write riddles about their class-mates. A sample riddle might be: *This person has brown hair. She wears her hair in braids. She likes to jump rope.* Help children write three clues and then ask others to guess.

Lesson Overview

Week 4

Mud Fun

Phonics	Comprehension	Vocabulary
• Initial /u/*u*; Medial /u/*u* • Blending	• Compare and Contrast	• do

Literature Resources

Big Books

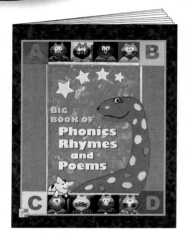

Big Book of Phonics Rhymes and Poems
pages 52, 53

ABC Big Book
pages 223A–223B

Literature Big Book
pages 225A–225B

Reading for Information Big Book
page 30

Read Aloud

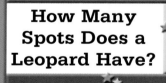

How Many Spots Does a Leopard Have?

page 227A

Student Books

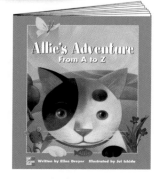

ABC Little Book
pages 223A–223B

Pam and the Pup

Easy
page 233A
Decodable

Mud Fun

Independent
pages 229/230A–229/230B, 233A
Decodable
Story also available in Pupil Edition

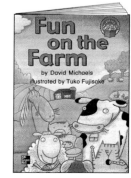

Fun on the Farm
by David Michaels
illustrated by Tuko Fujisake

Challenge
page 233B
Patterned

222C

Mud Fun

Daily Schedule
Today is: Tuesday

Good Morning	Good Afternoon
Circle Time	Rest
Center Time	Outdoor Play
Snack	Center Time
Music	Sharing Time
Story	
Lunch	

blocks

a Bb Cc Dd Ee

6   7

Center Activities for the Week

Center Activities

Activities take 15–20 minutes each.

Phonics

Picture This!

Objective: Identify initial sounds and letters.

◆ Have children draw a picture of one or two places that Allie visits.

◆ Help children arrange the pictures to show story sequence.

◆ Ask them to tell the beginning sound and letter of the locations.

MATERIALS

- *Allie's Adventure from A to Z*
- **White paper**
- **Crayons**

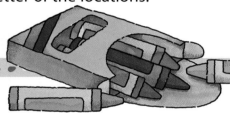

Writing

Words and Pictures

Objective: Write a word and illustrate it.

◆ Place the cards face down in the center.

◆ Children choose a card, read the word, and copy it in their journal.

◆ Have them illustrate their word.

MATERIALS

- **Six index cards with one medial /u/, /a/, /i/, or /o/ word written on each; for example:** *sun, cot, fan, sit, pup, cap.*

Reading and Listening

Self-Selected Reading

Objective: Hold a book upright.

Place the literature for the week and the corresponding audiocassettes or CDs in the Reading Center. You may also include the following books from the Theme Bibliography on pages T54–T55.

◆ *Fireflies, Fireflies Light My Way* by Jonathan London

◆ *I Took a Walk* by Henry Cole

◆ *What's This?* by Caroline Mockford

MATERIALS

- **Listening Library cassettes and CDs**
- **Books**

Math

May I Measure?

Objective: Estimate how many cups the pot will hold.

MATERIALS
- Measuring cups of varying sizes
- Small cooking pot
- Bag of pasta shells

◆ Have children work in small groups. Have them choose a measuring cup.

◆ Ask them to estimate how many cups of shells the pot will hold.

◆ Then have them check to see whether their estimates were correct.

Science

Nature Alphabet

Objective: Form the letters *Uu*, using items from nature.

MATERIALS
- Twigs and leaves
- Glue
- One sheet of construction paper per child

◆ Have children draw a large-scale *Uu* on their paper.

◆ Ask them to outline the letters in glue. Then have them cover the glue with bits of leaves and twigs.

Working with Words

High-Frequency Words

Objective: Practice reading and writing high-frequency words.

MATERIALS
- Letter cards that spell *to, me, go,* and *do*
- Pencils

◆ Place the letter cards in the middle of the Center.

◆ Ask children to read the words and use each one in a sentence.

◆ Children should write all four words in their journals.

Mud Fun

READING AND LANGUAGE ARTS

- **Phonological Awareness**

- **Phonics** initial and medial /u/*u*; blending with short *a, i, o*

- **Comprehension**

- **Vocabulary**

- **Beginning Reading Concepts**

- **Listening, Speaking, Viewing, Representing**

DAY 1

Focus on Reading Skills

Develop Phonological Awareness, 222I–222J
"Umbrellas" *Big Book of Phonics Rhymes and Poems*, 52

Phonics Introduce Initial /u/u, 222K–222
- ◆ Practice Book, 222
- ◆ Phonics/Phonemic Awareness Practice Book, 117–118

- ◆ **Phonics CD-ROM**

Read the Literature

Read *Allie's Adventure from A to Z* **Big Book,** 223A–223B
Shared Reading

Build Skills
- ☑ Up, Down, 223C–223
- ◆ Practice Book, 223

DAY 2

Focus on Reading Skills

Develop Phonological Awareness, 224A–224B
"Snug as a Bug" *Big Book of Phonics Rhymes and Poems*, 53

Phonics Introduce Medial /u/u, 224C–224
- ◆ Practice Book, 224
- ◆ Phonics/Phonemic Awareness Practice Book, 119–120

- ◆ **Phonics CD-ROM**

Read the Literature

Read *Nature Spy* **Big Book,** 225A–225B
Shared Reading

Build Skills
- ☑ Compare and Contrast, 225C–225
- ◆ Practice Book, 225

- **Cross Curriculum**

◆ **Activity** Science, 223B

◆ **Activity** Math, Science, 222F

- **Writing**

◆ **Writing Prompt:** Write your own adventure story of being on a farm.

Letter Formation, 222K

◆ **Writing Prompt:** Pick something in nature to write about.

Journal Writing, 225B
Letter Formation, 224C

◆ = **Whole-Day classrooms may extend the day with these optional activities!**

☑ = **Skill Assessed in Unit Test**

DAY 3

How Many Spots Does a Leopard Have?

Focus on Reading Skills

Develop Phonological Awareness, 226A–226B
"Snug as a Bug" and "Umbrellas" *Big Book of Phonics Rhymes and Poems,* 53, 52

 Review /u/u, 226C–226
◆ Practice Book, 226
◆ Phonics/Phonemic Awareness Practice Book, 117–120

◆  **CD-ROM**

Read the Literature

 Read "How Many Spots Does a Leopard Have?" Teacher Read Aloud, 227A–227B
Shared Reading
Read the Reading for Information Big Book, 30–31
Map

Build Skills

☑ High-Frequency Word: *do* 227C–227
◆ Practice Book, 227

◆ **Activity** Cultural Perspectives, 227B

 Writing Prompt: Do you have a favorite way to count? Write about how you do it.

DAY 4

Mud Fun

Focus on Reading Skills

Develop Phonological Awareness, 228A–228B
"A Pup Named Tom"

 **Introduce Blending with Short *u*,** 228C–228
◆ Practice Book, 228
◆ Phonics/Phonemic Awareness Practice Book, 121

◆ **CD-ROM**

Read the Literature

Read "Mud Fun" On-Level Decodable Story, 229/230A–229/230B

☑ Medial /u/u; Blending
☑ Compare and Contrast
☑ High-Frequency Words: *do*
Concepts of Print

Build Skills

☑ Compare and Contrast, 231A–231
◆ Practice Book, 231

◆ **Activity** Science, 229/230B

 Writing Prompt: What would you make if you were playing with mud? Write about it.

Journal Writing, 229–230B
Letter Formation Practice Book, 229–230

DAY 5

Pam and the Pup

Mud Fun

Focus on Reading Skills

Develop Phonological Awareness, 232A–232B
"A Pup Named Tom"

 **Review Blending with Short *u, o*,** 232C–232
◆ Practice Book, 232
◆ Phonics/Phonemic Awareness Practice Book, 122

◆ **CD-ROM**

Read the Literature

Read "Pam and the Pup" Easy Decodable Story, 233A
Reread "Mud Fun" On-Level Decodable Story, 233A
Read "Fun on the Farm" Challenge Patterned Book, 233B
Guided Reading
☑ Medial /u/u; Blending
☑ Compare and Contrast
☑ High-Frequency Word: *do*
Concepts of Print

Build Skills

☑ High-Frequency Words: *do, go, I, and, me,* 233C–233
◆ Practice Book, 233

◆ **Activity** Math, 233B

 Writing Prompt: If you could visit a farm, what animal would you most like to see? Write about it.

Interactive Writing, 234A–234B

Listen

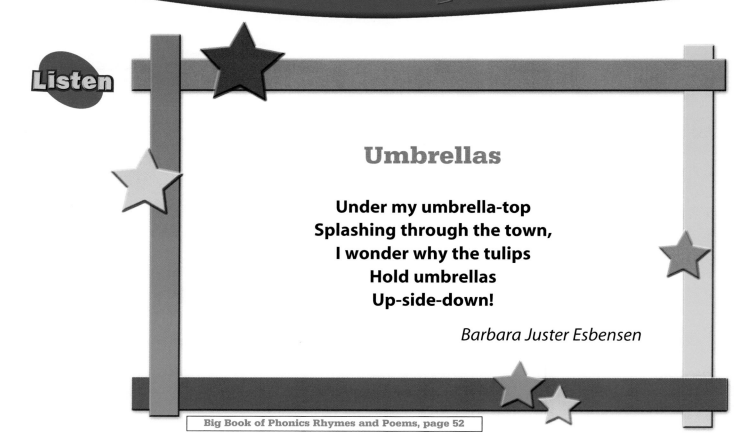

Umbrellas

**Under my umbrella-top
Splashing through the town,
I wonder why the tulips
Hold umbrellas
Up-side-down!**

Barbara Juster Esbensen

Big Book of Phonics Rhymes and Poems, page 52

Identify Rhyming Words

Phonological Awareness

Teach Have the children listen as you read "Umbrellas." Have them say which two words rhyme. *(town/down)*

MODEL: Listen as I read the poem again. You tell me what word I have left out. "Under my umbrella-top / Splashing through the town, / I wonder why the tulips / Hold umbrellas / Up-side-_____!" *(down)*

Practice Say each word below. Have children turn to a partner and say a rhyme for the word. Then have a few volunteers share their words with the class. Remind the children to produce rhymes that have the same ending sounds, such as *town* and *down*.

find	fox	hold
flip	fun	hill

Listen for Beginning Sounds

MATERIALS
• puppet

Teach Tell children to listen to the beginning sound of the word *up*. Tell children the word *up* begins with the /u/ sound. Have children say the following: /u/; *up*.

Practice Tell children that the puppet is going to say several words. They should put their hands up in the air if they hear the puppet say a word that begins with the /u/ sound. You might use these words for the activity: *under, umbrella, town, uncle, give, ugly, take*.

INFORMAL ASSESSMENT Observe children as they produce rhyming words and identify beginning sounds. If children have difficulty, see Alternate Teaching Strategies on T31 and T33.

Read Together

From Phonemic Awareness to Phonics

Objective: Identify /u/ U, u

IDENTIFY THE LETTER FOR THE SOUND

• Explain to children that the letters *U, u* stand for the sound /u/. Say the sound and have children say it with you.

• Display the Big Book of Phonics Rhymes and Poems, page 52. Point to the letters in the corner. Identify them, and have children say the /u/ sound.

REREAD THE POEM

• Reread the poem. Have children repeat the word when they hear a word that begins with /u/.

CAN YOU FIND A *U*?

• Invite children to find words that begin with *U* or *u* in the poem. Have children frame the word with their index fingers.

Uu **Umbrellas**

Under my umbrella-top,
Splashing through the town,
I wonder why the tulips
Hold umbrellas
Up-side-down!

Barbara Juster Esbensen

Big Book of Phonics Rhymes and Poems, page 52

Initial /u/ *u*

Uu
umbrella

Phonics Picture Posters and Cards

OBJECTIVES

TESTED

Children will:
- ☑ identify the letters *U, u*
- ☑ identify /u/ *U, u*
- ☑ form the letters *U, u*

MATERIALS

- Phonics Picture Posters
- umbrella-shaped cutouts

ADDITIONAL RESOURCES

- Practice Book, page 222
- Phonics/Phonemic Awareness Practice Book, pages 117–118
- Phonics CD-ROM

Phonics Song

Uncle Joe's Umbrella

Climb up the hill with Uncle Joe,
Uncle Joe, Uncle Joe,
Up the hill in the rain we go,
Under his umbrella!

Sung to the tune of "Here We Go 'Round the Mulberry Bush"

From **Songs from A to Z**

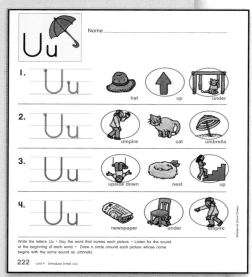

Introduce

TEACH

Phonemic Awareness Warm-Up Have children sing the song "Uncle Joe's Umbrella" with you. Sing it again and have children give a "thumbs up" every time they sing a word that begins with the /u/ sound.

Identify /u/ *U, u* Display the Phonics Picture Poster for umbrella and explain that *U, u* stands for the /u/ sound. Point to the letters and have children repeat the /u/ sound after you.

Form *U, u* Review the capital and lowercase forms with children. With your back to them, trace each letter in the air with your fingers. Give children umbrella-shaped paper cutouts, and ask them to color the umbrellas. Then, have them write the letters *U, u* on the reverse side.

PRACTICE

What Goes Under?

- ◆ Give children objects and ask them to put them under other objects. For example: *Put the pencil under the chair. Put the bear under the desk.*

- ◆ Emphasize the /u/ sound as you say each direction.

- ◆ After children complete the activity, ask them to write the letters *U, u*.

ON LEVEL

✓ ASSESS/CLOSE

Have children complete page 222 of the Pupil Edition or the Practice Book. For a different approach to this skill, see page T34 for the **Alternate Teaching Strategy.**

Activities

Glitter *U*'s

Materials: drawing paper, crayons, glue stick, glitter

- ◆ Have each child write *U, u* on a piece of paper.

- ◆ Ask children to trace the *U, u* with a glue stick and then sprinkle glitter on the glue.

- ◆ After it dries, have children trace the letters and say the sound they stand for.

EASY

The Action Word Game

Materials: *U, u* letter cards from the Word Building Manipulative Cards

- ◆ Have pairs of children take turns acting out words that begin with /u/. (*unlock, under, umbrella, up, umpire, untie*)

- ◆ After the game, children should trace *U, u* on the Word Building Cards as they say the name and the sound the letter stands for.

CHALLENGE

Thumbs Up!

- ◆ Ask children to turn their thumbs up and say "thumbs up" when they hear a word that begins with /u/.

- ◆ Then say words such as: *up, at, man, under, bend, ugly, umpire, rat, sat, unlock.*

- ◆ After the game, have children trace *U, u* as they say its name and sound.

LANGUAGE SUPPORT

Shared Reading

Allie's Adventure
From A to Z

Written by Ellen Dreyer   Illustrated by Jui Ishida

Big Book

TESTED

OBJECTIVES

Children will:
☐ identify the title page.
☐ recognize that names begin with capital letters.
☑ recognize main idea.
☐ listen and respond to the story.

Build Background

Develop Oral Language   Show children the cover and title of the book. Ask them, "What kinds of adventures does Allie have? Where does she go?" Write children's responses on the board in a word web.

Read the Big Book

Set Purposes   Tell children that as they reread the story, they should notice all the places Allie goes. Ask them to note which animal she meets in each place.

Read the Story   Before you read the story, turn to the title page and discuss the information that is found on it. *Concepts of Print*

MODEL: The title of the story is on the title page, too: *Allie's Adventure From A to Z*. I also see the name of the author and the illustrator. The name at the bottom is the company who made the book.

Ask children to compare the title page and the front cover. How are they alike? *Concepts of Print*

Point out that *Allie* begins with a capital letter. Can children recall why? (Names begin with capital letters.) Have them look for other names as you reread the story. *Letter Identification*

Allie wakes **up**.

She hears a **voice**.

Allie's Adventure, pages 24–25

Literature Response

LISTENING/SPEAKING

Discuss the Story Where is Allie when she sees an insect? (Allie is in the field behind the barn.) Where is she when she sees the cow? (Allie is in the barn.) *Literal: Use Illustrations*

What is the story about? (It is about a cat who walks around the farmyard, chasing a butterfly, a mouse and other animals until she is tired.) *Inferential: Main Idea*

Why does the word *Zack* begin with a capital letter? (Names begin with capital letters.) *Concepts of Print*

WRITING

Invite children to draw a picture map of Allie's travels through the farmyard and garden. Have them label different parts of the map with words from the story.

Allie sees an **insect**.

Allie's Adventure, page 11

INFORMAL ASSESSMENT

IDENTIFY THE TITLE PAGE

How to Assess
Ask children what information can be found on the title page. Use the Big Book as a reference.

Follow-Up
Have children locate the title page in other books and point to the title and the names of the author and illustrator.

 **Activity**

Cross Curricular: Science

MAKE A MURAL Ask children to draw or cut out pictures of different types of cats. Have them present their work, discussing how the cats are alike and different.

Up, Down

Nature Spy

^{TESTED} **OBJECTIVES**

Children will:

☑ describe *up* and *down*

MATERIALS

• *Nature Spy*

TEACHING TIP

INSTRUCTIONAL Use *up* and *down* throughout the day. For example, if you are walking down the steps, say what you are doing out loud. Ask children to repeat the sentences after you.

Introduce

TEACH

Identify Up and Down Display the Big Book *Nature Spy* and recall the story with children. Take a picture walk through the book, discussing illustrations that show the concept of up and down. For example: *The girl is walking down the steps; the girl is looking up at the tree.* Then ask children to look up and ask them to describe what they see. Have them look down and do the same thing. Talk about what they would see if they looked up and down outside on the playground.

PRACTICE

Find Up and Down

Materials: magazines

◆ Ask children to look at the pictures and find examples of both *up* and *down*.

◆ Ask children to cut out one *up* picture and one *down* picture and paste them on paper. Have them show the class which is *up* and which is *down*.

ON LEVEL

✓ ASSESS/CLOSE

Have children complete page 223 of the Pupil Edition or Practice Book. For a different approach to teaching this skill, see page T35 for the **Alternate Teaching Strategy.**

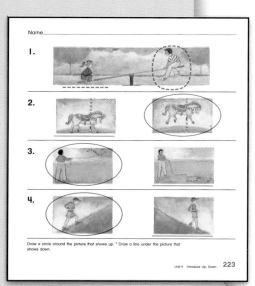

Pupil Edition page 223

#174 09-22-2009 1:50PM
Item(s) checked out to Buescher, Michell

TITLE: Macmillan/McGraw-Hill reading
BARCODE: 0005100010809
DUE DATE: 10-20-09

          Blackburn College
       (217) 854-3231, x4317

DAY 1

Up the Stairs

Materials: model drawing of a staircase

- ◆ Help children draw their own staircase.
- ◆ Have children use their fingers to walk up the steps. Ask them to use a sentence to explain what they are doing: *I am climbing up the steps.*
- ◆ Then, children use their fingers to climb down the steps.

EASY

It's a Bird!

Materials: drawing paper, pencils, crayons

- ◆ Invite children to draw a picture of an outdoor scene. Ask them to include things that could be *up* (*a bird, an airplane, a nest in a tree, a kite*) and *down* (*a bike, a car, flowers, a dog*).
- ◆ Ask children to describe their pictures using the words *up* and *down*.

CHALLENGE

Up and Down Rhyme

- ◆ Read aloud the nursery rhyme "Hickory, Dickory, Dock":
  Hickory, dickory, dock.
  The mouse ran up the clock.
  The clock struck one and down he came.
  Hickory, dickory, dock.
- ◆ Have children move their hands up and down to illustrate the story.

LANGUAGE SUPPORT

223

Listen

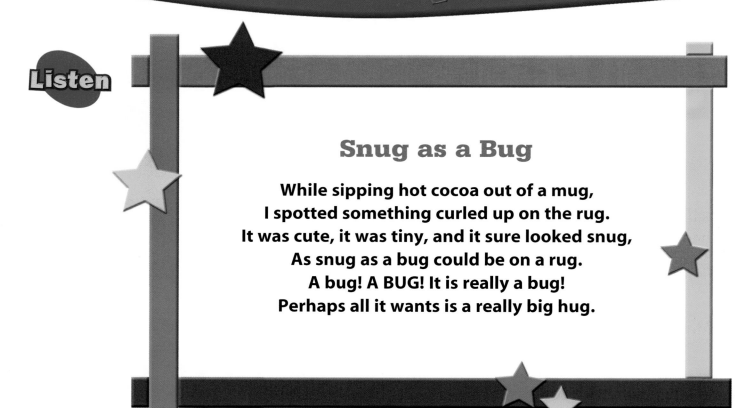

Snug as a Bug

While sipping hot cocoa out of a mug,
I spotted something curled up on the rug.
It was cute, it was tiny, and it sure looked snug,
As snug as a bug could be on a rug.
A bug! A BUG! It is really a bug!
Perhaps all it wants is a really big hug.

Big Book of Phonics Rhymes and Poems, page 53

Segment Syllables

Phonological Awareness

Teach Chant "Snug as a Bug" and have children chant with you. Then have children count the number of syllables they hear in some words from the poem.

MODEL: Listen to these words, *tiny* and *cocoa*. Close your eyes, and I'll say them again. This time, tap your nose for each syllable you hear. Did everyone tap twice for both words?

Practice Play "Mother May I?" Show the picture cards one at a time. Children should name the picture, count the syllables, and move forward that many steps. If they are wrong, they should take a step backwards. If children need help counting syllables, encourage them to tap their noses.

MATERIALS
• Phonics Picture Cards

Listen for Middle Sounds

Teach   Use the puppet to emphasize and hold the short /u/ sound in bug; for example, /b/ - /uuuuuuu/ - /g/. Have the children repeat after you. Do the same with another word from the poem such as *rug* or *mug*.

Practice   Have each child use his or her hand as a puppet. Slowly call out a set of words. Ask the class to repeat the words that have the sound /u/ in the middle, using their hand as a puppet. Use the words *fun, tug, sat, hum, lid,* and *tub*.

MATERIALS
- **puppet**

INFORMAL ASSESSMENT   Observe children as they count the number of syllables in a word and identify middle sounds. If children have difficulty, see Alternate Teaching Strategies: Unit 1, T24; and Unit 4, T33.

 **Read Together**

From Phonemic Awareness to Phonics

Objective: Identify /u/*u*

IDENTIFY THE LETTER FOR THE SOUND
- Explain to children that the letter *u* stands for the sound /u/. Invite children to say the sound with you.

- Display the Big Book of Phonics Rhymes and Poems, page 53. Point to the letters in the upper right corner and identify them. Have children say the sound /u/ with you.

REREAD THE POEM
- Reread the poem. Frame each word that has a medial *u*, and emphasize the /u/ sound. Have children say the words with you.

FIND WORDS WITH /u/
- Make word cards for words in the poem with medial *u*: *mug, rug, snug, bug, hug.* Invite volunteers to find the words in the poem. Read them together.

| snug | bug |
| mug | rug |

Snug as a Bug   Uu

While sipping hot cocoa
Out of a mug,
I spotted something
Curled up on the rug.
It was cute, it was tiny,
And it sure looked snug,
As snug as a bug
Could be on a rug.
A bug! A BUG!
It is really a bug!
Perhaps all it wants
Is a really big hug.

53

Big Book of Phonics Rhymes and Poems, page 53

224B

Medial /u/ u

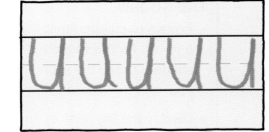

_u_

sun

Phonics Picture Posters and Cards

OBJECTIVES
Children will:
- ☑ identify the letter *U, u*
- ☑ identify /u/ *u*
- ☑ form the letter *U, u*

MATERIALS
- letter cards
- Phonics Picture Posters

ADDITIONAL RESOURCES
- Practice Book, page 224
- Phonics/Phonemic Awareness Practice Book, pages 119–120
- **Phonics** CD-ROM

TEACHING TIP
INSTRUCTIONAL Reread "Snug as a Bug" from the Big Book of Phonics Rhymes and Poems. Give each child a paper cup and marbles. Have them place a marble in the cup each time they hear you say a word with medial /u/.

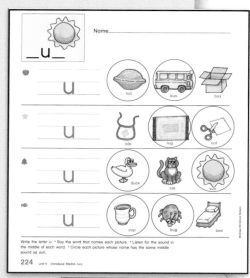

Pupil Edition page 224

224C *Mud Fun*

Introduce

TEACH

Phonemic Awareness Warm-Up Tell children the words *sun* and *run* rhyme because they have the same ending sound *–un*. Have children hold up their arms to make a circle over their heads when they hear you say a word that rhymes with *sun*. Say these words: *fun, man, bun, cat, him, won* and *pun*.

Identify /u/ *U, u* Display the Phonics Picture Poster for *sun*. Point to the letter *u* and explain that *u* stands for the /u/ sound. Have children repeat the /u/ sound after you.

Form *U, u* Review how to form the letters *Uu* with children. Have them practice writing the letters with their finger on the desk. Distribute sheets of paper and have children draw pictures of things that have the medial /u/ sound. Have children label their pictures _u_.

PRACTICE

Where is the *U*?

- ◆ Ask children to answer each question with a word that has /u/ *u* in the middle. For example: *What do you do with scissors? (cut) What shines in the sky? (sun) What do you drink hot chocolate from? (cup or mug)*
- ◆ For each answer, have children say the /u/ sound and write *u*.

ON LEVEL

✓ ASSESS/CLOSE

Have children complete page 224 of the Pupil Edition or the Practice Book. For a different approach to this skill, see page T34 for the **Alternate Teaching Strategy.**

Meeting Individual Needs
Activities

What Is Fun?

Materials: drawing paper, crayons

◆ Ask children to draw a picture of something that is fun to do.

◆ Children can label their pictures with *u* and say the word *fun* when they are finished.

◆ Invite children to talk about their pictures with a partner.

EASY

Color the *u* Word

Materials: drawing paper, crayons

◆ Ask children to pick an object that has *u* in the middle of its name and draw its picture.

◆ When they are finished, children should write the letter *u* under the picture and name the object.

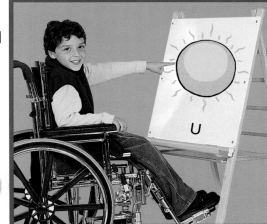

CHALLENGE

Listen to Learn!

Materials: objects or pictures whose names have a medial *u* sound

◆ Display objects or pictures whose names include a medial *u*. *(duck, cup, bug)*

◆ Point to each object, say its name, have children say /u/, and repeat the word.

◆ Write the words on the board. Then have children draw a line under the *u* in each word and trace *u* in the air.

LANGUAGE SUPPORT

Big Book

Build Background

Fingerplay Share the following fingerplay with the children.

Beehive

Here is the beehive, where are the bees? *(Hold out a fist.)*
Hidden away where nobody sees! *(Look at your fist.)*
Here they come creeping out of the hive, *(Open fist gradually.)*
One, two, three, four, five, ZOOM, ZOOM, ZOOM, see they're alive! *(Flutter fingers)*

Develop Oral Language After children perform the fingerplay, display a copy of "Nature Spy." Ask children to recall some of the things that the girl sees in the story.

Read the Big Book

Set Purposes MODEL: We know that this story is mainly about a girl who looks closely at nature. When we read the story today, let's find out more about the animals in the story.

Reread the Story As you read the story, track the print. *Concepts of Print*

Reread pages 8–9. Point to the comma on page 8, and note the period on page 9. Explain that this sentence does not end on one page, but carries over the two pages. *Concepts of Print*

OBJECTIVES

Children will:
- ☐ distinguish between real and make-believe
- ☑ compare and contrast
- ☐ listen responsively to a story.
- ☐ develop vocabulary to describe things

LANGUAGE SUPPORT

ESL Use illustrations in the book to review words that describe color, position, and size. Ask questions such as: *What color are the lily pads? Are corn kernels big or small?*

or the golden eye of a frog.

16

Nature Spy, pages 16–17

Literature Response

LISTENING/SPEAKING

Ask the children to name some of the animals in the story. Ask them to describe what the animals look like. Encourage children to assist each other with the vocabulary needed to describe things accurately.

Discuss the Story What covers the dog's body? (The dog's body is covered with fur.)
Literal: Story Details

Ask children to look at the three photographs of the frog. *How does the frog look the same and different in the photographs?* (Answers will vary.) *Inferential: Compare and Contrast*

MODEL: When I look at the pictures, I notice that I can see more details in the frog's eye in the third picture than I can in the first picture.

Look at the animals in the story. Which would make a good pet? Why? (Answers will vary.) *Critical Thinking*

Do you think the book tells about things that are real or things that are make-believe? (It tells about things that are real.)
Tell one reason why you think so. (Answers will vary.)

I notice the feathers of a bird.
14

Nature Spy, page 14

TEACHING TIP

INSTRUCTIONAL Collect books and other easy references on the five senses and place them in the Learning Center library. Invite children to select materials to read or look at for pleasure.

Writing

JOURNAL WRITING Ask children to choose an animal from the story and draw a picture of it. Have them write a sentence that describes the animal, such as: The frog is <u>green</u>. The spider is <u>small</u>.

The spider is small.

ASSESSMENT

How to Assess
If a child is having difficulty with compare and contrast, use the skills lesson on page 225C.

Compare and Contrast

Nature Spy

Nature Spy

TESTED OBJECTIVES

Children will:

☑ compare and contrast information from a story

MATERIALS

• *Nature Spy*

TEACHING TIP

SCIENCE Show children how to use a magnifying glass properly, moving the glass away to enlarge the item that is being examined.

Review

TEACH

Compare and Contrast Display the cover of *Nature Spy* and ask children to recall the story. Turn to pages 18 and 19 and ask the children to identify and describe both pictures. Talk about how tree bark is different from a hornet's nest. Then discuss how are they the same. Then compare the seed and the rock.

PRACTICE

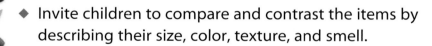

Alike and Different

Materials: leaves, pebbles, or flowers

◆ Display different leaves, pebbles, or flowers.

◆ Invite children to compare and contrast the items by describing their size, color, texture, and smell.

◆ Record their observations on the chalkboard under the headings *Same* and *Different*.

ON LEVEL

✓ ASSESS/CLOSE

Have children complete page 225 of the Pupil Edition or the Practice Book. For a different approach to this skill, see page T30 for the **Alternate Teaching Strategy.**

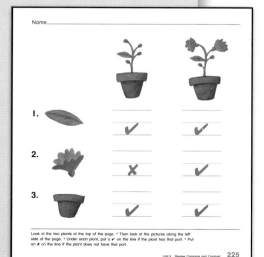

Name _____

1.	✓	✓
2.	✗	✓
3.	✓	✓

Look at the two plants at the top of the page. • Then look at the pictures along the left side of the page. • Under each plant, put a ✓ on the line if the plant has that part. • Put an ✗ on the line if the plant does not have that part.

Unit 4 Review Compare and Contrast 225

Pupil Edition page 225

Meeting Individual Needs
Activities

All About Animals

Materials: pictures of animals

◆ Display pictures of animals from nature books or magazines.

◆ Invite children to select two pictures of animals.

◆ Have children explain how the animals are the same and different.

EASY

Same and Different Drawings

Materials: pictures of plants and animals, drawing paper, crayons

◆ Have children fold their paper in half.

◆ Have them choose a plant or animal and draw it on one half of the paper.

◆ Then have them draw the same plant or animal on the other half using different colors, sizes, shapes, etc.

◆ Ask children how their pictures are the same and different.

CHALLENGE

Up Close and Far Away

Materials: magnifying glass, leaves, flowers, marbles

◆ Encourage children to select one of the objects, look at it in their hand, and then study it more closely with a magnifying glass.

◆ Encourage children to tell you how the object looks the same and different.

LANGUAGE SUPPORT

Listen

Snug as a Bug
a poem

While sipping hot cocoa
Out of a mug,
I spotted something
Curled up on the rug.
It was cute, it was tiny,
And it sure looked snug,
As snug as a bug
Could be on a rug.
A bug! A BUG!
It is really a bug!
Perhaps all it wants
Is a really big hug.

Umbrellas
a poem

Under my umbrella-top,
Splashing through the town,
I wonder why the tulips
Hold umbrellas
Up-side-down!

Barbara Juster Esbensen

Big Book of Phonics Rhymes and Poems, pages 53, 52

Delete Syllables

Phonological Awareness

Teach Read the poems. Have the children count the syllables in the words *tulips* and *splashing*. Then take away one of the syllables and have the children count again. Follow the model below.

MODEL: How many syllables does the word *tulips* have? *(two)* If I take away the beginning sound /tū/, what word is left? *(lips)* How many syllables does this word have? *(one)*

Practice Call out a word from the box. Ask children to count the syllables in the word. Then remove a syllable from the word, and ask children to say the part of the word that is left.

| freezer | firefly | hamster | computer |
| firefighter | flashlight | frightening | umbrella |

flash light

two

Listen for Beginning and Middle Sounds · · · · · · · ·

Teach Display a Word Building Box with three sections. Say the word /b/ - /u/ - /g/. Touch the first, middle, and last blocks on the Word Building Box as you say the individual sounds. Ask children whether they hear /b/ at the beginning or in the middle of the word. *(beginning)* Point to the first box. Then ask whether they hear the /u/ sound at the beginning or in the middle. *(middle)* Point to the middle box.

Practice Children should have their Word Building Boxes in front of them. Use these words: *cut, gum, hug, hum, run, duck.* After each word, ask about the beginning and medial sounds. To answer, children should point to the correct box.

MATERIALS
- **Word Building Boxes from** *Word Building Cards*

· ·

**INFORMAL ASSESSMENT** Observe children as they delete syllables and discriminate beginning and middle sounds. If children have difficulty, see Alternate Teaching Strategies on T22 and T33.

Read Together

From Phonemic Awareness to Phonics

Objective: Identify /u/ U, u

IDENTIFY THE LETTERS
Display the Big Book of Phonics Rhymes and Poems, pages 52 and 53. Point to the letters as you identify them. Tell children that the letters *U* and *u* stand for the /u/ sound.

REREAD THE POEMS Reread the poems. Point to each word, emphasizing those with /u/.

FIND WORDS WITH U, u Have children find words with *U* or *u* in the poems. Provide them with self-stick dots to place under the words.

Uu **Umbrellas**

Under my umbrella-top,
Splashing through the town,
I wonder why the tulips
Hold umbrellas
Up-side-down!

Barbara Juster Esbensen

Snug as a Bug Uu

While sipping hot cocoa
Out of a mug,
I spotted something
Curled up on the rug.
It was cute, it was tiny,
And it sure looked snug,
As snug as a bug
Could be on a rug.
A bug! A BUG!
It is really a bug!
Perhaps all it wants
Is a really big hug.

52   53

Big Book of Phonics Rhymes and Poems, pages 52, 53

226B

/u/ u

Phonics Picture Posters and Cards

OBJECTIVES

Children will:

- ☑ identify /u/ *U, u*
- ☑ discriminate between initial and medial *u*
- ☑ write and use letters *U, u*

MATERIALS

- letter cards
- Phonics Picture Posters

ADDITIONAL RESOURCES

- Practice Book, page 226
- Phonics/Phonemic Awareness Practice Book, pages 117–120
- **Phonics** CD-ROM

TEACHING TIP

DISCRIMINATE SOUNDS

Create a picture wall of initial and medial /u/ *u* words. Have children draw pictures or cut them from magazines, and post them on the wall with word cards.

Review

TEACH

Phonemic Awareness Warm-Up Remind children that the /u/ sound can be at the beginning or middle of words. Have children put their thumbs up if they hear the /u/ sound in the following words: *up, cat, pup, bun, under, button, pal, truck, seal, cow, fun.*

Identify and Discriminate Between Initial and Medial /u/ *U, u* Display the Phonics Picture Poster for *Uu.* Have children name the picture and say /u/ with you. Write __u__ on one part of the chalkboard and *u*__ on another part. Say the following words and ask children to point to the part of the chalkboard that shows the position of /u/ in each word: *sun; up; Gus; pup; run; uncle.*

Form *U, u* Display letter cards for *U* and *u* and review the capital and lowercase forms with children. Have children fold a sheet of paper in half and copy the headings from the chalkboard: __u__ and *u*__. Then have them draw a picture of something that has each sound.

PRACTICE

Placing the /u/ Sound

- ◆ Have children fold a piece of paper and write __u__ and *u*__ as the column heads.
- ◆ Show pictures of these objects and have children name the words as a group: *mud, umbrella, up (arrow), cup,* and *nut.*
- ◆ Have children draw one of these objects below each heading.

ON LEVEL

✓ ASSESS/CLOSE

Have children complete page 226 of the Pupil Edition or the Practice Book. For a different approach to this skill, see page T34 for the **Alternate Teaching Strategy.**

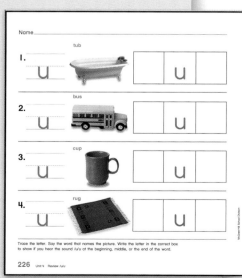

Name ___

1. tub | u | | u |
2. bus | u | | u |
3. cup | u | | u |
4. rug | u | | u |

Trace the letter. Say the word that names the picture. Write the letter in the correct box to show if you hear the sound /u/ at the beginning, middle, or end of the word.

226 Unit 4 Review /u/

Meeting Individual Needs
Activities

Short *u* Mobiles

Materials: hangers, paper clips, index cards, crayons or markers

◆ Have children write __u__ and u__ on index cards.

◆ Then have children draw pictures for initial and medial /u/ on index cards.

◆ Make a *Uu* mobile by hooking the __u__ card and its drawings onto a hanger with paper clips. Have children repeat for u__.

EASY

_u_

Riddle Me!

Materials: tape recorder, blank tape, drawing paper, crayons or markers

◆ Tell children to make up riddles for /u/ *u* words, such as: *This word has /u/ in the middle. It means "to move very fast." (run)*

◆ Have partners create riddles and record them. Children can draw a picture to show the answer.

◆ Have children listen to the tapes and guess other children's riddles.

CHALLENGE

Choose a Word

Materials: picture cards for /u/ *u* words

◆ Put out pairs of picture cards for /u/ *u* words. Say one of the words and have volunteers point to the picture that shows that word. Have children tell if the /u/ sound is at the beginning or in the middle of the word.

◆ Have children tell or show what the word means.

◆ Repeat for other pairs of pictures.

LANGUAGE SUPPORT

u

Listen

How Many Spots Does a Leopard Have?

an African folk tale retold by Julius Lester

One morning Leopard was doing what he enjoyed doing most. He was looking at his reflection in the lake. How handsome he was! How magnificent was his coat! And, ah! The spots on his coat! Was there anything in creation more superb?

Leopard's rapture was broken when the water in the lake began moving. Suddenly Crocodile's ugly head appeared above the surface.

Leopard jumped back. Not that he was afraid. Crocodile would not bother him. But then again, one could never be too sure about Crocodile.

"Good morning, Leopard," Crocodile said. "Looking at yourself again, I see. You are the most vain creature in all of creation."

Leopard was not embarrassed. "If you were as handsome as I am, if you had such beautiful spots, you, too, would be vain."

"Spots! Who needs spots? You're probably so in love with your spots that you spend all your time counting them."

Continued on page T4

Oral Comprehension

LISTENING AND SPEAKING Use these questions to encourage children to respond to the folk tale. Remind children to be polite and listen quietly when others are speaking.

• Why does Leopard look at his reflection in the lake? (He thinks he is very handsome and likes to look at himself.)

• Why does Leopard want to count his spots? (Leopard thinks his spots are so beautiful that he wants to know exactly how many he has.)

• Which animal wins the prize for counting Leopard's spots? How many spots does the animal say Leopard has? (Rabbit wins. He says Leopard has two spots—the dark spots and the light spots.)

• Do you think Rabbit counted correctly? (Possible answer: Rabbit counted the number of kinds of spots. There are many ways the spots can be counted.)

Activity Help children to make a class chart that shows how some animals are alike and different. Create headings such as *two legs, four legs, fur, feathers, flies,* and *runs.* Ask children to cut out magazine pictures of animals and sort them into the proper sections of the chart.

▶**Logical/Spatial**

Reading for Information

Help the leopard cub
find its way to its mother!

Reading for Information Big Book, pages 30–31

Objective: Read a Map

DISCUSS THE BIG BOOK Talk with children about leopards. Remind them that the main character in the story "How Many Spots Does a Leopard Have?" is a leopard.

- Turn to pages 30 and 31 in the Big Book and show children the map of Africa. Explain to children that a map indicates the best way to get from one point to another.

- Read aloud the statement on page 31. Look at the pictures and discuss the map.

- Ask: *What is the best route for the leopard cub to take to get to his mother? What animals will the leopard cub pass while traveling to his mother?* (The cub will pass the zebras, the crocodile, and the hippo.) *Will the leopard cub pass by any trees?* (no)

CULTURAL PERSPECTIVES

COUNTING People have used different methods for adding through the years. Long ago, people used sticks and rocks to add. Others dug marks into clay tablets or on cave walls to keep count of objects. In China and the Middle East, people used an abacus. Today, people use paper and pencil, a calculator, or a computer.

Activity Provide beans, an abacus, counting cubes, blocks, a calculator, and paper. Invite children to experiment with different methods of counting beans. Ask them to draw and write about their favorite counting tool.

▶ **Mathematical/Spatial**

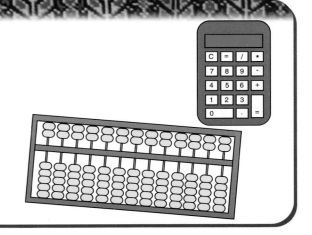

Vocabulary: *do*

do

Vocabulary Cards

OBJECTIVES

Children will:
- ☑ identify and read the vocabulary word *do*

MATERIALS
- word cards
- pocket chart

TEACHING TIP

WORD WALL Add the word *do* to the Word Wall. Have children make their own word card for *do*. Then have them search through books to find at least one example of the word.

Introduce

TEACH

Introduce *do* Write the following sentences on the chalkboard: *How do you do? What do you do?* Read them aloud with children several times, emphasizing the word *do*.

Put word cards in a pocket chart, and practice reading them aloud with children. Give each child a *do* word card. Role-play asking and answering the questions; for example: *How do you do? I am fine. What do you do? I am a student.* Have children hold up the *do* cards each time the word is said.

PRACTICE

Simon Says

Materials: *do* word card

- ◆ Use *do* when giving commands. (*Simon says do a spin*).
- ◆ Children respond by holding up their card and doing the action.
- ◆ For commands that do not include the words *Simon says*, don't use the word *do* (*Spin around*).

ON LEVEL

✓ ASSESS/CLOSE

Have children complete page 227 of the Pupil Edition or Practice Book. For a different approach to teaching this skill, see page T26 for the **Alternate Teaching Strategy.**

Name _____   do

1. <u>Do</u> you have a cat?

2. I <u>do</u> not have a cat.

3. <u>Do</u> you have a pup?

4. I <u>do</u> have a tan pup!

Read the sentence. • Draw a line under the word *do* in the sentence.

Unit 4 Introduce High-Frequency Words: *do*   **227**

Pupil Edition page 227

Meeting Individual Needs
Activities

Collage

Materials: magazines, scissors, glue or paste, art paper

◆ Have children, working in pairs, look through the magazines for the word *do*.

◆ Have them cut out the words and paste several of them onto the paper to make a collage.

EASY

Count the *Dos*

◆ Write the following words on chart paper or the chalkboard: *do, to, does, do, go, dot, do, did, do, so, do, do, go.*

◆ Have children come up and circle the word *do* each time it appears.

◆ Have them count how many times the word appears and write the number.

CHALLENGE

Answer Questions

◆ Help children practice using *do* orally in questions and statements.

◆ First, ask something that is true, and encourage children to answer it using the word *do*. For example: *Do you have a pencil? Yes, I do.*

◆ Give children word cards for *do* and have them hold them up each time they hear the word *do*.

LANGUAGE SUPPORT

Listen

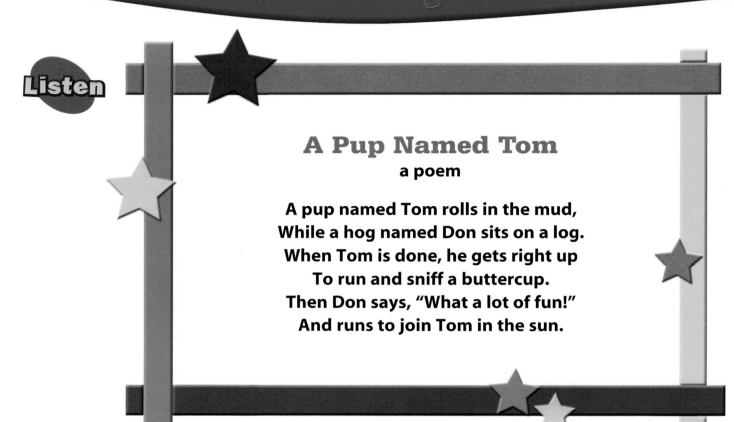

A Pup Named Tom
a poem

A pup named Tom rolls in the mud,
While a hog named Don sits on a log.
When Tom is done, he gets right up
To run and sniff a buttercup.
Then Don says, "What a lot of fun!"
And runs to join Tom in the sun.

Blend Sounds · · · · · · · · · · · · · · Phonemic Awareness · · · · · · · · ·

/p/   /u/   /p/

Teach Read "A Pup Named Tom." Finish by repeating the word *mud*. Draw out the phonemes so that the children can hear all three: /m/-/u/-/d/. Tell children the word *mud* has three sounds: /m/-/u/-/d/. Have children say the sounds with you.

Practice Have three children stand. Have the first child say /p/. Tell the second child to say /u/ and the third child to say /p/. As you touch the children, have them say their assigned phonemes. Repeat a little faster, until they've blended the sounds to form the word, *pup*. Repeat with the following words.

| fog | tip | mud | fig |
| log | fin | fan | leg |

Segment Sounds

Teach Say the word *Don*. Place a cube on the table as you say /d/. Place a second cube down as you say /o/. Place a third cube down as you say /n/. Explain that each cube stands for one sound in the word.

Practice Have children set out colored cubes for each sound they hear in these words: /h/ - /u/ - /g/, hug; /m/ - /u/ - /t/, mutt; /f/ - /u/ - /n/, fun; and /s/ - /u/ - /n/, sun. For each word ask how many sounds children hear and what the sounds are.

MATERIALS
- colored cubes

A̲SSESSMENT Observe children as they blend phonemes to make words and segment sounds. If children have difficulty, see Alternate Teaching Strategies on T31 and T33.

Read Together

From Phonemic Awareness to Phonics

Objective: Identify Word Endings

LISTEN FOR RHYMING WORDS Read the last two lines of "A Pup Named Tom," emphasizing the rhyming words at the end of each line. Write the words on an overhead projector transparency.

fun sun

IDENTIFY THE LETTERS Invite a volunteer to place rubber bands around the letters that are the same in each word. *(un)* Identify the letters, and ask children to say the sounds these letters stand for.

"RUBBER BAND" OTHER WORDS Ask children to name other words that rhyme with *fun* and *sun*. Add the rhyming words that end in *-un* to the overhead. Use new rubber bands to encircle *un* in these words. Invite children to repeat each word after you say it.

bun spun run

Short u
Blending

TESTED

OBJECTIVES

Children will:
- ☑ identify /u/ *u*
- ☑ blend and read short *u* words
- ☑ write short *u* words

MATERIALS
- letter cards

ADDITIONAL RESOURCES
- Practice Book, page 228
- Phonics/Phonemic Awareness Practice Book, pages 121–122
- 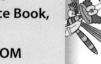 **Phonics** CD-ROM

TEACHING TIP

WORD FAMILIES Make cards for the ending letters: –*ut*, –*up*, –*ud*, and –*un*. Make cards for the beginning letters: *c, f, m, n, p,* and *s*. Have small groups match beginning and ending letters to make words.

Name_____

1. s u n | sun | ☀

2. c u p | cup | 🥣

3. n u t | nut | 🥜

4. p u p | pup | 🐶

Blend the sounds and write the word. Say the word that names each picture.

228 Unit 4 Introduce Blending with Short u

Introduce

TEACH

Model Blending with Short u Display the *u* letter card and say /u/. Have children repeat the sound /u/ as you point to the *u* card.

Place the *n* card to the right of the *u* card. Point to each letter as you blend the sounds together and have children repeat after you: *un*.

u n   u n

Place the *f* card to the left of *un* to show *fun*. Point to the cards as you blend to read *fun*, and have children repeat after you.

f u n   f u n

Continue modeling and guided practice using *cup, mud, nut, run, sun,* and *pup*.

PRACTICE

Choose a Word

Materials: letter cards for *c, d, f, m, n, p, r, s, t, u*

- ◆ Give each child a letter card. Say the word *sun*. Have children holding the letters that make the word go to the front of the room, arrange themselves in order to make the word, and then say the word as you track the print on their cards.
- ◆ Repeat for other /u/ *u* words.

ON LEVEL

✓ ASSESS/CLOSE

Have children complete page 228 of the Pupil Edition or the Practice Book. For a different approach to this skill, see page T34 for the **Alternate Teaching Strategy.**

Meeting Individual Needs
Activities

Match a Word

Materials: picture cards for /u/ *u* words such as *mud, run, cup, nut,* and *up*

- ◆ Divide paper into four sections. Write one /u/ *u* word from the picture cards per section.

- ◆ Give children four /u/ *u* picture cards.

- ◆ Have them blend the sounds to read each word and find the picture that matches it by placing it over the word.

EASY

List Your Words

Materials: letter cards *c, d, f, m, n, p, r, s, t, u*

- ◆ Have children fold a piece of paper in half. At the top of columns have them write __*u*__ and *u*__.

- ◆ Have partners use the letter cards to make as many /u/ *u* words as they can. Have them list the words in the correct column.

CHALLENGE

Short u Concentration

Materials: word cards and picture cards for medial /u/u words

- ◆ Display each picture card. Say each word and have children repeat. Ask volunteers to tell what each word means.

- ◆ Show each word card. Help children blend the sounds and match each to its picture.

- ◆ Have partners use the cards to play concentration. To keep a match, children must blend the sounds.

LANGUAGE SUPPORT

Read the Story

☑ **Medial /u/ u, Blending with /u/ u**

☑ **High-Frequency Word:** *do*

☑ **Compare and Contrast**

☐ **Concepts of Print**

PREVIEW AND PREDICT

Have children look at the cover and read the title. Ask if they see any mud in the picture and who they think will have fun with it. Then take a picture walk through the first few pages.

Mud Fun

SET PURPOSES

Discuss with children what they want to find out as they read. Ask *Do you think it would be fun to play in the mud?*

AS YOU READ

Remind children to track print as they read the story. Point out the question mark when it appears, and explain that it shows that someone is asking a question. Then use these prompts:

- **Page 2** Before reading the page, ask children to point to the word *do*. *High-Frequency Words*

- **Pages 5 and 7** Have children compare the pictures of the little girl on pages 5 and 7. *Compare and Contrast*

- **Page 7** Ask children to find a word on the page that has the sound /u/. Have children blend the word. *Medial u, Blending with u*

- **Page 8** If children have difficulty reading the word *fun,* remind them to look at the first letter to help them. *Graphophonic Cues*

Nan, do you have a pot?

2

You can have a pot, Pam.

3

Pupil Edition pp. 229–230

Nan, do you have a cup?

4

You can have a cup, Pam.

5

LANGUAGE SUPPORT

ESL Develop story vocabulary by playing the following game with children. Give each child a small object, such as a toy. Have children ask each other questions using the following sentence frame: *Do you have a (name of object)?* Encourage each child to answer using the following sentence frame: *Yes, I have a (name of object).*

You sat in the mud!

6

I did sit in the mud.

7

Mud is fun, fun, fun!

8

Cross Curricular: Science

PLANTING IN MUD Mud is made when rain mixes with the soil. As a class, plant seeds in muddy, dry, and moist soil. Observe the plants once a week, and draw illustrations to record plant growth. After a few weeks, discuss which type of soil is best for plant growth.

▶ **Visual/Logical**

 inter NET **CONNECTION** Help children log on to **www.mhschool.com/reading,** where they can learn more about flower gardens.

Read the Story

4

RETURN TO PREDICTIONS

Ask children to remember the beginning of the story and their predictions. Did children predict that the two girls would be playing in the mud?

RETELL THE STORY

Guide children to retell the story by asking the following questions: *What did the little girl want first?* (a pot) *What did she want next?* (a cup) *What did she do next?* (play in the mud) *What happened at the end of the story?* (Both girls played together.)

WRITING

Journal Writing Have children write a sentence about playing in the mud in their journal. Invite children to illustrate their sentence, as well.

HIGH-FREQUENCY WORDS

HOW TO ASSESS Ask children to read pages 2–4 and then point to the word *do* wherever it appears on the pages.

FOLLOW UP Add the word *do* to your Word Wall. Ask children to make up questions that begin with the word.

Compare and Contrast

Mud Fun

OBJECTIVES

Children will:
☑ compare and contrast to understand a story

MATERIALS

- *Mud Fun*

TEACHING TIP

INSTRUCTIONAL Display pairs of picture cards of plants, animals, and people. Ask children to identify what is the same and different in various picture pairs. Have them use words such as *same, different,* and *alike*.

Review

TEACH

Compare and Contrast Story Characters Display the cover of *Mud Fun* and ask children to recall the story. Read pages 2–3 and ask how Pam and Nan are alike and how they are different. Repeat the comparing and contrasting process as you continue to read the story.

PRACTICE

How to Build Castles

- ◆ Display blocks, boxes, and sand. Point out that all these materials can be used to make castles.

- ◆ Ask children to name other materials they might use to build castles. *(clay, craft sticks)*

- ◆ Have children compare and contrast the different materials.

ON LEVEL

ASSESS/CLOSE

Have children complete page 231 of the Pupil Edition or the Practice Book. For a different approach to this skill, see page T30 for the **Alternate Teaching Strategy.**

Name

1.
2.
3.

Look at the two snails at the top of the page. • Then look at the pictures along the left side of the page. • Under each snail, put a ✔ on the line if the snail has that part. • Put an ✗ on the line if the snail does not have that part.

Unit 9   Review Compare and Contrast   231

Pupil Edition page 231

Meeting Individual Needs
Activities

The Same and Different

Materials: pairs of different blocks, toy trucks, stuffed animals

◆ Have pairs of children choose the two blocks, trucks, or animals.

◆ Have children describe how the two items are the same and how they are different.

EASY

Make Your Own Castle

Materials: pictures of castles, modeling clay

◆ Display pictures of sand, clay, or mud castles.

◆ Have pairs of children use modeling clay to make a castle.

◆ Then have children describe the ways their castles are the same and ways they are different.

CHALLENGE

Same and Different

Materials: kitchen utensils, such as different-sized pots, lids, measuring cups, bowls

◆ Display the kitchen utensils in class.

◆ Discuss the purpose of each. Encourage children to contribute to the discussion.

◆ Ask children to tell how two different utensils are the same and how they are different.

LANGUAGE SUPPORT

Phonological
Awareness

Listen

A Pup Named Tom
a poem

A pup named Tom rolls in the mud,
While a hog named Don sits on a log.
When Tom is done, he gets right up
To run and sniff a buttercup.
Then Don says, "What a lot of fun!"
And runs to join Tom in the sun.

Blend Sounds

Phonemic Awareness

Teach   Chant "A Pup Named Tom" and have children chant along with you if they can. Then check to see if they hear all sounds in words.

MODEL: Listen to these sounds, /s/ - /u/ - /n/. I'll say them again. You hold up a finger for every sound you hear, /s/ - /u/ - /n/. How many fingers should you have up? *(three)* Now listen as I say the sounds faster and faster, /s/ - /u/ - /n/. What word do your hear? *(sun)*

Practice   Have the children say the words from the box with you. Ask them to put up their fingers to show they hear the phonemes. Say the sounds slowly the first time, repeat, and blend the sounds more quickly.

fed	hog	fun	pup
fib	mud	log	pig

Segment Sounds

Teach Put three pieces of construction paper on the floor in front of you, as if they are stepping stones. Then segment sounds out loud and take a step for every sound, /f/ - /u/ - /n/.

MATERIALS
- construction paper

Practice Have children put three pieces of construction paper in front of them. Be sure they understand the rules of the "Stepping-stone" game. Begin segmenting sounds so that everyone can hear. (These words will work well for the activity; *run, bug, fog, fad, dog, fig.*) Remind students to take a step each time they hear a new sound.

**ASSESSMENT** Observe children as they blend sounds to make words and segment sounds. If children have difficulty, see Alternate Teaching Strategies on T31 and T33.

Read Together

From Phonemic Awareness to Phonics

Objective: Associate Sounds with Letters

IDENTIFY LETTERS Encourage children to listen as you read the first line in the poem. Ask them to tell you which word is a name. *(Tom)* Then ask which word tells what you have when you add water to dirt. *(mud)* When children identify the words *Tom* and *mud*, write them on the chalkboard.

MAKE LETTER CARDS Point to the letters in each word, name them, and ask children what sound each letter represents. Make a set of six index cards for each child. Each set should include *T, o, m, m, u, d.*

PLAY "SIMON SAYS" Play a letter/sound version of "Simon Says," by giving directions such as the following:

Simon says, "Touch the first letter in the word *mud*."
Simon says, "Place the *d* on your head."
Simon says, "Place the letter that says /t/ on your foot."
Simon says, "Turn over the letter that says /o/."

PLAY "SIMON SAYS" WITH A PARTNER Divide the group into pairs. Have children take turns playing "Simon Says" with their partners, giving directions for identifying both letters and sounds.

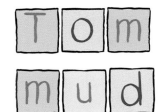

Short u, o
Blending

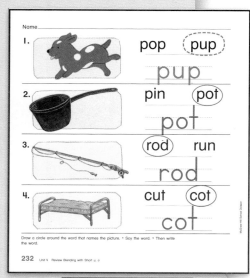

OBJECTIVES

Children will:
- ☑ identify /u/ *u*, /o/ *o*
- ☑ blend and read short *u* and *o* words
- ☑ write short *u* and *o* words

MATERIALS
- letter cards

ADDITIONAL RESOURCES
- Practice Book, page 232
- Phonics/Phonemic Awareness Practice Book, page 122
- **Phonics** CD-ROM

TEACHING TIP

WRITE WORDS On adding machine tape, write the endings –*ud*, –*un*, –*up*, and –*ut*. Have volunteers write the beginning sound next to the word endings. Say m<u>u</u>d, s<u>u</u>n, f<u>u</u>n, p<u>u</u>p, c<u>u</u>p, c<u>u</u>t, n<u>u</u>t, and r<u>u</u>t.

Review

TEACH

Model Blending with Short *u* and *o* Display the *u* letter card and say /u/. Have children repeat the /u/ sound as you point to the *u* card. Place the *t* card to the right of the *u* card. Point to each letter as you blend the sounds together and have children repeat after you: *ut*.

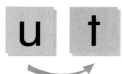

Place the *n* card to the left of *ut* to show *nut*. Point to the cards as you blend to read *nut*, and have children repeat after you.

Continue modeling and guided practice for short *u* and *o* using *sun, mop, pot, cut, mud, nod,* and *pup*.

PRACTICE

Take a Word

Materials: paper bag, slips of paper with short *u* and *o* words

- ◆ Put the slips of paper in the bag.
- ◆ Pass the bag around, and have each child take a slip of paper.
- ◆ Ask a volunteer to read the word and then use it in a sentence.

ON LEVEL

✓ ASSESS/CLOSE

Have children complete page 232 of the Pupil Edition or the Practice Book. For a different approach to this skill, see page T34 for the **Alternate Teaching Strategy.**

Pupil Edition page 232

Meeting Individual Needs
Activities

Sticky-Note Match

Materials: self-stick notes, picture cards for /u/ *u* and /o/ *o* words

◆ Prepare word notes by writing the name of each picture card on a self-stick note.

◆ Have children blend the sounds of each word and read the word aloud.

◆ Have children place each self-stick note on its picture.

EASY

Looks the Same

Materials: one letter card each for *u* and *o*, two letter cards each for *m, n, p,* and *t*

◆ Have children fold a piece of paper in half. At the top of the columns have them write __u__ and __o__.

◆ Have children make /u/ *u* and /o/ *o* words. Have them list the words in the correct column.

◆ Have them circle any words that use the same letter at the beginning and end of the word.

CHALLENGE

Show Me How You...

Materials: word cards for /u/*u* and /o/ *o* words

◆ Display the word cards. Track the print as children blend the sounds for each word. Have volunteers tell each meaning.

◆ Point to one card at a time, and give children directions to follow. For example, say: *Show me how you (use a fishing rod).*

LANGUAGE SUPPORT

Leveled Books

Meeting Individual Needs

EASY

Guided Reading

Pam and the Pup

McGraw Hill

OBJECTIVES

☑ Blend with Short *u*
☑ Compare and Contrast
☑ Vocabulary: *do*
☐ Concepts of Print

PREVIEW AND PREDICT Ask children to look at the cover illustration and predict what the story might be about. Point to each word as you read the title aloud. Then conduct a picture walk through the first few pages. Have children speculate why Pam called her pup Mop Top. Before reading, remind children to point to each word as they read it.

READ THE BOOK Use the following prompts to guide children's reading:

Page 2 Ask children to find the question mark. Have them practice reading the question aloud with the correct expression. *Concepts of Print*

Page 2 Have children find the word with the short *u*. Model how to blend the sounds: p-u-p; pup. *Phonics*

Page 7 Point to the word *do* on the page. *Let's read this word together:* do. *Vocabulary*

Page 8 *How does Mop Top look on this page compared to how he looks on page 3?* *Compare and Contrast*

LITERARY RESPONSE Ask children to draw pictures of what Pam and Mop Top might do next.

INDEPENDENT

Mud Fun

McGraw Hill

OBJECTIVES

☑ Blend with Short *u*
☑ Compare and Contrast
☑ Vocabulary: *do*
☐ Concepts of Print

REREAD THE BOOK FOR FLUENCY
Encourage children to reread the book alone or with a partner.

Page 2 Ask children to point to the word *do* on this page. *Vocabulary*

Guided Reading

Page 4 Ask children what kind of sentence is on this page. How can they tell? *Concepts of Print*

Page 6 *How do the girls look alike in this picture? How do they look different?* *Compare and Contrast*

Page 7 *Can you point to the word that has a short u sound? Let's blend the sounds: m-u-d; mud.* *Phonics*

LITERARY RESPONSE Ask children to draw something to make in the mud.

CHALLENGE

Fun on the Farm

by David Michaels
illustrated by Tuko Fujisake

Guided Reading

PREVIEW AND PREDICT Ask children to look at the cover illustration and predict what the story might be about. Read the title and author's and illustrator's names as you point to each word. Then conduct a picture walk through the first few pages.

READ THE BOOK Use the following prompts to guide children's reading:

Pages 2–3 *Point to the last word on each page. Let's read it together:* do. *Vocabulary*

Pages 4–5
How are the pigs and the sheep the same? How are they different? (They both live on the farm; The pigs are in the mud and the sheep are in the grass.) *Compare and Contrast*

Page 7 Ask children to point to the word with the short *u* sound. *Let's blend these sounds together:* s-u-n; sun. *Phonics*

Page 8 Ask children to point to the question marks in the story. *What word begins each of these sentences? Concepts of Print*

LITERARY RESPONSE Ask children to talk about what they would like to see and do at a farm. Have them draw a picture and share it with the class.

TESTED OBJECTIVES

☑ **Blend with Short *u***
☑ **Compare and Contrast**
☑ **Vocabulary:** *do*
☐ **Concepts of Print**

INFORMAL ASSESSMENT

BLENDING WITH SHORT *u*

HOW TO ASSESS Have children locate words in the stories containing short *u*. Ask them to blend the sounds to read the words.

FOLLOW UP Help children locate words containing short *u* by placing a small dot under those words. Help children blend the sounds to read the words.

CENTER Activity

Cross Curricular: Math

CATS OF A DIFFERENT COLOR Cut out small and large circular cat faces in red, green, blue, and yellow. Invite children to sort the cat faces by size and color. Encourage children to make their own color and size patterns.

▶ **Logical/Mathematical**

Vocabulary:
do, go, I, and, me

Vocabulary Cards

TESTED **OBJECTIVES**

Children will:
☑ identify and read the vocabulary words *do, go, I, and, me*

MATERIALS
- word cards

TEACHING TIP

WORD WALL Point to the words *and, do, go, me,* and *I* on the Word Wall. Have children give a clue about a word, such as: "The word rhymes with *no*." Another child identifies the word.

Review

TEACH

Review do, go, I, and, me Teach children this silly rhyme: *I like you./ Yes I do./Go with me./And hear cows moo.* Repeat the rhyme several times with children. Then pass out the word cards.

Read the rhyme aloud again, asking children to hold up the word cards as you say each high-frequency word. Ask them to say the words after you.

PRACTICE

Illustrate Words

◆ Write the rhyme from the Teach section on the chalkboard. Ask children to copy one of the lines from it.

◆ Have them circle the words *do, go, I, and, me.*

◆ Then have them draw an illustration for the rhyme.

ON LEVEL

✓ ASSESS/CLOSE

Have children complete page 233 of the Pupil Edition or Practice Book. For a different approach to teaching this skill, see Unit 4, page T26 and Unit 2, page T28 for the **Alternate Teaching Strategies.**

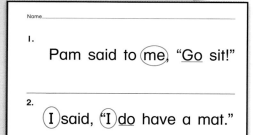

Name _____

1.
  Pam said to me, "Go sit!"

2.
  I said, "I do have a mat."

3.
  Pam and I do sit.

Read each sentence. 1. Draw a circle around the word me. Draw a line under the word go.
2. Draw a circle around the word I each time you see it. Draw a line under the word do.
3. Draw a circle around the word do. Draw a line under the word and.

Unit 4 Review do, go, I, and, me **233**

Pupil Edition page 233

233C *Mud Fun*

Meeting Individual Needs

Activities

What Do We Do?

Materials: drawing paper, crayons or markers

◆ Write the word *do* on the chalkboard and read it aloud with children.

◆ Ask questions about activities using the word *do*: *What do we do after snack? What do we do before we go home?*

◆ Invite children to illustrate an activity and label it with the word *do*.

EASY

Role Play

◆ Write the following rhyme on the chalkboard and read it aloud: *I go/To the zoo,/And you can come/With me, too./What will we do/At the zoo?*

◆ Have children repeat, emphasizing the words *do, go, I, me, and*.

◆ Working in pairs, have children act out something they might do at the zoo.

CHALLENGE

What Do You Like?

◆ Write the word *do* on chart paper and read it together.

◆ Ask questions such as: *Do you like to paint? Do you like to run?*

◆ Have children reply using sentence starters such as: *Yes, I do like to …* or *No, I do not like to …*

LANGUAGE SUPPORT

233

Interactive Writing

Write a Question

GRAMMAR/SPELLING CONNECTIONS
Model using the correct tense when asking and answering questions so that children will gain increasing control of grammar when speaking and writing.

TEACHING TIP
Ask children a few questions using different question words, such as: *Who is standing beside me? What is he doing? Why is he holding a pencil?* Write the questions on the chalkboard, and point out the question mark. Explain that all questions end with a question mark.

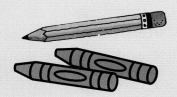

Prewrite

REVIEW THE STORY Help children recall the story *Nature Spy,* discussing the items shown in the book. Ask: *Which things in the book do you know quite a lot about? Which things do you know very little about?* Tell children that they are going to write a question about something in nature that they want to know more about.

BRAINSTORM Invite children to help you make a list of nature topics they are curious about. If necessary, prompt children by asking if they would like to learn more about specific things, such as the moon, rainbows, or volcanoes. Display several reference sources about nature for children to browse through as they generate ideas. Write children's topics on the chalkboard.

the moon
rainbows
volcanoes

Draft

WRITE A QUESTION Tell children that they are going to write a question about something in nature they have wondered about.

- On chart paper, write the title *We Want to Know!* and read the words with children, tracking the print.

- Call children's attention back to the chalkboard list and read it together as you track the print. Have each child think of a question about one of the topics on the list.

- Write the "5 Ws" of question words on the chalkboard and read them with children. (who, what, where, when, why) Explain that these are words that begin a question.

- Model writing a question on chart paper about one of the topics, such as *Why does the moon change its shape?* Point out the question word and the question mark. Explain that all questions begin with a capital letter and end with a question mark.

- Have each child dictate a question. Then provide each child with a piece of construction paper that has ruled write-on lines drawn on the bottom. Have each child copy their question from the chart paper.

- Invite children to illustrate their questions on the top part of their papers.

Revise

Before publishing the questions, read each child's question aloud as you track the print. Then ask:

- Does your question begin with a capital letter and end with a question mark?

- Does your picture match your question?

Publish

Display the questions on a nature bulletin board. Read them as a class. Track the print as the class reads each question.

Why do fish have scales?

Presentation Ideas

MAKE A CLASS BOOK Help children **GROUP** create a class book that includes all of their questions. Have volunteers make a cover with the title *We Want to Know!* Have children take turns reading the pages to the class.

DO RESEARCH Arrange a visit to the **GROUP** library, giving the librarian a list of the children's questions in advance. Ask the librarian to have ready several nature reference books, videos, laser disks, and CD-ROMs. Help children work together to find the answers to their questions. Arrange for classroom visits from "experts" to answer questions that cannot be answered during the library visit.

Listening and Speaking

- Model for children the proper voice inflection for asking a question. Have children practice with a classmate's question.

- Remind children to listen carefully and make eye contact as the librarian helps them find answers to their questions.

TECHNOLOGY TIP

Show children a variety of science web sites by logging on and taking a virtual tour. Preview and bookmark the web sites. This will not only save you time, but will also ensure that the content is age-appropriate.

LANGUAGE SUPPORT

ESL Provide speaking practice with the target vocabulary needed for this lesson by teaching children to play "I Spy." Give clues and have children guess an item of nature.

Meeting Individual Needs for Writing

EASY

Make Predictions Have children predict the answers to their questions. Then have them draw pictures or simple diagrams to show their predictions.

ON-LEVEL

Sort Nature Items Have children sort their question pictures into two categories: living and nonliving.

CHALLENGE

Question Quest Have children pick one nature topic and take turns thinking of as many questions as they can on that topic. Then have them write the questions in list form.

Week 5

Ron and Me

Phonics	Comprehension	Vocabulary
• Initial /r/r, /p/p, /l/l; Final /p/p • Blending	• Main Idea • Compare and Contrast	• to • me • go • do

Literature Resources

Big Books

Big Book of Phonics Rhymes and Poems
pages 32, 41, 42, 45

ABC Big Book
pages 235A–235B

Literature Big Book
pages 237A–237B

The Apple Pie Tree
by Zoe Hall
ILLUSTRATED BY Shari Halpern

Reading for Information Big Book
page 24

Reading for Information

Read Aloud

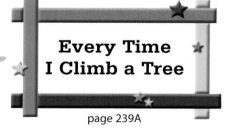

Every Time I Climb a Tree

page 239A

Student Books

ABC Little Book
pages 235A–235B

Allie's Adventure From A to Z

Easy
page 245A
Decodable

We Have Fun!

Independent
pages 241/242A–241/242B, 245A
Decodable
Story also available in Pupil Edition

Ron and Me

Challenge
page 245B
Patterned

Ron's Radishes
by Ray Tanner
illustrated by Andrea Wallace

Ron and Me

Center Activities

Activities take 15–20 minutes each.

Phonics

MATERIALS
- Letter cards for *Rr, Pp,* and *Ll*

Brainstorming Words

Objective: Identify words that begin with /r/, /p/, and /l/.

◆ Show one card at a time.

◆ Ask children to identify the letter and its phonemic sound.

◆ Ask children to think of a word that begins with this sound.

Writing

MATERIALS
- Construction paper
- Crayons

Make an *Rr* Book

Objective: Make a book of *Rr* letters and pictures.

◆ Staple together five pieces of paper. Cut it into the shape of a rabbit.

◆ Have children write *Rr* on each page and draw a picture of an object that begins with *r*.

Reading and Listening

Self-Selected Reading

Objective: Identify a book's cover, title, author/illustrator, and title page.

Place the literature for the week and the corresponding audiocassettes or CDs in the Reading Center. You may also include the following books from the Theme Bibliography on pages T54–T55.

◆ *A Pig Is Big* by Douglas Florian

◆ *When the Wind Stops* by Charlotte Zolotow

◆ *Zoo in the Sky: A Book of Animal Constellations* by Jacqueline Mitton

MATERIALS
- Listening Library cassettes and CDs
- Books

Science

Sun Spots

Objective: Find out what happens when the sun is blocked by an object.

◆ Have children place objects on construction paper, and put the paper in direct sunlight.

◆ Remove the objects at the end of the day.

◆ Have children circle the spots that are lighter than the others.

MATERIALS
- Dark construction paper
- Paper clips, erasers, and counting cubes

Social Studies

Map Time

Objective: Use spatial skills to label a map.

◆ Provide partners with a map of the classroom.

◆ Have them place and draw objects in the classroom.

◆ Have children share their maps.

MATERIALS
- Simple map of the classroom, one per pair of children
- Pencils

Working with Words

Word Hunting

Objective: Locate and count the number of times the words *to* and *me* appear in a book.

◆ Invite children to search a book for the words *to* and *me.*

◆ Have them mark the words with self-stick notes.

◆ Ask children to count how many times each word was used.

MATERIALS
- Various picture books
- Small self-stick notes

Ron and Me

Suggested Lesson Planner

💿 **Available on CD-ROM**

READING AND LANGUAGE ARTS

- Phonological Awareness
- Phonics review
- Comprehension
- Vocabulary
- Beginning Reading Concepts
- Listening, Speaking, Viewing, Representing

DAY 1

Allie's Adventure From A to Z
Written by Ellen Dreyer Illustrated by Jui Ishida

Focus on Reading Skills

Develop Phonological Awareness, 234I–234J
"R is for Ribbon" and "The Lazy Little Lion" *Big Book of Phonics Rhymes and Poems,* 32, 45

 **Review Initial /r/r, /p/p, /l/l,** 234K–234
- ◆ Practice Book, 234
- ◆ Phonics/Phonemic Awareness Practice Book, 123–124
- ◆ 💿 **Phonics** CD-ROM

Read the Literature

 **Read** *Allie's Adventure from A to Z* Big Book, 235A–235B
Shared Reading

Build Skills
- ☑ Positional Terms, 235C–235
- ◆ Practice Book, 235

DAY 2

The Apple Pie Tree
BY Zoe Hall
ILLUSTRATED BY Shari Halpern

Focus on Reading Skills

Develop Phonological Awareness, 236A–236B
"Chicken Soup" *Big Book of Phonics Rhymes and Poems,* 42

 **Review Final /p/p,** 236C–236
- ◆ Practice Book, 236
- ◆ Phonics/Phonemic Awareness Practice Book, 123–124
- ◆ 💿 **Phonics** CD-ROM

Read the Literature

Read *The Apple Pie Tree* Big Book, 237A–237B
Shared Reading

Build Skills
- ☑ Main Idea, 237C–237
- ◆ Practice Book, 237

- Cross Curriculum

◆ **Activity** Art, 235B

◆ **Activity** Science, Social Studies, 234F

- Writing

 Writing Prompt: Write your own story about a cat.

 Journal Writing, 235B
Letter Formation, 234K

 Writing Prompt: Write about a place in nature that you have been.

 Journal Writing, 237B
Letter Formation, 236C

DAY 3

Every Time I Climb a Tree

Focus on Reading Skills

Develop Phonological Awareness, 238A–238B
"The Lazy Little Lion" and "Pease Porridge Hot" *Big Book of Phonics Rhymes and Poems,* 32, 41
 **Review /r/r, /p/p, /l/l,** 238C–238
◆ Practice Book, 238
◆ Phonics/Phonemic Awareness Practice Book, 123–124
◆ **Phonics CD-ROM**

Read the Literature

Read "Every Time I Climb a Tree" Teacher Read Aloud, 239A–239B
Shared Reading
Read the Reading for Information Big Book, 24–25
Maps

Build Skills

☑ High-Frequency Words: *to, me, go, do,* 239C–239
◆ Practice Book, 239

Activity Social Studies, 239B

 Writing Prompt: Do you have a favorite place you like to visit? Write about it.

DAY 4

Ron and Me

Focus on Reading Skills

Develop Phonological Awareness, 240A–240B
"Making Mud Pies"
 **Review Blending with Short** *u,* 240C–240
◆ Practice Book, 240
◆ Phonics/Phonemic Awareness Practice Book, 125–126
◆ **Phonics CD-ROM**

Read the Literature

Read "Ron and Me" On-Level Decodable Story, 241/242A–241/242B

☑ Review *p, u;* Blending
☑ Compare and Contrast
☑ High-Frequency Words: *to, me, go, do*
Concepts of Print

Build Skills

☑ Compare and Contrast, ◆ 243A–243
Practice Book, 243

Activity Math, 241/242B

 Writing Prompt: Write about a time you made a mess

 Journal Writing, 241/242B
Letter Formation Practice Book, 241–242

DAY 5

We Have Fun!
Ron and Me
...on's Radishes
by Ray Tanner
illustrated by Andrea Wallace

Focus on Reading Skills

Develop Phonological Awareness, 244A–244B
"Making Mud Pies"
 **Review Blending with Short** *u, o, i,* 244C–244
◆ Practice Book, 244
◆ Phonics/Phonemic Awareness Practice Book, 125–126
◆ **Phonics CD-ROM**

Read the Literature

Read "We Have Fun!" Easy Decodable Story, 245A
Reread "Ron and Me" On-Level Decodable Story, 245A
Reread "Ron's Radishes" Challenge Patterned Book, 245B
Guided Reading
☑ Initial /r/ r; Blending
☑ Main Idea
☑ High-Frequency Word: *to*
Concepts of Print

Build Skills

☑ High-Frequency Words: *to, me, go, do,* 245C–245
◆ Practice Book, 245

Activity Science, 245B

 Writing Prompt: Draw a picture of something you like to wonder about.

Interactive Writing, 246A–246B

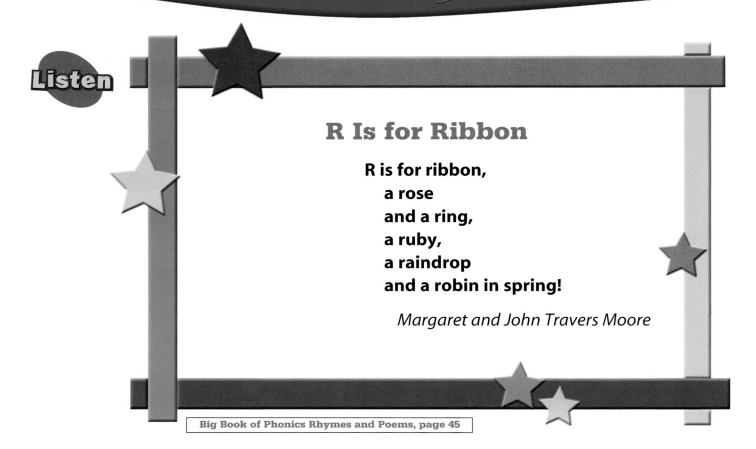

Listen

R Is for Ribbon

R is for ribbon,
   a rose
   and a ring,
   a ruby,
   a raindrop
   and a robin in spring!

Margaret and John Travers Moore

Big Book of Phonics Rhymes and Poems, page 45

Identify Rhyming Words

Phonological Awareness

Teach   Read "R Is for Ribbon" aloud and ask children to say the lines with you. Then say the words *ring* and *spring*. Tell children these words rhyme. Tell children that *sing, bring,* and *wing* also rhyme with *ring* and *spring*.

MODEL: Listen as I say *rose*. Does *nose* rhyme with *rose*? *(yes)* What about the word *run?* (no) *Rose* and *nose* rhyme because they end with the same sounds.

Practice   Place Picture Cards for *lamp* and *pig* as well as other pictures in a basket. Let children close their eyes to pick a picture. Have them think of words that rhyme with the picture they chose. Invite them to share the rhyming words with a partner.

lamp	pig	rake
rug	pan	leg

MATERIALS
- Phonics Pictures from *Word Building Cards*

Listen for Beginning Sounds

Teach Review these initial phonemic sounds: /r/, /l/, /i/, and /u/. Ask children if they remember words that begin with these phonemes. Each time a child offers a word, repeat it and stress the sound of the initial phoneme.

Practice Divide children into four groups. Give each group one sound and ask children to work together to come up with three words that begin with their sound. When everyone has finished, have group members tell the class their words. Ask, *"Does each word begin with /r/?" (/l/, /i/, or /u/)*

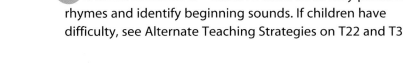

rabbit, rose, rooster

INFORMAL ASSESSMENT Observe children as they produce rhymes and identify beginning sounds. If children have difficulty, see Alternate Teaching Strategies on T22 and T31.

Read Together

From Phonemic Awareness to Phonics

Objective: Review Initial /l/ L, l

IDENTIFY THE LETTER Remind children that the letter *l* stands for the sound /l/. Display the Phonics Rhyme poem, "The Lazy Little Lion." Point to the letters *L, l* in the top corner. Have children make the sound the letters stand for.

READ THE POEM Read the poem through once and ask children to listen for the /l/ sound. Then read the poem again and point to each word. Exaggerate the words that begin with *l*.

LOOKING FOR *L*'S Have children repeat the poem title with

you, drawing out the initial /l/ sounds. Then ask a volunteer to come up and point to the letters in the title that make the /l/ sound at the beginning of the words. Continue, reading the poem line by line and inviting different children to find the *l*'s. If children notice that there are *l*'s in other parts of some words such as *little,* confirm that they are correct; the sound of /l/ can occur in other parts of a word as well as the beginning.

Ll

The Lazy Little Lion

The lazy little lion likes
To rest and lie around.
He likes to lounge
In piles of leaves
Or sprawl out on the ground.

The lazy little lion naps
With other lions, too.
Lions love to sleep a LOT!
That's just what lions do.

32

Big Book of Phonics Rhymes and Poems, page 32

234J

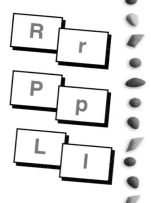

lion

Phonics Picture Posters and Cards

✓TESTED

☑ OBJECTIVES

Children will:

☑ identify and discriminate between /r/ R, r, /p/ P, p, /l/ L, l

☑ write and use letters R, r, P, p, L, l

MATERIALS

• Phonics Picture Posters

ADDITIONAL RESOURCES

• Practice Book, page 234

• Phonics/Phonemic Awareness Practice Book, pages 99, 105, 111

• **Phonics** CD-ROM

TEACHING TIP

INSTRUCTIONAL Give children Tactile ABC Cards for the letters R, r, P, p, and L, l. Ask children to trace each letter as you say the letter sound. Have children repeat the sound after you.

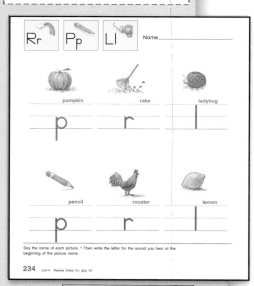

| Rr | Pp | Ll | Name_____ |

pumpkin   rake   ladybug

p   r   ___

pencil   rooster   lemon

p   r   ___

Say the name of each picture. • Then write the letter for the sound you hear at the beginning of the picture name.

234 Unit 6 Review Initial /r/, /p/, /l/

Pupil Edition page 234

234K *Ron and Me*

Review

TEACH

Phonemic Awareness Warm-Up Say the word *pot* and then say the onset and rime: *p-ot*. As you say the words: *rot, pot, rat, pat, ran, pan, pad, lad, rid,* and *lid*, have children repeat the words and then follow you in saying their beginning and ending sounds, such as *rot/r-ot*.

Identify and Discriminate Between /r/ R, r, /p/ P, p, /l/ L, l Say the word *ran*, emphasizing the initial sound. Write *R, r* on the board and explain that *R, r* stands for the sound /r/. Point to the letters and have the children repeat the /r/ sound after you. Repeat the procedure for /p/ *P, p* and /l/ *L, l.*

Write and Use R, r, P, p, L, l Display Phonics Picture Posters *R, r, P, p* and *L, l.* Review the capital and lowercase forms with children. Have children trace the letters on their desks with their fingers. Then have children suggest words that begin with the letters *R, P,* or *L.* For each word, have a child write the initial letter on a letter strip.

PRACTICE

Clap for Letters

Materials: letter cards *Rr, Pp, Ll*

◆ Randomly hold up the letter cards for *R, r, P, p* and *L, l.*

◆ Ask children to clap if they see both forms of the same letter.

◆ Have children name a word that begins with each letter.

| R | r |

| P | p |

| L | l |

ON LEVEL

✓ ASSESS/CLOSE

Have children complete page 234 of the Pupil Edition or the Practice Book. For a different approach to this skill, see pages T23, T28, T32, and T34 for the **Alternate Teaching Strategies.**

Meeting Individual Needs
Activities

Color the Letters

Materials: drawing paper folded in thirds, crayons

◆ Ask children to use different color crayons to print *R, r, P, p* and *L, l* in the three sections of their drawing paper.

◆ Partners should take turns pointing to letters and saying the sound each letter makes.

EASY

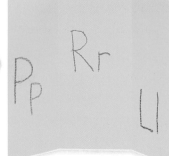

At Home with Letters

Materials: drawing paper, crayons

◆ Have children brainstorm things they might find at home that begin with *r, p,* and *l*, such as: *rug, rope, pan, pen, lamp.*

◆ Have children draw a picture of a room at home and label the appropriate objects with *r, p,* or *l.*

◆ As children point to each label, have them say /r/, /p/, or /l/.

CHALLENGE

Show the Right Letter

Materials: paper squares

◆ Have children write the letters *r* and *l* on two paper squares.

◆ Then say a word that begins with /r/ or /l/, such as *lip, rag, ran, leg, rain,* and *lap.*

◆ As you read each word, have children repeat it and hold up the square with the letter that matches the beginning sound.

LANGUAGE SUPPORT

Allie's Adventure
From A to Z

Written by Ellen Dreyer   Illustrated by Jui Ishida

Big Book

TESTED OBJECTIVES

Children will:
- ☐ recognize that print conveys meaning.
- ☑ recognize uppercase and lowercase letters.
- ☐ understand sequence of events.
- ☐ listen and respond to the story.

Build Background

Develop Oral Language   Prompt children to remember the story by displaying the Big Book cover and title. Ask, "What happens to Allie in the story?" Write down children's responses in a list on the board.

Read the Big Book

Set Purposes   Tell children that, as they read the story, they should think about how Allie might be feeling.

Read the Story   Ask children to look at page 12 and tell you what Allie is doing in the illustration. Then point out the word above the picture and connect the word to the action. *Concepts of Print*

MODEL: I see that Allie is jumping in this picture. I bet this word above the picture tells me what Allie is doing. *Concepts of Print*

Ask children to find the lowercase *j* on the page. *Letter Identification*

Point out the exclamation point on page 12 and identify it. Discuss its use. *Concepts of Print*

Allie **jumps**!

12

A hole is no place for a **kitten**.

13

Allie's Adventure, pages 12–13

Literature Response

LISTENING/SPEAKING

Discuss the Story How does Allie feel at the beginning of the story? (She is happy.) Why? (She is playing.) *Inferential: Story Events*

What happens at the end of the story? (Zack finds Allie.) How does Allie feel? (Allie is excited.) *Literal: Sequence of Events*

On page 12, what does the mark at the end of the sentence mean? (It means the sentence should be read with excitement.) Have volunteers read it aloud. *Concepts of Print*

WRITING

Journal Writing Have children draw and write about how Allie might have felt when she saw the insect.

Allie **jumps!**

12

Allie's Adventure, page 12

INFORMAL ASSESSMENT

IDENTIFY CAPITAL AND LOWERCASE LETTERS

How to Assess
Point to each letter on page 32 of the Big Book and have children identify them.

Follow-Up
Look at page 3 in the Big Book. Have children point out the capital and the lowercase *Aa*. Continue with other letters.

Cross Curricular: Art

PAPERBAG PUMPKIN Invite children to follow these steps to make a pumpkin.

1. Fill a small paper bag with crumpled paper.
2. Tie the top with a string.
3. Paint the bag orange and brown.
4. Glue on paper leaves and a vine.

Encourage children to share their pumpkins.

Positional Terms

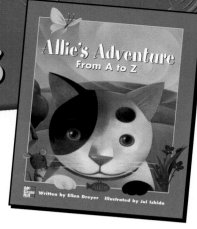

Allie's Adventure From A to Z

Written by Ellen Dreyer Illustrated by Jui Ishida

Allie's Adventure from A to Z

TESTED
OBJECTIVES

Children will:
- ☑ identify positions

MATERIALS

- *Allie's Adventure from A to Z*
- small classroom objects

TEACHING TIP

INSTRUCTIONAL Write positional terms on the chalkboard. Give children a secret signal, such as "thumbs up," to use when they hear you say one of these words during the day.

Review

TEACH

Identify Positions Display the Big Book *Allie's Adventure from A to Z,* and ask children to recall the story. Ask them where the cow is. *(inside the barn)* Take a picture walk through the book, and have children look for examples of *on, off; inside, outside; over, under;* and *up, down.*

PRACTICE

Hide and Seek

◆ Play a special game of "Hide and Seek." Hide an object and give clues, such as: *The book is inside a drawer. The cube is under a rug.*

◆ Then have children take turns hiding objects and giving clues.

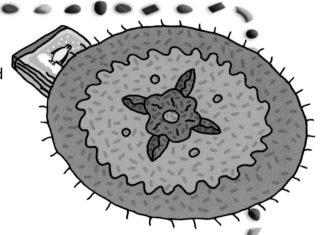

ON LEVEL

✓ ASSESS/CLOSE

Have children complete page 235 of the Pupil Edition or Practice Book. For a different approach to teaching this skill, see pages T24, T29, and T35 for **Alternate Teaching Strategies.**

Name

1.

2.

3.

4.

1. Draw a circle around the person who is on the couch. Draw a line under the person who is off the couch. 2. Draw a circle around the dog that is inside. Draw a line under the dog that is outside. 3. Draw a circle around the bird that is *over* the tree. Draw a line under the bird that is under the tree. 4. Draw a circle around the kite that is up. Draw a line under the kite that is down.

Unit 6 Review Positional Terms   235

Pupil Edition page 235

Meeting Individual Needs

Activities

Hide-and-Seek

Materials: animals from Phonics Picture Cards

◆ Place picture cards around the classroom so they are hidden and invite children to play hide-and-seek.

◆ Name an animal and ask children to look carefully around the room to find it. As each picture is found, have a volunteer describe where it is using the words *on, off, inside, outside, over, under, up, down.*

EASY

Simon says...

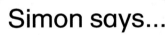

Book of Positions

Materials: magazines, glue or paste, scissors, paper, pencil

◆ Invite children to create a picture book of positional terms.

◆ Have children cut pictures from magazines that show different positional terms *(inside, outside, up, down, on, off, under, over).*

◆ Compile and label pictures in a book.

CHALLENGE

Play Simon Says

◆ Play a game of "Simon Says," using positional words. *(Simon says put your hands on your head. Simon says put your finger under your chin. Simon says reach up.)*

◆ Let volunteers take turns giving the commands for the rest of the group.

LANGUAGE SUPPORT

Listen

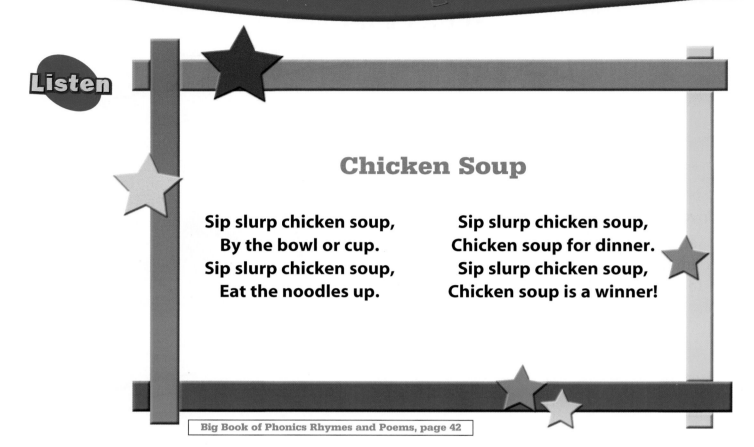

Chicken Soup

Sip slurp chicken soup,
By the bowl or cup.
Sip slurp chicken soup,
Eat the noodles up.

Sip slurp chicken soup,
Chicken soup for dinner.
Sip slurp chicken soup,
Chicken soup is a winner!

Big Book of Phonics Rhymes and Poems, page 42

Segment Syllables · · · · · · · · · · Phonological Awareness

Teach   Have children listen as you recite "Chicken Soup." Then ask them to segment the syllables of these words along with you: *chicken (chick-en)*, *noodles (noo-dles)*, *banana (ba-nan-a)*, and *tomato (to-ma-to)*.

MATERIALS
• colored chalk

Practice   Draw two bowls on the board. Write the numerals 2 and 3 on the bowls. Tell children that one bowl is for words with two syllables and the other bowl is for words with three syllables. Say the name of a food. Have children clap the syllables. Then have a volunteer use chalk to draw a tally mark inside the correct bowl.

| cracker | apple | pretzel | hamburger |
| cucumber | biscuit | orange | donut |

Listen for Ending Sounds

Teach Show the picture side of the Phonics Picture Card for *cap*. Ask, "What sound do you hear at the end of *cap*?" Have children say the word with you, segmenting the sounds: /k/-/a/-/p/. Emphasize the final /p/. Repeat with the picture of the *ship*.

Practice Review the poem with children by asking questions that provide the opportunity for them to use words with /p/. For example:

- What kind of food is this poem about? (*soup*)
- What noise do you make while eating soup? (*sip*)
- What sounds do *soup* and *sip* end with? (/p/)

Ask children to show you how they use their lips to form the /p/ sound.

MATERIALS

- Phonics Picture Cards

INFORMAL ASSESSMENT Observe children as they segment words into syllables and identify final sounds. If children have difficulty, see Alternate Teaching Strategies: Unit 2, T29; and Unit 4, T27.

Read Together

From Phonemic Awareness to Phonics

Objective: Review Final /p/ *p*

IDENTIFY THE LETTER Review with children that the letter *p* stands for the sound /p/. Display the Phonics Rhyme poem on page 42, and point out the letters in the upper right corner. Repeat the /p/ sound as you tell children that this is the letter capital and lowercase *p*.

REREAD THE POEM As you reread the poem, track the print. Draw children's attention to each word that ends with the letter *p* and the sound /p/.

FIND THE LETTERS Call on volunteers to come up and point to *p* as you say the lines of the poem. Have children tell where in the word they find the letter. Have them say the word to show where the /p/ sound occurs.

Pp **Chicken Soup**

Sip slurp chicken soup,
By the bowl or cup.
Sip slurp chicken soup,
Eat the noodles up.

Sip slurp chicken soup,
Chicken soup for dinner.
Sip slurp chicken soup,
Chicken soup is a winner!

Big Book of Phonics Rhymes and Poems, page 42

236B

Final /p/ p

✓TESTED

OBJECTIVES

Children will:
- ☑ identify and review /p/ *P, p*
- ☑ write and use the letter *P, p*

MATERIALS
- letter cards
- Word Building Cards

ADDITIONAL RESOURCES
- Practice Book, page 236
- Phonics/Phonemic Awareness Practice Book, page 107
- **Phonics** CD-ROM

TEACHING TIP

INSTRUCTIONAL Ask children to write *p* on several self-stick labels and place the labels on classroom objects that end in /p/.

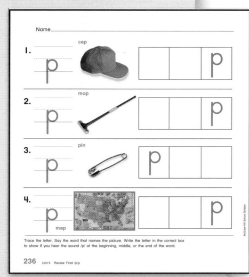

Name

1. cap

2. mop

3. pin

4. map

Trace the letter. Say the word that names the picture. Write the letter in the correct box to show if you hear the sound /p/ at the beginning, middle, or the end of the word.

236 Unit 4 • Review Final /p/p

Pupil Edition page 236

Review

TEACH

Phonemic Awareness Warm-Up Tell children *cap* and *lap* rhyme because they have the same ending sound. Tell children you will say three words and they should repeat the two words that rhyme. Use these words: *lip, tip, cat; hop, ball, top; tree, fun, run; shop, lid, stop.*

Identify /p/ *p* Point to the *p* on the Word Building Card and review with children that *p* stands for the sound /p/. Point to the letter and have children repeat the /p/ sound after you. Tell children the word *cap* has the /p/ sound at the end of the word.

Write and Use *p* Give each child a paper square and have them write a *p* on it. Then ask children to listen as you say some words. If they hear you say a word that ends in /p/, they hold up their *p* letter card. Use these words and others: *cup, sip, dog, lip, ball, map, top.*

PRACTICE

Find *P* Rhymes

Materials: Letter strips

◆ Say a word that ends in *p* and ask children to name a word that rhymes with it, such as *mop (top, stop).* Repeat with other words.

◆ Each time someone makes a rhyme, have children write *p* on a letter strip.

ON LEVEL

✓ ASSESS/CLOSE

Have children complete page 236 of the Pupil Edition or the Practice Book. For a different approach to this skill, see pages T23, T28, T32 and T34 for the **Alternate Teaching Strategies.**

Meeting Individual Needs
Activities

Make *P*

Materials: yarn, glue, paper, pencils

◆ Have children write *p* on their paper and trace it with glue.

◆ Have children place a piece of yarn over the *p* while glue is still wet.

◆ Children can trace the *p* with their fingers when the glue is dry.

EASY

Tell a Story

Materials: drawing paper, crayons

◆ Invite pairs of students to make up a silly story about a pup named Fred. The story should include three words that end in *p*.

◆ Have children make a drawing to accompany their story.

◆ Different pairs of children can tell their silly stories and show their pictures to the rest of the group.

CHALLENGE

Act Out the *P* Words

◆ Play "Simon Says" by naming action words that end in *p*. For example, *Simon says hop. Simon says skip.*

◆ Have children repeat final *p* words and follow your gestures.

◆ After each action, have children trace *p* in the air with their fingers. Continue with words such as *jump, tap,* and *drop.*

LANGUAGE SUPPORT

Shared Reading

The Apple Pie Tree
BY Zoe Hall
ILLUSTRATED BY Shari Halpern

Big Book

TESTED

OBJECTIVES

Children will:

☐ develop vocabulary to reflect a growing range of knowledge

☑ understand the main idea of the selection

☑ compare and contrast information

☐ listen and respond to a story

TEACHING TIP

WORD WEB Begin a word web on the chalkboard. Write the word *apple* in the center. Then add the words from the "Develop Oral Language" discussion in the web.

Build Background

Develop Oral Language Hold two apples as though your arms were branches of a tree. Then have children repeat with you the apple fingerplay found on pages 201A–201B. Have children describe their favorite types of apples and ways to eat them (in pies, in applesauce, etc.)

Read the Big Book

Set Purposes Have children determine a new purpose for reading "The Apple Pie Tree." For example, they may want to read to compare and contrast the weather in the four seasons.

Read the Story Use your finger to track the print as you read the story to the children. *Concepts of Print*

Ask children to look at the pictures of the baby robins on pages 10 and 17. Talk about how the robins have changed. *Compare and Contrast*

The branches bend down low.
They are covered with
big, round apples.

The Apple Pie Tree, pages 22–23

Literature Response

LISTENING/SPEAKING

Ask children to face the class as they respond to the story.

Discuss the Story Look at pages 10–11. Ask where to begin reading and where to end. Point out that this sentence begins on page 10 and ends on page 11. *Concepts of Print*

After you finish the story, ask the children to tell how the apples got from the tree to the pie. *Literal: Story Details*

MODEL: The story and the pictures tell me that someone picked the apples from the tree. Then they must have washed them, peeled them and sliced them before they put the apples in the pie.

Have the children compare and contrast the two girls in the story. *Inferential: Compare and Contrast*

Review with children the main idea of the selection. *Inferential: Main Idea*

WRITING

Journal Writing Have children write or draw about their favorite parts of the story. Give them an opportunity to share what they wrote with the class.

M y sister and I have a tree that grows the best part of apple pie.

Can you guess what that is?

The Apple Pie Tree, page 3

INFORMAL **ASSESSMENT**

How to Assess
If a child is having difficulty identifying the main idea, use the skills lesson on pages 237C–237.

Expand Vocabulary

Invite children to create riddles. Distribute a variety of pictures of fruits that grow on trees and have children work in pairs to create a riddle with two or three clues. Encourage them to end the riddle by asking, *What is it?* Have children share their riddles with a another pair, keeping the picture hidden until the riddle has been solved.

DAY 2 Main Idea

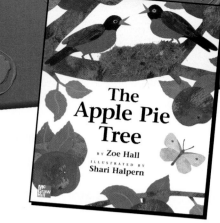

The Apple Pie Tree

OBJECTIVES

Children will:

☑ understand the main idea of a story

MATERIALS

- *The Apple Pie Tree*

TEACHING TIP

INSTRUCTIONAL Display some familiar books and read the titles aloud. Ask children to tell what the books are about. Confirm that they have been identifying the main idea of the story.

Review

TEACH

Understand Main Idea Display the cover of the Big Book *The Apple Pie Tree*, and ask children to recall the story. Draw their attention to details in the story, such as the bare trees in winter. Point out that these details make the story interesting. Details are part of the story, but the main idea tells what a story is mainly about. Ask children what happens to the apple tree in each of the four seasons. Work with children to restate the main idea of *The Apple Pie Tree*. *(The apple tree changes in every season.)*

PRACTICE

All About Pictures

Materials: Pictures showing people performing activities

◆ Display pictures of people doing activities; for example, pictures of athletes playing sports.

◆ Invite children to talk about what is happening in each picture.

ON LEVEL

✓ ASSESS/CLOSE

Have children complete page 237 of the Pupil Edition or the Practice Book. For a different approach to this skill, see page T25 for the **Alternate Teaching Strategy.**

Name_____

1. My cat ran to Dad.
   My pup ran to Pam.

2. The cat can nap on the cot.
   The pup is in the mud.

3. The pup can fit on the mat.
   The pup can fit in the cap.

Look at each picture. • Then read the sentences. • Draw a line under the sentence that tells what the picture is all about.

Unit 4 Review Main Idea **237**

Pupil Edition page 237

Meeting Individual Needs
Activities

The Room Riddle

Materials: drawing paper, crayons

◆ Ask children to think of a room in their house and describe it without saying its name.

◆ Ask the other children to guess the room.

◆ Invite children to make a drawing of the room.

EASY

Make a Four Seasons Poster

Materials: drawing paper, crayons

◆ Encourage children to brainstorm activities they do in each of the four seasons.

◆ Ask pairs of children to divide their paper into four sections and draw a picture of one seasonal activity in each section.

CHALLENGE

Spring, Summer, Fall, Winter

Materials: *The Apple Pie Tree*

◆ Use the story to introduce or review the words for the seasons.

◆ Read the passages that tell what happens in each season.

◆ Encourage the children to tell what they like to do in each season.

LANGUAGE SUPPORT

Listen

The Lazy Little Lion
a poem

The lazy little lion likes
To rest and lie around.
He likes to lounge in piles of leaves
Or sprawl upon the ground.
The lazy little lion naps
With other lions, too.
Lions love to sleep a LOT!
That's just what lions do.

Pease Porridge Hot
a poem

Pease porridge hot,
Pease porridge cold,
Pease porridge in the pot,
Nine days old.
Some like it hot,
Some like it cold,
Some like it in the pot,
Nine days old.

Big Book of Phonics Rhymes and Poems, pages 32, 41

Delete Syllables

Phonological Awareness

Teach After you read the poems, draw two boxes that are attached side-by-side on the chalkboard. Place a sticky note in each box. Point to the appropriate sticky notes and say *lion*. Then say /lī/ and /ən/. Remove the second sticky note and say, *lion* take away the /ən/ is /lī/. Replace the note and say the word *lion*.

Practice Say one of the words that follows and specify for children which syllable to take away. Have children remove the sticky note from the appropriate box as they take away the syllable. Then have them say the remaining syllable.

a-round	por-ridge
lit-tle	hot-ter
nap-time	break-fast

MATERIALS
- sticky notes

Listen for Beginning Sounds

Teach Say *rat*, stressing the initial /r/ sound. Tell children that the word *rat* begins with the /r/ sound. Repeat with /p/ and *pig*, /l/ and *lion*.

Practice Display the picture of the pig and have children name it. Then sing the following song about a pig to the tune of "Muffin Man."

Do you hear a /p/ in *pig*?
A /p/ in *pig*? A /p/ in *pig*?
Do you hear a /p/ in *pig*?

Then say the word right now! *(Pig!)*

Ask children where they hear the /p/ sound. *(beginning)* Display objects that begin with /p/, /r/, or /l/. Sing the song several times, using the name of one of the objects in place of *pig* each time.

INFORMAL ASSESSMENT Observe children as they delete syllables in words and identify beginning sounds. If children have difficulty, see Alternate Teaching Strategies on T22, T27, T31 and T33.

MATERIALS
- **Phonics Picture Card:** *pig*
- objects that begin with /p/, /r/, or /l/

Read Together

From Phonemic Awareness to Phonics

Objective: Associate /p/ *P, p* and /l/ *L, l*

IDENTIFY THE LETTERS
Display the Big Book of Phonics Rhymes and Poems, pages 32 and 41. On each page, point to the letters, identify them, and say their sounds: /p/ and /l/.

REREAD THE POEMS Reread the poems, tracking the print and emphasizing the words with initial or final /p/ or initial /l/.

FIND WORDS WITH *P, p* and *L, l* Write the letters *P, p* and *L, l* on cards, and have children match them with letters in words in the poems.

Ll

The Lazy Little Lion

The lazy little lion likes
To rest and lie around.
He likes to lounge
In piles of leaves
Or sprawl out on the ground.

The lazy little lion naps
With other lions, too.
Lions love to sleep a LOT!
That's just what lions do.

Pease Porridge Hot Pp

Pease porridge hot,
Pease porridge cold,
Pease porridge in the pot,
Nine days old.
Some like it hot,
Some like it cold,
Some like it in the pot,
Nine days old.

Big Book of Phonics Rhymes and Poems, pages 32, 41

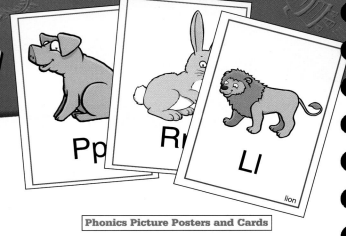

Phonics Picture Posters and Cards

OBJECTIVES

TESTED

Children will:

☑ identify and discriminate between /r/ R, r, /p/ P, p, and /l/ L, l

☑ write and use letters R, r, P, p, and L, l

MATERIALS

- letter cards
- Phonics Picture Posters

ADDITIONAL RESOURCES

- Practice Book, page 238
- Phonics/Phonemic Awareness Practice Book, pages 99, 105, 111
- **Phonics** CD-ROM

TEACHING TIP

INSTRUCTIONAL Give children Tactile ABC Cards R, r, P, p, L, and l. Ask children how the capital letters are alike and different. Then have them match each capital letter to the corresponding lowercase letter.

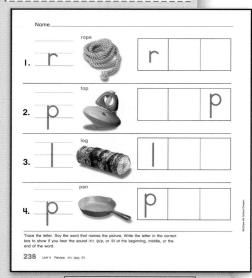

Review

TEACH

Phonemic Awareness Warm-Up Tell children they will clap when they hear the initial sound r. Say: *rod, rip, top, rat*. Repeat for the initial sounds *p*, and *l* with: *pod, pot, pit, lid, lip,* and *lap*. Then have them clap for the ending sound *p* in: *nap, lip, cap, cup,* and *sap*.

Identify and Discriminate Between /r/ R, r, /p/ P, p, and /l/ L, l Display the Phonics Picture Poster for *Rr*. Point to and identify each letter. Have children name the picture and say /r/ with you. Repeat for /p/ P, p, and /l/ L, l. Ask children to point to the correct poster for the initial sound of each of these words: *lid, lip, rip, rod, pad,* and *pot*. Then have them tap their tables when they hear words with final /p/ p.

Form R, r, P, p, L, and l Display letter cards for R, r, P, p, L, and l and review making each capital and lowercase form. Give each child three index cards. Have them write capital R, P, and L on one side of each card and the lowercase form on the reverse of each card. Say names that begin with R, P, or L. Have children show the correct capital letter.

PRACTICE

Pass the Hat

Materials: a hat, slips of paper

◆ Give children slips of paper and have them write *r, p,* or *l* on each one. Have children put their papers in a hat and mix them up.

◆ Form a circle and pass the hat around. Have each child pull out a slip of paper and name a word that begins with the letter on it.

ON LEVEL

ASSESS/CLOSE

Have children complete page 238 of the Pupil Edition or the Practice Book. For a different approach to this skill, see pages T23, T28, T32 and T34 for the **Alternate Teaching Strategies.**

Meeting Individual Needs
Activities

Fun with *P, p, R, r, L, l*

Materials: index cards, crayons, three boxes, picture cards for *pot, pin, rainbow, ring, lion,* and *ladder*

◆ Label boxes with *Rr, Pp,* and *Ll.* Have children put pictures in the boxes by initial sound.

◆ Have children write *r, p,* and *l* on separate cards and draw items that begin with each letter.

◆ Partners can play concentration with their cards.

EASY

Category Mural

Materials: mural paper, scissors, magazines, glue

◆ Label sections of mural paper with categories, such as *food, animals,* and *clothing.*

◆ Have children brainstorm words that begin with /r/ *r,* /p/ *p,* and /l/ *l* for each category.

◆ Have children cut pictures from magazines and paste them in the correct categories.

CHALLENGE

Puppet Show!

Materials: craft sticks, scissors, glue, crayons or markers, drawing paper, picture cards for /r/ *r,* /p/ *p,* and /l/ *l*

◆ Display the picture cards. Review by having children say each word and its initial sound and letter.

◆ Say *lion, rabbit,* and *puppet.* Have children name the letter that begins each one.

◆ Have children make a lion or rabbit stick puppet and have the puppet say a sentence with an /r/ *r,* /p/ *p,* or /l/ *l* word in it.

LANGUAGE SUPPORT

Listen

Every Time I Climb a Tree

a poem by David McCord

Every time I climb a tree
Every time I climb a tree
Every time I climb a tree
I scrape a leg
Or skin a knee
And every time I climb a tree
I find some ants
Or dodge a bee
And get the ants
All over me
And every time I climb a tree
Where have you been?
They say to me
But don't they know that I am free
Every time I climb a tree?
I like it best

To spot a nest
That has an egg
Or maybe three
And then I skin
The other leg
But every time I climb a tree
I see a lot of things to see
Swallows rooftops and TV
And all the fields and farms there be
Every time I climb a tree
Though climbing may be good for
   ants
It isn't awfully good for pants
But still it's pretty good for me
Every time I climb a tree

Oral Comprehension

LISTENING AND SPEAKING Use these questions to encourage children to respond to the poem. Invite children to listen for musical elements of language such as rhyme, repetition, and patterns.

- What things can the speaker see from the tree? (swallows, rooftops, TV, fields, and farms)

- What does the speaker mean when he says climbing "isn't awfully good for pants"? (He has probably ripped his pants while climbing a tree.)

- Is this poem make-believe or could it really happen? Why? (It could happen. Answers will vary.)

- What do you think would be the best part about climbing a tree? (Answers will vary.)

Activity Have children choose their favorite images from the poem and draw pictures to match. Then have them write words describing what they've drawn.

▶**Spatial**

Reading for Information

Can you follow the footsteps?
Start at **X**.

24   25

> **Reading for Information Big Book, pages 24–25**

Objective: Read a Map

DISCUSS THE BIG BOOK Remind children that the footsteps create a path for the boy in the poem to follow.

• Turn to pages 24 and 25 in the Big Book and show children the map. Explain again that a map is used to show how to get to different places.

• Reread the question at the bottom of page 25. Then discuss the map. Have children name objects the boy will pass on the way to his bicycle.

• Ask: *Why do you think maps are important? What are some maps you have seen at home? What are some maps you've seen at school?* (Answers will vary.)

CENTER Activity

Cross Curricular: Social Studies

OUR TOWN Provide children with a simple map of their town. Have them:

• label the map using words and/or pictures to indicate important buildings.

• include special places on the map, such as an ice cream parlor, movie house, toy store, or book shop.

• write a sentence that describes the street.

▶ Interpersonal/Spatial

*inter*NET
CONNECTION Help children log on to **www.mhschool.com/reading,** where they can access links to schools in other towns.

Vocabulary:
to, me, go, do

TESTED OBJECTIVES

Children will:
- ☑ review high-frequency words *to, me, go, do*

MATERIALS
- word cards
- chart paper
- magazines

TEACHING TIP

WORD WALL Point to the words *to, me, go,* and *do* on the Word Wall. Partners use letter cards *t, o, m, e, g,* and *d,* and take turns building and spelling the words.

Review

Vocabulary cards

TEACH

Review *to, me, go, do* Say the following rhyme with children: *Go, go, go./Do, do, do./It's from me./I give it to you!* Repeat it several times.

Give each child a set of *to, me, go, do* word cards. Say the rhyme again. Ask children to hold up the appropriate card each time you say one of the vocabulary words.

PRACTICE

Places to Go/Things to Do

The beach is a place to go.

- ◆ Divide a piece of chart paper in half, labeling one side "Places to <u>Go</u>" and one "Things to <u>Do</u>."

- ◆ Have children cut pictures from magazines.

- ◆ Have each child place a picture in each category. Help them label it using this sentence frame: _____ *is a place to <u>go</u>.* _____ *is a thing to <u>do</u>.*

ON LEVEL

✓ ASSESS/CLOSE

Have children complete page 239 of the Pupil Edition or Practice Book. For a different approach to teaching this skill, see page T26 for the **Alternate Teaching Strategy.**

Name_____

1. (do)	that	to	my
2. me	we	is	(to)
3. go	you	said	(me)
4. have	has	for	(go)

Read the words. 1. Draw a circle around the word do. 2. Draw a circle around the word to. 3. Draw a circle around the word me. 4. Draw a circle around the word go.

Unit 4 Review to, me, go, do **239**

Pupil Edition page 239

Meeting Individual Needs

Activities

All About Me

Materials: drawing paper, pencils, markers

◆ Write the heading "All About Me" on sheets of paper.

◆ Have children draw pictures to illustrate the heading.

◆ Ask children to share their pictures and tell about themselves, pointing out the word *me* in the heading.

EASY

I go to the zoo.

Clues to Use

Materials: word cards *to, me, go, do*

◆ Give children the following clues. As you say each one, have them hold up the card with the correct high-frequency word: 1. It sounds just like the number *two. (to)* 2. It is the opposite of *you. (me)* 3. It rhymes with *no. (go)* 4. Can you _____ that? *(do)*

Sorting Go and Do

Materials: picture cards

◆ Make a set of picture cards, some that show places and some that show activities.

◆ Have children sort them into *Go* and *Do* piles.

◆ Invite children to make up a sentence about something they can do and somewhere they can go.

LANGUAGE SUPPORT

The boys____to the store.

CHALLENGE

Phonological Awareness

Making Mud Pies
a poem

Find a lot of sand.
Add a cup of water.
Make a lot of mud pies,
And sell them for a quarter.
After mud pies have baked in the sun,
Run into the lake and have some fun!

Blend Sounds · Phonemic Awareness · · · · · · · · · · · ·

Teach Read the poem with children aloud. Then tell children that the poem is about /m/-/u/-/d/. Can they guess what you are saying? *(mud)* Tell children that you are going to say all of the sounds in a word from the poem.

MODEL: *Say /s/-/u/-/n/. This is something very hot that bakes the mud pies. I will blend the sounds to make the word: /s/-/u/-/n/, /sun/, sun.*

Practice Tell children to listen as you say the sounds of the following words. Ask for a volunteer to blend and say the word.

/b/-/ā/-/k/; (bake)	/d/-/ī/-/m/; (dime)
/m/-/ā/-/k/; (make)	/k/-/u/-/p/; (cup)
/l/-/ā/-/k/; (lake)	/r/-/u/-/n/; (run)

Segment Sounds

Teach Display the Word Building Box with three sections. Say the word *sun*. Put a button on the first box as you say /s/. Move the button to the second box as you say /u/, and the third box as you say /n/. Repeat and have children point to the boxes as they say the phonemes with you. Repeat with the words *pat* and *tug*.

Practice Have children move buttons on their own Word Building Boxes as you say *bug*: /b/ - /u/ - /g/. Have children segment sounds in words such as *hug, dip, net, nut,* and *fan*.

MATERIALS
- Word Building Boxes from *Word Building Cards*
- buttons

INFORMAL ASSESSMENT Observe children as they blend sounds to make words and segment sounds. If children have difficulty, see Alternate Teaching Strategies on T22, T27, T31 and T33.

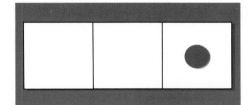

Read Together

From Phonemic Awareness to Phonics

Objective: Identify Word Endings

LISTENING FOR RHYMING WORDS Read the last two lines of the poem "Making Mud Pies," stressing the rhyming words. Ask children to name the words that rhyme and write them. (sun, fun, run)

IDENTIFY THE LETTERS Invite a volunteer to circle the letters in the words that are the same and then identify them. Ask children to say the sound each letter stands for.

NAME OTHER RHYMING WORDS Invite children to name other words that rhyme with *sun,* *run,* and *fun.* Write their suggestions on the board, circling the letters *un* to show that these words also have the same ending letters.

> **bun   run   spun**

IDENTIFY OTHER WORD ENDINGS Write the word *hum* on the board as you demonstrate its meaning. Say the word aloud. Invite children to suggest words that rhyme with *hum.* Write their responses on the board. Help children see that these words all end with the letters *um.*

SORT THE WORDS Write all the *um* words and *un* words on index cards. Have children sort the cards into rhyming families.

Short u
Blending

TESTED

OBJECTIVES
Children will:
- ☑ identify /u/ *u*
- ☑ blend and read short *u* words
- ☑ write short *u* words

MATERIALS
- letter cards

ADDITIONAL RESOURCES
- Practice Book, page 240
- Phonics/Phonemic Awareness Practice Book, page 119
- **Phonics** CD-ROM

TEACHING TIP
WORD FAMILIES Make a set of cards with _u_, and the letters: *c, d, f, m, n, p, s,* and *t.* Have small groups work to put the letters together and make as many words as they can.

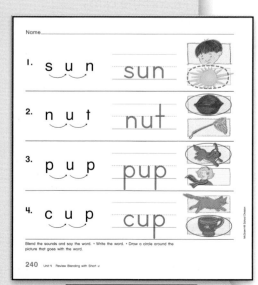

¹. s u n	sun	
². n u t	nut	
³. p u p	pup	
⁴. c u p	cup	

Blend the sounds and say the word. • Write the word. • Draw a circle around the picture that goes with the word.

240 Unit 4 Review Blending with Short u

Pupil Edition page 240

240C *Ron and Me*

Review

TEACH

Model Blending with Short *u* Display the *u* letter card and say /u/. Have children repeat the sound /u/ as you point to the *u* card.

Place the *t* card to the right of the *u* card. Point to each letter as you blend the sounds together and have children repeat after you: *ut*.

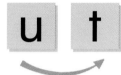

Place the *c* card to the left of *ut* to show *cut*. Point to the cards as you blend to read *cut,* and have children repeat after you.

Continue modeling and guided practice with other /u/ words.

PRACTICE

Make a Word

Materials: letter cards *c, d, f, m, n, p, r, s, t, u*

- ◆ Display cards. Make the word *mud* with the cards. Have children blend the sounds as you track the print.
- ◆ Then make the word *fun*. Ask volunteers to change one letter to make a new word. Repeat with other words.

ON LEVEL

✓ ASSESS/CLOSE

Have children complete page 240 of the Pupil Edition or the Practice Book. For a different approach to this skill, see pages T23, T28, T32, and T34 for the **Alternate Teaching Strategies.**

Meeting Individual Needs
Activities

Match a Word

Materials: drawing paper, crayons or markers, two boxes, word cards such as *nap, nut, nod, sip, pup, mud,* **and** *sun*

◆ Label one box __u__. Have children put /u/ *u* words in that box and the rest of the words in the other box.

◆ Have children blend the sounds and read the words with short *u*.

EASY

Change a Word

Materials: word cards *fin, Ron, mad, cop*

◆ Have children fold a piece of paper in half.

◆ Children take a word card, write the word on one half of the paper, and draw a line under the letter in the middle of the word.

◆ Then children rewrite their words with a *u* in the middle instead of the underlined letter.

CHALLENGE

Short *u* Sentences

Materials: *u* **letter card, short** *u* **word cards**

◆ Have children hold up their letter card each time they hear the sound /u/. Say: *The pup is in the sun. The pup is having fun.*

◆ Write the sentences on the chalkboard. Read them and track the print. Ask children what the sentences mean.

◆ Ask volunteers to circle each /u/ *u* word and underline the *u* in each.

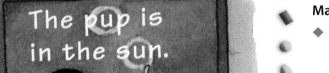

LANGUAGE SUPPORT

240

Read the Story

- ☑ **Review Initial /r/ *r*, /l/ *l*; Initial/Final *p*, Medial *u*, Blending**
- ☑ **High-Frequency Words:** *to, go*
- ☑ **Compare and Contrast**
- ☐ **Concepts of Print**

PREVIEW AND PREDICT

Ask children to look at the cover as you read the title. Have them count the number of words in the title. Ask *Who is Ron? What do you think Ron and the girl will do?*

Ron and Me

SET PURPOSES

Discuss with children what they want to find out as they read. Then say *Sometimes pets help people. How might Ron help the girl in the story?*

AS YOU READ

Remind children to track print as they read the story. Then use the following prompts:

- **Page 2** If children have difficulty reading *Ron,* guide them to cover the letter *R* and blend *o-n* to make *on.* Model how to add the /r/ sound to make *Ron. Graphophonic Cues*

- **Page 3** Ask *Which word ends in /p/? (lap) Which word has the sound /u/? (Run) Which words begin with /r/? (Run, Ron)* **Final** p, **Medial** u, **Initial** r

- **Page 5** Have children point to the words *to* and *Go. High-Frequency Words*

- **Page 8** Ask children to compare Ron to a real dog. *Can a real dog mop the floor? Why or why not? Compare and Contrast*

Ron is my pup.

2

Run to my lap, Ron.

3

Pupil Edition pp. 241–242

We have fun in the mud!

4

Go to the mop, Ron.

5

LANGUAGE SUPPORT

ESL Familiarize children with the story by inviting them to pretend to be Ron and his owner and pantomime each page as you read it aloud. Then invite some children to read the story as others pantomime the actions of Ron and his owner.

We can mop the mud!

6

Mop the mud, Ron.

7

We can mop, mop, mop!

8

Cross Curricular: Math

DOG PICTURES To reinforce one-to-one correspondence, ask children to write the numbers one to five along the bottom of a piece of construction paper. Then have children cut out five magazine pictures of dogs, and glue each picture above a number.

▶ **Logical/Mathematical**

 inter NET Help children log on to **www.mhschool.com/reading**
CONNECTION to learn about pet care.

Read the Story

RETURN TO PREDICTIONS
Remind children of their predictions and ideas before reading the story. Ask *Did anyone predict what Ron and the girl would do? Did anyone predict how Ron would help the girl?*

RETELL THE STORY
Divide the class into two groups. Have one group tell what Ron and the girl did before they played in the mud. Have the second group tell what Ron and the girl did after they played in the mud.

WRITING
Journal Writing Have children write a sentence about a time when they splashed or played in the mud. Invite children to illustrate their sentences.

HIGH-FREQUENCY WORDS

HOW TO ASSESS Invite children to scan the story for each of the following words: *to, go.* Each time they see a word, they should point to it and read it.

FOLLOW UP Have children look at the two words and identify how they are the same and how they are different.

241/242B

Compare and Contrast

TESTED OBJECTIVES

Children will:
☑ compare and contrast to understand a story

MATERIALS

* *Ron and Me*

TEACHING TIP

INSTRUCTIONAL Invite children to describe any pets they have. Write the various types of pets on the board. Discuss how the pets are alike and different, using the words *same, different,* and *alike.*

Ron and Me

Ron and Me

Review

TEACH

Compare and Contrast Display the cover of *Ron and Me* and ask children to recall the story. Reread the story together. After reading, have children compare the scenes on pages 4 and 8. Ask, *What is the same in the pictures? What is different?* (Answers will vary.)

Compare Feelings Ask children, *How did the girl feel at the end of the story? How did Ron feel? How do you know?*

PRACTICE

Clean Up

◆ Invite children to talk about the different ways to clean the floor, such as with different types of mops, vacuum cleaners, dust mops, and brooms.

◆ Write the responses on the chalkboard.

◆ Point out two of the items and ask children to tell what is the same and different about them. Continue with the remaining items.

ON LEVEL

✓ ASSESS/CLOSE

Have children complete page 243 of the Pupil Edition or the Practice Book. For a different approach to this skill, see page T30 for the **Alternate Teaching Strategy.**

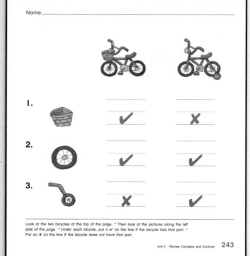

Name _____

1. ✔   ✗
2. ✔   ✔
3. ✗   ✔

Look at the two bicycles at the top of the page. • Then look at the pictures along the left side of the page. • Under each bicycle, put a ✔ on the line if the bicycle has that part. • Put an ✗ on the line if the bicycle does not have that part.

Unit 4 • Review Compare and Contrast   **243**

Pupil Edition page 243

Meeting Individual Needs

Activities

Dog Drawings

Materials: drawing paper, crayons

◆ Have children think of two different dogs that they have seen.

◆ Ask children to fold their paper in half and draw one dog on each half.

◆ Invite children to describe how the two dogs are the same and how they are different.

EASY

A Muddy Story

Materials: drawing paper, crayons

◆ Invite children to think of ways they can have fun with mud.

◆ Have children fold their paper into fourths and number the squares.

◆ Ask children to draw and illustrate a story involving mud. Have them compare and contrast the story with a classmate's.

CHALLENGE

Comparing Books

◆ Invite each child to choose two books from the classroom library.

◆ Guide a discussion in which children compare and contrast the books they chose. Ask questions such as: *Are the books about the same thing? Do both books have pictures? How else are they the same? How are they different?*

LANGUAGE SUPPORT

Listen

Making Mud Pies
a poem

Find a lot of sand.
Add a cup of water.
Make a lot of mud pies,
And sell them for a quarter.
After mud pies have baked in the sun,
Run into the lake and have some fun.

Blend Sounds

Phonemic Awareness

Teach   Read "Making Mud Pies" aloud to children. Then tell the class that you are going to make "word pies" with sounds. Explain that your ingredients are /m/, /u/, and /d/. Can students hear the word you create when you blend these sounds? (*mud*)

MODEL: I want to make a "word pie." Listen as I name my three ingredients: /f/, /u/, and /n/. I'll take these three ingredients and blend them together. What word have I created? (*fun*)

Practice   Ask volunteers to make "word pies" using phonemic "ingredients" that you provide. To keep the activity simple, use words from the poem.

Ingredients	Word Pies
/s/ - /e/ - /l/	sell
/l/ - /o/ - /t/	lot
/r/ - /u/ - /n/	run

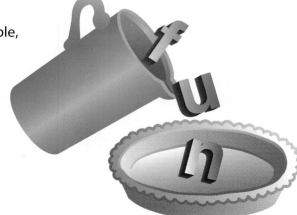

Segment Sounds · · · · · · · · · · · · · · · · · · Phonemic Awareness · · · · · · · · · · · · ·

Teach Gather children in a circle around an empty container. Explain that the beanbags in your hand represent the word *rip*. Toss the first beanbag into the container and say /r/. Toss the second and say /i/. Toss the third and say /p/. Then repeat the sounds you tossed: /r/ - /i/ - /p/, *rip*.

MATERIALS
- empty container
- three beanbags

Practice Pass the beanbags to the child on your right and ask him or her to repeat the activity for the word *done* (/d/ - /u/ - /n/). Continue the game with these words: *ran, rim, pop, pick, puck, sun,* and *bun*.

/r/

ASSESSMENT Observe children as they blend sounds to make words and segment words sounds. If children have difficulty, see Alternate Teaching Strategies on T22, T27, T31, and T33.

Read Together

From Phonemic Awareness to Phonics

Objective: Associate Sounds with Letters

LISTEN FOR A RHYMING WORD Read the first line of the poem "Making Mud Pies." Ask: *What word rhymes with* rot*?* Write the words *lot* and *rot* on the chalkboard.

> lot   rot

IDENTIFY THE LETTERS Invite a volunteer to circle the letters in the words that are the same. Then identify the letters. Ask children to say the sound each letter stands for.

NAME OTHER RHYMING WORDS Invite children to name other words that rhyme with *lot* and *rot*. Write their responses on the chalkboard. Have a volunteer circle the ending letters that are the same in all the words.

> not dot tot cot
> pot got hot jot

MORE RHYMING WORDS Have children suggest rhyming words for *dim, tin,* and *cut*. Work on one rhyming family at a time. Write their suggestions on the chalk-

board. Circle the ending letters to show that all the words that rhyme have the same ending letters.

> him Jim Kim rim Tim slim

> bin fin pin chin shin skin

> but hut nut shut

SORT RHYMING WORDS Write all the words from the chalkboard on index cards, one word per card. Shuffle the cards. Have children work together to sort the cards into rhyming families.

244B

Short u, o, i
Blending

OBJECTIVES

Children will:

☑ identify /u/ *u*, /o/ *o*, /i/ *i*

☑ blend and read short *u, o, i* words

☑ write short *u, o, i* words

MATERIALS

- letter cards

ADDITIONAL RESOURCES

- Practice Book, page 244
- Phonics/Phonemic Awareness Practice Book, pages 119, 122
- **Phonics** CD-ROM

TEACHING TIP

WORD FAMILIES Make a set of cards for each child with _u_, _o_, and _i_. Say *sun/fun/run/pup; pot/pop/rod/nod; pin/lip/tip/sip.* Have children write the whole word under the medial letter it contains.

Review

TEACH

Model Blending with Short u, o, i Display the *o* letter card and say /o/. Have children repeat the sound /o/ as you point to the *o* card.
Place the *d* card to the right of the *o* card. Point to each letter as you blend the sounds together and have children repeat after you: *od.*

Place the *n* card to the left of *od* to show *nod.* Point to the cards as you blend to read *nod,* and have children repeat after you.

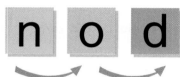 

Continue modeling and guided practice using *sip, cut, pod, lid, fin, mop,* and *run.*

PRACTICE

Make a Word

Materials: a hat, slips of paper

◆ Write short *u, o, i,* words on separate slips of paper. Put the words in a hat.

◆ Form a circle and pass the hat around. Have each child take a paper from the hat.

◆ Have each child read aloud the word on the paper and use his/her word in a sentence.

ON LEVEL

✓ ASSESS/CLOSE

Have children complete page 244 of the Pupil Edition or the Practice Book. For a different approach to this skill, see pages T23, T28, T32, and T34 for the **Alternate Teaching Strategies.**

Meeting Individual Needs
Activities

Make a Poster

Materials: drawing paper, crayons or markers, glitter or confetti, glue, picture cards and word cards for short *u, i, o* words

◆ Have children copy a word from a word card and draw a picture of that word next to it.

◆ Tell children to trace the *u, o,* or *i* in the word with glue and sprinkle on glitter or confetti.

EASY

cup

Build Words

Materials: drawing paper, crayons or markers, letter cards *c, d, f, i, l, m, n, o, p, r, s, t, u*

◆ Have children work in small groups to build words with *u, o,* and *i* in the middle.

◆ Have children record their words in a list.

CHALLENGE

up

cup

pup

Rhyming Ladders

Materials: chart paper

◆ Draw a ladder on chart paper. Write the phonogram *-up* at the top of the ladder.

◆ Write on the rungs of the ladder rhyming words for *-up*, such as *cup* and *pup*. Have children blend the sounds as you track the print.

◆ Repeat with other word families, such as *-ut, -un, -ot, -od, -ip,* and *-it.*

LANGUAGE SUPPORT

Leveled Books

Meeting Individual Needs

We Have Fun!

EASY

Guided Reading

TESTED OBJECTIVES

☑ Initial /r/r, /p/p, /l/l; final /p/p; medial /u/u.

☑ Blend with Short *u*

☑ Compare and Contrast

☑ Vocabulary: *to, me, go, do*

☐ Concepts of Print

PREVIEW AND PREDICT Ask children to look at the cover illustration and predict what the story might be about. Point to each word as you read aloud the title. Then conduct a picture walk through the first few pages. Have children predict what the boy and girl in the story will do. Before reading, remind children to point to each word as they read it.

READ THE BOOK Use the following prompts to guide children's reading:

Pages 2–3 Have children point to the words that are the same on these two pages. *Concepts of Print*

Pages 4–5 *How is the way the kids are using the lid and tin can the same? How is it different? Compare and Contrast*

Page 6 *Point to the word* go *on this page. Vocabulary*

Page 7 Ask children to blend the sounds *f-u-n* and say the word. *Phonics*

Page 8 Point to the second word and have children read it with you. *Vocabulary*

LITERARY RESPONSE Children can draw what the kids might do next.

INDEPENDENT

Ron and Me

Guided Reading

TESTED OBJECTIVES

☑ Initial /r/r, /p/p, /l/l; final /p/p; medial /u/u.

☑ Blend with Short *u*

☑ Compare and Contrast

☑ Vocabulary: *to, go, do*

☐ Concepts of Print

REREAD THE BOOK FOR FLUENCY
Encourage children to reread the book.

Page 4 Ask children to find the exclamation mark on this page. *Concepts of Print*

Page 4 Have children point to the two words with the short *u* sound. Ask them to blend the sounds and read the words. (fun, mud) *Phonics*

Page 5 Have children find the words *Go* and *to* on this page. *Vocabulary*

Pages 7–8 *How is what the girl and Ron are doing the same? Compare and Contrast*

LITERARY RESPONSE Ask children to draw a picture of something they might do with a puppy.

CHALLENGE

Fun on the Farm
by David Michaels
illustrated by Tuko Fujisake

Guided Reading

SELF-SELECTED READING   Have children select one or more Challenge Books to read.

REREAD THE BOOK   Use the following prompts to guide children's reading:

Have children find and name words that begin with /r/ *r*, /p/ *p*, /l/ *l*, have the short /u/ *u* sound, or end with /p/ *p*. *Phonics*

Have children tell you the main idea of the story. *Main Idea*

Invite children to choose one of the story characters and make up a sentence using one or more of these words: *to, me, go, do*. *Vocabulary*

LITERARY RESPONSE   Have children who read different books work in pairs to compare their stories. Have them talk about these questions: *How were the main ideas the same or different? Did the stories take place inside or outside?*

TESTED OBJECTIVES

☑ Initial /r/*r*, /p/*p*, /l/*l*; final /p/*p*; medial /u/*u*.

☑ Blend with Short *u*

☑ Main Idea; Compare and Contrast

☑ Vocabulary: *to, me, go, do*

☐ Concepts of Print

INFORMAL ASSESSMENT

BLENDING

HOW TO ASSESS
Write the following rhyming words on the chalkboard: *run, fun, sun*. Ask children to blend the sounds and read each word.

FOLLOW UP   For those children who are experiencing difficulty, work with them individually to blend short *u* words.

CENTER Activity

Cross Curricular: Science

KINDER-GARDEN   Start a class garden. Help children plant and label various seeds, such as carrot, tomato, and cucumber. Children can take turns with the daily upkeep of the plants. Have a veggie feast at "harvest time."

▶ **Logical/Interpersonal**

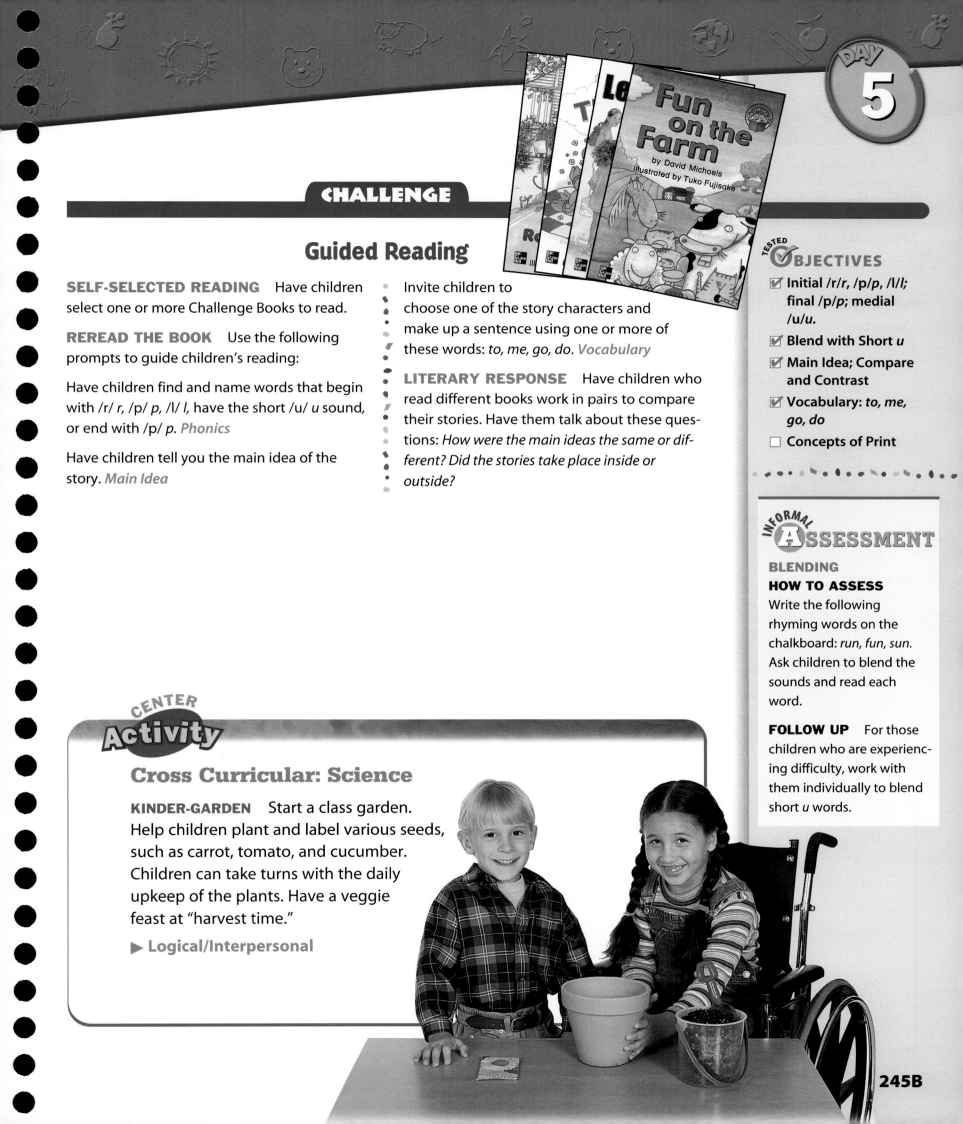

Vocabulary:
to, me, go, do

Vocabulary Cards

TESTED OBJECTIVES

Children will:
☑ identify and read the high-frequency words *to, me, go, do*

MATERIALS
- word cards

TEACHING TIP

WORD WALL Point to the words *to, me, go,* and *do* on the Word Wall. Say a sentence that contains two of the words, such as: "*Go to* bed." Then have children identify the words that were used.

Review

TEACH

Review to, me, go, do Tell children that you are going to say some lines from a play.

> Kyle: What can we *do*?
> Lyle: Will you play with *me*?
> Kyle: We can *go to* the park.

Say the lines aloud with children several times. Pass out word cards *to, me, go, do.*

Repeat the lines (or assign them to student actors). As you (or they) say each word, have children hold up the appropriate word card.

PRACTICE

Words in Context

Materials: word cards

- ◆ Hold up one of the word cards, and ask children to read it.

- ◆ Ask volunteers to make up a sentence using the word as you write the sentence on chart paper.

- ◆ Have children read the sentences aloud, holding up their word cards when they come to a vocabulary word.

ON LEVEL

✓ ASSESS/CLOSE

Have children complete page 245 of the Pupil Edition or Practice Book. For a different approach to teaching this skill, see page T26 for the **Alternate Teaching Strategy.**

Name _____

1.	go	my	do	(go)	to
2.	me	we	go	my	(me)
3.	to	(to)	do	the	is
4.	do	I	a	to	(do)

Say the first word in the row. • Draw a circle around the word where you see it in the same row.

Unit 4 Review *to, me, go, do*   245

Pupil Edition page 245

Meeting Individual Needs
Activities

Sparkle Letters

Materials: construction paper, glue sticks, glitter, word cards *to, me, go, do*

◆ Give each child a word card and review the words aloud.

◆ Have them copy each word from their cards, writing it with a glue stick and then sprinkling on glitter.

EASY

Match Words to Books

Materials: a selection of books, self-stick notes, word cards *to, me, go, do*

◆ Give each child a word card.

◆ Have children look through the books to find matches for their word cards.

◆ Ask children to mark the words they find with self-stick notes and share them with the rest of the group.

CHALLENGE

Match Game

Materials: word cards for *to, me, go, do*

◆ Make two sets of word cards for each pair of children.

◆ Have children turn over two cards, read the words, and pick them up if they match.

LANGUAGE SUPPORT

Interactive Writing

Write a Sentence Using Exclamation

GRAMMAR/SPELLING CONNECTIONS

During the Draft Step, explain to children that a character's spoken words are often shown in two ways, with quotation marks around their words, or with speech balloons. As an example, show children a comic strip that uses speech balloons.

TEACHING TIP

Ask two students to have a brief conversation about *Allie's Adventure from A to Z*. On the chalkboard, write one child's response using quotation marks. Then explain the use of quotation marks as a way to point out the words that characters say in stories.

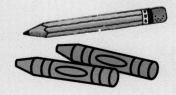

Prewrite

REVIEW THE STORY Reread *Allie's Adventure from A to Z* to children. Talk about the pattern of the story—that every page of the story has a letter of the alphabet and that Allie sees something that begins with the sound of that letter. Point out that Allie is very excited about what she sees.

BRAINSTORM Ask children to help you make a list of characters from the story. Write each one on the chalkboard as children respond.

Allie
Cow
Mouse
Zack

Draft

WRITE CHARACTER DIALOGUE USING EXCLAMATIONS Explain to children that they are going to be like authors and write some words for the characters in the story to say. They will put the words inside speech balloons.

- Display the Big Book and talk about what each character might be saying on a few pages.

- Explain that sentences that show excitement or surprise are called exclamations, and that they end with an exclamation mark. Write a sample sentence on chart paper, such as *Run fast little mouse!*

- Ask each child to think of an exclamation for a story character, being sure that the sentence contains "talking words." Have children help you write each sentence on chart paper.

- Help each child draw the character on construction paper and copy the exclamation above the character's head. Then have them draw a speech balloon around the words. Remind them to use an exclamation mark as end punctuation.

Revise

Before publishing children's work, read their dialogue as you track the print. Then ask:

- Does your sentence show excitement or surprise?

- Does your sentence begin with a capital letter and end with an exclamation mark?

Publish

Invite children to make a book cover titled *Allie's Friends Talk!* and bind the pages together to make a class book. Display the completed book in your classroom library.

Presentation Ideas

MAKE PUPPETS Have each child make a puppet with construction paper, tape, and a craft stick to show the story character for which he or she created dialogue. Ask children to read their dialogue and act out their scenes with the puppets.

CREATE A RESPONSE Read aloud each child's exclamatory sentence. Invite volunteers to think of and say appropriate dialogue responses for each sentence.

Listening and Speaking

- Tell children that actors in a play speak loudly enough so that everyone in the audience can hear. Remind them to do this as they put on their puppet shows.

- Remind children to listen carefully as you read aloud their exclamatory sentences.

TECHNOLOGY TIP

Help children type their dialogue into a script format next to each character's name. Then show them how to highlight the text they will deliver by changing the color of the type.

LANGUAGE SUPPORT

ESL Participate in dialogue with ESL children to show them common greetings or telephone etiquette. Take turns with children to say *Hello. How are you today? Fine, thank you. How are you?*

Meeting Individual Needs for Writing

EASY

Write Dialogue Have children work with a partner to create a two-character cartoon with speech balloons. Help them write the words each character speaks.

ON-LEVEL

Describe It! Have children write as many words as they can to describe one of the characters in the story.

CHALLENGE

Allie's Journal Have children pretend to be Allie and write a journal entry about something she might do during the day.

Wrap Up
the Theme

I Wonder

We can make discoveries about the wonders of nature in our own backyard.

REVIEW THE THEME Read the theme statement to children. Engage them in a conversation about some of the nature discoveries they have made during the past few weeks.

READ THE POEM Read the poem "Shell" aloud. Try to bring in a conch shell and pass it around so that children can have the experience of "hearing the water sound."

DISCUSS THE POEM Before rereading "Shell," ask children to listen for words that give clues about where Adam found the shell. Ask why the beach is a good place to find shells.

LOOKING AT GENRE: NONFICTION (INFORMATIONAL STORIES) The Literature Big Books *The Apple Pie Tree* and *Nature Spy* are stories that contain information about nature. Discuss how some books may have fictional characters but may also contain valuable information that children can learn from.

SHELL

When it was time
for Show and Tell,
Adam brought a big
  pink shell.

He told about
the ocean roar
and walking on the
  sandy shore.

And then he passed
the shell around.
We listened to the
  water sound.

And that's the first
  time
I could hear
the wild waves
  calling to my ear.

Myra Cohn Livingston

Listening Library

Research *and* Inquiry

Theme Project: Nature Collage

Give the Presentation Display all the nature collages in the classroom. Work with each pair as they practice telling about their collage. Then invite another class to hear the presentations.

PARTNERS

Draw Conclusions Encourage questions from the visiting class. Ask the visitors to tell what they learned about nature. Create a list of conclusions from their feedback.

Ask More Questions Ask children how they would like to expand their research about nature. Some suggestions for topics include Types of Fruit Trees and Caring for Nature. Encourage each group to research and present its findings in an imaginative way.

HIGH-FREQUENCY WORDS

GROUP Display the word cards *to, me, go, do*. Track print as you read each word with children. Ask them to point to the word that makes sense in this sentence: *Can you _____ this?* After they identify the word *do*, play a game in which you make a gesture, or other physical movement, and then ask: *Can you do this?* Have children imitate your movement.

Unit Review

You Are IT!
to

Is It You?
me

Go, Lad, Go!
go

Mud Fun
do

Ron and Me
review: *to, me, go, do*

☑ SKILLS & STRATEGIES

Phonics and Decoding
- ☑ Initial /r/r, /p/p, /l/l, /u/u
- ☑ Final /p/p
- ☑ Medial /u/u
- ☑ Blending with Short *a, i, o, u*

Comprehension
- ☑ Main Idea
- ☑ Compare and Contrast

Vocabulary
- ☑ High-Frequency Words: *to, me, go, do*

Beginning Reading Concepts
- ☑ On, Off
- ☑ Inside, Outside
- ☑ Over, Under
- ☑ Up, Down

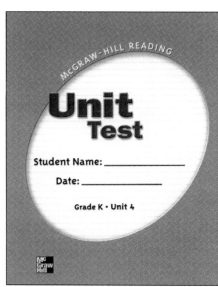

McGRAW-HILL READING

Unit Test

Student Name: _____

Date: _____

Grade K · Unit 4

Mc Graw Hill

UNIT 4 ASSESSMENT

Assessment
Follow-Up

Use the results of the informal and formal assessment opportunities in the unit to help you make decisions about future instruction.

SKILLS AND STRATEGIES	Alternate Teaching Strategies
Phonological Awareness	
Identifying rhyming words	T31
Identifying sounds: initial, final, and medial	T22, T27, T31, T33
Segmenting (syllables, sounds)	T27, T33
Blending (onset/rime, sounds)	T22, T31
Deleting syllables	T22
Phonics and Decoding	
Initial /r/r, /f/f, /p/p, /l/l, /u/u	Unit 3 T22, T27, T31, T32, T33
Final /p/p, Medial /u/u	T27, T33
Blending with Short a, i, o, u	Unit 1 T36, Unit 2 T35, Unit 3 T32, T33
Comprehension	
Main Idea	T25
Compare and Contrast	T30
Vocabulary	
High-Frequency Words: to, me, go, do	T26
Beginning Reading Concepts	
On, Off	T24
Inside, Outside	T24
Over, Under; Up, Down	T29
Writing	
Letter Formation	T36

McGraw-Hill School

 CD-ROM Provides extra phonics support.

 Research & Inquiry Ideas. Visit **www.mhschool.com/reading**

Cover Illustration: Mary Jane Begin

The publisher gratefully acknowledges permission to reprint the following copyrighted material:

"Annie's Pet" by Barbara Brenner. Text copyright © 1989 by Bank Street College of Education. Used by permission of Random House Children's Books, a division of Random House, Inc.

ANY KIND OF DOG by Lynn Whisnant Reiser. Copyright © 1992 by Lynn Whisnant Reiser. Reprinted by permission of William Morrow & Company. Used by permission of HarperCollins Publishers.

THE APPLE PIE TREE by Zoe Hall. Text copyright ©1996 by Zoe Hall. Illustrations copyright ©1996 by Shari Halpern. Reproduced by permission of Scholastic Inc.

CAPS FOR SALE by Esphyr Slobodkina. Copyright © 1940 and 1947, © renewed 1968, by Esphyr Slobodkina. Reprinted by permission of HarperCollins Publishers, Inc.

THE CHICK AND THE DUCKLING. This edition is reprinted by arrangement with Simon & Schuster Books for Young Readers, Simon & Schuster Children's Publishing Division. Text copyright © 1972 by Mirra Ginsburg. Illustrations copyright © 1972 by Jose Aruego and Ariane Dewey. All rights reserved.

"Clay" from A SONG I SANG TO YOU by Myra Cohn Livingston. Copyright © 1958, 1959, 1965, 1967, 1969, 1984 by Myra Cohn Livingston. Used by permission of Marian Reiner for the author.

"The Clever Turtle" retold by Margaret H. Lippert from CHILDREN'S ANTHOLOGY. Copyright © 1988 by Macmillan Publishing Company. Used by permission of McGraw-Hill, Inc.

THE EARTH AND I by Frank Asch. Copyright © 1994 by Frank Asch. Reprinted by permission of Harcourt Brace & Company.

"Engine, Engine, Number Nine"; "Gobble, Gobble"; "Miss Mary Mack"; "Nicholas Ned"; "Pease Porridge Hot"; "Sing a Song of Sixpence" and "Wee Willie Winkie" from BIG BOOK OF ALPHABET RHYMES AND CHIMES © 1993 by Macmillan/McGraw-Hill School Publishing Company, New York. Reproduced with permission of The McGraw-Hill Companies, Inc.

THE ENORMOUS CARROT by Vladimir Vagin. Copyright © 1998 by Vladimir Vagin. Reproduced by permission of Scholastic Inc.

"Every Time I Climb a Tree" from ONE AT A TIME by David McCord. Copyright © 1952 by David McCord. Reprinted by permission of Little, Brown & Company.

"50 Simple Things Kids Can Do to Save the Earth" from 50 SIMPLE THINGS KIDS CAN DO TO SAVE THE EARTH by The EarthWorks Press. Reprinted with permission of Andrews McMeel Publishing. All rights reserved

"Five Little Seeds" from THIS LITTLE PUFFIN compiled by Elizabeth Matterson. Copyright © 1969 by Puffin Books. Reprinted by permission of Penguin Putnam Inc.

FLOWER GARDEN by Eve Bunting. Text copyright ©1994 by Eve Bunting, illustrations copyright ©1994 by Kathryn Hewitt. Reprinted by permission of Harcourt Brace & Company.

"The Hare and the Tortoise" from WHAT YOUR KINDERGARTNER NEEDS TO KNOW by E.D. Hirsch, editor. Copyright © 1996 by The Core Knowledge Foundation. Used by permission of Doubleday, a division of Random House, Inc.

"Helping" from WHERE THE SIDEWALK ENDS by Shel Silverstein. Copyright © 1974 by Evil Eye Music, Inc. Reprinted by permission of HarperCollins Publishers.

"The Hokey Pokey" written by Taftt Baker, Larry LaPrise, and Charles P. Macak. Copyright 1950, Renewed 1978 Acuff-Rose Music, Inc. International Rights Secured. All Rights Reserved. Used by permission.

"How Many Spots Does a Leopard Have?" from HOW MANY SPOTS DOES A LEOPARD HAVE AND OTHER STORIES by Julius Lester. Copyright © 1989 by Julius Lester. Reprinted by permission of Scholastic Inc.

"Hungry Spider and the Turtle" from THE COW-TAIL SWITCH AND OTHER WEST AFRICAN STORIES by Harold Courlander and George Herzog. Illustrated by Madye Lee Chastain. Copyright © 1947 by Holt, Rinehart and Winston, Inc.

"Jennifer Bing, Why Won't You Sing?" from LADYBUG: THE MAGAZINE FOR YOUNG CHILDREN by Kimberly Thomas. Illustrated by Jada Rowland. Copyright © 1997 by Carus Publishing Company.

"A Kite" from READ-ALOUD RHYMES FOR THE VERY YOUNG. Copyright © 1986 by Alfred A. Knopf, Inc.

"Learning" by M. Lucille Ford from POETRY PLACE ANTHOLOGY published by Instructor Books, an imprint of Scholastic Professional Books, a division of Scholastic Inc. Copyright © 1983 by Edgell Communications Inc. Reproduced by permission of Scholastic Inc.

"Little Brown Rabbit" from THIS LITTLE PUFFIN compiled by Elizabeth Matterson. Copyright © 1969 by Puffin Books. Reprinted by permission of Penguin Putnam Inc.

"The Little Red Hen" from WHAT YOUR KINDERGARTNER NEEDS TO KNOW edited by E. D. Hirsch. Copyright © 1996 by The Core Knowledge Foundation. Used by permission of Doubleday, a division of Random House, Inc.

"The Little Red House" from A WORLD OF CHILDREN'S STORIES by Carolyn Sherwin Bailey. Edited by Anne Pellowski and illustrated by Gloria Ortiz. Copyright © 1993 by Friendship Press.

"The Little Turtle" from COLLECTED POEMS by Vachel Lindsay. Copyright © 1920 by Macmillan Publishing Co., Inc., renewed 1948 by Elizabeth C. Lindsay.

"Making Friends" from NATHANIEL TALKING. Copyright © 1988 by Eloise Greenfield. Reprinted by permission of Scott Treimel New York.

"Mary Had a Little Lamb" from WHAT YOUR KINDERGARTNER NEEDS TO KNOW edited by E. D. Hirsch, Jr., and John Holdren. Copyright © 1996 by The Core Knowledge Foundation. Used by permission of Delta Books, a division of Bantam Doubleday Dell Publishing Group, Inc.

"Mr. Sun," traditional, from SINGABLE SONGS FOR THE VERY YOUNG, courtesy of Homeland Publishing company, a division of Troubadour Records Ltd.

THE MITTEN retold by Alvin Tresselt, illustrated by Yaroslava. Adapted from the version by E. Rachov. Copyright © 1964 by Lothrop, Lee and Shepard Co., Inc.

"Morning Verse" from THE KINDERGARTEN SERIES. Edited by Margret Meyerkort. Copyright ©1983 by Wynstones Press. Published in England by Wynstones Press.

NATURE SPY by Shelley Rotner and Ken Kreisler. Text copyright © 1992 by Shelley Rotner and Ken Kreisler. Illustrations copyright © 1992 by Shelley Rotner. Reprinted by permission of Simon & Schuster Children's Publishing Division.

PEANUT BUTTER AND JELLY by Nadine Bernard Westcott. Copyright ©1987 by Nadine Bernard Westcott. Reprinted by permission of Dutton Children's Books, a division of Penguin Books USA Inc.

"The Playground of the Sun and Moon" from TUCK-ME-IN-TALES: BEDTIME STORIES FROM AROUND THE WORLD by Margaret Read MacDonald. Illustrated by Yvonne Davis. Text copyright © 1996 by Margaret Read MacDonald. Illustrations © 1996 by Yvonne Davis. Published 1996 by August House LittleFolk.

PRETEND YOU'RE A CAT by Jean Marzollo, illustrated by Jerry Pinkney. Text copyright © 1990 by Jean Marzollo. Paintings copyright © 1990 by Jerry Pinkney. Reprinted by permission of Dial Books for Young Readers, a division of Penguin Putnam Inc.

"R Is for Ribbon" from John Travers Moore Collection, Special Collections Dept., University of Virginia Library.

"Shell" from WORLDS I KNOW AND OTHER POEMS by Myra Cohn Livingston. Copyright © 1985 by Myra Cohn Livingston. Reprinted by permission of Margaret K. McElderry Books, an imprint of Simon & Schuster Children's Publishing Division.

SHOW AND TELL DAY by Anne Rockwell. Text copyright © 1997 by Anne Rockwell. Illustrations copyright © 1997 by Lizzy Rockwell. Reprinted by permission of HarperCollins Publishers.

"The Squeaky Old Bed" from CROCODILE! CROCODILE! STORIES TOLD AROUND THE WORLD by Barbara Baumgartner. Text copyright © 1994 by Barbara Baumgartner. Used by permission of Dorling Kindersley Publishing.

"The Soup Stone" from THE SOUP STONE by Maria Leach (Funk and Wagnalls Company). Copyright © 1954 Reprinted by permission of Harper and Row, Publishers, Inc.

"The Three Little Pigs" by Joseph Jacobs, illustrated by Tomie dePaola, from TOMIE DEPAOLA'S FAVORITE NURSERY TALES by Tomie dePaola. Copyright © 1986 by Tomie dePaola. Used by permission of G.P. Putnam's Sons, a division of Penguin Putnam Inc.

"Tommy" from BRONZEVILLE BOYS AND GIRLS by Gwendolyn Brooks. Copyright © 1956 by Gwendolyn Brooks Blakely.

"The Town Mouse and the Country Mouse" retold and illustrated by Lorinda Bryan Cauley. Copyright © 1984 by Lorinda Bryan Cauley. Used by permission of G.P. Putnam's Sons, a division of Penguin Putnam Inc.

"Umbrellas" from SWING AROUND THE SUN by Barbara Juster Esbensen. Copyright 1965 by Lerner Publications. Used by permission of the Publisher. All rights reserved.

Untitled from JUNE IS A TUNE THAT JUMPS ON A STAIR by Sarah Wilson. Copyright © 1993 by Sarah Wilson.

"The Velveteen Rabbit; or, How Toys Become Real" from WHAT YOUR KINDERGARTNER NEEDS TO KNOW by E. D. Hirsch, editor. Copyright © 1996 by The Core Knowledge Foundation. Used by permission of Doubleday, a division of Random House, Inc.

WARTHOGS IN THE KITCHEN by Pamela Duncan Edwards. Text ©1998 by Pamela Duncan Edwards. Illustrations ©1998 by Henry Cole. Reprinted by Hyperion Books for Children.

"Whistling" from RAINY RAINY SATURDAY by Jack Prelutsky. Text copyright © 1980 by Jack Prelutsky. Used by permission of HarperCollins Publishers.

WHITE RABBIT'S COLOR BOOK by Alan Baker. Copyright © 1994 by Alan Baker. Reprinted by permission of Larousse Kingfisher Chambers, Inc.

"Wonderful World" by Eva Grant from POETRY PLACE ANTHOLOGY published by Instructor Books, an imprint of Scholastic Professional Books, a division of Scholastic Inc. Copyright © 1983 by Edgell Communications Inc. Reproduced by permission of Scholastic Inc.

"The Yak" from ZOO DOINGS by Jack Prelutsky. Copyright © 1967, 1983 by Jack Prelutsky. Reprinted by permission of Greenwillow Books, a division of William Morrow & Company. Used by permission of HarperCollins Publishers.

"Yesterday's Paper" by Mabel Watts from READ-ALOUD RHYMES FOR THE VERY YOUNG. Copyright © 1986 by Alfred A. Knopf, Inc.

HANDWRITING
ZB Font Method Copyright © 1996 Zaner-Bloser. Manuscript handwriting models. Used by permission.

ILLUSTRATION
Jennifer Emery, 106A; Eugenie Fernandes, 6N, 18F, 42F, 54E, 78E, 90F, 114E, 130A, 140B, 144A, 212A 180B, 184B, 260B, 286B, 304A; Dara Goldman, 332B, 360B; Jean Hirashima, R18, 189B, 237B; Meredith Johnson, 152A, 164A, 200B, 216B, 226B, 228A, 258J, 268A, 270J, 294J; Richard Kolding, R1, 55B, 66T, 79B, 102F, 131B, 138F, 151B, 155B, 210E, 210F, 211B, 215B, 222F, 234F, 246S, 246T, 258E, 258F, 270E, 270F, 271B, 282E, 287B, 294F, 323B, 335B; Vicki Learner, 93B, 117B, 330I; Anne Lederhos, R7, R15, R23, R27, R31, R38, 7B, 316B, 318J, 342I, 354J, 358A; Taia Morley, 6J, 34A, 44B, 48B, 92A, 118A, 118B, 210B, 243, 246P, 322B, 324A, 340A, 348A, 360A, 363A; Blanche Sims, 95B, 96B, 108B, 112B, 114B, 120B, 124B, 132A, 132B, 142A, 148B, 167B, 178A, 198B, 219A, 219, 240A, 244A, 268A, 270J, 275B, 294J, 306S, 306T, 311B, 318E, 318F, 330E, 330F, 342F, 347B, 354E, 354F; Susan Spellman, 19B, 31B, 66T, 78E, 90F, 102F, 114E, 115B, 187B, 199B, 223B, 235B; Steve Sullivan, R3, 141B, 184A, 196B, 204B, 236A, 244A, 248B, 298A, 335, 357B, 365; Linda Weller, R14, 57B, 69B, 126S, 126T, 138F, 150F, 153B, 162F, 174F, 186S, 198E, 213B, 307B, 321B, 327, 333B, 343B

All other illustrations in Unit 1 are by Bernard Adnet, KenBowser.com, Nan Brooks, Valérie Cardon, Karol Kaminsky, Laura Kraning, Anthony Lewis, Claude Martinot, Sharon McKenna, Paula Sjöblom, and Nancy Woodman.

PHOTOGRAPHY
All photographs are by the Macmillan/McGraw-Hill School Division (MMSD), Mike Gaffney for MMSD, Richard Haynes for MMSD, Richard Hutchings for MMSD, Titus Kang for MMSD, Ken Karp for MMSD, Dave Mager for MMSD, Anna Nielson for MMSD, Mike Peters for MMSD, Mike Provost for MMSD, John Serafin for MMSD, and Clara Von Aich for MMSD, and Francis Westfield for MMSD except as noted below.

Unit 1: 59B: b.: Robert W. Madden/National Geographic Society

Unit 5: 282D: Jose L. Pelaez Inc./The Stock Market

Contents

Every Time I Climb a Tree
by David McCord

Every time I climb a tree
Every time I climb a tree
Every time I climb a tree
I scrape a leg
Or skin a knee
And every time I climb a tree
I find some ants
Or dodge a bee
And get the ants
All over me

And every time I climb a tree
Where have you been?
They say to me
But don't they know that I am free
Every time I climb a tree?
I like it best
To spot a nest
That has an egg
Or maybe three

And then I skin
The other leg
But every time I climb a tree
I see a lot of things to see
Swallows rooftops and TV
And all the fields and farms there be
Every time I climb a tree
Though climbing may be good for ants
It isn't awfully good for pants
But still it's pretty good for me
Every time I climb a tree

The Playground of the Sun and Moon
a myth by Margaret Read MacDonald

Some people say that high in the sky, the sun lives in a palace of gold.

Sun looks out his window each morning to see if Moon is in sight.

"Where are you, little Moon? Are you hiding in the nighttime fields? Or are you playing in my blue day skies?"

Sometimes Moon is nearby, drifting pale in the bright daytime. She answers sweetly: "Did you call me, Sun?"

"Sure I called you!" Sun shoots his rays toward her.

"What do you want to play today?" asks Moon shyly.

"Ring of Fortune!" That is what Sun calls his game of chase.

"Oh? And how is it played?"

Then Sun begins to chant the directions:

"I have two rings

▶ that are two paths.

One is day,

The other, night.

Tell me, Moon,

Which do you take?

The gold is day,

the silver, night."

Moon never hesitates at all. "Me? I take the night!"

The Sun jumps up, laughing, "Then run, run, run! And if I catch you, I get your silver ring!"

So Moon dances off through the blue sky and Sun runs happily after. Of course Sun never catches Moon. Moon crosses the sky and slips away into her lovely fields of darkness. There she dances and sings all night long, drifting gently among the shadows.

Watch the sky and you will see...there goes Moon in the daytime sky, with Sun trailing behind. But never will you see Sun move within the nighttime sky.

The night belongs to Moon and Moon alone.

The Clever Turtle
a Hispanic folk tale retold by Margaret H. Lippert

Wheet-weedle-whoo, wheet-weedle-whoo, wheet-wheet-wheet-whoo. Every day, Turtle sat by the Amazon River and played her flute. All the birds and animals loved to listen to her play.

One day, a man walking through the forest heard her beautiful music. Wheet-weedle-whoo, wheet-weedle-whoo, wheet-wheet-wheet-whoo.

He stopped to listen. When he saw that a turtle was playing the flute, he thought about dinner.

"Turtle soup would be a treat tonight," he thought. So he picked Turtle up and carried her home.

He put Turtle into a cage made of branches and closed the lid. "Don't let the turtle out of the cage," he said to his children. "Tonight we will have turtle soup." Then the father picked up his hoe and went to work in the garden. The children played in the yard.

Turtle did not want to be made into soup. She started to play her flute. Wheet-weedle-whoo, wheet-weedle-whoo, wheet-wheet-wheet-whoo. The children stopped their game and listened.

"Turtle is playing the flute!" they shouted.

"I can dance as well as I can play," called Turtle. "I can even play and dance at the same time. If you open the lid you can watch me." The children opened the lid, and Turtle started to dance.

Wheet-weedle-whoo. Crash-bam. Wheet-weedle-whoo. Crash-bam. Turtle's shell banged against the sides of the cage as she danced.

The children laughed and clapped.

Turtle danced for a while, then she stopped. "I am stiff from dancing in this little cage," she said. "I need to stretch my legs. Let me go for a short walk. Then I will dance some more for you."

The children wanted to see Turtle dance again. They lifted Turtle out of the cage. "Don't go far," they said. Turtle walked around and around the yard. She walked closer and closer to the forest. Then she crawled under some leaves and disappeared.

The children looked and looked for Turtle. "Turtle! Turtle!" they called. But there was no answer. "Father will be angry," they said. "What can we do now?"

The children found a big smooth stone and painted it to look like a turtle. Then they put the painted stone in Turtle's cage. "It is dark in the cage," they said. "Father will think that the turtle is still in there."

When the father came home, he lit a fire and put some water in a pot. "Bring me the turtle," he said. The children brought the painted stone and threw it in the pot. CRASH! "The shell is hard," said the father. "But the meat will be soft when it is cooked."

After some time, the father decided the soup must be ready. He spooned the painted stone out of the pot. The stone fell onto his dish and broke it.

The father looked at the silent children. "You let the turtle go," he said. "Now we have nothing to eat tonight. But tomorrow is another day. In the morning I will try to find the turtle."

The next day the father walked into the forest. He looked and looked for Turtle. Then he got tired and went home. Do you think he ever found Turtle again?

How Many Spots Does a Leopard Have

an African folk tale retold by Julius Lester

One morning Leopard was doing what he enjoyed doing most. He was looking at his reflection in the lake. How handsome he was! How magnificent was his coat! And, ah! The spots on his coat! Was there anything in creation more superb?

Leopard's rapture was broken when the water in the lake began moving. Suddenly Crocodile's ugly head appeared above the surface.

Leopard jumped back. Not that he was afraid. Crocodile would not bother him. But then again, one could never be too sure about Crocodile.

"Good morning, Leopard," Crocodile said. "Looking at yourself again, I see. You are the most vain creature in all of creation."

Leopard was not embarrassed. "If you were as handsome as I am, if you had such beautiful spots, you, too, would be vain."

"Spots! Who needs spots? You're probably so in love with your spots that you spend all your time counting them."

▶ Now there was an idea that had not occurred to Leopard. "What a wonderful idea!" he exclaimed. "I would very much like to know how many spots I have." He stopped. "But there are far too many for me to count myself."

The truth was that Leopard didn't know how to count. "Perhaps you will count them for me, Crocodile?"

"Not on your life!" answered Crocodile. "I have better things to do than count spots." He slapped his tail angrily and dove beneath the water.

Leopard chuckled. "Crocodile doesn't know how to count, either."

Leopard walked along the lakeshore until he met Weasel. "Good morning, Weasel. Would you count my spots for me?"

"Who? Me? Count? Sure. One-two-three-four."

"Great!" exclaimed Leopard. "You can count."

Weasel shook his head. "But I can't. What made you think that I could?"

"But you just did. You said, 'One-two-three-four.' That's counting."

Weasel shook his head again. "Counting is much more difficult than that. There is something that comes after four, but I don't know what it is."

"Oh," said Leopard. "I wonder who knows what comes after four."

"Well, if you ask at the lake when all the animals come to drink, you will find someone who can count."

"You are right, Weasel! And I will give a grand prize to the one who tells me how many spots I have."

"What a great idea!" Weasel agreed.

That afternoon all the animals were gathered at the lake to drink. Leopard announced that he would give a magnificent prize to the one who could count his spots.

Elephant said he should be first since he was the biggest and the oldest.

"One-two-three-four-five-six-seven-eight-nine-ten," Elephant said very loudly and with great speed. He took a deep breath and began again. "One-two-three-four-five-si–"

"No! No! No!" the other animals interrupted. "You've already counted to ten once."

Elephant looked down his long trunk at the other animals. "I beg your pardon. I would appreciate it if you would not interrupt me when I am counting. You made me forget where I was. Now, where was I? I know I was somewhere in the second ten."

"The second ten?" asked Antelope. "What's that?"

"The numbers that come after the first ten, of course. I don't much care for those 'teen' things, thirteen, fourteen, and what have you. It is eminently more sensible to count ten twice and that makes twenty. That is multiplication."

None of the other animals knew what Elephant was talking about.

"Why don't you start over again?" suggested Cow.

Elephant began again and he counted ten twice and stopped. He frowned and looked very confused. Finally he said, "Leopard has more than twenty spots."

"How many more than twenty?" Leopard wanted to know.

Elephant frowned more. "A lot." Then he brightened. "In fact, you have so many more spots than twenty that I simply don't have time to count them now. I have an important engagement I mustn't be late for." Elephant started to walk away.

"Ha! Ha! Ha!" laughed Mule. "I bet Elephant doesn't know how to count higher than twenty."

Mule was right.

"Can you count above twenty?" Leopard asked Mule.

"Who? Me? I can only count to four because that's how many legs I have."

Leopard sighed. "Can anyone count above twenty?" he asked plaintively.

Bear said, "Well, once I counted up to fifty. Is that high enough?"

Leopard shrugged. "I don't know. It might be. Why don't you try and we will see."

Bear agreed. "I'll start at your tail. One-two-three-four-five-six . . . . Hm. Is that one spot or two spots?"

All the animals crowded around to get a close look. They argued for some time and finally agreed that it should only count as one.

"So, where was I?" asked Bear.

"Five," answered Turkey.

"It was six, you turkey," said Chicken.

"Better start again," suggested Crow.

Bear started again and got as far as eleven. "Eleven. That's a beautiful spot right there, Leopard."

"Which one?" Leopard wanted to know.

"Right there. Oh, dear. Or was it that spot there?

They're both exquisite. My, my. I don't know where I left off counting. I must start again."

Bear counted as far as twenty-nine this time and then stopped suddenly. "Now, what comes after twenty-nine?"

"I believe thirty does," offered Turtle.

"That's right!" exclaimed Bear. "Now, where did I leave off?"

"You were still on the tail," offered Lion.

"Yes, but was that the twenty-ninth spot, or was it this one here?"

The animals started arguing again.

"You'd better start again," suggested Cow.

"Start what again?" asked Rabbit who had just arrived.

The animals explained to Rabbit about the difficulty they were having in counting Leopard's spots.

"Is that all?" Rabbit said. "I know the answer to that."

"You do?" all the animals, including Leopard, exclaimed at once.

"Certainly. It's really quite simple." Rabbit pointed to one of Leopard's spots. "This one is dark." He pointed to another. "This one is light. Dark, light, dark, light, dark, light." Rabbit continued in this way until he had touched all of Leopard's spots.

"It's simple," he concluded. "Leopard has only two spots—dark ones and light ones."

All the animals remarked on how smart Rabbit was, all of them, that is, except Leopard. He knew something was wrong with how Rabbit counted, but unless he learned to count for himself, he would never know what it was.

Leopard had no choice but to give Rabbit the magnificent prize.

What was it?

What else except a picture of Leopard himself!

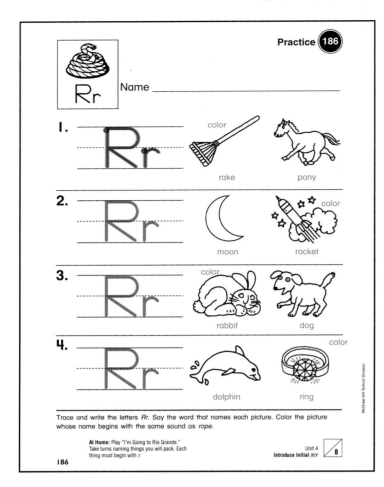

Practice 186

Name _____

1. R r — color — rake — pony

2. R r — moon — color — rocket

3. R r — color — rabbit — dog

4. R r — dolphin — color — ring

Trace and write the letters *Rr*. Say the word that names each picture. Color the picture whose name begins with the same sound as *rope*.

At Home: Play "I'm Going to Rio Grande." Take turns naming things you will pack. Each thing must begin with *r*.

Unit 4
Introduce Initial /r/r 8

186

Practice 187

Name _____

Look at the picture. Color the items that are *on* the tree. Draw a circle around the things that are *off* the tree.

9 Unit 4
Introduce On, Off

At Home: Place common objects on a table and on the floor. Together, talk about the items that are on the table and those that are off.

187

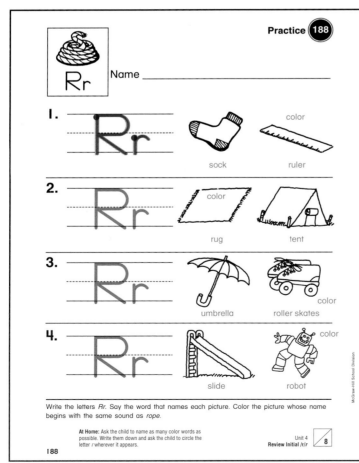

Practice 188

Name _____

1. R r — sock — color — ruler

2. R r — color — rug — tent

3. R r — umbrella — color — roller skates

4. R r — slide — color — robot

Write the letters *Rr*. Say the word that names each picture. Color the picture whose name begins with the same sound as *rope*.

At Home: Ask the child to name as many color words as possible. Write them down and ask the child to circle the letter *r* wherever it appears.

Unit 4
Review Initial /r/r 8

188

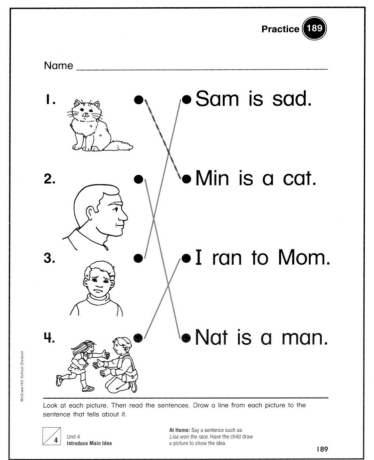

Practice 189

Name _____

1. Sam is sad.

2. Min is a cat.

3. I ran to Mom.

4. Nat is a man.

Look at each picture. Then read the sentences. Draw a line from each picture to the sentence that tells about it.

4 Unit 4
Introduce Main Idea

At Home: Say a sentence such as: *Lisa won the race.* Have the child draw a picture to show the idea.

189

Annotated Workbooks

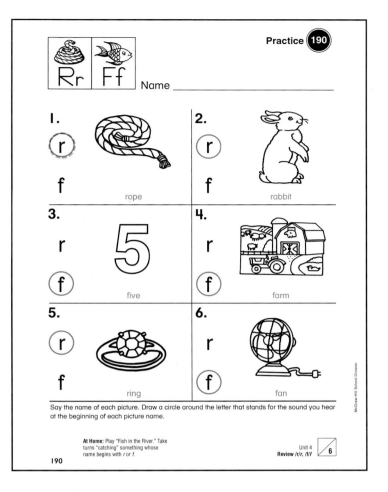

Practice 190

Name _____

1. (r) f rope

2. (r) f rabbit

3. r (f) five

4. r (f) farm

5. (r) f ring

6. r (f) fan

Say the name of each picture. Draw a circle around the letter that stands for the sound you hear at the beginning of each picture name.

At Home: Play "Fish in the River." Take turns "catching" something whose name begins with r or f.

Unit 4
Review /r/r, /f/f 6

190

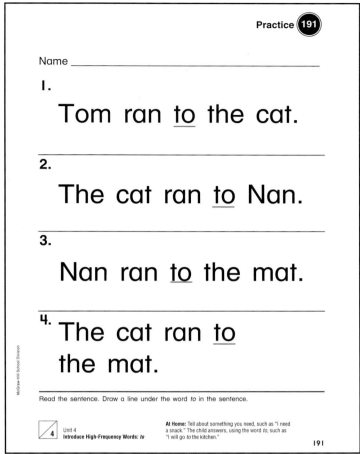

Practice 191

Name _____

1.

Tom ran <u>to</u> the cat.

2.

The cat ran <u>to</u> Nan.

3.

Nan ran <u>to</u> the mat.

4. The cat ran <u>to</u> the mat.

Read the sentence. Draw a line under the word *to* in the sentence.

4 Unit 4
Introduce High-Frequency Words: *to*

At Home: Tell about something you need, such as "I need a snack." The child answers, using the word *to*, such as "I will go *to* the kitchen."

191

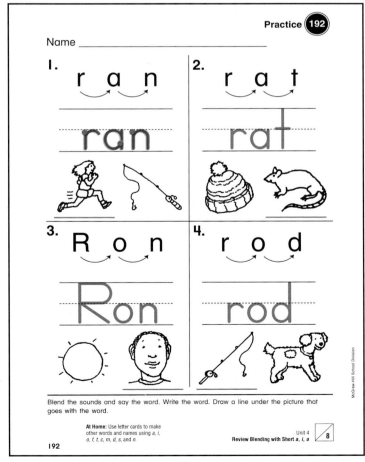

Practice 192

Name _____

1. r a n

ran

2. r a t

rat

3. R o n

Ron

4. r o d

rod

Blend the sounds and say the word. Write the word. Draw a line under the picture that goes with the word.

At Home: Use letter cards to make other words and names using *a, i, o, f, t, c, m, d, s,* and *n.*

Unit 4
Review Blending with Short *a, i, o* 8

192

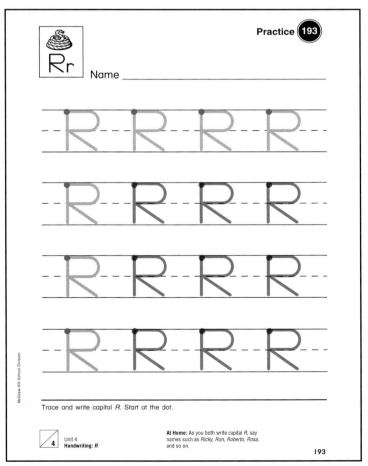

Practice 193

Rr Name _____

R R R R

R R R R

R R R R

R R R R

Trace and write capital *R*. Start at the dot.

4 Unit 4
Handwriting: *R*

At Home: As you both write capital *R*, say names such as *Ricky, Ron, Roberto, Rosa,* and so on.

193

Practice 194

Rr

Name _____

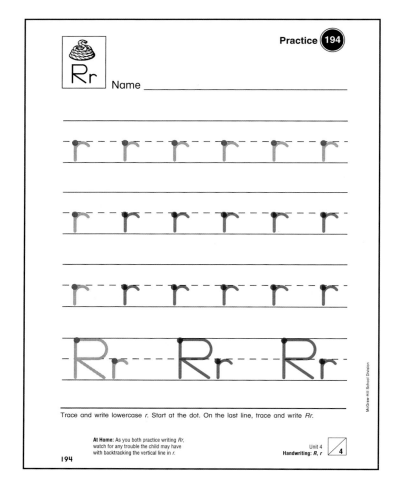

Trace and write lowercase *r*. Start at the dot. On the last line, trace and write *Rr*.

At Home: As you both practice writing *Rr*, watch for any trouble the child may have with backtracking the vertical line in *r*.

Unit 4
Handwriting: R, r 4

194

Practice 195

Name _____

1. ● ● Sid did not fit.

2. ● ● Ron ran to Tom.

3. ● ● The cat ran.

4. ● ● Tam is mad.

Look at each picture. Then read the sentences. Draw a line from each picture to the sentence that tells about it.

4 Unit 4
Review Main Idea

At Home: Together, pick a picture from a photo album. Have the child say a sentence that tells what the picture is about.

195

Practice 196

Name _____

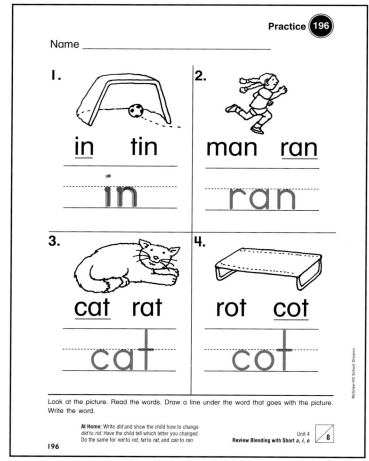

1. in   tin

in

2. man   ran

ran

3. cat   rat

cat

4. rot   cot

cot

Look at the picture. Read the words. Draw a line under the word that goes with the picture. Write the word.

At Home: Write *did* and show the child how to change *did* to *rid*. Have the child tell which letter you changed. Do the same for *not* to *rot*, *fat* to *rat*, and *can* to *ran*.

Unit 4
Review Blending with Short *a, i, o* 8

196

Practice 197

Name _____

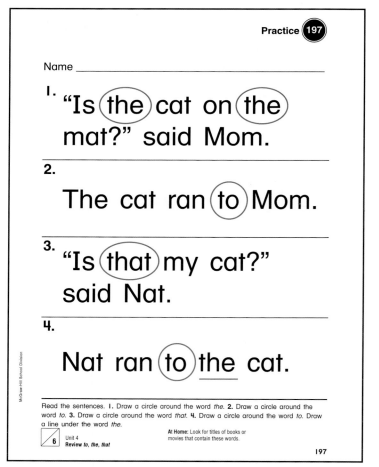

1. "Is (the) cat on (the) mat?" said Mom.

2. The cat ran (to) Mom.

3. "Is (that) my cat?" said Nat.

4. Nat ran (to) the cat.

Read the sentences. **1.** Draw a circle around the word *the*. **2.** Draw a circle around the word *to*. **3.** Draw a circle around the word *that*. **4.** Draw a circle around the word *to*. Draw a line under the word *the*.

6 Unit 4
Review *to, the, that*

At Home: Look for titles of books or movies that contain these words.

197

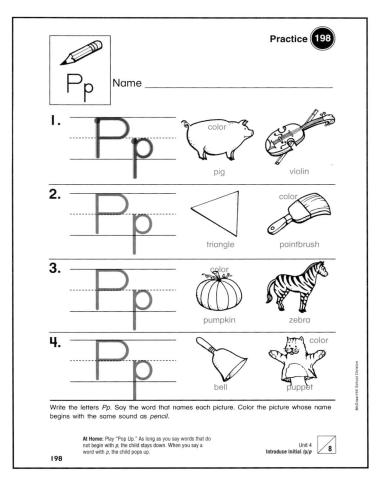

Practice 198

Pp Name _____

1. P p   color — pig   violin
2. P p   triangle   color — paintbrush
3. P p   color — pumpkin   zebra
4. P p   bell   color — puppet

Write the letters *Pp*. Say the word that names each picture. Color the picture whose name begins with the same sound as *pencil*.

At Home: Play "Pop Up." As long as you say words that do not begin with *p*, the child stays down. When you say a word with *p*, the child pops up.

Unit 4
Introduce Initial /p/p   8

198

Practice 199

Name _____

1.
2.
3.

Look at the picture on the left. Draw a circle around the picture on the right that shows something you would find inside the building. Draw a line under the picture on the right that shows something you would find outside the building.

Unit 4
Introduce Inside, Outside   6

At Home: Take a walk around the block. Have the child choose a building. Take turns naming what might be inside the building. Would it have an elevator? Do people work there?

199

Practice 200

–p Name _____

cup — p
sock —
mop — p

cap — p
top — p
pot —

Say the name of each picture. Write the letter *p* under each picture that has the same ending sound as *map*.

At Home: Take turns saying the name of something that ends with the sound the letter *p* stands for.

Unit 4
Introduce Final /p/p   6

200

Practice 201

Name _____

Look at the bear on the left. Then look at the pictures below it. Draw a circle around the items found on the bear. Cross out the items that are not on the bear. Do the same thing for the bear on the right. Then use the items to tell how the two bears are the same and different.

Unit 4
Introduce Compare and Contrast   8

At Home: Have the child compare his or her clothing with another person's clothing. Help the child see similarities and differences in pants, shirts, shoes and so on.

201

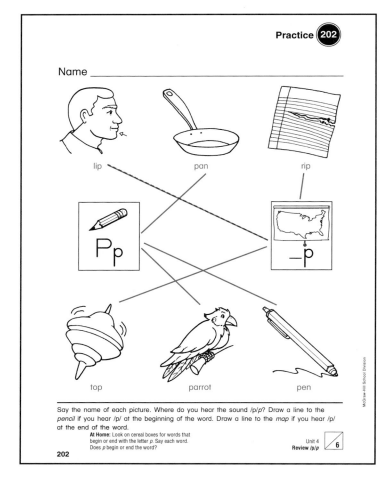

Practice 202

Name _____

lip   pan   rip

Pp   _p

top   parrot   pen

Say the name of each picture. Where do you hear the sound /p/p? Draw a line to the *pencil* if you hear /p/ at the beginning of the word. Draw a line to the *map* if you hear /p/ at the end of the word.

At Home: Look on cereal boxes for words that begin or end with the letter *p*. Say each word. Does *p* begin or end the word?

202

Unit 4
Review /p/p   6

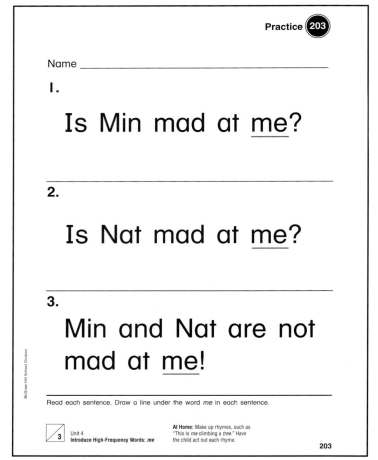

Practice 203

Name _____

1.

Is Min mad at me?

_____

2.

Is Nat mad at me?

_____

3.

Min and Nat are not mad at me!

_____

Read each sentence. Draw a line under the word *me* in each sentence.

3   Unit 4
Introduce High-Frequency Words: *me*

At Home: Make up rhymes, such as "This is *me* climbing a *tree*." Have the child act out each rhyme.

203

Practice 204

Name _____

1. P a m

Pam

2. r i p

rip

3. t o p

top

4. p i n

pin

Blend the sounds and say the word. Write the word. Draw a line under the picture that goes with the word.

At Home: Together, write words that begin and end with the same letters. Take turns using some of the words in sentences.

204

Unit 4
Review Blending with Short *a, i, o*   8

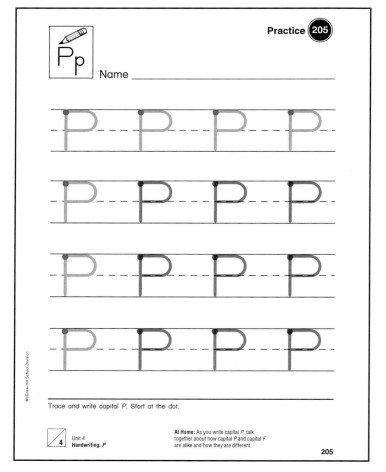

Practice 205

Pp

Name _____

P - P - P - P

P   P   P   P

P   P   P   P

P   P   P   P

Trace and write capital *P*. Start at the dot.

4   Unit 4
Handwriting: *P*

At Home: As you write capital *P*, talk together about how capital *P* and capital *F* are alike and how they are different.

205

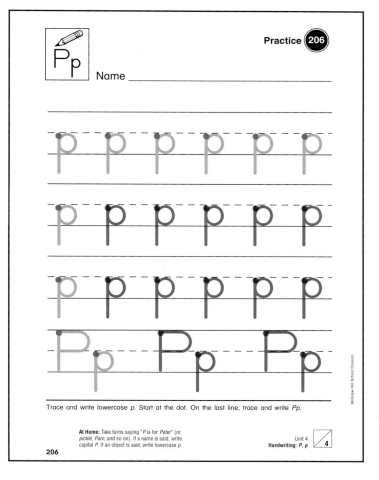

Trace and write lowercase p. Start at the dot. On the last line, trace and write *Pp*.

At Home: Take turns saying "*P* is for *Peter*" (or *pickle*, *Pam*, and so on). If a name is said, write capital *P*. If an object is said, write lowercase *p*.

Unit 4
Handwriting: P, p 4

206

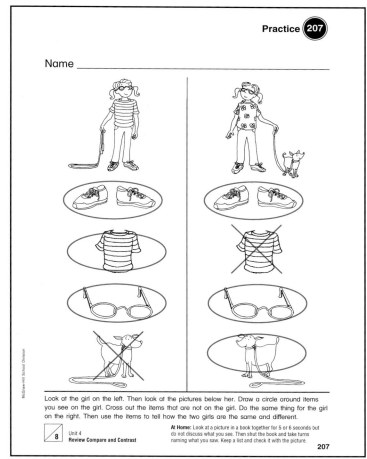

Look at the girl on the left. Then look at the pictures below her. Draw a circle around items you see on the girl. Cross out the items that are not on the girl. Do the same thing for the girl on the right. Then use the items to tell how the two girls are the same and different.

Unit 4
Review Compare and Contrast 8

At Home: Look at a picture in a book together for 5 or 6 seconds but do not discuss what you see. Then shut the book and take turns naming what you saw. Keep a list and check it with the picture.

207

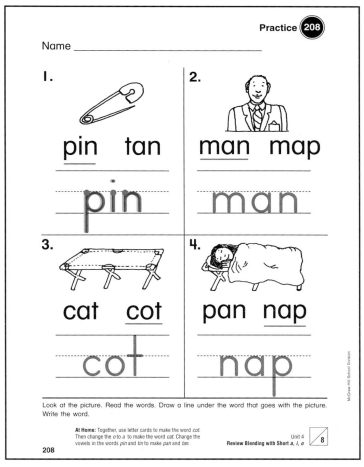

1.
pin   tan

pin

2.
man   map

man

3.
cat   cot

cot

4.
pan   nap

nap

Look at the picture. Read the words. Draw a line under the word that goes with the picture. Write the word.

At Home: Together, use letter cards to make the word *cot*. Then change the *o* to *a* to make the word *cat*. Change the vowels in the words *pin* and *tin* to make *pan* and *tan*.

Unit 4
Review Blending with Short a, i, o 8

208

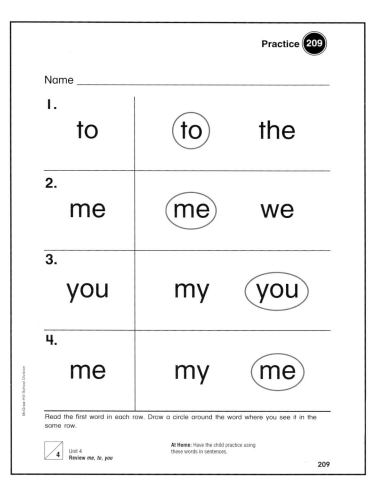

1.
to   (to)   the

2.
me   (me)   we

3.
you   my   (you)

4.
me   my   (me)

Read the first word in each row. Draw a circle around the word where you see it in the same row.

Unit 4
Review me, to, you 4

At Home: Have the child practice using these words in sentences.

209

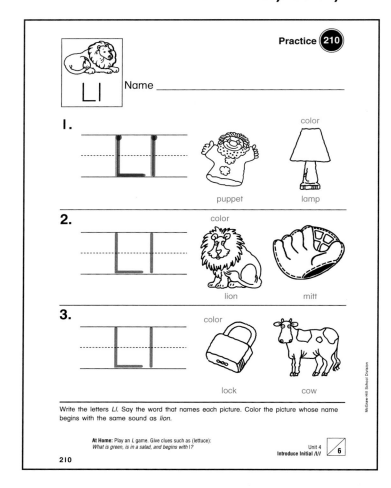

Practice 210

Ll Name _____

1. color / puppet / lamp

2. color / lion / mitt

3. color / lock / cow

Write the letters *Ll*. Say the word that names each picture. Color the picture whose name begins with the same sound as *lion*.

At Home: Play an *l* game. Give clues such as (lettuce): *What is green, is in a salad, and begins with l?*

Unit 4
Introduce Initial /l/ 6

210

Practice 211

Name _____

1. _____ color

2. color _____

3. _____ color

Color the picture that shows *over*. Draw a line under the picture that shows *under*.

6 Unit 4
Introduce Over, Under

At Home: Find and talk about items over or under another item, such as a chair or a table.

211

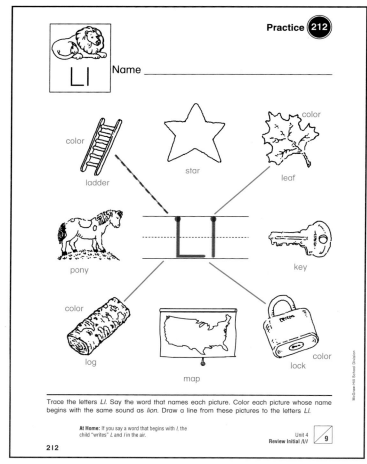

Practice 212

Ll Name _____

color — ladder / star / leaf

pony / Ll / key

color — log / map / lock — color

Trace the letters *Ll*. Say the word that names each picture. Color each picture whose name begins with the same sound as *lion*. Draw a line from these pictures to the letters *Ll*.

At Home: If you say a word that begins with *l*, the child "writes" *L* and *l* in the air.

Unit 4
Review Initial /l/ 9

212

Practice 213

Name _____

1. • • Ron is mad.

2. • • I have a dip.

3. • • The lid can fit.

4. • • I have a nap.

Look at each picture. Then read the sentences. Draw a line from each picture to the sentence that tells about it.

4 Unit 4
Review Main Idea

At Home: Read a story together. Have the child say the main idea of the story: "This story is about ___."

213

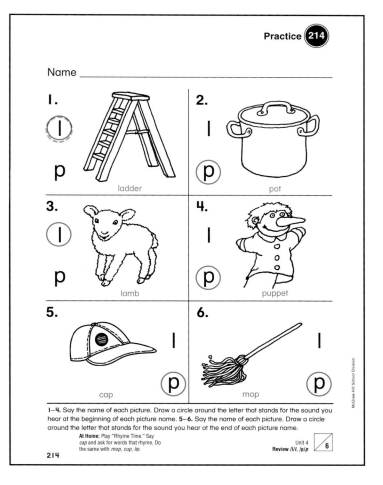

Practice 214

Name _____

1. ladder
2. pot
3. lamb
4. puppet
5. cap
6. mop

1–4. Say the name of each picture. Draw a circle around the letter that stands for the sound you hear at the beginning of each picture name. 5–6. Say the name of each picture. Draw a circle around the letter that stands for the sound you hear at the end of each picture name.

At Home: Play "Rhyme Time." Say cap and ask for words that rhyme. Do the same with mop, cup, lip.

Unit 4
Review /l/l, /p/p   6

214

Practice 215

Name _____

1. "Can we go in?" said Dan.

2. "We can go in," said Mom.

3. "Can the cat go in?" said Pam.

4. "The cat can go in," said Mom.

Read each sentence. Draw a line under the word go in each sentence.

Unit 4
Introduce High-Frequency Words: go

At Home: Use go in questions and answers, such as Can I go to the park? You can go to the park.

215

Practice 216

Name _____

1. l i t — lit
2. l i p — lip
3. f a n — fan
4. r o d — rod

Blend the sounds and say the word. Write the word. Draw a line under the picture that goes with the word.

At Home: Write not and dot. Have the child change dot to lot and tell how it was done. Do the same for dad to lad, did to lid, and tap to lap.

Unit 4
Review Blending with Short a, i, o   8

216

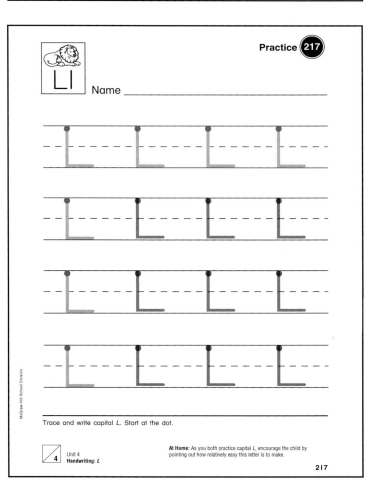

Practice 217

Ll   Name _____

L L L L
L L L L
L L L L
L L L L

Trace and write capital L. Start at the dot.

Unit 4
Handwriting: L

At Home: As you both practice capital L, encourage the child by pointing out how relatively easy this letter is to make.

217

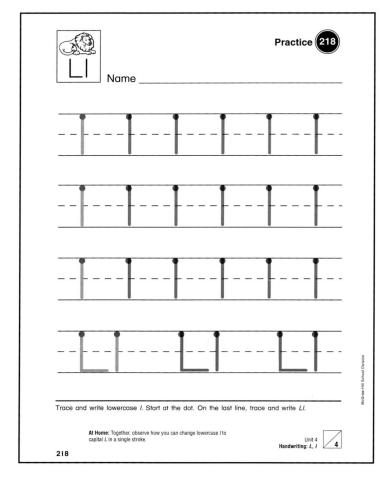

Practice 218

Ll

Name _____

Trace and write lowercase *l*. Start at the dot. On the last line, trace and write *Ll*.

At Home: Together, observe how you can change lowercase *l* to capital *L* in a single stroke.

Unit 4
Handwriting: L, l   4

218

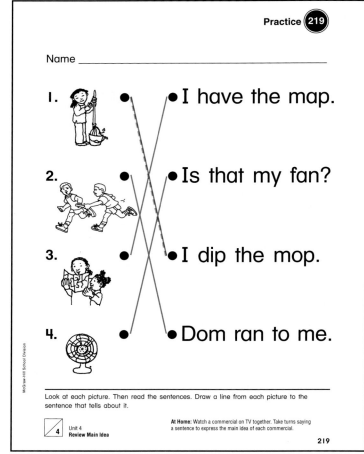

Practice 219

Name _____

1. • •I have the map.

2. • •Is that my fan?

3. • •I dip the mop.

4. • •Dom ran to me.

Look at each picture. Then read the sentences. Draw a line from each picture to the sentence that tells about it.

Unit 4
Review Main Idea   **At Home:** Watch a commercial on TV together. Take turns saying a sentence to express the main idea of each commercial.

219

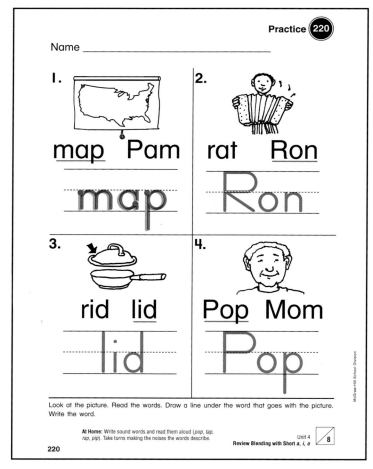

Practice 220

Name _____

1.   map Pam
map

2.   rat Ron
Ron

3.   rid lid
lid

4.   Pop Mom
Pop

Look at the picture. Read the words. Draw a line under the word that goes with the picture. Write the word.

At Home: Write sound words and read them aloud (*pop, tap, rap, pip*). Take turns making the noises the words describe.

Unit 4
Review Blending with Short a, i, o   8

220

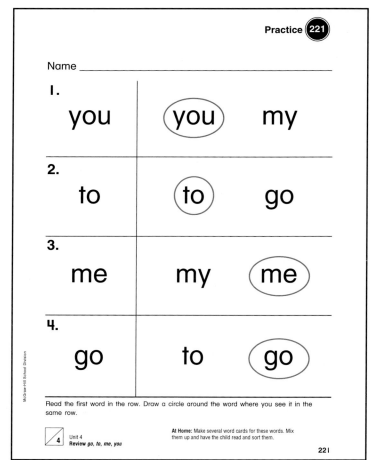

Practice 221

Name _____

1. you   (you)   my

2. to   (to)   go

3. me   my   (me)

4. go   to   (go)

Read the first word in the row. Draw a circle around the word where you see it in the same row.

Unit 4
Review go, to, me, you   **At Home:** Make several word cards for these words. Mix them up and have the child read and sort them.

221

Mud Fun • PRACTICE

Name _____

1. Uu

color
vase

under

2. Uu

color
umpire

mitt

3. Uu

astronaut

color
up

Write the letters *Uu*. Say the word that names each picture. Color the picture whose name begins with the same sound as *umbrella*.

At Home: Play "Jack-in-the-Box." When you say a word that begins with /u/, such as *up*, the child jumps up.

Unit 4
Introduce Initial /u/u 6

222

Name _____

color   color   color   color   color

Look at the picture. Draw a circle around the things in the picture that are up in the air. Color the things that are down on the ground.

Unit 4
Introduce Up, Down 10

At Home: Name some things that are up (books on shelves, etc.) and some things that are down (rugs, grass, etc.).

223

_u_ Name _____

u

color   color
ham   pup   rug

sock   mug   tub
         color   color

cat   hug
              color

Write the letter *u*. Say the word that names each picture. Listen for the sound in the middle of the word. Color each picture whose name has the same middle sound as *sun*.

At Home: Play "Rhyme Time." Say *sun* and ask for words that rhyme. Do the same for *nut* and *rug*.

Unit 4
Introduce Medial /u/u 9

224

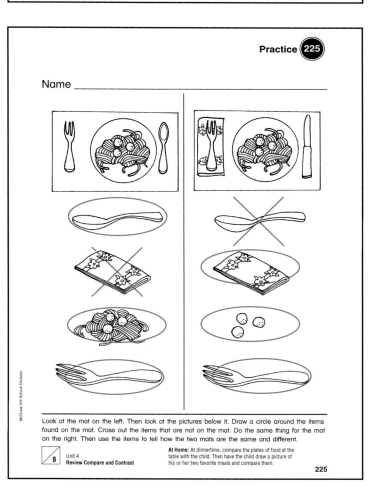

Name _____

Look at the mat on the left. Then look at the pictures below it. Draw a circle around the items found on the mat. Cross out the items that are not on the mat. Do the same thing for the mat on the right. Then use the items to tell how the two mats are the same and different.

Unit 4
Review Compare and Contrast 8

At Home: At dinnertime, compare the plates of food at the table with the child. Then have the child draw a picture of his or her two favorite meals and compare them.

225

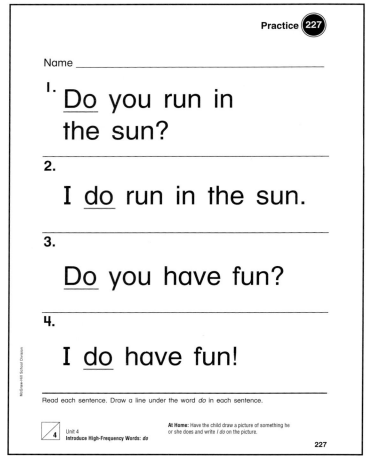

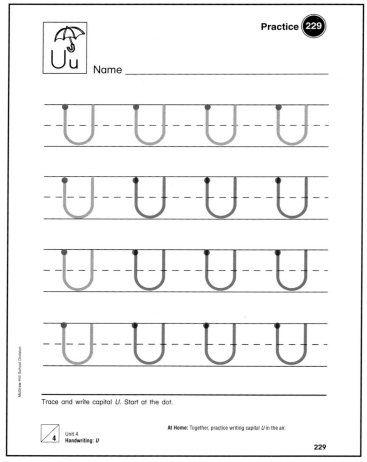

Mud Fun • PRACTICE

Name _____

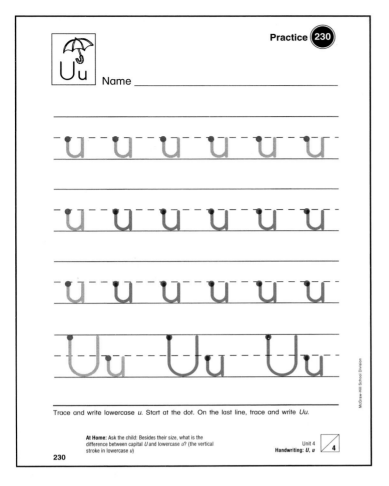

Trace and write lowercase *u*. Start at the dot. On the last line, trace and write *Uu*.

At Home: Ask the child: Besides their size, what is the difference between capital *U* and lowercase *u*? (the vertical stroke in lowercase *u*)

Unit 4
Handwriting: *U, u*   4

230

Name _____

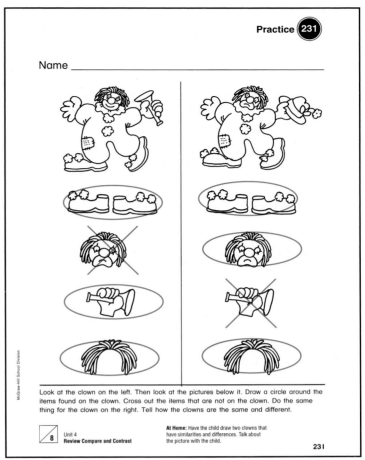

Look at the clown on the left. Then look at the pictures below it. Draw a circle around the items found on the clown. Cross out the items that are not on the clown. Do the same thing for the clown on the right. Tell how the clowns are the same and different.

8   Unit 4
Review Compare and Contrast

At Home: Have the child draw two clowns that have similarities and differences. Talk about the picture with the child.

231

Name _____

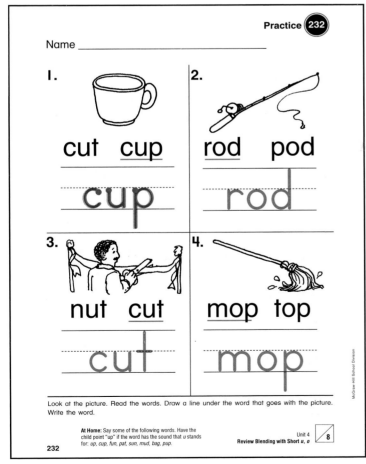

1. cut cup → cup
2. rod pod → rod
3. nut cut → cut
4. mop top → mop

Look at the picture. Read the words. Draw a line under the word that goes with the picture. Write the word.

At Home: Say some of the following words. Have the child point "up" if the word has the sound that *u* stands for: *up, cup, fun, pat, sun, mud, bag, pup.*

Unit 4
Review Blending with Short *u, o*   8

232

Name _____

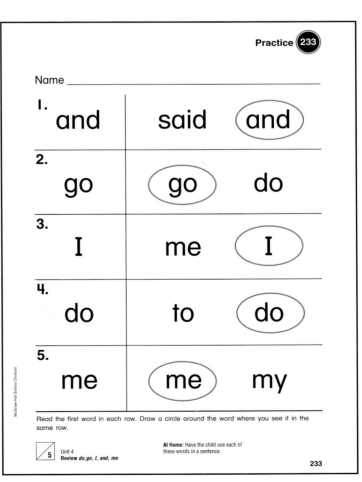

1. and	said	(and)
2. go	(go)	do
3. I	me	(I)
4. do	to	(do)
5. me	(me)	my

Read the first word in each row. Draw a circle around the word where you see it in the same row.

5   Unit 4
Review *do, go, I, and, me*

At Home: Have the child use each of these words in a sentence.

233

Ron and Me • PRACTICE

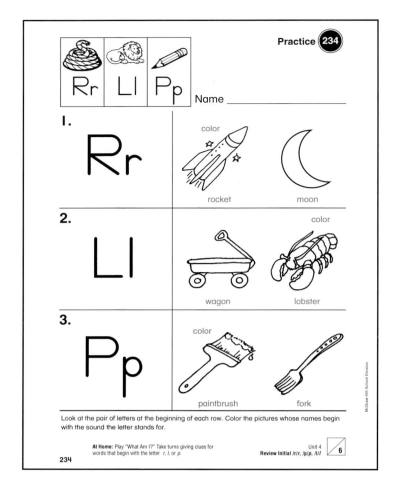

R r — rocket, moon (color)

L l — wagon, lobster (color)

P p — paintbrush, fork (color)

Name _____

Look at the pair of letters at the beginning of each row. Color the pictures whose names begin with the sound the letter stands for.

At Home: Play "What Am I?" Take turns giving clues for words that begin with the letter *r, l,* or *p.*

Unit 4
Review Initial /r/r, /p/p, /l/l 6

234

Name _____

1. Draw a circle around the stairs going *up.* Draw a line under the stairs going *down.* Color the window *over* the stairs blue. Color the window *under* the stairs red. **2.** Draw a circle around the squirrel *on* the roof. Draw a line under the squirrel *off* the roof. Color the bird *inside* the birdhouse red. Color the bird *outside* the birdhouse blue.

Unit 4
Review Positional Terms 8

At Home: Put a spoon on the kitchen counter. Ask the child to find another spoon that is inside a drawer. Have the child tell which spoon is outside the drawer and which one is inside.

235

Name _____

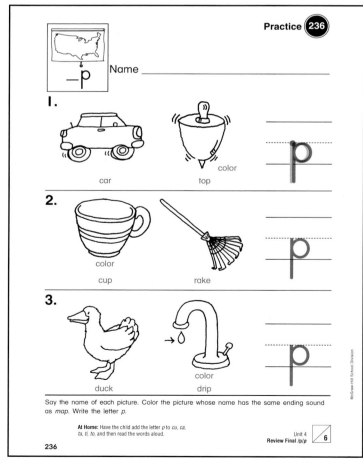

1. car, top (color) — p
2. cup, rake (color) — p
3. duck, drip (color) — p

Say the name of each picture. Color the picture whose name has the same ending sound as *map.* Write the letter *p.*

At Home: Have the child add the letter *p* to *cu, ca, ta, ti, to,* and then read the words aloud.

Unit 4
Review Final /p/p 6

236

Name _____

1. • ——— • I run in the mud.

2. • ——— • It is fun in the sun.

3. • ——— • Pup sat on the mat.

4. • ——— • We have a nap.

Look at each picture. Then read the sentences. Draw a line from each picture to the sentence that tells about it.

Unit 4
Review Main Idea 4

At Home: Write a sentence such as *I am in the mud.* Have the child draw a picture to show what the sentence is about.

237

T18 *Annotated Workbooks*

Ron and Me • PRACTICE

Name _____

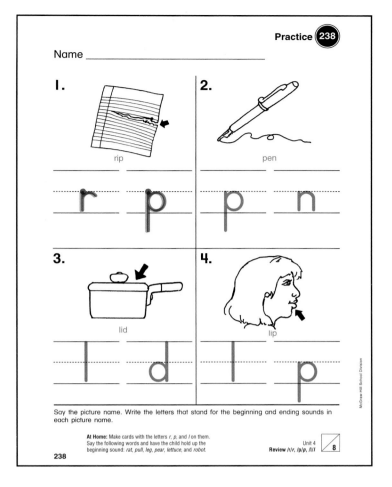

1. rip

2. pen

3. lid

4. lip

r | r | p
p | n
l | d
l | p

Say the picture name. Write the letters that stand for the beginning and ending sounds in each picture name.

At Home: Make cards with the letters *r*, *p*, and *l* on them. Say the following words and have the child hold up the beginning sound: *rat*, *pull*, *leg*, *pear*, *lettuce*, and *robot*.

Unit 4
Review /r/r, /p/p, /l/l | 8

238

Name _____

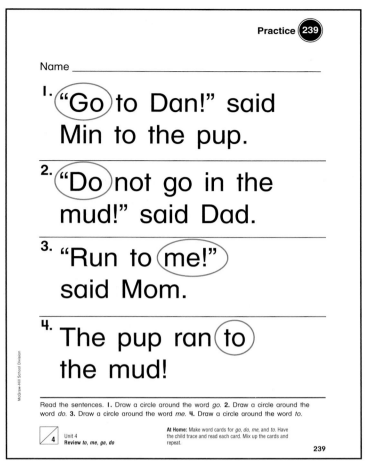

1. "(Go) to Dan!" said Min to the pup.

2. "(Do) not go in the mud!" said Dad.

3. "Run to (me)!" said Mom.

4. The pup ran (to) the mud!

Read the sentences. **1.** Draw a circle around the word *go*. **2.** Draw a circle around the word *do*. **3.** Draw a circle around the word *me*. **4.** Draw a circle around the word *to*.

Unit 4
Review *to, me, go, do*

At Home: Make word cards for *go*, *do*, *me*, and *to*. Have the child trace and read each card. Mix up the cards and repeat.

239

Name _____

1. u p — up

2. c u p — cup

3. n u t — nut

4. m u d — mud

Blend the sounds and say the word. Write the word. Draw a line under the picture that goes with the word.

At Home: Write *up* in the air and blend the sounds as you write. Continue with *mud* and *cup*. Use the words in sentences.

Unit 4
Review Blending with Short *u* | 8

240

Name _____

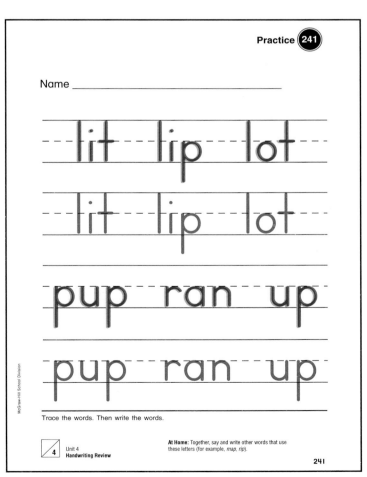

lit lip lot
lit lip lot

pup ran up
pup ran up

Trace the words. Then write the words.

Unit 4
Handwriting Review

At Home: Together, say and write other words that use these letters (for example, *map*, *rip*).

241

T19

Practice 242

Name _____

Run to Pat.

Run to Pat.

Mud is fun!

Mud is fun!

_____

Trace the words in the sentence. Then write the words.

At Home: Make sure that the child is holding his/her pencil comfortably and correctly.

Unit 4
Handwriting Review / 4

242

Practice 243

Name _____

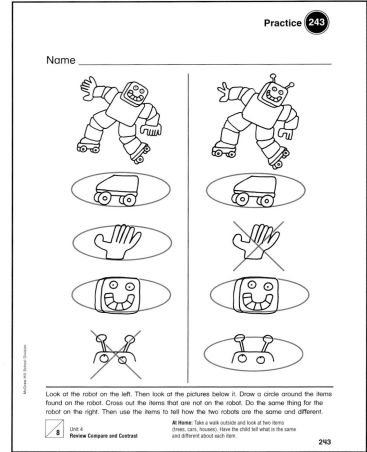

Look at the robot on the left. Then look at the pictures below it. Draw a circle around the items found on the robot. Cross out the items that are not on the robot. Do the same thing for the robot on the right. Then use the items to tell how the two robots are the same and different.

/ 8 Unit 4
Review Compare and Contrast

At Home: Take a walk outside and look at two items (trees, cars, houses). Have the child tell what is the same and different about each item.

243

Practice 244

Name _____

1. fun fin
    fun

2. Mom mop
    Mom

3. rut run
    run

4. top tip
    tip

Look at the picture. Read the words. Draw a line under the word that goes with the picture. Write the word.

At Home: Write *fin*. Ask the child to change *fin* to *fun*. Take turns. Change *fun* to *run* and change *fun* to *sun*.

Unit 4
Review Blending with Short *u, o, i* / 8

244

Practice 245

Name _____

1. go   do   (to)

2. we   <u>me</u>   my

3. to   go   (do)

4. <u>go</u>   the   is

1. Draw a circle around the word *to*. 2. Draw a line under the word *me*. 3. Draw a circle around the word *do*. 4. Draw a line under the word *go*.

/ 4 Unit 4
Review *to, me, go, do*

At Home: Write the words *to, me, go,* and *do* on a sheet of paper. Have the child read the words and name the words that rhyme (*to, do*).

245

Phonological Awareness

OBJECTIVES Children will practice deleting sounds in words, listening for beginning sounds, and blending sounds in words.

Alternate Activities

Delete Sounds

RENNY THE RABBIT

GROUP **Materials:** Phonics Picture Card for *rabbit*
Use this activity to give children practice in deleting beginning sounds of words.

- Place the Phonics Picture Card for *rabbit* on the chalk rail or in a pocket chart. Explain that this is Renny the Rabbit.

- Tell children that Renny the Rabbit is playing a game and he wants you to help. He likes to take away the beginning sound of a word.

- Use Renny the Rabbit to model deleting the beginning sound of a word: If I take away the /r/ from *run*, I have /un/. If I take away the /r/ from *red*, I have *ed*.

- Ask children to say the following words, taking away the beginning sound: *ran, rug, rock,* and *rag*.

Listen for Beginning Sounds: /r/

RAIN, RAIN, GO AWAY

GROUP This activity will give children practice identifying the beginning sound of a word.

- Say a variation of "Rain, Rain, Go Away" with children, such as *Rain, rain, go away. Come again another day. Little Rosie wants to play. Rain, rain, go away.*

- Ask children what sound they hear at the beginning of the name *Rosie*. Have children think of other names that begin with /r/, such as *Rachel, Rick,* or *Rob*. Substitute those names in the rhyme.

- Repeat the rhyme by substituting the names of children in the class, even those that do not begin with /r/. Have children determine what sound is at the beginning of each name that is used.

Blend Sounds

FIND THE PICTURE

GROUP **Materials:** pictures of objects that have one-syllable names that begin with /r/, such as: *rag, rain, rake, red, rice, rock*

This activity will help children practice blending sounds in words.

- Place the pictures on the chalk rail or in a pocket chart.

- Tell children that you are going to name an object, saying each sound of its name. Children should blend the sounds together and say the object's name. For example, ask *Who can point to the /r/-/o/-/k/?*

- Have children come to the chalkboard or pocket chart, name the object, and point to the picture.

Initial *r*

OBJECTIVES   Children will apply letter/sound associations for *r*. They will identify words that begin with *r*.

Alternate

Activities

Visual

R RIBBONS

Materials: red ribbon or strips of red construction paper, markers, pictures or objects whose names begin with *r,* masking tape

Have children write *r* on a ribbon and label a picture or object whose name begins with *r*.

- Gather other pictures and objects whose names begin with *r*.

- Give each child a ribbon or strip of red construction paper. Point out that *red* and *ribbon* both begin with *r*.

Have children label their red ribbon *r*.

- Invite them to use masking tape to attach their *r* ribbon to a picture or object whose name begins with r.

- Invite each child to share the name of their object or picture as you lead children in singing a variation of a round. Have each child sing the name of the object or picture to the tune of "Row, Row, Row Your Boat." ▶**Linguistic**

Auditory

RICE

Materials: unsweetened crisp rice cereal, napkins

Children will listen to a list of words and respond by moving a piece of rice cereal to a napkin if the word begins with *r*.

- Give each child two napkins, one with a small pile of rice cereal.

- Say a list of words, some that begin with *r,* and some that do not.

- Tell children to move a piece of the rice cereal to the clean napkin when they hear a word that begins with *r*, as in *rice*. ▶**Bodily/Kinesthetic**

Kinesthetic

RAINBOW ROAD

Materials: large sheets of colored butcher paper, markers

Children will blend sounds as they walk along a path of letters to read words that begin with *r*.

- On large sheets of colored butcher paper, write letters children can blend to form words that begin with *r*, such as r*an, r*at, r*od, r*id. Allow space between each letter to create a path for children to walk along.

- Set up letters to create a "rainbow road" of colors. Point out that *rainbow* and *road* both begin with *r*.

- Have pairs of children take turns walking along a path, saying each letter's sound to blend and read the words. ▶**Bodily/Kinesthetic**

Phonics CD-ROM

On, Off

 **OBJECTIVES** Children will demonstrate the concepts of *on* and *off* as they respond to a variety of directions.

Alternate Activities

Visual

SWITCHING OFF AND ON

 Materials: construction paper, markers

Children will create light switch covers that are labeled *off* and *on*.

- Give each child a pre-cut light switch cover made of construction paper.

- Have a volunteer demonstrate turning the lights off and on. Ask children to notice the position of the switch when the lights are off and when they are on.

 WRITING On the chalkboard, write the words *off* and *on*. Have children create a design for their switch cover that includes the labels. Children may wish to dictate other words, phrases, or sentences for you to record. ▶**Spatial**

Auditory

SIMON SAYS ON/OFF

Children will respond to directions that include *off* and *on*.

- Lead children in playing *Simon Says*. In each direction, include *on* or *off*. For example, *Simon says put your hands on your head. Take your hands off your head.*

- Have volunteers take turns being Simon and giving directions to classmates. ▶**Interpersonal**

Kinesthetic

OFF/ON GAME

Materials: butcher paper, construction paper, scissors, tape, paper plate, paper arrow, brad

Children will use the words *on* and *off* as they play a game.

- Choose four colors of construction paper. Cut four large circles of each color. Tape the circles in rows to a large sheet of butcher paper.

- Use a paper plate to create a spinner. Divide the plate into four sections with a drawing to represent left hand, left foot, right hand, right foot. Within each section, show each color. Attach a paper arrow with a brad to complete the spinner.

- Spin the arrow for children. As each child takes a turn, have the child use the words *off* and *on* to describe his or her movements, such as *I'm taking my left hand off green and putting it on yellow.* ▶**Bodily/Kinesthetic**

Main Idea

OBJECTIVES Children will identify the main idea in several stories.

Alternate Activities

Auditory

MAIN IDEA IN A SONG

 Materials: cassette player, cassette tapes

PARTNERS Partners will work together to identify the main idea of a story they hear and use the main idea to complete a patterned song.

- Have pairs of children listen to a brief story, either one you read aloud or a story on tape. Assign a different story to each pair of children.

- Have partners discuss what the story was about.

- Ask pairs to complete a song about the story to a familiar tune. For example, the following words can be sung to the tune of "Twinkle, Twinkle, Little Star."

  Listen, listen, to this tale

  It is about a _____ who _____.

- Invite pairs to share with classmates the title of their book and their song. ▶**Musical**

Kinesthetic

MAIN IDEA TABLEAU

 Materials: magazine pictures, props featured in magazine pictures

GROUP

Children will work in groups to portray the main idea of a magazine picture.

- Gather several magazine pictures.

- Organize the class into small groups, and give each group a picture. Have the groups discuss what the picture is mainly about.

- Have each group arrange themselves and props to show the main idea of the picture.

- Have groups show the picture, discuss the action or scene, and answer questions their classmates ask. ▶**Bodily/Kinesthetic**

Visual

MAIN IDEA HEAD BANDS

ONE **Materials:** sentence strips, stapler or tape, markers or crayons, construction paper, scissors

Children will dictate the main idea of a story and use art materials to create a head band.

- Lead children in a discussion about a story you have recently read together, or introduce a new story.

- **WRITING** Give each child a sentence strip about 18 inches long. Have children write or dictate a sentence that tells about the main idea of the story.

- Ask children to draw or cut and paste shapes onto the sentence strip to show the main idea.

- Tape or staple the strips to create head bands for children to wear while they reread or discuss the story. ▶**Intrapersonal**

Vocabulary: *to, me, go, do*

✓OBJECTIVES Children will practice reading the high-frequency words *to, me, go,* and *do.*

Alternate Activities

Visual

BOOKWORM PULL-THROUGHS

ONE **Materials:** oak tag, marker, paper, scissors

Children will make a pull-through game to practice reading high-frequency words.

- Make an oak tag bookworm or other character cutout for each child. Cut two slits in the cutout. Give each child a strip of paper or oak tag that is the same width as the slits.

WRITING Write the high-frequency words *to, me, go, do* on the chalkboard. Have children write the words on their strips of paper.

- Show children how to feed the paper strip through the slits in the character cutout to reveal one word at a time.

- Have children use their strips to practice reading the words. ▶**Spatial**

Kinesthetic

HOPSCOTCH WITH WORDS

GROUP **Materials:** chalk, stone or other marker

Children will play a variation of *Hopscotch* and read high-frequency words.

- In an outdoor area, draw a *Hopscotch* grid with four squares. In each square, write a high-frequency word: *me, to, go, do.*

- Have groups of children take turns playing the game. Children must read the word in the box where his or her stone lands and then hop to that box. ▶**Bodily/Kinesthetic**

Auditory

ROUND ROBIN STORY

PARTNERS **Materials:** index cards, markers

Children will incorporate high-frequency words into an oral story.

- Write the high-frequency words *me, to, go,* and *do* on individual index cards, and give pairs of children each a set of the cards.

- Have the pairs turn the cards face down. Have one child begin the story with a story starter, such as *One day, something strange happened on the way to school.*

- Have partners take turns turning over a card and using the high-frequency word in a sentence that continues the story.

- Have children return the cards to the pile and play until they feel their story is complete.

- Invite partners to share their stories with the rest of the class. ▶**Linguistic**

Phonological Awareness

 **OBJECTIVES** Children will practice listening for beginning sounds, listening for ending sounds, and segmenting sounds.

Alternate Activities

Listen for Beginning Sounds: /p/

FIND THE PIG

 Materials: Phonics Picture for *pig* from Word Building Manipulative Cards

Use this activity to give children practice in identifying the beginning sound of a word.

- Provide copies of the Phonics Pictures, for *pig*. Have children find the picture of the pig. Ask children what sound they hear at the beginning of the word *pig*. (/p/) Tell children to color the pig *pink*. Help them recognize that *pink* also begins with /p/.

- Challenge children to name other words that begin with /p/, such as *pass* or *pin*.

Listen for Ending Sounds: /p/

LISTEN FOR /P/

 Materials: Word Building Boxes from the Word Building Manipulative Cards, markers such as pennies

This activity will give children practice in identifying the ending sound of a word.

- Provide Word Building Boxes and a place marker for each child.

- Slowly say the following list of words: *pan, cap, sip, party, mop, zip, pick, nap, lip.*

- Repeat each word separately. Ask children to listen carefully for the /p/ sound. If the /p/ sound is at the beginning of the word, then have them place the marker in the first box. If the /p/ sound is at the end of the word, then have children place the marker in the last box.

Segment Sounds

ACTION WORD CHARADES

 This activity will give children more practice segmenting sounds.

- Help children think of action words that begin or end with /p/, such as *hop, rip, pat, tap, dip, pet,* and *pack.*

- Allow a volunteer to act out his or her word.

- Invite a child to guess the action word by segmenting the sounds, such as *I can see you like to /h-/o-/p/.*

- Repeat until each child has a turn.

Initial and Final /p/ p

OBJECTIVES Children will apply letter/sound associations for /p/ p. They will identify words that begin or end with p.

Alternate Activities

Auditory

TONGUE TWISTERS

Materials: p letter cards

PARTNERS Children will make letter/sound associations as they say tongue twisters. Partners will collaborate on an original tongue twister that uses the repeated sound of p.

- Lead children in saying "Peter Piper."

  Peter Piper picked a peck of pickled peppers.

  If Peter Piper picked a peck of pickled peppers,

  How many pickled peppers did Peter Piper pick?

- Give children p letter cards. Have them raise their cards when they hear a word that begins with p.

- Lead children in brainstorming additional words that begin with p. Encourage pairs of children to incorporate some of those words in a sentence to make a tongue twister.

- Invite pairs to share their tongue twisters with classmates. ▶**Linguistic**

Visual

PICNIC PUZZLES

Materials: paper plates, magazine pictures of foods whose names begin with p, scissors, glue, markers

Children will match puzzle pieces of foods that begin with p with their labels.

- Gather magazine pictures of foods whose names begin with p, such as *pizza, pineapple, pear* and *pie*.

- On one half of a paper plate, glue a picture. On the other half, write p and the object's label.

- Cut apart the picture and label in a way that creates a unique puzzle with only one match.

- Mix the puzzle pieces for children to assemble. When children complete each puzzle, ask them to say the object's name and point to the letter that stands for its beginning sound. ▶**Spatial**

Kinesthetic

WORD GROUPS

Materials: construction paper, hole punch, **GROUP** yarn, markers

Small groups of children will wear letter necklaces and arrange themselves to build words. Other children will blend the sounds to read the words.

- Organize children into groups of three. Give each child a "letter necklace" (construction paper with a letter; holes punched and yarn tied to make a necklace). Arrange the letters so the group can spell words that begin or end with p.

- Have groups arrange themselves so they spell a word from left to right when facing the class.

- Have the class blend the sounds to read the words. ▶**Bodily/Kinesthetic**

 **CD-ROM**

Inside, Outside

 **OBJECTIVES** Children will discriminate between inside and outside as they respond to directions.

Alternate Activities

Kinesthetic

HOKEY POKEY

GROUP Children will apply the concepts of *inside* and *outside* as they play a traditional musical circle game.

- Have children form a circle. Point out areas that are inside the circle and those that are outside the circle.

- Lead children in singing the "Hokey Pokey" and performing the moves. You may wish to begin with your right hand and invite children to suggest other body parts to continue the song.
▶**Musical**

Visual

IN AND OUT

PARTNERS **Materials:** large plastic play hoop or masking tape, index cards, markers, various classroom objects

Pairs of children will arrange objects to match a scene drawn on a card you give them.

- Create a set of cards that show various classroom objects, including children, inside or outside a circle. For example, the cards might include a stick-figure child standing in the circle, a pencil placed outside the circle, a book placed inside the circle, and so on.

- Make a large masking-tape circle on the floor, or use a plastic hoop.

- Provide children with the objects depicted in the drawings on the cards. Have pairs work together to arrange the objects to create a scene that matches the drawing. ▶**Spatial**

Auditory

INSIDE/OUTSIDE GAME

ONE Children will share examples to demonstrate *inside* and *outside*.

- Review the concepts of inside and outside with children. Stand inside an area, such as the reading center. Describe your position with an oral sentence, such as *I am inside the reading center*. Then change your position and describe it, such as *I am outside the reading center*.

- Encourage children to think of and demonstrate other examples. If children need help, you might whisper some suggestions, such as standing inside/outside a closet, inside/outside a big box, or putting a small object inside/outside a cup.
▶**Bodily/Kinesthetic**

Compare and Contrast

OBJECTIVES Children will compare and contrast different people and objects. They will sort objects based on similarities and differences.

Alternate Activities

Auditory

COMPARE CHARACTERS

Materials: two large plastic play hoops

GROUP Children will participate in a discussion to compare and contrast two characters from literature. They will assist in completing a Venn diagram.

- Tape together two large plastic hoops to create a three-dimensional Venn diagram. Set the hoops on the chalk rail. Alternatively, draw a large Venn diagram on the chalkboard or on chart paper.

- Identify two characters in stories children have recently read.

- Label each circle with one character's name. Label the area where the circles intersect *Both*. Explain to children that a Venn diagram can be used to tell how people or objects are the same and different.

- Lead children in discussing how the characters are alike and different, and record their responses in the appropriate places on the diagram. ▶**Spatial**

Visual

MAKE THEM THE SAME

Materials: construction paper, scissors

PARTNERS Children will manipulate geometric shapes to make two different patterns the same.

- Cut a variety of geometric shapes from construction paper. Make a pattern by arranging four colored shapes in a row. Beneath that row, create the same pattern with one exception.

- Have children identify how the pattern in the second row is different from that in the first row. Have a volunteer replace the shape so the two patterns are identical.

- Have pairs of children work together. Have one partner create a new pattern in one row and duplicate it with one exception in the second row. Have the other partner replace one shape to make the two patterns the same. Then have partners switch roles. ▶**Logical/Mathematical**

Kinesthetic

SHOE SORT

 Children will compare and contrast shoes in

GROUP the classroom, sorting them by category.

- Have children stand in a circle and notice all the different types of shoes. Discuss how the shoes are alike. (They are worn to protect the feet.) Then discuss differences in color and style.

- Have children choose a criterion, such as color or style. Ask them to arrange themselves in groups by category. For example, children with black shoes will stand together. ▶**Interpersonal**

Phonological Awareness

OBJECTIVES Children will practice identifying rhyming words, listening for beginning sounds, and blending sounds in words.

Alternate Activities

Identify Rhyming Words

RHYME TIME

 Use this activity to give children practice in identifying rhyming words.

- Remind children that rhyming words share the same ending sound. Have children listen carefully to the following word pairs: *leg/beg, log/fog, land/lane, lift/sift, light/sight, lap/loop, lip/flip.*

- Repeat each pair, one at a time. Tell children to slap their legs each time they hear a word pair that rhymes.

Listen for Beginning Sounds: /l/

WHERE'S THE LAMP?

 Materials: Phonics Picture for *lamp* from Word Building Manipulative Cards

This activity will give children practice in identifying the beginning sound of a word.

- Provide copies of the Phonics Picture for *lamp*. Have children find the picture of the lamp. Then have them color it and cut out the card. Ask what sound they hear at the beginning of the word *lamp.* (/l/)

- Tell children that this lamp goes in an imaginary house. However, it can only go in rooms that begin with the same sound as *lamp.*

- Have children listen carefully to the following list of rooms: *laundry room, living room, kitchen, library, bedroom.*

- Ask children to lift their picture of the lamp each time they hear a place that begins with /l/.

Blend Sounds

FIND IT!

 Materials: pictures of objects that have one-syllable names that begin with /l/, such as: *lid, lace, lamb, lock, leaf, log*

This activity will help children practice blending sounds in words.

- Place the pictures on the chalk rail or in a pocket chart.

- Tell children that you are going to say the name of one of the pictures by saying each sound of its name. Children will then have to blend the sounds together to determine which picture you are asking for.

- Model by saying *I want the /l/-/a/-/m/.* Have the class name the object: *lamb.*

- Have children point to the picture and name the object. Repeat until all pictures are named.

Initial *l*

 OBJECTIVES Children will apply letter/sound associations for *l*. They will identify words that begin with *l*.

 **Alternate Activities**

Visual

TOWERING L

 Materials: boxes or blocks, self-stick notes, crayons, markers

Children will build a tower in the shape of the letter *l*. They will attach pictures and labels to the tower.

- Have children use stacks of boxes or blocks to build a tower resembling the letter *l*.

Give each child a self-stick note. Ask children to draw a picture of something that begins with *l*. Help children label their drawings.

- Invite children to share their drawings and attach them carefully to the tower. ▶**Interpersonal**

Auditory

DID YOU EVER SEE AN *L* WORD?

Children will suggest phrases that contain words beginning with *l* to sing a variation of "Did You Ever See a Lassie?"

- Lead children in singing "Did You Ever See a Lassie?" Guide them to realize that *lassie* begins with *l*.

- Tell children that you want to sing a new version of the song that uses more words that begin with *l*. Provide several examples, such as *lick a lollipop, lose a letter,* or *lie on the lawn*. Encourage children to suggest additional phrases. Sing the new phrases to the tune of "Did You Ever See a Lassie?" ▶**Musical**

Kinesthetic

L LADDERS

Materials: index cards, markers, step ladder or paper ladder

Children will blend sounds to read words that begin with *l* as they "climb" a ladder.

- On index cards, write words beginning with *l*, such as *lip, lid, lit, lap,* and *lot*. Attach each card to the rung of a step ladder. Alternatively, you may wish to attach labels to a playground ladder, or one you draw on butcher paper.

- Have children blend the sounds to read the words as they climb up and down the ladder. ▶**Bodily/Kinesthetic**

 CD-ROM

Phonological Awareness

 **OBJECTIVES** Children will practice listening for beginning sounds, listening for middle sounds, and segmenting individual sounds.

Alternate

Listening for Beginning Sounds: /u/

HANDS UP!

 Materials: Phonics Picture Card for *umbrella* Use this activity to give children practice in identifying the beginning sound of a word.

- Place the Phonics Picture Card for *umbrella* on the chalk rail or in a pocket chart. Have children tell what sound they hear at the beginning of the word *umbrella*. (/u/)

- Invite a volunteer to name another word that begins with the same sound as *umbrella*, such as *under* or *up*.

- Continue by having children put their hand up each time they hear you say a word that begins with the sound /u/. Say the following words: *up, ran, uncle, fit, under, unless, dot, us, until*.

Listen for Middle Sounds: /u/

COVER THE BUG

Materials: drawing paper, crayons, markers, such as pennies

This activity will give children practice identifying the middle sound of a word.

- Have each child draw a bug that has three body parts—a head, a thorax (or middle part), and an abdomen. Ask children what sound they hear in the middle of the word *bug*. (/u/)

- Have children listen to the following list of words: *run, us, sun, mud, up, cut, fun, up, cup.*

- Give each child a place marker. Repeat the words separately, telling children to listen for the /u/ sound.

- If a word has the /u/ sound at the beginning, children should place the marker on the bug's head. If the word has a /u/ sound in the middle, children should place the marker on the bug's thorax.

Segment Sounds

CLAP FOR SOUNDS

Use this activity to help children practice segmenting individual sounds.

- Say the following words slowly: *hug, cup, sun, mud, pup, nut.*

- Repeat a word. Invite a volunteer to say how many sounds he or she hears in the word, and then identify each sound and clap for it; for example, *hug* has three sounds, /h/ (clap), /u/ (clap), /g/ (clap).

- Repeat with the rest of the words.

Initial and Medial Short *u*

OBJECTIVES Children will apply letter/sound associations for short *u*. They will identify words that have short *u* in the initial and medial positions.

Alternate Activities

Visual

POP-UPS

 Materials: construction paper, scissors, crayons or markers

Children will create a pop-up page with illustrations of words containing the short *u* sound.

- For each child, prepare a pop-up card. Fold a piece of construction paper in half across the width. Two inches from the top of the page, make a two-inch cut toward the fold. Cut an arch, similar to a quarter circle, to the top of the page. Open the card. Press the half circle down into the card. When reopened, it's a pop-up.

 Have children open the card and label the half-circle pop-up *u*. Have children draw pictures whose names contain the short *u* sound in the initial and medial positions. ▶Spatial

Auditory

RHYME WITH SHORT *U*

 Children will identify words with the short *u* sound in the initial and medial positions in a finger play.

- Share the following words and movements:

  We had no umbrella as we walked to the bus.
  (swing arms by your side)

  Suddenly the rain started pouring on us!
  (flutter fingers down in front of you)

  Let's get an umbrella to hold up high.
  (pretend to hold handle of umbrella)

  If we stand under it, then we will be dry.
  (pretend to flick rain from each shoulder)

- Repeat each line. Ask volunteers to identify words that contain the short *u* sound. Have children tell whether they hear the sound at the beginning or in the middle of the word. ▶Bodily/Kinesthetic

Kinesthetic

UNDER THE UMBRELLA

Materials: umbrella, yarn, paper clips, index cards, markers

Partners will take turns selecting word cards for each other to blend and read.

- Prepare an umbrella prop by tying three pieces of yarn to spokes on an umbrella. At the end of each piece of yarn, tie a paper clip.

- On index cards, write words with the short *u* sound in the initial or medial positions, for example, *up, us, cup, mud, sun, fun, run* and *cut*.

- Have partners take turns choosing three cards and attaching them to the clips hanging from the umbrella. Have the partner who chose the words stand under the open umbrella. The other partner blends the sounds to read the words. Have children switch roles. ▶Linguistic

 CD-ROM

Over, Under, Up, Down

 **OBJECTIVES** Children will distinguish *over, under, up,* and *down* as they respond to directions.

Alternate
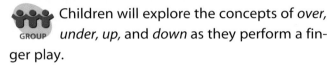

Auditory

UNDER/OVER FINGER PLAY

GROUP Children will explore the concepts of *over, under, up,* and *down* as they perform a finger play.

- Share the following words and movements with children:

  Under the water, down deep,
  (point hand down as if diving into water)

  What kinds of animals might you see?
  (raise hands and tilt head)

  Over the water, up in the air,
  (gesture toward sky)

  What kinds of animals might like it there?
  (raise hands and tilt head)

- Repeat each line and have children echo after you.

- Invite children to suggest what kinds of animals they might see in each place mentioned in the finger play. ▶**Musical**

Kinesthetic

LIMBO BEAT

GROUP **Materials:** wooden stick or string
Children will explore the concepts of *over, under, up,* and *down* as they play a traditional *Limbo* game.

- Have two volunteers hold the string or bar. Lead children in a discussion about things in the room that are *over* the line and things that are *under* the line. Point out that to describe an object's position, children can tell someone to look *up* or *down.*

- Demonstrate for children how you can step *over* or go *under* the bar.

- Guide children in playing *Limbo.* Have them bend backward to go under the bar. After everyone has had a turn, lower the bar. If someone touches the bar, he or she is out of the game.
  ▶**Bodily/Kinesthetic**

Visual

I SPY

PARTNERS Children will give each other clues about objects using the position words *over, under, up,* and *down.*

- Model for children playing the game *I Spy* using the position words *over, under, up,* and *down* in the clues.

- Have pairs of children play the game in the classroom or on the playground. ▶**Spatial**

Writing Readiness

Before children begin to write, fine motor skills need to be developed. Here are examples of activities that can be used:

- **Simon Says** Play Simon Says using just finger positions.
- **Finger Plays and Songs** Sing songs such as "Where Is Thumbkin" or "The Eensie, Weensie, Spider" or songs that use Signed English or American Sign Language.
- **Mazes** Use or create mazes, especially ones that require moving the writing instruments from left to right.

The Mechanics of Writing

POSTURE

- Chair height should allow for the feet to rest flat on the floor.
- Desk height should be two inches above the elbows.
- There should be an inch between the child and the desk.
- Children sit erect with the elbows resting on the desk.
- Letter models should be on the desk or at eye level.

PAPER POSITION

- **Right-handed children** should turn the paper so that the lower left-hand corner of the paper points to the abdomen.

- **Left-handed children** should turn the paper so that the lower right-hand corner of the paper points to the abdomen.

- The nondominant hand should anchor the paper near the top so that the paper doesn't slide.
- The paper should be moved up as the child nears the bottom of the paper. Many children won't think of this.

The Writing Instrument Grasp

For handwriting to be functional, the writing instrument must be held in a way that allows for fluid dynamic movement.

FUNCTIONAL GRASP PATTERNS

- **Tripod Grasp** The writing instrument is held with the tip of the thumb and the index finger and rests against the side of the third finger. The thumb and index finger form a circle.
- **Quadrupod Grasp** The writing instrument is held with the tip of the thumb and index finger and rests against the fourth finger. The thumb and index finger form a circle.

INCORRECT GRASP PATTERNS

- **Fisted Grasp** The writing instrument is held in a fisted hand.

- **Pronated Grasp** The instrument is held diagonally within the hand with the tips of the thumb and index finger but with no support from other fingers.

- **Five-Finger Grasp** The writing instrument is held with the tips of all five fingers.

- **Flexed or Hooked Wrist** Flexed or bent wrist is typically seen with left-handed writers but is also present in some right-handed writers.

- To correct wrist position, have children check their writing posture and paper placement.

TO CORRECT GRASPS

- Have children play counting games with an eye dropper and water.
- Have children pick up small objects with a tweezer.
- Do counting games with children picking up small coins using just the thumb and index finger.

Evaluation Checklist

Formation and Strokes

- ☑ Does the child begin letters at the top?
- ☑ Do circles close?
- ☑ Are the horizontal lines straight?
- ☑ Do circular shapes and extender and descender lines touch?
- ☑ Are the heights of all upper-case letters equal?
- ☑ Are the heights of all lower-case letters equal?
- ☑ Are the lengths of the extenders and descenders the same for all letters?

Directionality

- ☑ Do the children form letters starting at the top and moving to the bottom?
- ☑ Are letters formed from left to right?

Spacing

- ☑ Are the spaces between letters equidistant?
- ☑ Are the spaces between words equidistant?
- ☑ Do the letters rest on the line?
- ☑ Are the top, bottom and side margins on the paper even?

Write the Alphabet
Trace and write the letters.

Trace and write the letters.

Trace and write the letters.

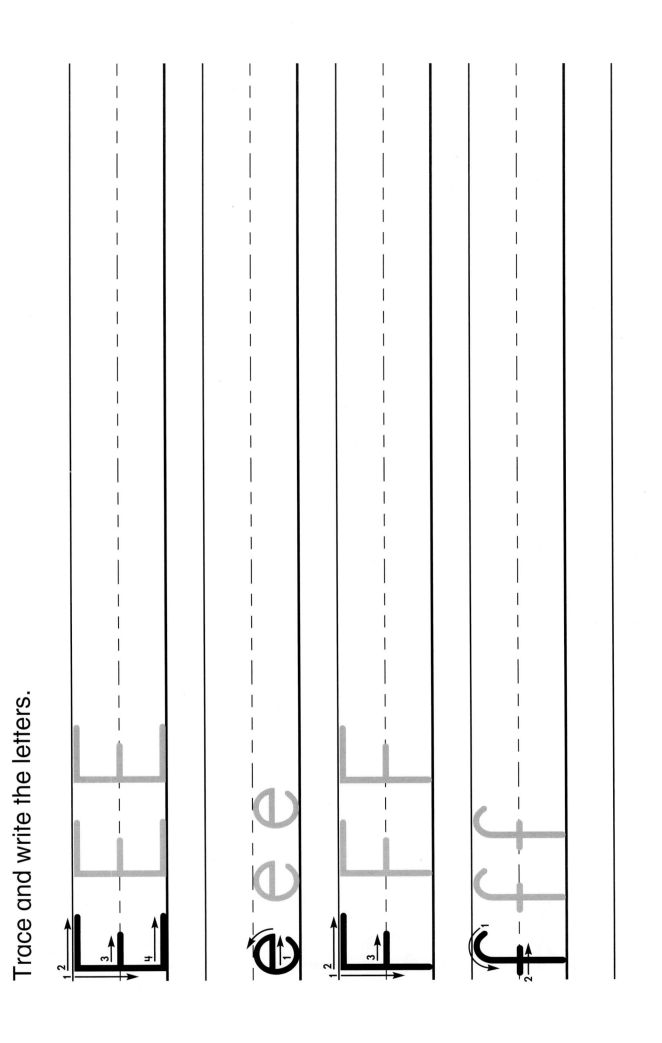

Trace and write the letters.

G G G

g g g

H H H

h h h

Trace and write the letters.

Trace and write the letters.

Trace and write the letters.

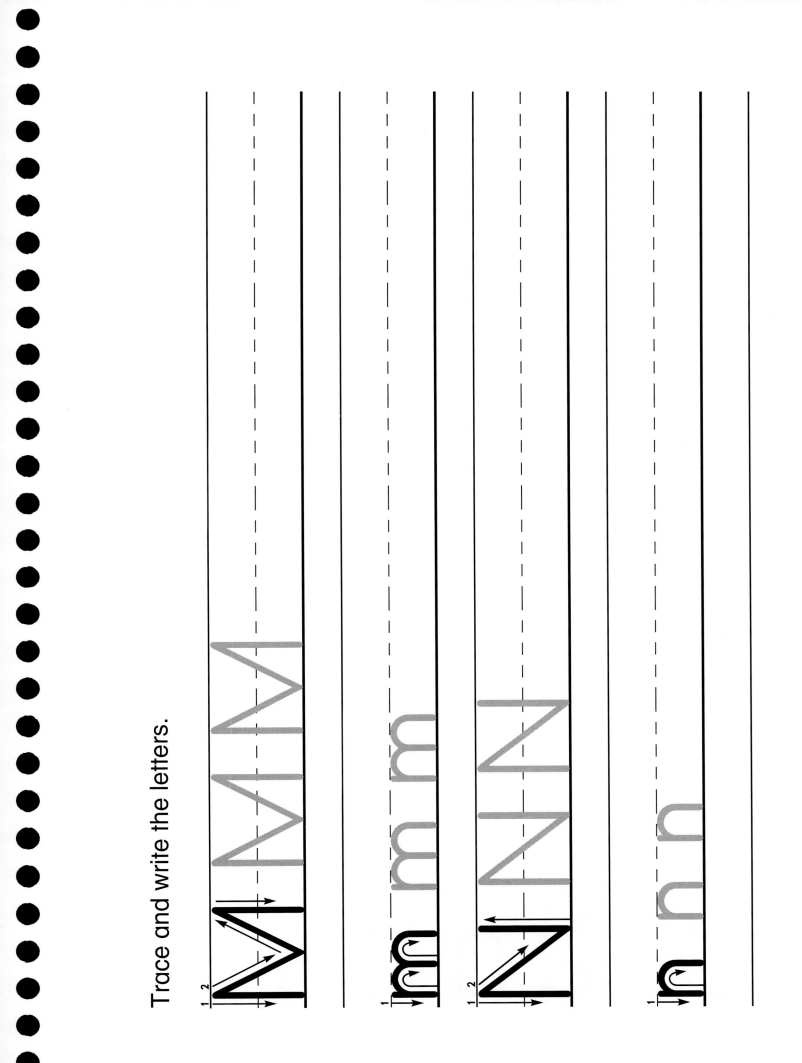

Trace and write the letters.

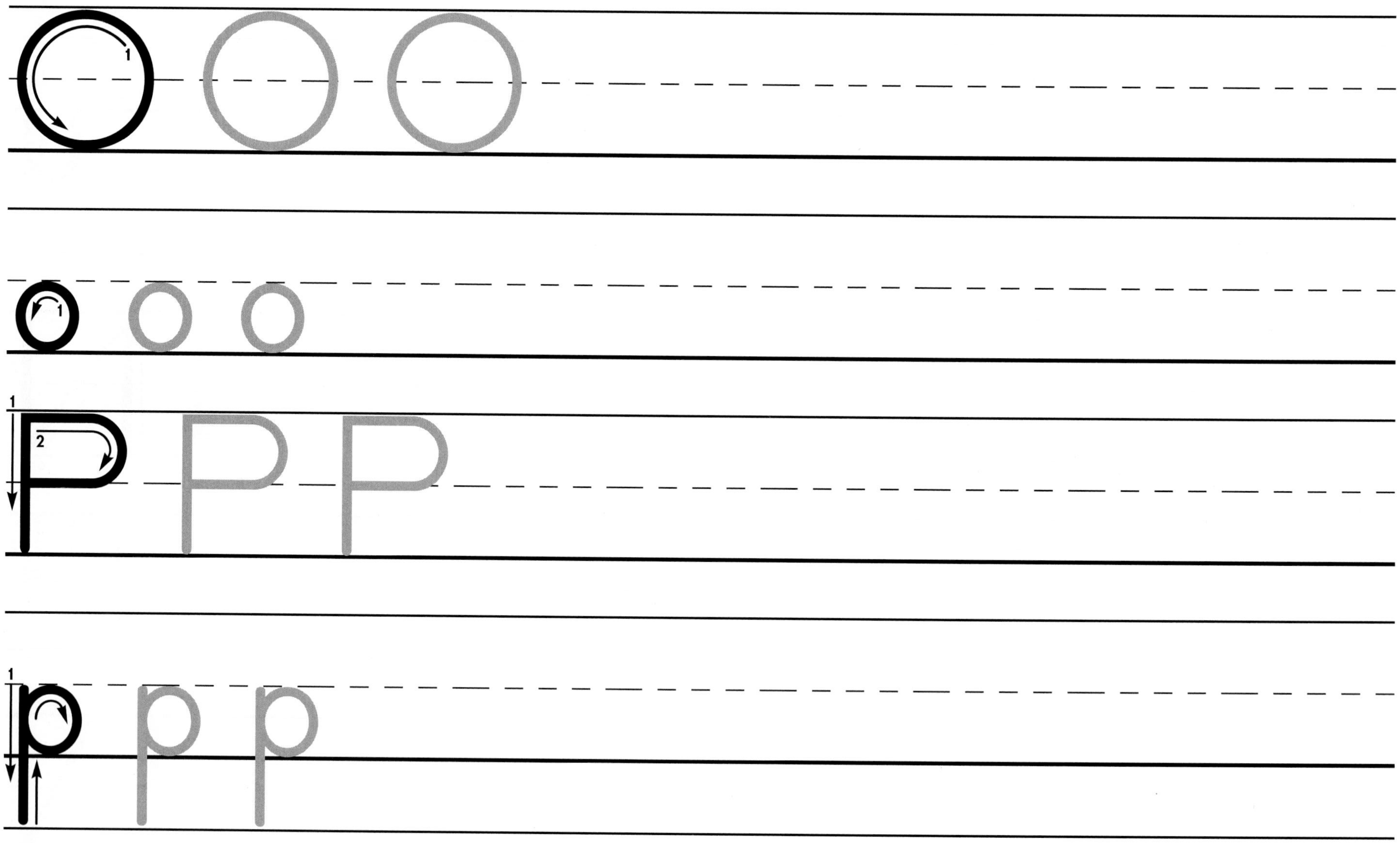

O O O

o o o

P P P

p p p

Trace and write the letters.

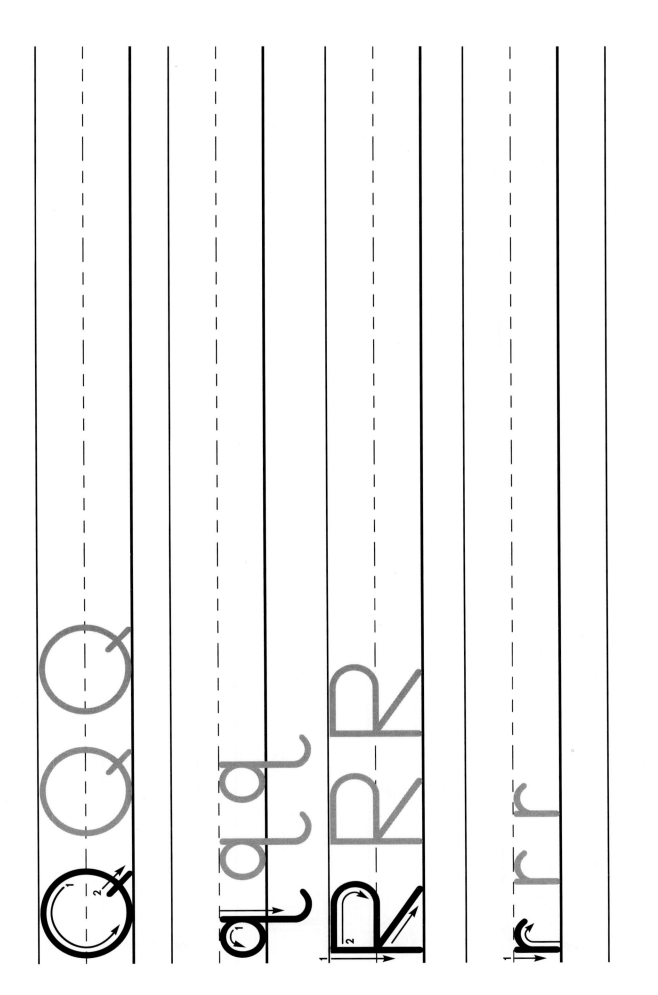

Trace and write the letters.

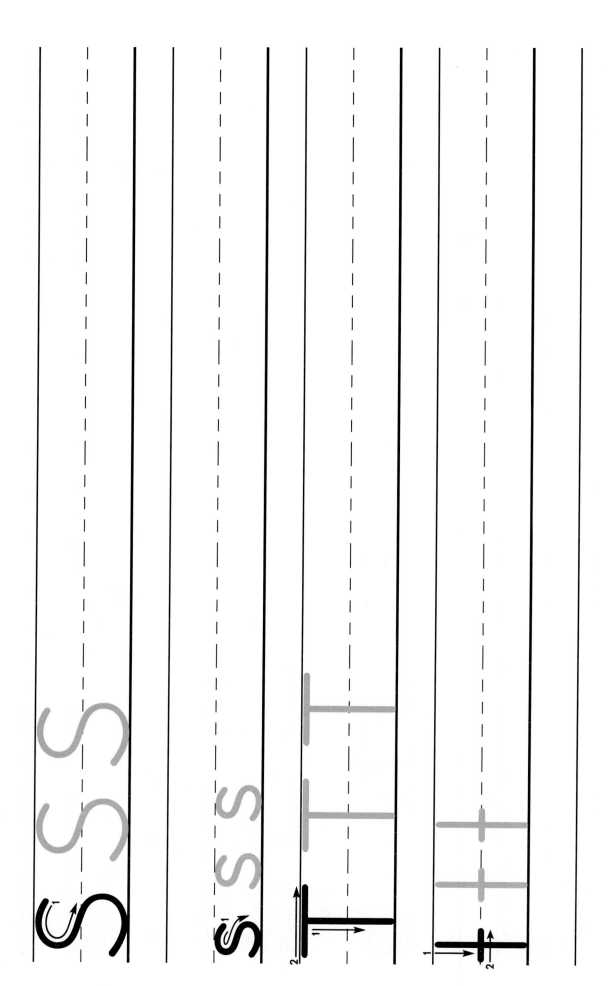

Trace and write the letters.

Trace and write the letters.

Trace and write the letters.

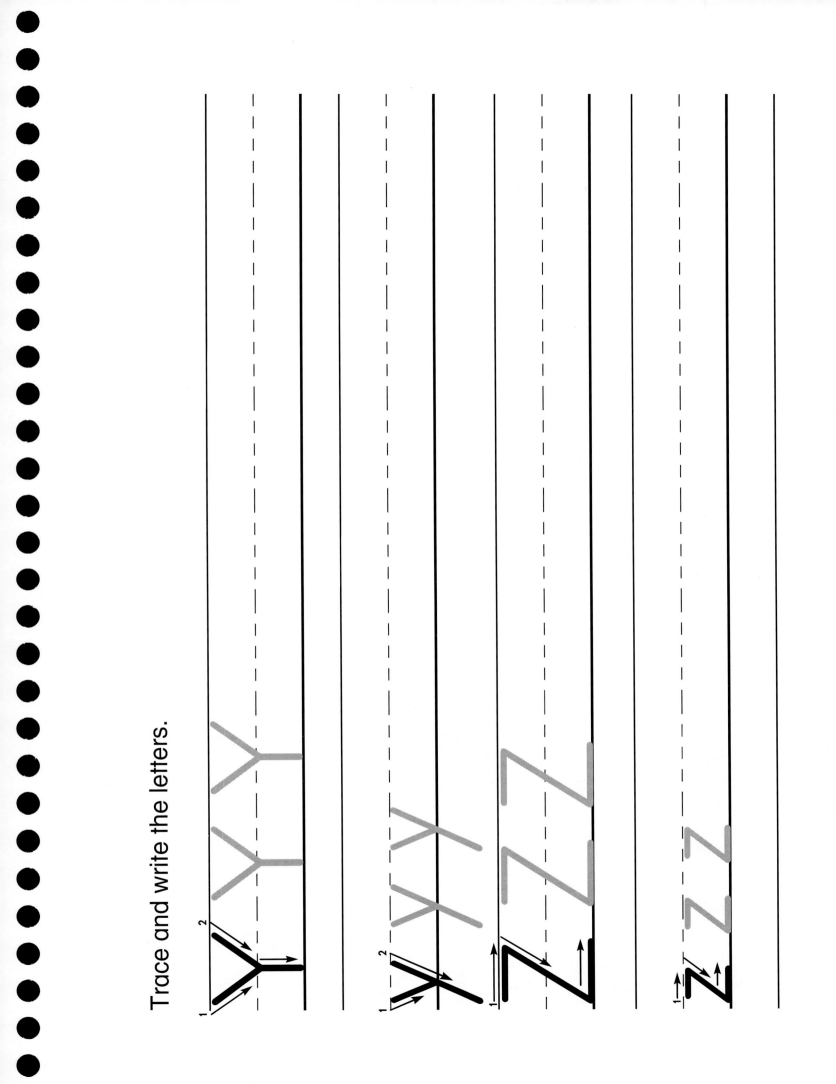

Handwriting Models—Slant Manuscript

Aa Bb Cc Dd Ee

Ff Gg Hh Ii Jj Kk

Ll Mm Nn Oo Pp

Qq Rr Ss Tt Uu

Vv Ww Xx Yy Zz

Selection Titles

Honors, Prizes, and Awards

SHOW AND TELL DAY
by **Anne Rockwell**

Author/Illustrator Anne Rockwell, winner of American Booksellers' Award Pick of the List for *Boats* (1985) and *Cars* (1986); National Science Teachers Association Award for Outstanding Science Trade Book for Children (1988) for *Trains*

THE CHICK AND THE DUCKLING
by **Mirra Ginsburg**
Illustrated by **Jose Aruego and Ariane Dewey**

Illustrators: Jose Aruego and Ariane Dewey, winners of Boston Globe-Horn Book Honor (1974) for *Herman the Helper*

FLOWER GARDEN
by **Eve Bunting**
Illustrated by **Kathryn Hewitt**

Author: Eve Bunting, winner of ALA Notable Book (1990), IRA-CBC Children's Choice, IRA-Teachers' Choice, School Library Journal Best Book (1989) for *The Wednesday Surprise;* Mark Twain Award (1989) for *Sixth Grade Sleepover;* ALA Notable (1990) for *Wall;* ALA Notable (1992) for *Fly Away Home;* Edgar Allen Poe Juvenile Award (1993) for *Coffin on a Case;* ALA Notable, Caldecott Medal (1995) for *Smoky Night;* Booklist Editors' Choice (1995) for *Spying on Miss Müller;* ALA Notable, Booklist Editors' Choice (1997) for *Train to Somewhere;* National Council for Social Studies Notable Children's Book Award (1998) for *Moonstick,* and *I Am the Mummy Heb-Nefert,* and *On Call Back Mountain;* Young Reader's Choice Award (1997) for *Nasty Stinky Sneakers*
Illustrator: Kathryn Hewitt, winner of Association of Booksellers for Children, Children's Choice Award (1998) for *Lives of the Athletes: Thrills, Spills (And What the Neighbors Thought);* ALA Notable (1994) Boston Globe-Horn Book Honor (1993) for *Lives of the Musicians: Good Times, Bad Times (and What the Neighbors Thought)*

PRETEND YOU'RE A CAT
by **Jean Marzollo**
Illustrated by **Jerry Pinkney**

Author: Jean Marzollo, winner of 1998 Association of Booksellers for Children, Children's Choice Award for *I Spy Little Book*
Illustrator: Jerry Pinkney, winner of Coretta Scott King Award, ALA Notable, Christopher Award (1986) for *Patchwork Quilt;* Newbery Medal, Boston Globe-Horn Book Honor (1977) for *Roll of Thunder, Hear My Cry;* Boston Globe-Horn Book Honor (1980) *Childtimes: A Three Generation Memoir;* Coretta Scott King Award (1987) for *Half a Moon and One Whole Star;* ALA Notable (1988) for

Selection Titles	Honors, Prizes, and Awards
PRETEND YOU'RE A CAT (CONTINUED) by **Jean Marzollo** Illustrated by **Jerry Pinkney**	*Tales of Uncle Remus: The Adventures of Brer Rabbit;* ALA Notable, Caldecott Honor, Coretta Scott King Award (1989) for *Mirandy and Brother Wind;* ALA Notable, Caldecott Honor, Coretta Scott King Honor (1990) for *Talking Eggs: A Folktale for the American South;* Golden Kite Award Book (1990) for *Home Place;* ALA Notable (1991) for *Further Tales of Uncle Remus: The Misadventures of Brer Rabbit, Brer Fox . . .;* ALA Notable (1993) for *Back Home;* ALA Notable, Boston Globe-Horn Book Award, Caldecott Honor (1995) for *John Henry;* ALA Notable, Blue Ribbon, Booklist Editors' Choice (1997) for *Sam and the Tigers;* ALA Notable, Christopher Award, Coretta Scott King Award, Golden Kite Honor Book (1997) for *Minty: A Story of Young Harriet Tubman;* Aesop Prize (1997) for *The Hired Hand;* National Council for Social Studies Notable Children's Book Award (1998) for *The Hired Hand* and *Rikki-Tikki-Tavi* (also Children's Choice Award, Association of Booksellers for Children, and Booklist Editors' Choice, 1998); Rip Van Winkle Award (1998); 1998 Hans Christian Andersen nominee
ANY KIND OF DOG by **Lynn Reiser**	**Author/Illustrator: Lynn Reiser,** winner of ALA Notable (1995) for *The Surprise Family*
THE EARTH AND I by **Frank Asch**	**Author/Illustrator: Frank Asch,** winner of American Book Award Pick of the List Award (1997) for *Barnyard Animals*

THEME: I WONDER

SUBTHEME: IN MY BACKYARD

Trade Books

Additional fiction and nonfiction trade books related to each selection can be shared with children throughout the unit.

A Pig Is Big
Douglas Florian (Greenwillow, 2000)

Starting with the questions, "What is big?" and "What is bigger?" we travel through space in increments. First, a pig is big, then many other things are bigger, and finally we arrive at the Universe, which is the biggest thing of all.

When the Wind Stops
Charlotte Zolotow, illustrated by Stefano Vitali (HarperCollins, 1995)

In answer to her son's many questions, a mother explains that in nature an end is also a beginning.

Zoo in the Sky: A Book of Animal Constellations
Jacqueline Mitton, illustrated by Christina Balit (National Geographic, 1998)

Simple descriptions and shiny illustrations provide an introduction to astronomy for youngsters.

My Backyard Garden
Carol Lerner (Morrow, 1998)

Young readers are provided with details on how to start their own vegetable gardens.

My Spring Robin
Anne F. Rockwell, illustrated by Harlow and Lizzy Rockwell (Macmillan, 1989)

While searching for a robin in her backyard, a child discovers many interesting plants and creatures.

Planting a Rainbow
Lois Ehlert (Harcourt Brace Jovanovich, 1988)

A mother and child plant a rainbow of flowers in the family garden.

Technology

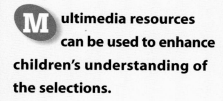

Multimedia resources can be used to enhance children's understanding of the selections.

 Where Do Animals Go in Winter? (National Geographic) Video, 17 min. Children learn about animal behaviors, appearances, and needs in this award-winning film.

 Where Does It Come From? (National Geographic) Video, 15 min. This award-winning film explains how raw materials are processed and used, from pizza to paper.

 Backyard Birds (National Geographic) Video, 15 min. One family observes both the migratory and non-migratory birds attracted to their backyard bird feeder.

 Backyard Bugs (National Geographic) Video, 15 min. This multiple-award-winning film introduces children to the numerous creatures that live in neighborhoods and backyards.

Fireflies, Fireflies Light My Way
Jonathan London, illustrated by Linda Messier (Viking, 1996)

Rhyming text features fireflies and other creatures in celebration of the interconnectedness of the natural world.

I Took a Walk
Henry Cole (Greenwillow, 1998)

A child recounts a nature trek through woods, meadow, stream, and pond.

What's This?
Caroline Mockford (Barefoot Books, 2000)

A little girl finds a sunflower seed and cares for it. After the summer ends, she takes her flower to school and discovers the seeds can be used to make a beautiful roomful of flowers for her class next year.

Me and My World (National Geographic) Video, 15 min. A young girl learns how things can be animals, vegetables, minerals, or all three.

Signs of Nature (National Geographic) Video, 20 min. An award-winning look at what nature's "signs" are and what we can learn from them.

Publishers Directory

Abdo & Daughters
4940 Viking Drive, Suite 622
Edina, MN 55435
(800) 800-1312 • www.abdopub.com

Aladdin Paperbacks
(Imprint of Simon & Schuster Children's Publishing)

Atheneum
(Imprint of Simon & Schuster Children's Publishing)

Bantam Doubleday Dell Books for Young Readers
(Imprint of Random House)

Blackbirch Press
260 Amity Road
Woodbridge, CT 06525
(203) 387-7525 • (800) 831-9183 •
www.blackbirch.com

Blue Sky Press
(Imprint of Scholastic)

Boyds Mills Press
815 Church Street
Honesdale, PA 18431
(570) 253-1164 • Fax (570) 253-0179 •
(800) 490-5111 • www.boydsmillspress.com

Bradbury Press
(Imprint of Simon & Schuster Children's Publishing)

BridgeWater Books
(Distributed by Penguin Putnam)

Candlewick Press
2067 Massachusetts Avenue
Cambridge, MA 02140
(617) 661-3330 • Fax (617) 661-0565 •
www.candlewick.com

Carolrhoda Books
(Division of Lerner Publications Co.)

Children's Press (Division of Grolier, Inc.)
P.O. Box 1795
Danbury, CT 06816-1333
(800) 621-1115 • www.grolier.com

Child's World
P.O. Box 326
Chanhassen, MN 55317-0326
(612) 906-3939 • (800) 599-READ •
www.childsworld.com

Chronicle Books
85 Second Street, Sixth Floor
San Francisco, CA 94105
(415) 537-3730 • Fax (415) 537-4460 •
(800) 722-6657 • www.chronbooks.com

Clarion Books
(Imprint of Houghton Mifflin, Inc.)
215 Park Avenue South
New York, NY 10003
(212) 420-5800 • (800) 225-3362 •
www.houghtonmifflinbooks.com/clarion

Crowell (Imprint of HarperCollins)

Crown Publishing Group
(Imprint of Random House)

Dial Books
(Imprint of Penguin Putnam Inc.)

Dorling Kindersley (DK Publishing)
95 Madison Avenue
New York, NY 10016
(212) 213-4800 • Fax (212) 213-5240 •
(888) 342-5357 • www.dk.com

Doubleday (Imprint of Random House)

E. P. Dutton Children's Books
(Imprint of Penguin Putnam Inc.)

Farrar Straus & Giroux
19 Union Square West
New York, NY 10003
(212) 741-6900 • Fax (212) 741-6973 •
(888) 330-8477

Four Winds Press
(Imprint of Macmillan, see Simon & Schuster Children's Publishing)

Greenwillow Books
(Imprint of William Morrow & Co, Inc.)

Grosset & Dunlap
(Imprint of Penguin Putnam, Inc.)

Harcourt Brace & Co.
6277 Sea Harbor Drive
Orlando, FL 32887
(407) 345-2000 • (800) 225-5425 •
www.harcourtbooks.com

Harper & Row (Imprint of HarperCollins)

HarperCollins Children's Books
1350 Avenue of the Americas
New York, NY 10019
(212) 261-6500 • Fax (212) 261-6689 •
(800) 242-7737 •
www.harperchildrens.com

Holiday House
425 Madison Avenue
New York, NY 10017
(212) 688-0085 • Fax (212) 421-6134

Henry Holt and Company
115 West 18th Street
New York, NY 10011
(212) 886-9200 • (212) 633-0748 • (888)
330-8477 • www.henryholt.com/byr/

Houghton Mifflin
222 Berkeley Street
Boston, MA 02116
(617) 351-5000 • Fax (617) 351-1125 •
(800) 225-3362 •
www.houghtonmifflinbooks.com

Hyperion Books
(Division of ABC, Inc.)
77 W. 66th Street, 11th Floor
New York, NY 10023
(212) 456-0100 • (800) 343-4204 •
www.disney.com

Ideals Children's Books
(Imprint of Hambleton-Hill Publishing, Inc.)
1501 County Hospital Road
Nashville, TN 37218
(615) 254-2451 • (800) 327-5113

Joy Street Books
(Imprint of Little, Brown & Co.)

Just Us Books
356 Glenwood Avenue
E. Orange, NJ 07017
(973) 672-7701 • Fax (973) 677-7570 •
www.justusbooks.com

Alfred A. Knopf
(Imprint of Random House)

Lee & Low Books
95 Madison Avenue, Room 606
New York, NY 10016
(212) 779-4400 • Fax (212) 683-1894

Lerner Publications Co.
241 First Avenue North
Minneapolis, MN 55401
(612) 332-3344 • Fax (612) 332-7615 •
(800) 328-4929 • www.lernerbooks.com

Little, Brown & Co.
3 Center Plaza
Boston, MA 02108
(617) 227-0730 • Fax (617) 263-2864 •
(800) 759-0190 • www.littlebrown.com

Lothrop Lee & Shepard
(Imprint of William Morrow & Co.)

Macmillan
(Imprint of Simon & Schuster Children's Publishing)

Marshall Cavendish
99 White Plains Road
Tarrytown, NY 10591
(914) 332-8888 • Fax (914) 332-1888 •
(800) 821-9881 •
www.marshallcavendish.com

William Morrow & Co.
(Imprint of HarperCollins)

Morrow Junior Books
(Imprint of HarperCollins)

Mulberry Books
(Imprint of HarperCollins)

National Geographic Society
1145 17th Street, NW
Washington, DC 20036
(202) 857-7345 • (800) 638-4077 •
www.nationalgeographic.com

Northland Publishing
(Division of Justin Industries)
P.O. Box 1389
Flagstaff, AZ 86002
(520) 774-5251 • Fax (800) 744-0592 •
(800) 346-3257 • www.northlandpub.com

Orchard Books (A Grolier Company)
95 Madison Avenue
New York, NY 10016
(212) 951-2600 • Fax (212) 213-6435 •
(800) 433-3411 • www.grolier.com

Owlet (Imprint of Henry Holt & Co.)

Penguin Putnam, Inc.
375 Hudson Street
New York, NY 10014
(212) 366-2000 • Fax (212) 366-2636 •
(800) 631-8571 •
www.penguinputnam.com

Willa Perlman Books
(Imprint of Simon & Schuster Children's Publishing)

Philomel Books
(Imprint of Penguin Putnam, Inc.)

Puffin Books
(Imprint of Penguin Putnam, Inc.)

G. P. Putnam's Sons Publishing
(Imprint of Penguin Putnam, Inc.)

Random House
1540 Broadway
New York, NY 10036
(212) 782-9000 • Fax (212) 302-7985 • (800)
200-3552 • www.randomhouse.com/kids

Scholastic
555 Broadway
New York, NY 10012
(212) 343-6100 • Fax (212) 343-6930 •
(800) SCHOLASTIC • www.scholastic.com

Charles Scribner's Sons
(Imprint of Simon & Schuster Children's Publishing)

Sierra Club Books for Children
85 Second Street, Second Floor
San Francisco, CA 94105-3441
(415) 977-5500 • Fax (415) 977-5793 •
(800) 935-1056 • www.sierraclub.org

Simon & Schuster Children's Books
1230 Avenue of the Americas
New York, NY 10020
(212) 698-7200 • (800) 223-2336 •
www.simonsayskids.com

Smith & Kraus
177 Lyme Road
Hanover, NH 03755
(603) 643-6431 • Fax (603) 643-1831 •
(800) 895-4331 • www.smithkraus.com

Teacher Ideas Press
(Division of Libraries Unlimited)
P.O. Box 6633
Englewood, CO 80155-6633
(303) 770-1220 • Fax (303) 220-8843 •
(800) 237-6124 • www.lu.com

Ticknor & Fields
(Imprint of Houghton Mifflin, Inc.)

Usborne (Imprint of EDC Publishing)
10302 E. 55th Place, Suite B
Tulsa, OK 74146-6515
(918) 622-4522 • (800) 475-4522 •
www.edcpub.com

Viking Children's Books
(Imprint of Penguin Putnam Inc.)

Walker & Co.
435 Hudson Street
New York, NY 10014
(212) 727-8300 • (212) 727-0984 • (800)
AT-WALKER

Watts Publishing
(Imprint of Grolier Publishing;
see Children's Press)

Albert Whitman
6340 Oakton Street
Morton Grove, IL 60053-2723
(847) 581-0033 • Fax (847) 581-0039 •
(800) 255-7675 • www.awhitmanco.com

Workman Publishing Co., Inc.
708 Broadway
New York, NY 10003
(212) 254-5900 • Fax (800) 521-1832 •
(800) 722-7202 • www.workman.com

Directory of Resources

Multimedia Resources

AGC/United Learning
1560 Sherman Ave., Suite 100
Evanston, IL 60201
(800) 323-9084 • (847) 328-6700 •
www.unitedlearning.com

AIMS Multimedia
9710 DeSoto Avenue
Chatsworth, CA 91311-4409
(800) 367-2467 • (818) 773-4300 •
www.aimsmultimedia.com

BFA Educational Media
(see Phoenix Learning Group)

Broderbund
(Parsons Technology;
also see The Learning Company)

Carousel Film and Video
260 Fifth Avenue, Suite 905
New York, NY 10001
(800) 683-1660 • Fax: (212) 683-1662 •
www.carouselfilms.com

Coronet/MTI
(see Phoenix Learning Group)

Davidson (see Knowledge Adventure)

Direct Cinema, Ltd.
P.O. Box 10003
Santa Monica, CA 90410-1003
(310) 636-8200
www.directcinema.com

Disney Interactive
(800) 900-9234 • www.disney.go.com/
DisneyInteractive

DK Multimedia (Dorling Kindersley)
95 Madison Avenue
New York, NY 10016
(212) 213-4800 • Fax: (800) 774-6733 •
(888) 342-5357 • www.dk.com

Edmark Corp.
P.O. Box 97021
Redmond, WA 98073-9721
(800) 691-2986 • www.edmark.com

Encyclopaedia Britannica Educational Corp.
310 South Michigan Avenue
Chicago, IL 60604
(800) 522-8656 • www.eb.com

ESI/Educational Software Institute
4213 S. 94th Street
Omaha, NE 68127
(800) 955-5570 • Fax: (402) 592-0217 •
www.edsoft.com

GPN/Reading Rainbow
University of Nebraska-Lincoln
P.O. Box 80669
Lincoln, NE 68501-0669
(800) 228-4630 • www.gpn.unl.edu

Hasbro Interactive
(800) 683-5847 • www.hasbro.com

Humongous
13110 NE 177th Pl., Suite B101, Box 180
Woodenville, WA 98072
(800) 499-8386 • www.humongous.com

IBM Corp.
New Orchard Road
Armonk, NY 10504
(877) 222-6426 • (888) 746-7426 •
www.ibm.com/pc/athome

Knowledge Adventure
19840 Pioneer Avenue
Torrence, CA 90503
(800) 542-4240 • (800) 545-7677 •
www.knowledgeadventure.com

The Learning Company
6160 Summit Drive North
Minneapolis, MN 55430
(800) 395-0277 • www.learningco.com

Library Video Company
P.O. Box 580
Wynnewood, PA 19096
(800) 843-3620 • www.libraryvideo.com

Listening Library
One Park Avenue
Greenwich, CT 06870-1727
(800) 733-3000 • www.listeninglib.com

Macmillan/McGraw-Hill
(see SRA/McGraw-Hill)

Maxis
2121 N. California Blvd
Walnut Creek, CA 94596-3572
(925) 933-5630 • Fax (925) 927-3736 •
(877) 324-2637 • www.maxis.com

MECC
(see the Learning Company)

Microsoft
One Microsoft Way
Redmond, WA 98052-6399
(800) 426-9400 • www.microsoft.com/kids

National Geographic Society Educational Services
P.O. Box 1041
Des Moines, IA 50340-0597
(800) 225-5647 •
www.nationalgeographic.com

National School Products
101 East Broadway
Maryville, TN 37804
(800) 251-9124

PBS Video
1320 Braddock Place
Alexandria, VA 22314
(800) 344-3337 • www.pbs.org

Phoenix Films
(see Phoenix Learning Group)

The Phoenix Learning Group
2349 Chaffee Drive
St. Louis, MO 63146
(800) 221-1274 • e-mail:
phoenixfilms@att.net

Pied Piper (see AIMS Multimedia)

Scholastic New Media
555 Broadway
New York, NY 10003
(800) 724-6527 • www.scholastic.com

Simon & Schuster Interactive
(see Knowledge Adventure)

SRA/McGraw-Hill
220 East Danieldale Road
De Soto, TX 75115
(888) 772-4543 • www.sra4kids.com

SVE/Churchill Media
6677 North Northwest Highway
Chicago, IL 60631
(800) 829-1900 • www.svemedia.com

Tom Snyder Productions (also see ESI)
80 Coolidge Hill Rd.
Watertown, MA 02472
(800) 342-0236 • www.teachtsp.com

Troll Associates
100 Corporate Drive
Mahwah, NJ 07430
(888) 998-7655 • Fax (800) 979-8765 •
www.troll.com

Voyager (see ESI)

Weston Woods
12 Oakwood Avenue
Norwalk, CT 06850
(800) 243-5020 • Fax (203) 845-0498

Zenger Media
10200 Jefferson Blvd., Room 94,
P.O. Box 802
Culver City, CA 90232-0802
(800) 421-4246 • Fax: (800) 944-5432 •
www.Zengermedia.com

UNIT 1

	Decodable Words				Vocabulary
THE HOUSE					**High-Frequency Words** the
A PRESENT					**High-Frequency Words** a
MY SCHOOL					**High-Frequency Words** my
NAN	an	**Nan**			**High-Frequency Words** that
THAT NAN!	Review				**High-Frequency Words** Review

UNIT 2

	Decodable Words				Vocabulary
DAN AND DAD	**Dad**	**Dan**			**High-Frequency Words** and
DAD, DAN, AND I	sad				**High-Frequency Words** I
I AM SAM!	**am** dam	mad	**man**	Sam	**High-Frequency Words** is
SID SAID	did dim	in	**Min**	Sid	**High-Frequency Words** said
IS SAM MAD?	Review				**High-Frequency Words** Review

Boldfaced words appear in the selection.

UNIT 3

	Decodable Words				Vocabulary
THAT TAM!	at it mat	Nat **sat** **sit**	**Tam** tan	**Tim** tin	**High-Frequency Words** **we**
NAT IS MY CAT	**can**	**cat**			**High-Frequency Words** **are**
ON A DOT	cot Dom **Don**	**dot** **Mom**	**not** **on**	**Tom** tot	**High-Frequency Words** **you**
WE FIT!	fan	fat	fin	**fit**	**High-Frequency Words** **have**
A TIN CAN	Review				**High-Frequency Words** Review

UNIT 4

	Decodable Words				Vocabulary
YOU ARE IT!	**ran** rat	rod	**Ron**	rot	**High-Frequency Words** **to**
IS IT YOU?	cap dip map mop nap	pad **Pam** pan **pat**	pod pot rip sap	sip tap tip top	**High-Frequency Words** **me**
GO, LAD, GO!	**lad** **lap**	lid	lit	lip	**High-Frequency Words** **go**
MUD FUN	**cup** cut	**mud** nut	**fun** rut	sun pup	**High-Frequency Words** **do**
RON AND ME	Review				**High-Frequency Words** Review

UNIT 5

Decodable Words

Vocabulary

TOM IS SICK

dock	lock	**pick**	**sock**
duck	luck	rack	tack
kid	Mack	rock	tick
Kim	Mick	sack	tock
kit	muck	**sick**	tuck
lick	pack		

High-Frequency Words

for

HE IS PUG

dug	gum	**Pug**	tag
fog	log	rag	tug
got	**mug**	rug	

High-Frequency Words

he

A PET FOR KEN

den	leg	Ned	**red**
fed	**let**	net	set
get	Meg	pen	Ted
Ken	men	**pet**	ten
led	met		

High-Frequency Words

she

A BIG BUG

bad	bet	bog	cub
bag	**big**	bud	Rob
bat	bin	**bug**	rub
bed	bit	**but**	tub
Ben	bus		

High-Frequency Words

has

PUP AND CAT

Review

High-Frequency Words

Review

UNIT 6

	Decodable Words				Vocabulary

HOP WITH A HOG

had	him	**hog**	**hug**
ham	hip	**hop**	**hum**
hat	**hit**	hot	hut
hen			

High-Frequency Words
with

WE WIN!

wag	wed	wig	**win**
web	wet		

High-Frequency Words
was

THE VET VAN

ax	fox	ox	**van**
box	**Max**	**Rex**	**vet**
fix	mix	six	wax

High-Frequency Words
see

JEN AND YIP

jam	job	quit	yum
Jan	**jog**	yam	Zack
Jen	jot	yet	Zeb
jet	jug	**Yip**	**zig-zag**
jig	**quack**	yuck	zip
Jim	**quick**		

High-Frequency Words
of

ZACK AND JAN

Review

High-Frequency Words
Review

Listening, Speaking, Viewing, Representing

☑ Tested Skill

Tinted panels show skills, strategies, and other teaching opportunities

	K	1	2	3	4	5	6
LISTENING							
Learn the vocabulary of school (numbers, shapes, colors, directions, and categories)							
Identify the musical elements of literary language, such as rhymes, repetition, onomatopoeia, alliteration, assonance							
Determine purposes for listening (get information, solve problems, enjoy and appreciate)							
Understand and follow directions							
Listen critically and responsively; recognize barriers to effective listening							
Ask and answer relevant questions (for clarification; to follow up on ideas)							
Listen critically to interpret and evaluate							
Listen responsively to stories and other texts read aloud, including selections from classic and contemporary works							
Connect and compare own experiences, feelings, ideas, and traditions with those of others							
Apply comprehension strategies in listening activities							
Understand the major ideas and supporting evidence in spoken messages							
Participate in listening activities related to reading and writing (such as discussions, group activities, conferences)							
Listen to learn by taking notes, organizing, and summarizing spoken ideas							
Know personal listening preferences							
SPEAKING							
Uses repetition, rhyme, and rhythm in oral texts (such as in reciting songs, poems, and stories with repeating patterns)							
Learn the vocabulary of school (numbers, shapes, colors, directions, and categories)							
Use appropriate language, grammar, and vocabulary learned to describe ideas, feelings, and experiences							
Ask and answer relevant questions (for clarification; to follow up on ideas)							
Communicate effectively in everyday situations (such as discussions, group activities, conferences, conversations)							
Demonstrate speaking skills (audience, purpose, occasion, clarity, volume, pitch, intonation, phrasing, rate, fluency)							
Clarify and support spoken messages and ideas with objects, charts, evidence, elaboration, examples							
Use verbal communication in effective ways when, for example, making announcements, giving directions, or making introductions							
Use nonverbal communication in effective ways such as eye contact, facial expressions, gestures							
Retell a story or a spoken message by summarizing or clarifying							
Connect and compare own experiences, ideas, and traditions with those of others							
Determine purposes for speaking (inform, entertain, compare, describe, give directions, persuade, express personal feelings and opinions)							
Recognize differences between formal and informal language							
Demonstrate skills of reporting and providing information							
Demonstrate skills of interviewing, requesting and providing information							
Apply composition strategies in speaking activities							
Monitor own understanding of spoken message and seek clarification as needed							
VIEWING							
Demonstrate viewing skills (focus attention, organize information)							
Understand and use nonverbal cues							
Respond to audiovisual media in a variety of ways							
Participate in viewing activities related to reading and writing							
Apply comprehension strategies in viewing activities, including main idea and details							
Recognize artists' craft and techniques for conveying meaning							
Interpret information from various formats such as maps, charts, graphics, video segments, technology							
Knows various types of mass media (such as film, video, television, billboards, and newspapers)							
Evaluate purposes of various media, including mass media (information, appreciation, entertainment, directions, persuasion)							
Use media, including mass media, to compare ideas, information, and points of view							
REPRESENTING							
Select, organize, or produce visuals to complement or extend meanings							
Produce communication using appropriate media to develop a class paper, multimedia or video reports							
Show how language, medium, and presentation contribute to the message							

Reading: Alphabetic Principle, Sounds/Symbols

☑ Tested Skill

☐ Tinted panels show skills, strategies, and other teaching opportunities

PRINT AWARENESS	K	1	2	3	4	5	6
Know the order of the alphabet							
Recognize that print represents spoken language and conveys meaning							
Understand directionality (tracking print from left to right; return sweep)							
Understand that written words and sentences are separated by spaces							
Know the difference between individual letters and printed words							
Understand that spoken words are represented in written language by specific sequence of letters							
Recognize that there are correct spellings for words							
Know the difference between capital and lowercase letters							
Recognize how readers use capitalization and punctuation to comprehend							
Recognize the distinguishing features of a letter, word, sentence, paragraph							
Understand appropriate book handling							
Recognize that parts of a book (such as cover/title page and table of contents) offer information							

PHONOLOGICAL AWARENESS	K	1	2	3	4	5	6
Listen for environmental sounds							
Identify spoken words and sentences							
Divide spoken sentence into individual words							
Produce rhyming words and distinguish rhyming words from nonrhyming words							
Identify, segment, and combine syllables within spoken words							
Blend and segment onsets and rimes							
Identify and isolate the initial, medial, and final sound of a spoken word							
Add, delete, or substitute sounds to change words (such as *cow* to *how*, *pan* to *fan*)							
Blend sounds to make spoken words							
Segment one-syllable spoken words into individual phonemes							

PHONICS AND DECODING	K	1	2	3	4	5	6
Alphabetic principle: Letter/sound correspondence	☑	☑	☑				
Blending CVC words	☑	☑					
Segmenting CVC words	☑						
Blending CVC, CVCe, CCVC, CCCC, CVVC words	☑	☑	☑				
Segmenting CVC, CVCe, CCVC, CCCC, CVVC words and sounds	☑	☑	☑				
Initial and final consonants: /n/n, /d/d, /s/s, /m/m, /t/t, /k/c, /f/f, /r/r, /p/p, /l/l, /k/k, /g/g, /b/b, /h/h, /w/w, /v/v, /ks/x, /kw/qu, /j/j, /y/y, /z/z	☑	☑					
Initial and medial short vowels: *a, i, u, o, e*	☑	☑	☑				
Long vowels: *a-e, i-e, o-e, u-e* (vowel-consonant-e)		☑	☑				
Long vowels, including *ay, ai; e, ee, ie, ea; o, oa, oe, ow; i, y, igh*		☑	☑				
Consonant Digraphs: *sh, th, ch, wh*		☑					
Consonant Blends: continuant/continuant, including *sl, sm, sn, fl, fr, ll, ss, ff*		☑					
Consonant Blends: continuant/stop, including *st, sk, sp, ng, nt, nd, mp, ft*		☑					
Consonant Blends: stop/continuant, including *tr, pr, pl, cr, tw*		☑					
Variant vowels: including /ù/oo; /ô/a, aw, au; /ü/ue, ew		☑	☑				
Diphthongs, including /ou/ou, ow; /oi/oi, oy		☑	☑				
r-controlled vowels, including /âr/are; /ôr/or, ore; /îr/ear			☑				
Soft *c* and soft *g*			☑				
nk		☑	☑				
Consonant Digraphs: *ck*	☑	☑					
Consonant Digraphs: *ph, tch, ch*			☑				
Short *e: ea*			☑				
Long *e: y, ey*			☑				
/ü/oo		☑	☑				
/är/ar; /ûr/ir, ur, er		☑	☑				
Silent letters: including *l, b, k, w, g, h, gh*			☑				
Schwa: /ər/er; /ən/en; /əl/le;			☑				
Reading/identifying multisyllabic words		☑	☑				
Using graphophonic cues							

Reading: Vocabulary/Word Identification

☑ Tested Skill

☐ Tinted panels show skills, strategies, and other teaching opportunities

WORD STRUCTURE	K	1	2	3	4	5	6
Common spelling patterns							
Syllable patterns							
Plurals		☑					
Possessives		☑					
Contractions		☑					
Root, or base, words and inflectional endings (-s, -es, -ed, -ing)		☑	☑	☑		☑	
Compound Words		☑	☑	☑	☑	☑	☑
Prefixes and suffixes (such as un-, re-, dis-, non-; -ly, -y, -ful, -able, -tion)			☑	☑	☑	☑	☑
Root words and derivational endings				☑	☑	☑	☑

WORD MEANING	K	1	2	3	4	5	6
Develop vocabulary through concrete experiences, word walls, other people							
Develop vocabulary through selections read aloud							
Develop vocabulary through reading							
Cueing systems: syntactic, semantic, graphophonic							
Context clues, including semantic clues (word meaning), syntactical clues (word order), and graphophonic clues	☑	☑	☑	☑	☑	☑	☑
High-frequency words (such as the, a, and, said, was, where, is)	☑	☑					
Identify words that name persons, places, things, and actions							
Automatic reading of regular and irregular words							
Use resources and references (dictionary, glossary, thesaurus, synonym finder, technology and software, and context)							
Classify and categorize words							
Synonyms and antonyms			☑	☑	☑	☑	☑
Multiple-meaning words			☑		☑	☑	☑
Figurative language			☑	☑	☑	☑	☑
Decode derivatives (root words, such as like, pay, happy with affixes, such as dis-, pre-, un-)							
Systematic study of words across content areas and in current events							
Locate meanings, pronunciations, and derivations (including dictionaries, glossaries, and other sources)							
Denotation and connotation							☑
Word origins as aid to understanding historical influences on English word meanings							
Homophones, homographs							
Analogies							☑
Idioms							

Reading: Comprehension

PREREADING STRATEGIES	K	1	2	3	4	5	6
Preview and predict							
Use prior knowledge							
Set and adjust purposes for reading							
Build background							

MONITORING STRATEGIES	K	1	2	3	4	5	6
Adjust reading rate							
Reread, search for clues, ask questions, ask for help							
Visualize							
Read a portion aloud, use reference aids							
Use decoding and vocabulary strategies							
Paraphrase							
Create story maps, diagrams, charts, story props to help comprehend, analyze, synthesize and evaluate texts							

(continued on next page)

☑ Tested Skill

Tinted panels show skills, strategies, and other teaching opportunities

(Reading: Comprehension continued)

SKILLS AND STRATEGIES	K	1	2	3	4	5	6
Recall story details, including character and setting	☑	☑					
Use illustrations	☑	☑					
Distinguish reality and fantasy	☑	☑	☑				
Classify and categorize	☑						
Make predictions	☑	☑	☑	☑	☑	☑	☑
Recognize sequence of events (tell or act out)	☑	☑	☑	☑	☑	☑	☑
Recognize cause and effect	☑	☑	☑	☑	☑	☑	☑
Compare and contrast	☑	☑	☑	☑	☑	☑	☑
Summarize	☑	☑	☑	☑	☑	☑	☑
Make and explain inferences		☑	☑	☑	☑	☑	☑
Draw conclusions		☑	☑	☑	☑	☑	☑
Distinguish important and unimportant information				☑	☑	☑	☑
Recognize main idea and supporting details	☑	☑	☑	☑	☑	☑	☑
Form conclusions or generalizations and support with evidence from text			☑	☑	☑	☑	☑
Distinguish fact and opinion (including news stories and advertisements)				☑	☑	☑	☑
Recognize problem and solution				☑	☑	☑	☑
Recognize steps in a process		☑	☑	☑	☑	☑	☑
Make judgments and decisions				☑	☑	☑	☑
Distinguish fact and nonfact				☑	☑	☑	☑
Recognize techniques of persuasion and propaganda							☑
Evaluate evidence and sources of information, including checking other sources and asking experts							☑
Identify similarities and differences across texts (including topics, characters, problems, themes, cultural influences, treatment, scope, or organization)							
Practice various questions and tasks (test-like comprehension questions)							
Paraphrase and summarize to recall, inform, and organize							
Answer various types of questions (open-ended, literal, interpretative, test-like such as true-false, multiple choice, short-answer)							
Use study strategies to learn and recall (preview, question, reread, and record)							
LITERARY RESPONSE							
Listen to stories being read aloud							
React, speculate, join in, read along when predictable and patterned selections are read aloud							
Respond to a variety of stories and poems through talk, movement, music, art, drama, and writing							
Show understanding through writing, illustrating, developing demonstrations, and using technology							
Connect ideas and themes across texts							
Support responses by referring to relevant aspects of text and own experiences							
Offer observations, make connections, speculate, interpret, and raise questions in response to texts							
Interpret text ideas through journal writing, discussion, enactment, and media							
TEXT STRUCTURE/LITERARY CONCEPTS							
Distinguish forms and functions of texts (lists, newsletters, signs)							
Use text features to aid comprehension							
Understand story structure							
Identify narrative (for entertainment) and expository (for information)							
Distinguish fiction from nonfiction, including fact and fantasy							
Understand literary forms (stories, poems, plays, and informational books)							
Understand literary terms by distinguishing between roles of author and illustrator							
Understand title, author, and illustrator across a variety of texts							
Analyze character, character's motive, character's point of view, plot, setting, style, tone, mood		☑	☑	☑	☑	☑	☑
Compare communication in different forms							
Understand terms such as *title, author, illustrator, playwright, theater, stage, act, dialogue,* and *scene*							
Recognize stories, poems, songs, myths, legends, folktales, fables, tall tales, limericks, plays, biographies, autobiographies							
Judge internal logic of story text							
Recognize that authors organize information in specific ways							
Recognize author's purpose: to inform, influence, express, or entertain							
Describe how author's point of view affects text				☑	☑	☑	☑
Recognize biography, historical fiction, realistic fiction, modern fantasy, informational texts, and poetry							
Analyze ways authors present ideas (cause/effect, compare/contrast, inductively, deductively, chronologically)							
Recognize literary techniques such as imagery, repetition, flashback, foreshadowing, symbolism							

(continued on next page)

T65

☑ Tested Skill

Tinted panels show skills, strategies, and other teaching opportunities

VARIETY OF TEXT	K	1	2	3	4	5	6
Read a variety of genres and understand their distinguishing features							
Use expository and other informational texts to acquire information							
Read for a variety of purposes							
Select varied sources when reading for information or pleasure							
Know preferences for reading literary and nonfiction texts							

FLUENCY	K	1	2	3	4	5	6
Read regularly in independent-level and instructional-level materials							
Read orally with fluency from familiar texts							
Self-select independent-level reading							
Read silently for increasing periods of time							
Demonstrate characteristics of fluent and effective reading							
Adjust reading rate to purpose							
Read aloud in selected texts, showing understanding of text and engaging the listener							

CULTURES	K	1	2	3	4	5	6
Connect own experience with culture of others							
Compare experiences of characters across cultures							
Articulate and discuss themes and connections that cross cultures							

CRITICAL THINKING	K	1	2	3	4	5	6
Experiences (comprehend, apply, analyze, synthesize, evaluate)							
Make connections (comprehend, apply, analyze, synthesize, evaluate)							
Expression (comprehend, apply, analyze, synthesize, evaluate)							
Inquiry (comprehend, apply, analyze, synthesize, evaluate)							
Problem solving (comprehend, apply, analyze, synthesize, evaluate)							
Making decisions (comprehend, apply, analyze, synthesize, evaluate)							

Study Skills

INQUIRY/RESEARCH AND STUDY STRATEGIES	K	1	2	3	4	5	6
Follow and give directions							
Use alphabetical order							
Use text features and formats to help understand text (such as boldface, italic, or highlighted text; captions; headings and subheadings; numbers or symbols)							
Use study strategies to help read text and to learn and recall information from text (such as preview text, set purposes, and ask questions; use SQRRR; adjust reading rate; skim and scan; use KWL)							
Identify/frame and revise questions for research							
Obtain, organize, and summarize information: classify, take notes, outline, web, diagram							
Evaluate research and raise new questions							
Use technology for research and/or to present information in various formats							
Follow accepted formats for writing research, including documenting sources							
Use test-taking strategies							
Use text organizers (book cover; title page—title, author, illustrator; contents; headings; glossary; index)		☑	☑	☑	☑	☑	☑
Use graphic aids, such as maps, diagrams, charts, graphs, schedules, calendars		☑	☑	☑	☑	☑	☑
Read and interpret varied texts, such as environmental print, signs, lists, encyclopedia, dictionary, glossary, newspaper, advertisement, magazine, calendar, directions, floor plans, online resources		☑	☑	☑	☑	☑	☑
Use print and online reference sources, such as glossary, dictionary, encyclopedia, telephone directory, technology resources, nonfiction books		☑	☑	☑	☑	☑	☑
Recognize Library/Media center resources, such as computerized references; catalog search—subject, author, title; encyclopedia index		☑	☑	☑	☑	☑	☑

Writing

☑ Tested Skill

Tinted panels show skills, strategies, and other teaching opportunities

MODES AND FORMS	K	1	2	3	4	5	6
Interactive writing							
Descriptive writing			☑				
Personal narrative			☑	☑	☑	☑	☑
Writing that compares		☑	☑	☑	☑	☑	☑
Explanatory writing			☑	☑	☑	☑	☑
Persuasive writing				☑	☑	☑	☑
Writing a story		☑	☑	☑	☑	☑	☑
Expository writing; research report		☑	☑	☑	☑	☑	☑
Write using a variety of formats, such as advertisement, autobiography, biography, book report/report, comparison-contrast, critique/review/editorial, description, essay, how-to, interview, invitation, journal/log/notes, message/list, paragraph/multi-paragraph composition, picture book, play (scene), poem/rhyme, story, summary, note, letter							

PURPOSES/AUDIENCES	K	1	2	3	4	5	6
Dictate sentences and messages such as news and stories for others to write							
Write labels, notes, and captions for illustrations, possessions, charts, and centers							
Write to record, to discover and develop ideas, to inform, to influence, to entertain							
Exhibit an identifiable voice							
Use literary devices (suspense, dialogue, and figurative language)							
Produce written texts by organizing ideas, using effective transitions, and choosing precise wording							

PROCESSES	K	1	2	3	4	5	6
Generate ideas for self-selected and assigned topics using prewriting strategies							
Develop drafts							
Revise drafts for varied purposes, elaborate ideas							
Edit for appropriate grammar, spelling, punctuation, and features of published writings							
Proofread own writing and that of others							
Bring pieces to final form and "publish" them for audiences							
Use technology to compose, revise, and present text							
Select and use reference materials and resources for writing, revising, and editing final drafts							

SPELLING	K	1	2	3	4	5	6
Spell own name and write high-frequency words							
Words with short vowels (including CVC and one-syllable words with blends CCVC, CVCC, CCVCC)							
Words with long vowels (including CVCe)							
Words with digraphs, blends, consonant clusters, double consonants							
Words with diphthongs							
Words with variant vowels							
Words with r-controlled vowels							
Words with /ər/, /əl/, and /ən/							
Words with silent letters							
Words with soft c and soft g							
Inflectional endings (including plurals and past tense and words that drop the final e and double a consonant when adding -ing, -ed)							
Compound words							
Contractions							
Homonyms							
Suffixes such as -able, -ly, -ful, or -less, and prefixes such as dis-, re-, pre-, or un-							
Spell words ending in -tion and -sion, such as station and procession						-	
Accurate spelling of root or base words							
Orthographic patterns and rules such as keep/can; sack/book; out/now; oil/toy; match/speech; ledge/cage; consonant doubling, dropping e, changing y to i							
Multisyllabic words using regularly spelled phonogram patterns							
Syllable patterns (including closed, open, syllable boundary patterns)							
Synonyms and antonyms							
Words from Social Studies, Science, Math, and Physical Education							
Words derived from other languages and cultures							
Use resources to find correct spellings, synonyms, and replacement words							
Use conventional spelling of familiar words in writing assignments							
Spell accurately in final drafts							

(continued on next page)

☑ Tested Skill

Tinted panels show skills, strategies, and other teaching opportunities

GRAMMAR AND USAGE

	K	1	2	3	4	5	6
Understand sentence concepts (word order, statements, questions, exclamations, commands)							
Recognize complete and incomplete sentences							
Nouns (common, proper, singular, plural, irregular plural, possessives)							
Verbs (action, helping, linking, irregular)							
Verb tense (present, past, future, perfect, and progressive)							
Pronouns (possessive, subject and object, pronoun-verb agreement)							
Use objective case pronouns accurately							
Adjectives							
Adverbs that tell how, when, where							
Subjects, predicates							
Subject-verb agreement							
Sentence combining							
Recognize sentence structure (simple, compound, complex)							
Synonyms and antonyms							
Contractions							
Conjunctions							
Prepositions and prepositional phrases							

PENMANSHIP

	K	1	2	3	4	5	6
Write each letter of alphabet (capital and lowercase) using correct formation, appropriate size and spacing							
Write own name and other important words							
Use phonological knowledge to map sounds to letters to write messages							
Write messages that move left to right, top to bottom							
Gain increasing control of penmanship, pencil grip, paper position, beginning stroke							
Use word and letter spacing and margins to make messages readable							
Write legibly by selecting cursive or manuscript as appropriate							

MECHANICS

	K	1	2	3	4	5	6
Use capitalization in sentences, proper nouns, titles, abbreviations and the pronoun *I*							
Use end marks correctly (period, question mark, exclamation point)							
Use commas (in dates, in addresses, in a series, in letters, in direct address)							
Use apostrophes in contractions and possessives							
Use quotation marks							
Use hyphens, semicolons, colons							

EVALUATION

	K	1	2	3	4	5	6
Identify the most effective features of a piece of writing using class/teacher-generated criteria							
Respond constructively to others' writing							
Determine how his/her own writing achieves its purpose							
Use published pieces as models for writing							
Review own written work to monitor growth as writer							

90I–J, 96B, 100B, 101A, 102I–J, 108B, 112B, 120B, 124B, 126W–X, 128, 130, 138I–J, 148B, 150A, 152, 150I–J, 160B, 160, 162I–J, 172B, 174B, 174I–J, 186W–X, 192C, 198I–J, 222I–J, 246W–X, 250C, 252B, 256, 257C, 267, 268B, 250C, 252B, 256B, 264B, 268, 269, 270I–J, 280B, 281C, 306W–X, 328B, 330I–J, 336B, 340B, 360B, 365, Unit 1:T37, Unit 3: T29, Unit 4:T31. *See also* Phonological awareness: rhyme production; rhyme recognition.

Science link. *See* Center activities.

Seasons, 61/62A–B, 75A, 237, 275B

Segmenting. *See* Phonics and decoding, Phonological awareness.

Self–selected reading, 6M, 18E, 30E, 42E, 54E, 65B, 66S, 78E, 90E, 102E, 114E, 126S, 138E, 150E, 162E, 176E, 186S, 198E, 210E, 222E, 234E, 246S, 258E, 270E, 282E, 294E, 306S, 318E, 330E, 342E, 354E, T56–57. *See also* Leveled books.

Semantic cues, 11C, 11, 17A, 17C, 17, 29C, 29, 35C, 35, 41A, 47C, 47, 59, 71C, 71, 83C, 83, 89A, 89, 125C, 126A, 131C, 131, 143C, 155C, 167C, 222F, 275

Sequence of events, analyzing. *See* Comprehension strategies.

Setting purposes, for reading, 7A, 9A, 13/14A, 19A, 21A, 25/26A, 31A, 33A, 37/38A, 43A, 45A, 49/50A, 55A, 57A, 61/62A, 67A, 69A, 73/74A, 79A, 81A, 85/86A, 91A, 93A, 97/98A, 103A, 105A, 109/110A, 115A, 117A, 121/122A, 127A, 129A, 133/134A, 139A, 141A, 145/146A, 151A, 153A, 157/158A, 163A, 165A, 169/170A, 175A, 177A, 181/182A, 187A, 189A, 193/194A, 199A, 201A, 205/206A, 211A, 213A, 217/218A, 223A, 225A, 229/230A, 235A, 237A, 241/242A, 247A, 249A, 253/254A, 259A, 261A, 265/266A, 271A, 273A, 277/278A, 283A, 285A, 289/290A, 295A, 297A, 301/302A, 307A, 309A, 313/314A, 319A, 321A, 325/326A, 331A, 333A, 337/338A, 343A, 345A, 349/350A, 355A, 357A, 361/362A

Shapes, R18, R38, 91C–91, 103C–103, 115C–115, 319C–319, 355C–355, Unit 2: T31, Unit 6: T26
  circle, R18, R38, 91C–91, 115C–115, Unit 2: T34
  square, R18, 103C–103, 115C–115, Unit 2: T34
  rectangle, R18, R38, 103C–103, 115C–115, Unit 2: T34
  triangle, R18, R38, 91C–91, 115C–115, Unit 2: T34

Shared reading, R5, R9, R13, R17, R21, R25, R29, R33, R37, R41, 7A–B, 9A–B, 19A–B, 21A–B, 29A–B, 31A–B, 33A–B, 43A–B, 45A–B, 55A–B, 57A–B, 67A–B, 69A–B, 79A–B, 81A–B, 91A–B, 93A–B, 103A–B, 105A–B, 115A–B, 117A–B, 127A–B, 129A–B, 139A–B, 141A–B, 151A–B, 153A–B, 163A–B, 165A–B, 175A–B, 177A–B, 187A–B, 189A–B, 199A–B, 201A–B, 211A–B, 213A–B, 223A–B, 225A–B, 235A–B, 237A–B, 247A–B, 249A–B, 259A–B, 261A–B, 271A–B, 273A–B, 283A–B, 285A–B, 295A–B, 297A–B, 307A–B, 309A–B, 319A–B, 321A–B, 331A–B, 333A–B, 343A–B, 345A–B, 355A–B, 357A–B

Short vowels. *See* Phonics and decoding.

Sight words. *See* High–frequency words.

Signs, reading, 35B, 47B

Social studies link. *See* Center activities.

Sorting, 20, 37/38B, 78F, 82, 102F, 109/110B, 115B, 142C, 166C, 198E, 250, 262C, 296, 316, 354, 354K, 364

Speaking and listening activities. *See* Listening and speaking activities, Listening and speaking strategies.

Spelling. *See* Grammar/spelling connection.

Story details. *See* Comprehension strategies.

Story structure. *See* Comprehension strategies.

Summarizing. *See* Comprehension strategies, Listening and speaking activities: retelling.

Syllables. *See* Phonological awareness.

Syntactic cues, 66T, 71, 83, 90F, 95C, 101C, 114A, 126A, 137, 149, 161C, 167, 173C, 173, 257C, 282F, 318E, 329, 342F, 354A

Teaching tips, 6S, 7E, 9G, 10C, 11C, 15A, 17C, 18A, 18K, 19C, 21C, 23C, 27A, 28C, 30A, 32C, 33G, 36C, 40C, 42A, 43C, 45B, 45C, 54A, 55C, 56C, 60C, 63A, 64C, 69E, 71C, 72C, 77C, 78A, 79C, 81B, 81C, 83C, 87A, 89C, 90A, 91C, 92C, 93E, 95C, 96C, 99A, 100C, 101C, 102A, 103C, 104C, 105B, 105C, 107C, 108C, 113C, 114A, 114K, 115C, 116C, 117B, 117C, 119C, 120C, 124C, 125C, 126A, 128C, 131C, 132C, 135A, 136C, 137C, 138A, 139C, 141B, 141C, 142C, 143C, 144C, 147A, 148C, 149C, 150A, 151C, 152C, 155C, 159A, 160C, 161C, 163C, 165B, 165C, 168C, 171A, 172C, 173B, 174A, 174K, 176C, 177C, 178C, 179C, 180C, 183A, 184C, 185C, 186A, 189E, 190C, 191C, 195A, 196C, 197C, 198A, 199C, 200C, 201B, 201C, 202C, 203C, 204C, 208C, 209C, 210A, 211C, 213G, 214C, 215C, 216C, 219C, 220C, 221C, 223A, 224C, 225B, 225C, 226C, 227C, 228C, 231A, 232C, 233C, 234A, 234K, 236C, 237A, 237C, 238C, 239C, 240C, 243A, 245C, 246A, 247E, 248C, 249G, 250C, 251C, 252C, 255C, 256C, 257C, 259C, 260C, 261B, 261C, 262C, 263C, 264C, 267C, 268C, 269C, 270A, 273C, 273I, 274C, 275C, 276C, 279A, 280C, 281C, 282A, 283C, 284C, 285A, 285C, 286C, 287C, 288C, 291C, 292C, 293C, 294A, 294K, 295C, 296C, 297A, 297C, 298C, 299C, 300C, 304C, 305C, 306A, 307E, 309G, 310C, 311C, 312C, 315A, 316C, 317C, 318A, 319C, 321B, 321C, 322C, 323C, 324C, 327A, 328C, 329C, 330A, 331C, 333G, 335C, 336C, 339A, 340C, 341C, 342A, 343C, 345B, 345C, 347C, 348C, 351A, 352C, 353C, 354A, 354K, 355C, 356C, 357B, 357C, 358C, 359C, 360C, 363A, 365C

Technology tips, 18B, 30B, 42B, 54B, 66B, 78B, 90B, 102B, 114B, 126B, 138B, 150B, 162B, 174B, 198B, 210B, 222B, 234B, 246B, 258B, 270B, 282B, 294B, 306B, 318B, 330B, 342B, 354B, 366B

Theme connections, 6I–J, 66C, 66O–P, 126C, 126O–P, 186C, 186O–P, 246C, 246O–P, 306C, 306O–P, 366C

Theme projects, 6J, 66C, 66P, 126C, 126P, 186C, 186P, 246C, 246P, 306C, 306P, 366C

Tracking print. *See* Concepts of print.

Uppercase letters. *See* Capital letters.

Viewing and representing, 18B, 30B, 42B, 54B, 66B, 78B, 90B, 102B, 114B, 126B, 138B, 150B, 162B, 174B, 198B, 210B, 222B, 234B, 246B, 258B, 270B, 282B, 294B, 306B, 318B, 330B, 342B, 354B, 366B

Vocabulary
  action words, 271C–271, 283C–283, 295C–295, Unit 5: T34
  developing, 7A, 9A, 33A, 69A, 127A, 153A, 247A, 273A, 307A, 309A, 333A
  high–frequency words, 11C–11, 17C–17, 23C–23, 29C–29, 35C–35, 41C–41, 47C–47, 53C–53, 59C–59, 65C–65, 71C–71, 77C–77, 83C–83, 89C–89, 95C–95, 101C–101, 107C–107, 113C–113, 119C–119, 125C–125, 131C–131, 137C–137, 143C–143, 149C–149, 155C–155, 161C–161, 167C–167, 173C–173, 179C–179, 185C–185, 191C–191, 197C–197, 203C–203, 209C–209, 215C–215, 221C–221, 227C–227, 233C–233, 239C–239, 245C–245, 251C–251, 257C–257, 263C–263, 269C–269, 275C–275, 281C–281, 287C–287, 293C–293, 299C–299, 305C–305, 311C–311, 317C–317, 323C–323, 329C–329, 335C–335, 341C–341, 347C–347, 353C–353, 359C–359, 365C–365

naming words, 247E–247, 259C–259, 295C–295, Unit 5: T26
position and direction words, R10, R30, 7E–7, 19C–19, 55C–55, 151C–151, 163C–163, 175C–175, 187E–187, 199C–199, 211C–211, 223C–223, 235C–235, Unit 1: T26, T31, Unit 3: T34, Unit 4: T24, T35
See also Beginning reading concepts: position and direction words; High–frequency words.

Word choice, 6I, 119A, 126O, 155A, 239A, 246A, 306A, 318A, 126O, 318B, 354A, 354B

Word endings, identifying, 156B, 160B, 196B, 228B, 240B

Word identification. *See* Concepts of print.

Word segmentation. *See* Phonological awareness.

Writing activities
  backyard map, 193/194B
  calendar, 102A–B
  captions/labels, 6J, 7B, 9B, 18B, 23A, 23B, 45B, 54A, 54B, 57B, 59A, 59B
  chart 210A–B
  class book, 30A–B, 66A, 137, 156, 185B, 222A–B, 252, 258A–B, 262, 270A–B, 342A–B, 366A–B
  class chart, 210A–B
  class letter, 138A–B
  class list, 42A–B
  class mural, 18A–B
  class story, 282A–B, 354B
  clues, 342B
  color cards, 354B
  completing sentence frames, 126A–B
  dialogue, 246B, 306A–B
  dictating words and messages, 6J, 7B, 13/14B, 15, 21B, 30B, 31B, 33B, 43B, 45B, 47, 61/62B, 66P, 73/74B, 105B, 119A, 129B, 129, 131A, 165B, 175B, 177B, 185A, 186P, 189, 198B, 219A, 221, 251A, 263B, 294A, 319B, 329, 331B
  directions, 30A, 30B
  exclamations, 246A–B
  friendship mural, 66P
  in complete sentences, 21B, 150F
  labels, captions, 6J, 7B, 18A, 23B, 25/26B, 54A, 59A, 59B, 91B, 105B, 107B, 114K, 115B, 121/122B, 126B, 129B, 139B, 143A, 143B, 145/146B, 163B, 167A, 167B, 174B, 203A, 203B, 211B, 215B, 233, 253/254B, 263A, 265/266B, 275A, 282K, 301/302B, 306B, 311A, 313/314B, 318B, 323A, 330B, 335A
  letter, 138A–B
  letters of the alphabet, 66B, 114A, 126S, 140A, 151B, 153B, 162B, 186B, 226C, 234K, 239C, 246A, 247B, 275B. *See also* Letter formation.
  lists, 11B, 23, 42A–B, 59B, 65B, 162B, 186B
  names, R6, 35, 41B, 95A, 342B, 354B, 361/362B, 366A
  news story, 282A–B
  poem, 97/98B, 150A–B, 354A
  poster, 143A, 174B, 198E, 221B, 318A, 321B, 330B
  questions, 47
  rebus phrase/sentence, 41A, 90B, 126T
  record, 49/50B
  rhymes, 128, 138B, 354B
  riddles, 222A–222B, 270B
  rule, 193/194B
  sentences, 85/86B, 109/110B, 114B, 131, 133/134B, 157/158B, 169/170B, 186A–B, 217/218B, 241/242B, 270A–B, 301/302B, 318A, 325/326B, 337/338B, 349/350B, 366B
  sign, 35B
  simile, 342B
  simple directions, 30A–B
  song, 330A–B
  story, 78A–B, 114A–B, 126B, 129, 186B, 205/206B, 282A–B, 357B, 366A–B
  words, 33B, 35, 53
  See also Center activities: writing, Drawing, Interactive writing, Journal writing, Letter formation.

Scoring Chart

The Scoring Chart is provided for your convenience in grading your students' work.

- Find the column that shows the total number of items.
- Find the row that matches the number of items answered correctly.
- The intersection of the two rows provides the percentage score.

TOTAL NUMBER OF ITEMS

NUMBER CORRECT	1	2	3	4	5	6	7	8	9	10	11	12	13	14	15	16	17	18	19	20	21	22	23	24	25	26	27	28	29	30
1	100	50	33	25	20	17	14	13	11	10	9	8	8	7	7	6	6	6	5	5	5	5	4	4	4	4	4	4	3	3
2		100	66	50	40	33	29	25	22	20	18	17	15	14	13	13	12	11	11	10	10	9	9	8	8	8	7	7	7	7
3			100	75	60	50	43	38	33	30	27	25	23	21	20	19	18	17	16	15	14	14	13	13	12	12	11	11	10	10
4				100	80	67	57	50	44	40	36	33	31	29	27	25	24	22	21	20	19	18	17	17	16	15	15	14	14	13
5					100	83	71	63	56	50	45	42	38	36	33	31	29	28	26	25	24	23	22	21	20	19	19	18	17	17
6						100	86	75	67	60	55	50	46	43	40	38	35	33	32	30	29	27	26	25	24	23	22	21	21	20
7							100	88	78	70	64	58	54	50	47	44	41	39	37	35	33	32	30	29	28	27	26	25	24	23
8								100	89	80	73	67	62	57	53	50	47	44	42	40	38	36	35	33	32	31	30	29	28	27
9									100	90	82	75	69	64	60	56	53	50	47	45	43	41	39	38	36	35	33	32	31	30
10										100	91	83	77	71	67	63	59	56	53	50	48	45	43	42	40	38	37	36	34	33
11											100	92	85	79	73	69	65	61	58	55	52	50	48	46	44	42	41	39	38	37
12												100	92	86	80	75	71	67	63	60	57	55	52	50	48	46	44	43	41	40
13													100	93	87	81	76	72	68	65	62	59	57	54	52	50	48	46	45	43
14														100	93	88	82	78	74	70	67	64	61	58	56	54	52	50	48	47
15															100	94	88	83	79	75	71	68	65	63	60	58	56	54	52	50
16																100	94	89	84	80	76	73	70	67	64	62	59	57	55	53
17																	100	94	89	85	81	77	74	71	68	65	63	61	59	57
18																		100	95	90	86	82	78	75	72	69	67	64	62	60
19																			100	95	90	86	83	79	76	73	70	68	66	63
20																				100	95	91	87	83	80	77	74	71	69	67
21																					100	95	91	88	84	81	78	75	72	70
22																						100	96	92	88	85	81	79	76	73
23																							100	96	92	88	85	82	79	77
24																								100	96	92	89	86	83	80
25																									100	96	93	89	86	83
26																										100	96	93	90	87
27																											100	96	93	90
28																												100	97	93
29																													100	97
30																														100

Guided Reading Support

★ **Leveled Books for Guided Reading**

Macmillan/McGraw-Hill Leveled Books

The Wright Group Leveled Books

★ **Guided Reading Lesson Plan**

Additional Theme Resources

Theme Book Lesson Plans

More books.

More success.

191288-2 191289-0 191291-2 191292-0 191293-9 191294-7

Guided Reading Support

Macmillan/McGraw-Hill Leveled Books

TITLE	READING LEVEL
Lin Did It!	B
The Mop Man	B
Ron Is In	B
Fun on the Farm	C
Go, Lad, Go!	C
Is It You?	C
Let's Go	C
Mud Fun	C
Pam and the Pup	C
The Picnic	C
Ron and Me	C
Ron's Radishes	C
We Have Fun!	C
You Are IT!	C

Additional Leveled Books from The Wright Group

TITLE	READING LEVEL
A Cat's Day	A
The Flower Box	A
A Garden	A
In the Air	A
My Fish	A
The Weather Chart	A
What Season Is This?	A
Bug Watching	B

To order these titles or other Wright Group Leveled Book titles, call 1-800-648-2970.

Guided Reading Lesson Plan

Story Introduction

(The teacher has the only copy of the book.)
- Read the title to children.
- Discuss cover and title page art with children. Invite children to participate, and acknowledge their responses.
- Encourage children to make predictions about the book's content, using the cover art and the title.
- As you talk, begin to bring in words, language patterns, and concepts from the book.

Picture Walk

(The teacher has the only copy of the book.)
- Discuss the pictures together, and highlight key book concepts.
- Allow children to share their prior knowledge. Look for ways to connect children with the story.
- Continue bringing in language from the book, especially unknown words or recurrent language patterns. Locate one or two unknown words or high-frequency words, and tell children: *This word says _____.* Have children repeat the word.
- Continue the picture walk. Encourage children to make predictions about the book's content, using the pictures.

First Reading

(The teacher has the only copy of the book.)
- Point to each word as you read it—to develop print awareness.
- Model the language pattern by reading the first two or three pages of the story. Bring in the artwork as it

interacts with the text (e.g., either before or after reading the text—whichever works best). Allow children to attempt to read the rest of the story.
- If the text is too difficult, use a cloze technique as you read the rest of the story. Pause at key points to allow children to supply what comes next. Encourage them to use the language pattern and artwork to predict text.

The Cloze Technique in Action

(The text is from I Have a Home *by Judy Ling. The child uses the language pattern and artwork to predict text.)*

Teacher: "I have a home," said the turtle. "I live in my shell." "I have a home," said the . . .
Child: . . . rabbit.
Teacher: "I live in my burrow."
(Notice that the teacher does not pause before burrow, *since the word is likely to be unfamiliar to children.)*
Teacher: "I have a . . ."
Child: ". . . home," said the bird.
(The teacher turns over more of the text to children.)

- Assist children in using cues as they read the text. Model the use of the following cues (see possible prompts at the top of page T107):
  > *picture cues* (use artwork to support text and gain an understanding of the story)
  > *visual cues* (use letter-sound relationships to figure out a word)
  > *structure cues* (use language patterns and grammatical structures to figure out a word)
  > *meaning cues* (associate language with experience to gain understanding of the story)

Possible Prompts for Discussing Strategies

- Does that look right? What letter/sound does that word start/end with? (visual cues)
- Did that sound right? What is another word that might fit here? Does that make sense? (structure cues and meaning cues)
- Did that make sense? Look at the pictures. What do you think the word might be? (meaning cues and picture cues)

- Reinforce the correct or attempted use of strategies. (Example: *I like the way you tried to say that word. What helped you read that word?*)

Second Reading

(Each child has a copy of the book.)
- Have children read the story orally together; however, allow each child to read at his or her own pace.
- Guide and observe children as they read, evaluating their use of concepts of print and word knowledge. Encourage children as you notice them cross-check or self-correct.
- As you did in the first reading, reinforce the correct or attempted use of strategies.

Discussion

- Relate the story to children's lives, whenever possible.
- Discuss the topic, ideas, and literary elements (setting, character, plot) found in the story.
- Give children the opportunity to retell the story.

Minilesson

- A minilesson can take place at any point in the Guided Reading process—whenever it is applicable and as needed by your children. For example, if a child needs help locating a known word, point to the word and say it. Then have the child locate it throughout the text.
- Possible focuses for the minilesson might be concepts of print, sight words, or beginning use of strategies.

Independent Practice

- Model fluent reading for children. Then have them practice fluency by reading the book independently or in pairs.
- Related activities should focus on a concept found in the book and should be done only occasionally (once or twice a week).

WORD-ATTACK STRATEGY PROMPTS

Focus on directionality.
- Where do you start reading?
- Put your finger on the first word.
- Which way do you go?
- Now where do you go?
- Can you find the title page?
- Point to the title.

Focus on one-to-one correspondence.
- Point to the words as you read.
- Were there enough words?
- Point to where the word begins. Point to where it ends. Notice the space between the words.

Focus on locating known words.
- Can you point to ___?
- Show me ___.
- How did you know?

Focus on locating unknown words.
- Watch me point to the word as I say it. Now you point to the word and say it.
- Find the word on other pages in the story.

Additional Theme Resources

Contents

Theme Book

SKILLS AND OBJECTIVES

Comprehension
Phonics and Decoding
High-Frequency Word
Concepts of Print

Analyze Setting
/s/Ss, /b/Bb
is
Sentences

Planting Seeds

Written by Amy Jo
Illustrated by Dorothy Donohue

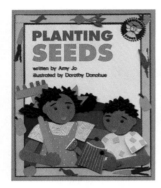

A brother and sister are busy planting vegetable seeds in their garden. After some time, they will have created a beautiful garden of many colors.

Before They Read
BUILDING BACKGROUND

Planting Seeds Bring in packets of seeds to show children. Ask: *What would you do with these seeds?* Encourage children to describe how they would get the ground ready to plant seeds and how they would take care of the growing plants. Ask children what plants they would most like to grow from seeds.

Seed Packet Display Cut out pieces of paper that are the size and shape of seed packets. Invite children to draw a fruit or vegetable on their seed packets. Label each packet with the name of the fruit or vegetable. Attach all the packets to a bulletin board. Encourage children to read each other's seed packets.

HIGH-FREQUENCY WORD: *is*

Focus on the high-frequency word *is* by naming an action word, such as *jump* or *walk,* and choosing a child to demonstrate the action. Then write on the board: _____ *is walking.* Read the sentence together and have a volunteer underline the word *is.* Repeat with other children and actions.

While They Read
GUIDED READING

Preview the Book Display the book *Planting Seeds* and read the title. Encourage children to talk about what the two children on the cover will do with the gardening tools. Point out the author's and illustrator's names.

Prediction Chart Invite children to suggest what the children shown on the book cover will plant. List their ideas.

Picture Walk Together, look through the illustrations. Ask children which vegetable will grow from each seed packet and what color it will be. Compare the predictions they made earlier with the vegetables they see.

First Reading of the Book Read the story aloud, tracking the print. Call attention to the capital letter that begins each sentence and the period that ends it. Explain to children that they can use the seed packet picture and the border art on the page to help read each vegetable's name. After reading the story, ask children why they think the author calls it a "garden of colors."

Second Reading of the Book Have children read the story. Use the following prompts to aid children who might need support.

Page 2: Read the sentence together. Invite children to point to the high-frequency word *is.* Ask: *Where is this story taking place?*

Page 3: Model how to read the vegetable name using picture clues. Say: *The fourth word on each page tells what vegetable will grow from the seeds. I see a picture of a carrot on the seed packet. I think the sentence says:* She is planting carrot seeds.

Pages 4–5: Invite children to compare the words on each page. Point out that the words *he* and *she* change to tell which child is doing the planting. Ask children what time of year they think it is. How can they tell? (It is probably spring, since many gardens are planted at that time.)

Pages 6–7: On page 6, point out the letter *s* in the word *seeds*. Invite children to read the sentence, emphasizing the initial *s* in *seeds*. On page 7, repeat this process for the sound and letter /b/*b* in the word *beet*. Ask children how they can tell where each sentence begins and ends. Have volunteers point to the capital letter and period in each sentence.

Page 8: Read the sentence together. Invite children to describe the garden in the picture. Have them point to and name the vegetables the boy and girl planted earlier. Then ask children what season they think it is now. (summer) How can they tell? (The girl and the boy are wearing shorts; time has passed.)

INDEPENDENT READING
Read Alone Ask children to read the story and to draw a garden of colors, using crayons of the same colors found in the story.

Read with a Partner Suggest that partners take turns reading pages 2–7, acting out how the boy and the girl plant the seeds. Have them read the last page together.

After They Read
COMPREHENSION: ANALYZE CHARACTER
Have children describe the garden in the story. Then invite them to make a mural of a garden by drawing vegetable plants at various stages of growth. Help them label their drawings. Invite children to tell about the plants and how they will grow. *(Spatial/Interpersonal)*

PHONICS AND DECODING: /s/*Ss*, /b/*Bb*
Brainstorm a list of words that begin with *s* and *b*. Have children illustrate one of the words on circle-shaped paper. Along the bottom of mural paper, draw flower stems. Then attach children's illustrations to the stems. Label each "flower" beneath its stem. Repeat the activity with letters previously learned. *(Linguistic/Spatial)*

HIGH-FREQUENCY WORD: *is*
On the board, write: *The cat is* _____. Have a volunteer circle the word *is*. Invite children to think of words to complete the sentence. Repeat with other sentences. *(Linguistic/Interpersonal)*

CONCEPTS OF PRINT: SENTENCES
Give partners a set of word cards and a period card for one story sentence. Have children shuffle the words, put the sentence back together and read it aloud to their partner. Remind children that the last word is followed by a period. *(Linguistic/Kinesthetic)*

Theme Book

SKILLS AND OBJECTIVES ▶

Comprehension
Phonics and Decoding
High-Frequency Word
Concepts of Print

Make Inferences
/i/Ii, /ks/Xx
has
Tracking Print

Izzy Has a Box

Written by Louisa Ernesto
Illustrated by Jared Lee

Izzy gets a big box in the mail. But he has to open many boxes before he finds the present inside.

Before They Read
BUILDING BACKGROUND

Surprise Packages Have children share experiences they have had receiving a surprise package. Then ask children to imagine that the mail carrier has just brought them a surprise package. Ask them to name things they would like to find inside.

What's in the Box? Draw outlines of many different-sized and different-shaped packages on pieces of blank paper. Invite children to choose an outline and draw a surprise inside. Remind them that their surprise should fit the size and shape of the box. Display their pictures and discuss other surprises that might fit inside each package.

HIGH-FREQUENCY WORD: *has*
Focus on the high-frequency word *has*. Invite several children to stand. Note the color of an article of clothing on each child. Write sentences on the board, using the following pattern: *Sally has a red shirt.* Read the sentences aloud. Have volunteers frame the word *has* in each sentence and then underline it.

While They Read
GUIDED READING

Preview the Book Invite children to describe what is happening on the cover illustration of *Izzy Has a Box*. Then read the title. Ask: *Why do you think Izzy is getting a package? What do you think will be inside?* Point out the author's and illustrator's names.

Picture Walk Together, look at the illustrations through page 7. Invite children to describe the boxes on each page. After pages 3 and 5, ask: *What do you think will be inside this new box?*

Predict the Story Ending Remind children that each box Izzy opens has a smaller box inside. Then invite them to predict what Izzy will find inside the last box. List children's ideas.

First Reading of the Book Read the story aloud. Model how to use the pictures to read each color word. Point to the pictures of Izzy and ask: *How do you think he is feeling about opening all these boxes?* After page 7, remind children of their predictions. Then turn the page and have children find out if their predictions were correct. Ask children how they think Izzy felt about receiving the jack-in-the-box.

Second Reading of the Book Have children read the story. You may wish to use some of the following prompts as children read.

Page 2: Read the first sentence. Have children point to the high-frequency word *has*. Then ask: *Where does the next sentence begin?* Read the second sentence, tracking the print. Ask: *Do you think Izzy is excited about receiving the box? How can you tell?*

Page 3: Ask: *How many boxes does Izzy have now?* Have children point to the color word that comes before the word *box*. Help them understand that it describes the box Izzy is holding.

Page 4: Read the first sentence together. Point to the *i* in *Izzy* and emphasize the /i/ sound. Read the second sentence. Ask children which words begin with the same sound as *Izzy*. Then ask: *How do you think Izzy is feeling now?*

Page 5: Say: *I know that the new word on this page names the color box Izzy is holding. I see a purple box. I think the word is* purple.

Pages 6–7: Help children compare the sentences on pages 6 and 7. Ask: *Which words are the same on both pages? Which sentence asks a question?* Point to the *x* in *box* and ask children what sound it makes.

Page 8: Read the sentence together. Ask: *How do you think Izzy felt about his gift? How can you tell?* Ask children why a jack-in-the-box is a good present to find inside all of those boxes. Try to elicit that a jack-in-the-box has a smaller surprise inside, just like all the boxes that came before.

INDEPENDENT READING

Read Alone As children read the story, have them count the number of boxes Izzy has to open before getting his gift.

Read with a Partner Give six blank squares to pairs of children. As they read the story, have them color a square to match each colored box that Izzy receives.

After They Read

COMPREHENSION: MAKE INFERENCES
Look through the book and invite children to describe how Izzy is feeling as he opens each new package. Try to elicit words such as *excited, curious,* or *confused.* Ask children to think of a new story ending and how Izzy would have felt. *(Logical/Spatial)*

PHONICS AND DECODING: /i/*Ii,* /ks/*Xx*
On the board, draw a picture of Izzy and a box and label each. Place word cards for *fox, it, Max, in, sax, mix, is, ox,* and *into* in a bag. Have children pick a word and tell whether it begins like *Izzy* or ends like *box.* Place each card under the appropriate drawing. *(Linguistic/Kinesthetic)*

HIGH-FREQUENCY WORD: *has*
Begin a circle game by giving a toy to one child and saying: *(Name of child) has a toy.* Have the child pass the toy to the next child. Invite everyone to repeat the sentence with you using the next child's name. Write the sentences on the board and ask volunteers to underline the word *has.* *(Linguistic/Kinesthetic)*

CONCEPTS OF PRINT: TRACKING PRINT
Print the verses of a familiar song, such as "Twinkle, Twinkle Little Star" on chart paper. Invite children to join you in singing. Track the print from left to right and from top to bottom as you sing. *(Musical/Kinesthetic)*

Theme Book

SKILLS AND OBJECTIVES ▶

Comprehension
Phonics and Decoding
High-Frequency Word
Concepts of Print

Compare and Contrast
/n/Nn, /u/Uu
in
Exclamation Points

Rain, Rain, Go Away!

Written by Fay Robinson
Illustrated by Erika LeBarre

Where do animals hide in the rain? You can find them under trees, leaves, steps, and other unexpected places.

Before They Read

BUILDING BACKGROUND

Rainy Days Ask children what they like about rainy days. Talk about the gray sky, the thunder, and the lightning that comes with the rain. Then ask children to name things they usually put on to keep themselves dry on a rainy day.

Weather Chart Invite children to keep track of the weather for a week or more on a calendar. Decide on weather symbols: a sun for a sunny day; raindrops for a rainy day; clouds for a cloudy day. Have children tell what the weather is each day, draw the symbol on the calendar, and describe the temperature.

HIGH-FREQUENCY WORD: *in*

Put an object in a box. Ask: *What is in the box?* Then ask a child to open the box. Write: *A (name of the object) is in the box.* Read aloud the sentence and ask a volunteer to underline the word *in*. Repeat with other objects.

While They Read

GUIDED READING

Preview the Book Display the book *Rain, Rain, Go Away!* and read the title with enthusiasm. Ask children when they might use this expression. Point out the names of the author and illustrator.

Prediction Chart On the board, list the story characters: *ladybugs, ants, frogs, cats, cows, children.* Tell children that they will all hide from the rain. Invite children to predict where each group will hide. List their suggestions.

Picture Walk Together, look at the illustrations through page 7. Invite children to tell who is on each page and what they are hiding under. After page 7, ask children what they think will happen on the last page of the book.

First Reading of the Book Read the story aloud with expression. Model using picture clues to read each new hiding place. Invite children to chime in on the second sentence. After page 8, ask: *Why did everyone come out from their hiding places?* Then ask children to recall where each animal hid and to tell which places most surprised them.

Second Reading of the Book Have children read the story. You may wish to use some of these prompts as children read.

Pages 2–3: Read the sentences. Ask: *Which words are the same on both pages?* Model how to use the picture clues to read the word on each page that is different. Say: *The new word in the first sentence tells what the animals hide under. On page 2, I see ladybugs under grass. I think the word is* grass. *On page 3, I see ants under nuts. I think the word is* nuts.

Pages 4–5: Point to the exclamation point that ends the second sentence. Model how to read the sentence. Ask: *Where are the animals now?* Have children find the high-frequency word *in*. Then ask: *Which hiding place do you think is drier? Which hiding place was built by people?*

Pages 6–7: Read page 6 with children and ask: *Who is hiding now? What are they hiding under?* Call attention to the two words on page 7 that begin with the letter *u* and the sound /u/. *(umbrellas, under)* Ask children to describe how umbrellas and trees have similar shapes.

Page 8: Read the sentences. Have children frame the word that begins with the sound /n/ and the letter *n*. *(Now)* Ask children what all the characters are doing now that the sun has come out. Have children contrast where the characters are now with where they were while it was raining.

INDEPENDENT READING

Read Alone Have children read the book. Ask them to draw two groups of animals from the story who hide under something that grows in the ground.

Read with a Partner Pair children. Invite them to take turns reading the first sentence on each page and to read *Rain, rain, go away!* together.

After They Read

COMPREHENSION: COMPARE AND CONTRAST
Recall with children where the animals and children hid in the story. Ask compare-and-contrast questions such as: *What was the smallest thing an animal hid under? What was the largest thing? What hiding places are things that grow?* *(Linguistic/Logical)*

PHONICS AND DECODING: /n/*Nn*, /u/*Uu*
Give each child a card with *Nn* on it. On the board, write *nut* and *now*. Say words that begin with *Nn* and words that do not. Have children hold up their cards when the word begins with /n/. Repeat with *Uu* cards. *(Linguistic/Kinesthetic)*

HIGH-FREQUENCY WORD: *in*
On the board, write: *What is in our classroom?* Underline *in*. Invite children to draw something in the classroom. Help them label their drawings: *A _____ is in our classroom.* Underline the word *in*. *(Linguistic/Spatial)*

CONCEPTS OF PRINT: EXCLAMATION POINTS
Have children draw a picture of themselves in a rainstorm. Label their drawings: *Rain, rain, go away.* Ask children to add the exclamation point that ends the sentence. Have them read the sentence with expression. *(Linguistic/Spatial)*

Theme Book

SKILLS AND OBJECTIVES

Comprehension
Phonics and Decoding
High-Frequency Word
Concepts of Print

Use Picture Clues
/l/Ll, /j/Jj
like
Sentences

Just Like a Rainbow

Written by Cynthia Rothman
Illustrated by Nicole Rutten

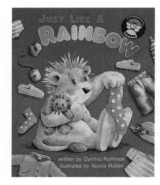

When Lion gets dressed, the results are very colorful. In fact, she looks just like a rainbow!

Before They Read

BUILDING BACKGROUND

Getting Dressed Invite children to pantomime putting on socks, shoes, shirts with buttons, jackets with zippers, and hats. Then ask volunteers to pantomime putting on one article of clothing. Ask classmates to guess which article of clothing is being put on.

Make an Outfit Ask each child to draw a colorful item of clothing. Help cut their drawings out. Display the cutouts on a table. Ask children to name articles of clothing that would make an outfit. Invite children to make new outfits with the cutouts in their free time.

HIGH-FREQUENCY WORD: *like*

On the board, draw a shirt and have children use colored chalk to decorate it. Then write: *The shirt is just like a rainbow.* Underline the word *like.* Read the sentence. Invite children to suggest other things that are colorful "just like a rainbow." Write each new sentence on the board and have children underline the word *like.* Invite children to illustrate a sentence.

While They Read

GUIDED READING

Preview the Book Display the book *Just Like a Rainbow* and read the title. Ask children what they think Lion will do with the clothing pictured on the cover. Point out the author's and illustrator's names.

Prediction Chart Ask children to predict what kind of outfit the lion in the story will put on. List their predictions on the board.

Picture Walk Together, look through the illustrations. On each page, ask: *What is Lion putting on?* Encourage children to respond by naming the color, or pattern, and the article of clothing. Ask: *Do you notice anything unusual about the way Lion is putting on her clothes? What do you think she will look like when she is finished getting dressed?*

First Reading of the Book Read the story aloud. Once children become familiar with the language pattern, invite them to chime in. Point out that the last words on each page name the article of clothing Lion is putting on and either its color or its pattern. After reading, ask children why Lion looks just like a rainbow.

Second Reading of the Book Have children read the story. You may wish to use some of the following prompts.

Pages 2–3: Ask: *Who is the story about?* Point to the *L* in *Lion.* Introduce the letter and sound /l/Ll. Then model how to use picture clues to figure out the last two words on page 2. Say: *The last two words on the page tell what the lion is putting on and its color or pattern. I see that Lion has shoes that are yellow. I think the two words are* yellow shoes. Point out the words *polka dot* on page 3. Explain that these words describe the pattern of the socks.

Pages 4–5: Have children point to the words *striped shirt.* Use the picture to discuss the meaning of the word *striped.* Ask: *What does Lion put on after the striped shirt? What do the pictures tell you that the words don't?*

Pages 6–7: On page 6, point out the letter and sound /j/*j* in *jacket.* Invite children to read the sentence, emphasizing the /j/ sound. Then ask: *Did Lion put on her jacket correctly?* Look at page 7, and ask: *Which words are the same as on page 6?* Help children use picture clues to figure out the words *orange hat.*

Page 8: Read the two sentences, tracking the print. Call attention to the exclamation points. Then point out the high-frequency word *like* in the second sentence. Ask: *What letter and sound does* like *begin with?* Discuss why Lion looks like a rainbow. Then ask children to use the picture to tell what Lion might be thinking when she looks in the mirror.

INDEPENDENT READING

Read Alone Have children read the story to themselves and draw a picture of something Lion puts on that begins with the letter *j.*

Read with a Partner Have partners read the repeated words *Lion put on* in unison and alternate reading the rest of each sentence. Invite them to pantomime Lion's actions as she puts on each article of clothing.

After They Read

COMPREHENSION: USE PICTURE CLUES

Help groups of children cut out a paper lion. Then ask group members to draw and cut out articles of clothing to fit the lion. Invite children to take turns placing articles of clothing on the lion. Have group members tell what Lion has on, using the story's language pattern: *Lion put on a* _____. *(Kinesthetic/Spatial)*

PHONICS AND DECODING: /l/*Ll*, /j/*Jj*

Invite children to look through the book for words that begin with *l* and *j.* *(lion, look, looks, like; jeans, jacket, just)* Then play "Leap or Jump." Say words that begin with /l/ or /j/. Encourage children to repeat each word and then either leap forward for *l,* or jump in place for *j.* *(Linguistic/Kinesthetic)*

HIGH-FREQUENCY WORD: *like*

Say: *I can growl like a lion.* Write this sentence on chart paper, underlining *like.* Read the sentences and have everyone act it out. Invite children to suggest things they can do like a lion. Have volunteers underline *like* in each new sentence. *(Linguistic/Kinesthetic)*

CONCEPTS OF PRINT: SENTENCES

Give partners a set of word cards for one sentence in the book. Have them help each other put the cards in order to make the sentence. Ask them to check it by finding the matching sentence in the little book. *(Linguistic/Kinesthetic)*

Theme Book

SKILLS AND OBJECTIVES

Comprehension
Phonics and Decoding
Concepts of Print

Main Idea and Supporting Details
/i/Ii, /ks/Xx
Sentences

What Insects Do

Written by Kana Riley

Through amazing close-up photographs and simple text, readers discover the wonderful things insects do.

Before They Read

BUILDING BACKGROUND

Insects Ask children to name different kinds of insects, such as ants, bees, flies, grasshoppers, beetles, caterpillars, and butterflies. Invite children to tell what they know about these insects. Share the following general information.

- All insects have six legs.
- There are more insects than any other group of animals.
- Insects can be found all over the world.

Then, have children use clay, or other materials, to make some six-legged insects of their own.

Favorite Insects Tally Draw or display pictures of common insects, such as a beetle, butterfly, ladybug, ant, or bee. Ask children to choose the insect they like best and draw it on a small square of paper. Make a chart, listing each insect name. Collect the papers and have volunteers help you sort them into groups. Count and record the number of drawings of each insect, using tally marks. Then ask questions, such as: *Which insect do most children like? Which insect is the least popular?*

While They Read

GUIDED READING

Preview the Book Display the book *What Insects Do* and read the title. Have children name and describe the insects they see. Point out the author's name.

Prediction Chart Invite children to predict what the insects on the cover will do in the story. Write their ideas on chart paper.

Picture Walk Together, look through and discuss the illustrations. On each page, invite children to name the insect, tell how many they see, and describe what the insects are doing. If children are interested, point out the real names of the insects in the photographs. (One palm beetle; two praying mantises; three monarch butterflies; four green lacewings; five leaf-cutter ants; six water striders)

First Reading of the Book Read the story aloud. Point out that there are two sentences on each page. As you read, model how to use the illustration to figure out the word in the first sentence that tells how many insects there are, and the word in the second sentence that tells what the insects are doing. After finishing the story, invite children to tell what they learned about insects from looking at and reading this book.

Second Reading of the Book Invite children to read the story. You may wish to use some of the following prompts as they read.

Pages 2–3: Have children compare the two sentences on page 2. Ask: *Which words are the same in both sentences? Why does the word* one *begin with a capital letter in the second sentence?* Repeat this process for page 3. Then ask children which word on each page tells what insects do.

Pages 4–5: On page 4, have children point to and read the number word in the sentence. Review how they can use the picture clue to figure out this word. On page 5, ask them to read the word that names the action, using the picture clue again. Ask how fluttering is different from flying. Explain that *flutter* means "to move wings quickly while staying in place."

Page 6: Discuss the letter and sound /i/*Ii* and ask children to find the word on the page that begins with that letter and sound.

Page 7: Have children count the number of insects. Then ask them to find the word *six*. Point out the sound and letter /ks/*x* in the word *six*. Ask children to describe how the insects are skating.

Page 8: Read the sentences aloud. Restate the main idea: *Insects do many things.* Ask children to look back through the story and read a sentence that tells one thing that insects do.

INDEPENDENT READING

Read Alone Invite children to read the story. Have them draw a picture of the insect they like best.

Read with a Partner Ask one partner to read the first sentence and the other to read the second sentence on each page. Then have them reverse roles.

After They Read

COMPREHENSION: MAIN IDEA AND SUPPORTING DETAILS

Restate the main idea: *Insects do many things.* Invite children to act out the story details. Assign children to groups, matching the number of children to the number of insects on each page. Have group members pantomime the insects' actions as you read the story. *(Kinesthetic/Linguistic)*

PHONICS AND DECODING: /i/*Ii,* /ks/*Xx*

Review the letters and sounds /i/*Ii* and /ks/*Xx*. Make letter cards for *i* and *x*. Give each child one letter card. Read aloud words that have beginning or medial *i,* or that end with *x*. Have children hold up their card if they hear their sound. *(Linguistic/Kinesthetic)*

CONCEPTS OF PRINT: SENTENCES

Place word cards for a story sentence in a bag. Invite partners to pick cards and place them on the table, from left to right. When all the cards are placed, have children rearrange them to form a story sentence. *(Linguistic/Kinesthetic)*

SHARED WRITING: INSECT REPORT

Share information from a resource book about one of the insects from the story. Invite children to dictate a sentence telling one thing they learned about the insect for a class report. Invite them to illustrate the sentence they contributed. *(Linguistic/Interpersonal)*

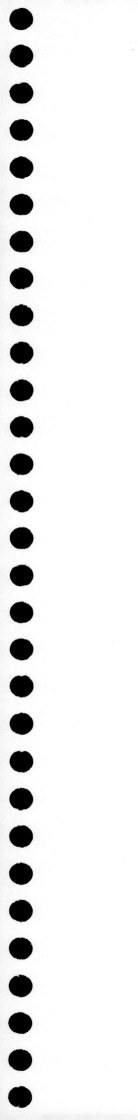

Segment Sounds · · · · · · · · · Phonemic Awareness · · · · · · · ·

Teach Hide the picture of the *van* behind your back. Have children try to guess the picture using these clues: *It begins with /v/. It has the /a/ sound in the middle. It ends with /n/.* Tell children that you can blend the sounds to make a word: /v/-/a/-/n/, *van.* Display the picture.

Practice Have children hide pictures of the *fox, pig, cat, bed, bib, top, wig, ham, fan,* and *cap.* Let them give clues for each new word and invite the other children to blend the sounds to make the word. Children may show pictures to confirm the new words.

MATERIALS

• Phonics Pictures from *Word Building Cards*

· · · · · · · · · · · · · · · · · · · ·

INFORMAL ASSESSMENT Observe children as they blend onsets and rimes and segment sounds. If children have difficulty, see Alternate Teaching Strategies: Unit 1, T33; and Unit 4, T27.

Read Together | **From Phonemic Awareness to Phonics**

Objective: Develop Letter/Sound Correspondence

LISTEN FOR SOUNDS Choose several CVC words from the poem, and write each on a sentence strip. Ask children to listen for the three sounds in each word as you read it aloud.

> nap cat cot did
> not map Sid pot Min

ECHO GAME Read a sentence-strip word. Guide children in echoing the word, stretching out each sound as if it is echoing from a mountain top.

MAKE A WORD Have children form pairs. Tell them there are three letters/sounds in the word they just echoed. On index cards, write one letter per card from each word children have echoed. Ask pairs to place three index card letters in front of them. Display a sentence-strip word, and have children hold up the letters that match the word. Continue the

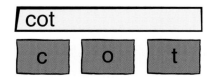

activity with the rest of the sentence-strip words.

RECORD THE WORDS Have children glue the index cards to construction paper. Invite pairs to read a favorite word while the class echoes their reading.

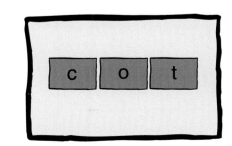

Short *a, i, o*
Blending

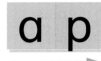

OBJECTIVES

Children will:

☑ identify /a/ *a,* /i/ *i,* and /o/ *o*

☑ blend and read short *a, i,* and *o* words

☑ write short *a, i,* and *o* words

MATERIALS

- letter cards

ADDITIONAL RESOURCES

- Practice Book, page 208
- Phonics/Phonemic Awareness Practice Book, pages 110, 116, 122
- **Phonics** CD-ROM

TEACHING TIP

WRITE WORDS Write *–ap,* *–ip,* and *–op* on the chalkboard. Say the words: *tap, pop,* and *rip.* Have volunteers write the beginning letters to complete the words.

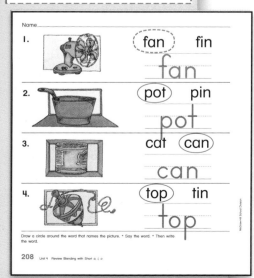

| Pupil Edition page 208 |

208C *Is It You?*

Review

TEACH

Model Blending with Short *a, i, o* Display the *a* letter card and say /a/. Have children repeat the sound /a/ as you point to the *a* card. Place the *p* card to the right of the *a* card. Point to each letter as you blend the sounds together and have children repeat after you: *ap.*

Place the *c* card to the left of *ap* to show *cap.* Point to the cards as you blend to read *cap,* and have children repeat after you.

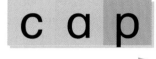

Continue modeling and guided practice using *tip, mop, rip, pod, nap, sip,* and *fan.*

PRACTICE

Backward Words

Materials: Word Building Cards for *pan, Pam, map, tap,* and *pat,* letter cards

◆ Give each child one of the word cards.

◆ Tell children to create a new word that has the first and last letter of their word in reverse order.

ON LEVEL

✓ ASSESS/CLOSE

Have children complete page 208 of the Pupil Edition or the Practice Book. For a different approach to this skill, see page T28 for the **Alternate Teaching Strategy.**